Student Edition

American
LITERATURE

ENCOURAGING THOUGHTFUL CHRISTIANS TO BE WORLD CHANGERS

By James P. Stobaugh

This Book is gratefully dedicated to
Karen
and
our four children:
Rachel, Jessica, Timothy, and Peter.

He has given us a ministry of reconciliation . . .
2 Corinthians 5:18

Students, to you 'tis given to scan the heights
Above, to traverse the ethereal space,
And mark the systems of revolving worlds.
Still more, ye sons of science ye receive
The blissful news by messengers from heav'n,
How Jesus blood for your redemption flows . . .

— Phillis Wheatley

ACKNOWLEDGMENTS

From the Broadman and Holman Home Education Division, I wish to thank Sheila Moss, whose editorial assistance and encouragement have been greatly appreciated; Matt Stewart, whose vision and perseverance have made this project possible; and Paul Gant and Mark Grover for their work with graphics and the DVD. Likewise, I thank my four children and my distance learning students who so graciously allowed me to use their essays. Finally, and most of all, I want to thank my best friend and lifelong editor, my wife, Karen. "Come, let us glorify the Lord and praise His name forever . . . ." (Psalm 34:3)

Contents

*Provided in the student textbook.

It is strongly suggested that students read most of the following books during the summer before taking this course:

Augustine, *Confessions*

Dostoevsky, *Crime and Punishment*

Goethe, *Tragedy of Foust*

Homer, *Iliad*

Homer, *Odyssey*

Paton, *Cry the Beloved Country*

Tolstoy, *War and Peace*

Virgil, *Aeneid*

Preface

INTRODUCTION

American Literature is a rhetoric level course. There are two distinctives of rhetoric level courses: they are content driven and they presume higher level thinking. In most cases, you will be reading in excess of 200 pages per week. Therefore, to ease your weekly schedule throughout the school year, most of this material should be read the summer before you begin this course.

In any event, you will need to read the whole book/literary work before the week's lesson begins. Sometimes this is not a very lengthy assignment (e.g., reading Phillis Wheatley's poetry, Lesson 5). In other cases it will take you more than a week to read the assigned text (e.g., *The Scarlet Letter*, Lesson 8 or *The Unvanquished*, Lesson 23).

If you have worked through the *Skills for Literary Analysis* and *Skills for Rhetoric* courses in this series, you already know how to accomplish elementary literary criticism. If you have not worked through the introductory courses and you are concerned, don't be. You will be reviewed on how to do literary analysis as the course progresses. Literary analysis questions are the most often asked questions in the study of literature, and in this course analysis type questions are divided into three main categories: Critical Thinking, Biblical Application, and Enrichment.

In *Merriam Webster's Collegiate Dictionary* (10th ed., 1993), *literature* is defined as "writings in prose or verse: especially having excellence of form or expression and expressing ideas of permanent or universal interest."

The person who examines, interprets, and analyzes literature is a *critic*. That is your job. A critic is a guide to the reader, not a prophet or a therapist. While it is the critic's right to express his preferences, and even his privilege to influence others, it is not his job to tell the reader what to like or not like. However, the critic is a helper, a guide helping the reader better understand the author's intention and art. In fact, the critic is concerned about the structure, sound, and meaning of the literary piece. These structures are described as genres: *narrative prose*, *essays*, *poetry*, and *drama*.

Literary analysis or criticism is a way to talk about literature. It is a way to understand literature better so that you can tell others about it. If you really want to understand something, you need to have a common language with everyone else. If you were talking about football, for instance, you would need to know about certain terminology and use it when describing the game. How lost you would be without knowing what a tackle is! Or how could you enjoy watching the game without knowing what the referee means when he shouts, "First and Ten!"

Literary Analysis employs *a common language* to take apart and to discuss literary pieces. You will learn that language with its literary terms as this course progresses over the year. A list of literary terms is found in the glossary at the end of this book.

You will be asked to participate in higher-level thinking and problem-solving. Saying, "I don't know" or "I can't think" or "I don't know how to do it" isn't problem solving!

Typically, you and your teachers/parents will decide on required essays for the lessons, choosing two or three essays per week. Remember to follow the writing suggestions in the appendices as you write the essays.

STUDENT ROLES AND RESPONSIBILITIES:

1. Read the assigned, whole literary piece before the first classroom assignment. You will need to read ahead: you cannot wait until two days before an assignment is due to read the material. At the end of each lesson, the Suggested Weekly Implementation boxes will prompt you concerning future assignments, but you will need to make sure you do the work in a timely way. In addition to the information in the Suggested Implementation box at the end of each lesson, you will be prompted at the beginning of each lesson in a text memo box. For example, in Lesson 1 the goal states, "You will examine several Puritan writings and understand their distinctive worldviews." You will also find in the memo box, "Reading Ahead: Students will review Worldviews for next lesson" and a "Guide Question: What are the distinctives of Bradstreet's writings?"

Your teacher/parent may try to help you occasionally with more difficult readings by providing unabridged book tape copies of the assigned text.

2. Read and discuss the guide question concerning future reading found in the text box on and at the end of each lesson. For example, the guide questions at the end of Lesson 1, concerning Lesson 2, are "What does the word *worldview* mean? What is your worldview? What worldviews do you encounter in the world around you?" These questions will guide you as you review (because you should have already *read*) the next reading assignments.

3. Discuss with your parent/educator the background material.

4. Discuss with your parent/educator the assigned questions. The highlighted term is defined in simple language and illustrated by a readable example. If you need more information, access other composition handbooks.

> Sample Text Box:
>
> You will analyze several Puritan writings and Native American voices.
>
> **Reading ahead:** No readings are necessary for Lesson 2 but students should review Religious Affections, Jonathan Edwards for Lesson 3.
>
> **Guide Questions:** What does the word worldview mean? What is your worldview? What worldviews do you encounter in the world around you?

5. Complete all assigned activities that teachers and students decide upon, choosing from three essay types:
Critical Thinking
Biblical Application
Enrichment

You will be writing two to three 1-2 page essays/week, depending on the level of accomplishment you and your parent educator decide upon. To experience the optimum from the course, you should be willing to write from all essay types—including the Enrichment essays. After you and your teachers/parents decide on the *required* essays, I recommend that you at least *outline* and/or *discuss* the remaining essays. Outline strategies are found in the Appendix at the back of this book.

6. Complete literary check-ups. You will be assigned particular works to read during this course; however, as time allows, read books from the enclosed list (see Appendix). You should read most of the books on the enclosed supplemental book list before you graduate from high school. After reading a literary work, for this course or for any other reason, you should complete a book checkup (see Appendix) as a record of your high school reading. The supplemental book list is not meant to be exhaustive but is intended as a guide to good reading. Reading 35-50 pages per night (or 200 pages per week), including the reading for this course, is a good plan to strengthen your reading protocol.

7. Create 3x5 vocabulary cards.
Part of the reason for reading so many challenging literary works is for you to increase your functional vocabulary. Your best means of increasing vocabulary is through reading a vast amount of classical, well-written literary works. I could give you 15 new words to learn every week, but studies show that most of you would forget those words within 24 hours. While reading literary works, you should harvest as many unknown words as you can. *You should use five new words in each essay you write.*

Then most conspicuous, when great things or small,/Useful or hurtful, prosperous or *adverse*/ We can create . . .	Harmful, Evil Adj., Adversity is Noun The <u>adverse</u> effects of smoking are great.
Front	Back

When you meet a new word, do your best to figure out the word in context; check your guess by looking in the dictionary; write a sentence with the word in it.

Use the illustration above to formulate your vocabulary cards of new words.

8. Write in a prayer journal. If you don't have a prayer journal, try using the prayer journal template in the appendix. Make 25-50 copies of this page and put it in a notebook. As often as you can—hopefully daily—file out one of these sheets on a biblical passage. You will find a sample format in the Appendices.

NOTE: Used along with the Biblical Application Questions, commitment to the daily process of Prayer Journaling could lead to a separate credit elective course. Be sure to discuss this option with your parent/educator.

9. Begin the final project. See appendix for more specific instructions.

Your **Final Portfolio** should include corrected essays, literary checkups, writing journal, vocabulary cards, pictures from field trips, and other pertinent material (see Lesson 35 for more details).

SUGGESTED WEEKLY IMPLEMENTATION SCHEDULE

If you follow this schedule, you will get all your work done in a timely way.

SUGGESTED
Weekly *Implementation*

DAY 1	DAY 2	DAY 3	DAY 4	DAY 5
Prayer journal.	**Prayer journal.**	**Prayer journal.**	**Prayer journal.**	**Prayer journal.**
Review the required reading(s) before the assigned lesson begins.	Review reading(s) from next lesson.	Write rough drafts of all assigned essays.	Rewrite corrected copies of essays due tomorrow.	Essays are due.
Teacher may want to discuss assigned reading(s) with students.	Outline essays due at the end of the week.	The teacher and/or a peer evaluator may correct rough drafts.		Take Lesson One test.
Teacher and students will decide on required essays for this lesson, choosing two or three essays.	Per teacher instructions, students may answer orally in a group setting some of the essays that are not assigned as formal essays.			Reading ahead: This will give you a reminder of what to be reading ahead for future lessons.
The rest of the essays can be outlined, answered with shorter answers, or skipped.				Guide: These questions will guide your thinking and study for the next lesson.
Review all readings for Assigned Lesson.				

NOTE: Remember to read ahead the requisite literary material for this course; many students read the required literature *during the summer* before the course begins.

SCOPE AND SEQUENCE
AMERICAN LITERATURE

LESSON	PERIOD/WORLDVIEW AUTHORS/ TEXTS
1	**The New Land to 1750: Puritanism and Native American Voices** *The History of Plimoth Plantation*, William Bradford.* *The Navajo Origin Legend;* Navajo Tribe, from *The Iroquois Constitution* * Iroquois Tribe
2	**Worldview Formation and Discernment** No Readings Required
3	**The New Land to 1750: Puritanism** *Religious Affections*, Jonathan Edwards; "Diary Entries,"* Esther Edwards; Poems* by Anne Bradstreet
4	**The Revolutionary Period, 1750-1800 (Part 1)** *The Autobiography of Benjamin Franklin*, Benjamin Franklin
5	**The Revolutionary Period, 1750-1800 (Part 2)** Poems* by Phillis Wheatley; *Speech in the Virginia Convention*,* Patrick Henry; *The Declaration of Independence*,* Thomas Jefferson; *Letter to Her Daughter from the* *New White House*,* Abigail Adams
6	**A Growing Nation, 1800-1840: National Period (Part 1)** "Thanatopsis,"* William Cullen Bryant; "The Devil and Tom Walker,"* Washington Irving
7	**A Growing Nation, 1800-1840: National Period (Part 2)** "The Fall of the House of Usher,"*and "The Tell Tale Heart,"* Edgar Allan Poe
8	**Romanticism: New England Renaissance, 1840-1855 (Part 1)** *The Scarlet Letter* and "Birthmark,"* Nathaniel Hawthorne
9	**Romanticism: New England Renaissance, 1840-1855 (Part 2)** Poems* by Henry Wadsworth Longfellow, Oliver Wendell Holmes, James Russell Lowell, John Greenleaf Whittier, and Emily Dickinson.
10	**Romanticism: New England Renaissance, 1840-1855 (Part 3)** Selected Poems,* Ralph Waldo Emerson
11	**Romanticism: New England Renaissance, 1840-1855 (Part 4)** *Walden*, Henry David Thoreau
12	**Romanticism: New England Renaissance, 1840-1855 (Part 5)** *Billy Budd*, Herman Melville

*Provided in the student textbook.

13	**Division, War, and Reconciliation, 1855-1865 (Part 1)** "O Captain, My Captain!"* Walt Whitman; "Go Down Moses,"* "Deep River,"* Roll Jordan, Roll,"* "Swing Low, Sweet Chariot;"* Negro Spirituals; "The Gettysburg Address,"* Abraham Lincoln; "I will Fight No More Forever,"* Chief Joseph
14	**Division, War, and Reconciliation, 1855-1865 (Part 2)** *Narrative of the Life of Frederick Douglass*, Frederick Douglass
15	**Realism, Naturalism, and The Frontier, 1865-1915 (Part 1)** *The Adventures of Huckleberry Finn*, Mark Twain
16	**Realism, Naturalism, and The Frontier, 1865-1915 (Part 2)** *The Adventures of Huckleberry Finn*, Mark Twain
17	**Realism, Naturalism, and The Frontier, 1865-1915 (Part 3)** *Red Badge of Courage*, Stephen Crane
18	**Realism, Naturalism, and The Frontier, 1865-1915 (Part 4)** *Red Badge of Courage*, Stephen Crane
19	**Realism, Naturalism, and The Frontier, 1865-1915 (Part 5)** "The Outcasts of Poker Flat,"* Bret Harte; "The Story of an Hour,"* Kate Chopin; "Richard Cory,"* Edwin Arlington Robinson; "Lucinda Matlock,"* Edgar Lee Masters
20	**The Modern Age, 1915-1946: Late Romanticism/ Naturalism (Part 1)** *Ethan Frome*, Edith Wharton
21	**The Modern Age, 1915-1946: Late Romanticism/ Naturalism (Part 2)** 20th Century Poetry
22	**The Modern Age, 1915-1946: Late Romanticism/ Naturalism (Part 3)** *A Farewell to Arms*, Ernest Hemingway
23	**The Modern Age, 1915-1946: Late Romanticism/ Naturalism (Part 4)** *Their Eyes Were Watching God*, Zora Neale Hurston
24	**The Modern Age, 1915-1946: Late Romanticism/ Naturalism (Part 5)** *The Unvanquished*, William Faulkner
25	**The Modern Age, 1915-1946: Late Romanticism/ Naturalism (Part 6)** *The Pearl*, John Steinbeck
26	**The Modern Age, 1946-1960: Late Romanticism/ Naturalism (Part 1)** 20th Century Drama: *The Emperor Jones*, Eugene Gladstone O'Neill

*Provided in the student textbook.

*Provided in the student textbook.

Audio presentations of most of the readings in the book may be obtained from Blackstoneaudio.com

American Literature Reading List

Additional texts, not included within the study, needed for this program:

Religious Affections by Jonathan Edwards
The Autobiography of Benjamin Franklin by Benjamin Franklin
Walden by Henry David Thoreau
Billy Budd by Herman Melville
Narrative of the Life of Frederick Douglass by Frederick Douglass
The Adventures of Huckleberry Finn by Mark Twain
Red Badge of Courage by Stephen Crane
Ethan Frome by Edith Wharton
A Farewell to Arms by Ernest Hemingway
Their Eyes Were Watching God by Zora Neale Hurston
The Unvanquished by William Faulkner
The Pearl by John Steinbeck
The Emperor Jones by Eugene Gladstone O'Neill
The Little Foxes by Lillian Hellman
The Glass Menagerie by Tennessee Williams
The Crucible by Arthur Miller
Cold Sassy Tree by Olive Ann Burns
The Chosen by Chiam Potok

My prayer for you is

"For this reason I bow my knees before the Father from whom every family in heaven and on earth is named. I pray that He may grant you, according to the riches of His glory, to be strengthened with power through His Spirit in the inner man, and that the Messiah may dwell in your hearts through faith. I pray that you, being rooted and firmly established in love, may be able to comprehend with all the saints what is the length and width, height and depth of God's love, and to know the Messiah's love that surpasses knowledge, so you may be filled with all the fullness of God. Now to Him who is able to do above and beyond all that we ask or think — according to the power that works in you — to Him be glory in the church and in Christ Jesus to all generations, forever and ever. Amen."
(Ephs. 3:14-21)

James Stobaugh

From the Editor

Developing appropriate curricula for a specific audience is a major and intricate endeavor. Doing so for the homeschool and Christian communities is perhaps even more difficult: homeschool approaches, methodology, and content are as diverse as traditional educational trends have ever dared to be. Homeschooling is complex—from unschooling to the Classical approach, there are myriads of opinions of what to teach, when to teach it, and how to teach it to whom at what age and at what level of development. Perhaps you struggle with choices between a *whole-book* approach to literature study or a more traditional and inclusive canon. Perhaps you are still wading through myriads of questions associated with homeschooling teenagers. However, perhaps your decision is final and you merely need a solid literature-and-writing-based English curriculum. Keep reading.

In one-year literature/writing-based courses, including all the quality literature that has ever been published is impossible—there is simply too much good literature and not enough space to include it; neither is there time enough to read it all. Regrettably, many selections of quality literature have not been included in this course—not because they are unworthy, but because they all cannot fit into the designated framework. The author and I have done our best to include whole-book or whole-work selections from the major genres of literature (prose, poetry, and drama). In the *Literary Analysis, Rhetoric,* and *American, British,* and *World Literature* courses in this series, literary selections incorporate many ethnicities from both male and female writers. We believe our selections inform the purpose of the curricula: *Encouraging Thoughtful Christians to be World Changers.*

According to a well-known author, homeschool conference speaker, and long-time homeschooling mom, two of the greatest needs in the homeschool community reside in curricula for high school and for special needs. These English curricula consider those needs; they were conceived in prayer, deliberated through educational experience, and nurtured with inspiration. We are providing unique five-year curricula for required English studies for the multifarious Christian community. Canonical and Classical literature is emphasized; students are meticulously guided through carefully honed steps of *critical thinking, biblical challenge for spiritual growth,* and even additional *enrichment* motivators. A major key to the successful completion of these courses falls in the statements, "Teachers and students will decide on required essays for this lesson, choosing two or three essays. All other essays may be outlined, discussed, or omitted." These statements, repeated in every lesson, allow tremendous flexibility for various levels of student maturity and interests. Since each lesson may offer 10-15 essays, choosing essays each week is vital.

In any literature course offered to Christian audiences there will be differences in opinions regarding acceptable and appropriate content, authors, poets, and playwrights. Some educators may object to specific works or specific authors, poets, or playwrights included in these curricula *even though we have been very conscientious with selections.* For that reason we highly encourage educators and students to confab—choose units according to students' maturity, ability, age, sensitivity, interests, educational intentions, and according to family goals. Educators decide how much they want to shelter their students or to sanction certain works or authors, poets, and playwrights.

On a broader note, our goal in this series is to provide parent educators and Christian schools with educationally sound, rigorous literature courses that equip students
1. to think critically about their world and their participation in it;
2. to write their thoughts, primarily through essays;
3. to articulate their thoughts through small group discussions with peers, families, broader communities, and through occasional formal speeches;
4. to enhance vocabulary through reading and studying quality literature;
5. to converse about the major worldviews of authors of literature, past and present;
6. to develop and refine their own worldviews through participating in biblical application and Christian principles in weekly studies.

Additionally, we provide educators with an instructional CD in the back of each teacher edition. Narrated by the author, the CD is designed to provide extra commentary on the unit studies.

Ideally, students will complete these entire curricula; however, parent educators and teachers are free to choose literary selections that best fit their goals with students. Regardless of the choices, I pray that students come away from studying *Skills for Literary Analysis*, *Skills for Rhetoric*, *American Literature*, *British Literature*, and *World Literature* not only highly educated but also equipped to participate in and contribute to their earthly home while preparing for their heavenly home.

Enjoy!
Sheila Moss

Introduction

I am profoundly enthusiastic about the future. Not only do I trust in our Mighty God, I am greatly encouraged by what I see in this generation. God is doing great things in the midst of students.

There is much need in our physical world. In his seminal work *The Dust of Death* (Downers Grove, Illinois: Intervarsity Press, 1973), social critic Os Guinness prophetically argues that "western culture is marked . . . by a distinct slowing of momentum . . . a decline in purposefulness. . . ." Guinness implies that ideals and traditions that have been central to American civilization are losing their compelling cultural authority. In short, there is no corpus of universally accepted morality that Americans follow. As Dallas Willard in *The Divine Conspiracy* (San Francisco: HarperCollins Publishers, 1997) states, ". . . there is no recognized moral knowledge upon which projects of fostering moral development could be based."

In his poem "The Second Coming" William Butler Yeats writes

The best lack all conviction, while the worst
Are full of passionate intensity
Turning and turning in the widening gyre;
The falcon cannot hear the falconer.

In the beginning of the twenty-first century, America is spinning out of control. She is stretching her wings adventurously but is drifting farther away from her God. America is in trouble. How do we know?

You are America's first generation to grow up when wholesale murder is legal; the first generation to access 130 channels and at the same time to access almost nothing of value. In 1993 in their book *The Day America Told the Truth* (NY: Simon & Schuster Publishers, Inc.), James Patterson and Peter Kim warned that 87% of Americans do not believe that the Ten Commandments should be obeyed and 91% of them tell at least one lie a day. Unfortunately, I doubt things are any better today than they were over 10 years ago. The challenge, the bad news, is that this is a time when outrage is dead. Whatever needs to be done, you and your friends are probably going to have to do it.

I think the good news is that we are turning a corner. I believe that in the near future Americans will be looking to places of stability and strength for direction. Besides, by default, those people whose lives are in reasonably good shape, who have some reason to live beyond the next paycheck, will have an almost inexorable appeal. Those who walk in the Light will draw others into the very-same Light. My prayer is that these curricula will help you walk in the Light in a modest way.

I believe that God is raising a mighty generation at the very time that many twenty-first century Americans are searching for truth—at the very time they are hungry for things of the Lord. You will be the culture-creators of the next century. You are a special generation, a special people.

Young people, I strongly believe that you are the generation God has called *for such a time as this* to bring a Spirit-inspired revival. God is stirring the water again at the beginning of this century. He is offering a new beginning for a new nation. I believe you are the personification of that new beginning.

You are part of one of the most critical generations in the history of Western culture. Indeed, only Augustine's generation comes close in importance to your generation. In both cases—today and during the life of Augustine, Bishop of Hippo—civilizations were in decline. Young Augustine lived through the decline of the Roman world; you are living through the decline of American cultural superiority. Even though the barbarians conquered Rome, the Christians conquered the barbarians.

Similar to Anne Bradstreet and other young Puritans who settled in 1630 Boston, you will need to replace this old, reprobate culture with a new God-centered, God-breathed society, or our nation may not survive another century.

While I was a graduate student at Harvard University in the mid-1970s, I attended a chapel service where the presenter self-righteously proclaimed that we Harvard students were the next generation of culture creators. Indeed. Perhaps he was right—look at the moral mess my generation created!

Evangelical scholars Nathan Hatch and George Marsden argue, and I think persuasively, that you young people will be the next generation of elites: important politicians, inspired playwrights, and presidents of Fortune 500 companies.

I profoundly believe and fervently hope that you young people will also be the new elite of culture creators. I define "elitism" as the ability and propensity of an individual or a group to assume leadership and culture-creation in a given society. In his essay "Blessed Are the History-Makers," theologian Walter Bruggemann reminds us that culture is created and history is made by those who are radically committed to obeying God at all costs.

Will you be counted among those who are radically committed—being smart, but above all, loving, worshipping, and being obedient to the Word of God? In your generation and for the first time in 300 years of American cultural history, the marriage of smart minds and born-again hearts is becoming visible. This combination is potent indeed and has revolutionary implications for twenty-first century cultural America. Now, as in the Puritan era, a spirit-filled elite with all its ramifications is exciting to behold.

This book is dedicated to the ambitious goal of preparing you to be a twenty-first century world changer for the Christ whom John Milton in *Paradise Lost* called "the countenance too severe to be beheld" (VI, 825).

James Stobaugh

LESSON 1

THE NEW LAND TO 1750: PURITANISM AND NATIVE AMERICAN VOICES

VARIOUS PURITAN WRITINGS

John Winthrop

The Puritan Separatists, incorrectly called *Pilgrims* by later generations, were members of a religious sect called *Puritans*. They separated from the Church of England and thus were called *Separatist Puritans*. Other Puritans—who settled in the Boston area—sought to *purify* the church, not to *withdraw* from it. They were merely called Puritans. The Pilgrims included all 1620 settlers at Plymouth, MA. The Puritans settled in Boston in 1630.

The Plymouth settlers included both religious saints—the Separatist Puritans—and secular adventurers. The Puritans, as well as the Separatist Puritans, then, were fervently religious people with a firm belief in God's omnipotence and in His abiding love. In this section we will look at several examples of Puritan literature. Some of us may think of Puritans as colorless, unhappy, stuffy white-collared, black-coated, frowning saints. Nothing could be farther from the truth. They were fun-loving, active people whose love of life was surpassed only by their love of God. Actually, the Puritan civilization was a successful marriage between cultural sonority and Christian devotion.

John Calvin believed that salvation was accomplished by the almighty power of the triune God. The Father chose a people, the Son died for them, the Holy Spirit made Christ's death effective by bringing the elect to faith and repentance, thereby causing them willingly to obey the Gospel. The entire process (election, redemption, regeneration) was the work of God and was by grace alone. Thus God, not man, determined who would be the recipients of the gift of salvation.

You will examine several Puritan writings and understand their distinctive worldview.

Reading ahead: No readings are necessary for Lesson 2.

For Lesson 3 students should review *Religious Affections*, Jonathan Edwards and Anne Bradstreet poetry in this text.

Guide Question: What does the word "worldview" mean? What is your worldview? What worldviews do you encounter in the world around you?

The historian Perry Miller wrote, "Without some understanding of Puritanism . . . there is no understanding of America." Indeed. But who were the Puritans?

Puritanism, a movement arising within the Church of England in the latter part of the 16th century, sought to carry the reformation of that church beyond the point the early Anglican or Church of England had reached. The Church of England was attempting to establish a middle course between Roman Catholicism and the ideas of the Protestant reformers. This attempt was unacceptable to a growing number of Puritan reformers, who wanted the Church of England to reject Anglicanism and embrace Calvinism. The term "Puritanism" was also used in a broader sense to refer to attitudes and values considered characteristic of these radical reformers. Thus, the Separatists in the 16th century, the Quakers in the 17th century, and Nonconformists after the Restoration were called Puritans, although they were no longer part of the established church. For the purposes of the American Literature course, Puritans will be referred to in two ways: Puritans and Pilgrims.

The stated purpose of the Puritan expedition to North America was to worship God in a place and in a fashion that was more conducive to their worldview. This worldview was decidedly Theistic/ Calvinistic. These religious Separatists believed that the true church was a voluntary company of the faithful under the spiritual direction of a pastor. In all Puritanism, including Separatism, there was not a clear distinction between what was secular and what was sacred. The Church and state were one, and the notion that they were separate was indeed a ludicrous thought to the Puritan. The Pilgrims, unlike the Puritans who settled in Boston, wanted to separate from the Church of England—not merely "purify" the church—but they did not wish to separate the Church from the state.

The Puritans, then, were committed Christians, but they were also loyal Englishmen. They came to the new world as English patriots with a strong faith in Jesus Christ.

In 1620, the Pilgrims, whose legal destination really laid 300 miles south in Virginia, mistakenly landed on Cape Cod. They called their new settlement Plimouth Plantation. In the first year of settlement, nearly half the settlers died of disease. Thanks to help from the local Natives, a few survived. Although none of their principal economic pursuits—farming, hunting, fishing, and trading—promised instant wealth, the Pilgrims became self-sufficient after only five years. They were free to focus on more eternal issues—advancing the Kingdom of God in a wilderness.

Before disembarking from the *Mayflower* in 1620, William Bradford demanded that all the adult males sign a compact promising obedience to a legal covenant promoting a very narrow theistic legal plan. The compact placed biblical law above British common law. The highly religious Mayflower Compact was an important step in the evolution of American democracy.

Like the Puritan Separatists, the Puritans of Boston in 1630 arrived in Massachusetts Bay. They had sailed to America to worship God freely. The Puritans did not desire to separate themselves from the Church of England but, rather, hoped to reform it. Nonetheless, the notions of freedom and equality, so precious to later New England patriots, were completely foreign to Puritan leaders. The leaders of the Massachusetts Bay enterprise never intended their colony to be a bastion of freedom and tolerance in the New World; rather, they intended it to be a "City on a Hill," a model of Christian felicity and enthusiasm.

"City upon a Hill"
1630

Now the onely way to avoyde this shipwracke and to provide for our posterity is to followe the Counsell of Micah, to doe Justly, to love mercy, to walke humbly with our God, for this end, wee must be knitt together in this worke as one man, wee must entertaine each other in brotherly Affeccion, wee must be willing to abridge our selves of our superfluities, for the supply of others necessities, wee must uphold a familiar Commerce together in all meekenes, gentlenes, patience and liberallity, wee must delight in eache other, make others Condicions our owne rejoyce together, mourne together, labour, and suffer together, allwayes haveing before our eyes our Commission and Community in the worke, our Community as members of the same body, soe shall wee keepe the unitie of the spirit in the bond of peace, the Lord will be our God and delight to dwell among us, as his owne people and will commaund a blessing upon us in all our wayes, soe that wee shall see much more of his wisdome power goodnes and truthe then formerly wee have beene acquainted with, wee shall finde that the God of Israell is among us, when tenn of us shall be able to resist a thousand of our enemies, when hee shall make us a prayse and glory, that men shall say of succeeding plantacions: the lord make it like that of New England: for wee must Consider that wee shall be as a Citty upon a Hill, the eies of all people are uppon us; soe that if wee shall deale falsely with our god in this worke wee have undertaken and soe cause him to withdrawe his present help from us, wee shall be made a story and a byword through the world, wee shall open the mouthes of enemies to speake evill of the wayes of god and all professours for Gods sake; wee shall shame the faces of many of gods worthy servants, and cause theire prayers to be turned into Cursses upon us till wee be consumed out of the good land whether wee are going: And to shutt upp this discourse with that exhortacion of Moses that faithfull servant of the Lord in his last farewell to Israell Deut. 30. Beloved there is now sett before us life, and good, deathe and evill in that wee are Commaunded this day to love the Lord our God, and to love one another to walke in his wayes and to keepe his Commaundements and his Ordinance, and his lawes, and the Articles of our Covenant with him that wee may live and be multiplyed, and that the Lord our God may blesse us in the land whether wee goe to possesse it: But if our heartes shall turne away soe that wee will not obey, but shall be seduced and worshipp other Gods our pleasures, and proffitts, and serve them, it is propounded unto us this day, wee shall surely perishe out of the good Land whether wee passe over this vast Sea to possesse it;

Therefore lett us choose life,
    that wee, and our Seede,
    may live; by obeyeing his voyce, and cleaveing to him,
    for hee is our life, and our prosperity.
www.mtholyoke.edu/acad/intrel/winthrop.htm

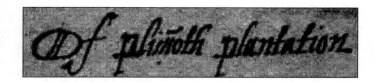

Massachusetts Bay was not a democracy; it was an autocracy under the law of the land and the perceived laws of the Bible. It was one of the first efforts to create a new society entirely on the Word of God. The first governor, John Winthrop, believed that it was the duty of the public officials of the commonwealth to act entirely according to the laws of the land and the laws of the World of God. The will of the people was suspect and even spurious when stacked against the Bible. Perhaps there will never again be such a people whose worldview was so manifestly evident in its literature and art. Enjoy . . .

The History of Plimoth Plantation

William Bradford

William Bradford went with his separatist English friends (called *Pilgrims*) for an eleven-year stay in Holland. Later, the Pilgrims returned to England. In 1620, Bradford led the historic pilgrims' group when it sailed from England to settle at Plymouth. William Bradford's *The History of Plimoth Plantation* is best termed a chronicle, a nonfictional literary genre showing a factual record of events in chronological order.

The following is a copy of Chapter Nine, *The History of Plimoth Plantation*.

September 6 (1620). These troubles being blown over, and now all being compact together in one ship, they put to sea again with a prosperous wind, which continued divers days together, which was some encouragement unto them; yet according to the usual manner many were afflicted with sea sickness. And I may not omit here a special work of God's providence. There was a proud and very profane young man, one of the sea-men, of a lusty, able body, which made him the more haughty; he would always be condemning the poor people in their sickness, and cursing them daily with grievous execrations, and did not let to tell them, that he hoped to help to cast half of them overboard before they came to their journey's end, and to make merry with what they had; and if he were by any gently reproved, he would curse and swear most bitterly. But it pleased God before they came half seas over, to smite this young man with a grievous disease, of which he died in a desperate manner, and so was himself the first that was thrown overboard. Thus his curses light on his own head; and it was an astonishment to all his fellows, for they noted it to be the just hand of God upon him.

After they had enjoyed fair winds and weather for a season, they were encountered many times with cross winds, and met with many fierce storms, with which the ship was shroudly shaken, and her upper works made very leaky; and one of the main beams in the mid ships was bowed and cracked,

> So they committed themselves to the will of God and resolved to proceed.

which put them in some fear that the ship could not be able to perform the voyage. So some of the chief of the company, perceiving the mariners to fear the sufficiency of the ship, as appeared by their mutterings, they entered into serious consultation with the master and other officers of the ship, to consider in time of the danger; and rather to return then to cast themselves into a desperate and inevitable peril. And truly there was great distraction and difference of opinion among the mariners themselves; fain would they do what could be done for their wages sake, (being now half the seas over), and on the other hand they were loath to hazard their lives too desperately.

But in examining of all opinions, the master and others affirmed they knew the ship to be strong and firm under water; and for the buckling of the main beam, there was a great iron screw the passengers

© Arttoday.com

brought out of Holland, which would raise the beam into his place; the which being done, the carpenter and master affirmed that with a post put under it, set firm in the lower deck, and other-ways bound, he would make it sufficient. And as for the decks and upper works they would caulk them as well as they could, and though with the working of the ship they would not long keep staunch, yet there would otherwise be no great danger, if they did not overpress her with sails. So they committed themselves to the will of God, and resolved to proceed. In sundry of these storms the winds were so fierce, and the seas so high, as they could not bear a knot of sail, but were forced to hull, for divers days together. And in one of them, as they thus lay at hull, in a mighty storm, a lusty young man (called John Howland) coming upon some occasion above the gratings, was, with a seele of the ship thrown into the sea; but it pleased God that he caught hold of the topsail halyards, which hung overboard, and ran out at length; yet he held his hold (though he was sundry fathoms under water) till he was hauled up by the same rope to the brim of the water, and then with a boat hook and other means got into the ship again, and his life saved; and though he was something ill with it, yet he lived many years after, and became a profitable member both in church and commonwealth. In all this voyage their died but one of the passengers, which was William Butten, a youth, servant to Samuel Fuller, when they drew near the coast. But to omit other things, (that I may be brief), after long beating at sea they fell with that land which is called Cape Cod; the which being made and certainly known to be it, they were not a little joyful. After some deliberation had amongst themselves and with the master of the ship, they tacked about and resolved to stand for the southward (the

wind and weather being fair) to find some place about Hudson's River for their habitation.

But after they had sailed that course about half a day, they fell amongst dangerous shoals and roaring breakers, and they were so far entangled therewith as they conceived themselves in great danger; and the wind shrinking upon them withal, they resolved to bear up again for the Cape, and thought themselves happy to get out of those dangers before night overtook them, as by God's providence they did. And the next day they got into the Cape-harbor where they rid in safety. A word or two by the way of this cape; it was thus first named by Captain Gosnold and his company, Anno. 1602, and after by Captain Smith was called Cape James; but it retains the former name amongst seamen. Also that point which first showed these dangerous shoals unto them, they called Point Care, and Tucker's Terror; but the French and Dutch to this day call it Malabar, by reason of those perilous shoals, and the losses they have suffered there.

Being thus arrived in a good harbor and brought safe to land, they fell upon their knees and blessed the God of heaven, who had brought them over the vast and furious ocean, and delivered them from all the per-

> Being thus arrived in a good harbor and brought safe to land, they fell upon their knees and blessed the God of heaven, who had brought them over the vast and furious ocean, and delivered them from all the perils and miseries thereof, again to set their feet on the firm and stable earth, their proper element.

ils and miseries thereof, again to set their feet on the firm and stable earth, their proper element. And no marvel if they were thus joyful, seeing wise Seneca was so affected with sailing a few miles on the coast of his own Italy; as he affirmed, that he had rather remain twenty years on his way by land, then pass by sea to any place in a short time; so tedious and dreadful was the same unto him.

But here I cannot but stay and make a pause, and stand half amazed at this poor people's present condition; and so I think will the reader too, when he well considers the same. Being thus passed the vast ocean, and a sea of troubles before in their preparation (as may be remembered by that which went before), they had now no friends to welcome them, nor inns to entertain or refresh their weather-beaten bodies, no houses or

© Arttoday.com

much less towns to repair to, to seek for succor. It is recorded in scripture as a mercy to the apostle and his shipwrecked company, that the barbarians showed no small kindness in refreshing them, but these savage barbarians, when they met with them (as after will appear) were readier to fill their sides full of arrows then otherwise. And for the season it was winter, and they that know the winters of that country know them to be sharp and violent and subject to cruel and fierce storms, dangerous to travel to known places, much more to search an unknown coast. Besides, what could they see but a hideous and desolate wilderness, full of wild beasts and wild men? and what multitudes there might be of them they knew not. Neither could they, as it were, go up to the top of Pigsah, to view from this wilderness a more goodly country to feed their hopes; for which way soever they turned their eyes (save upward to the heavens) they could have little solace or content in respect of any outward objects. For summer being done, all things stand upon them with a weather-beaten face; and the whole country, full of woods and thickets, represented a wild and savage hew. If they looked behind them, there was the mighty ocean which they had passed, and was now as a main bar and gulf to separate them from all the civil parts of the world. If it be said they had a ship to succor them, it is true; but what heard they daily from the master and company? But that with speed they should look out a place with their shallop, where they would be at some near distance; for the season was such as he would not stir from thence till a safe harbor was discovered by them where they would be, and he might go without danger; and that victuals consumed apace, but he must and would keep sufficient for themselves and their return. Yea, it was muttered by some, that if they got not a place in time, they would turn them and their goods ashore and leave them. Let it also be considered what weak hopes of supply and succor they left behind them, that might bear up their minds in this sad condition and trials they were under; and they could not but be very small. It is

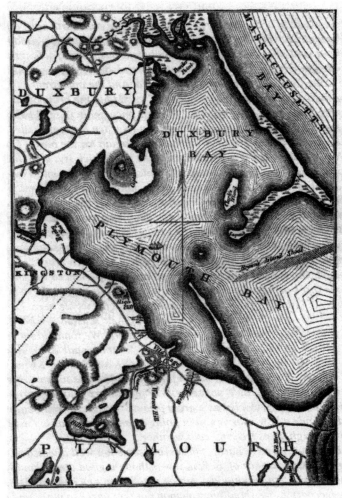

© Arttoday.com

May not and ought not the children of these fathers rightly say: "Our fathers were Englishmen which came over this great ocean, and were ready to perish in this wilderness; but they cried unto the Lord, and he heard their voice, and looked on their adversity, etc. Let them therefore praise the Lord, because he is good, and his mercies endure forever. Yea, let them which have been redeemed of the Lord, show how he hath delivered them from the hand of the oppressor. When they wandered in the desert wilderness out of the way, and found no city to dwell in, both hungry, and thirsty, their soul was overwhelmed in them. Let them confess before the Lord his loving kindness, and his wonderful works before the sons of men.

Mourt's Relation was written by Edward Winslow, although many scholars argue that William Bradford collaborated. Written between November 1620 and November 1621, *Mourt's Relation* describes in detail what happened to the Pilgrims. It is the only extant version of the first Thanksgiving. Why is it called *Mourt's Relation*? It was first published in London in 1622, presumably by George Morton (hence the title, *Mourt's Relation*).

"Wednesday, the sixth of September, the winds coming east north east, a fine small gale, we loosed from Plymouth, having been kindly entertained and courteously used by divers friends there dwelling, and after many difficulties in boisterous storms, at length, by God's providence, upon the ninth of November following, by break of the day we espied land which was deemed to be Cape Cod, and so afterward it proved. And the appearance of it much comforted us, especially seeing so goodly a land, and wooded to the brink of the sea. It caused us to rejoice together, and praise God that had given us once again to see land. And thus we made our course south south west, purposing to go to a river ten leagues to the south of the Cape, but at night the wind being contrary, we put round again for the bay of Cape Cod; and upon the 11th of November we came to an anchor in the bay, which is a good harbor and pleasant bay, circled round, except in the entrance which is about four miles over from land to land, compassed about to the very sea with oaks, pines, juniper, sassafras, and other sweet wood; it is a harbor wherein a thousand sail of ships may safely ride: there we relieved ourselves with wood and water, and refreshed our people, which our shallop was fitted to coast the bay, to search for a habitation; there was the greatest store of fowl that ever we saw.

And every day we saw whales playing hard by us, of which in that place, if we had instruments and means to take them, we might have made a very rich return, which to our great grief we wanted. Our master and his mate, and others experienced in fishing, professed we might have made three or four thousand pounds worth of oil; they preferred it before Greenland whale-fishing, and purpose the next winter to fish for whale here. For cod we assayed, but found none, there is good store, no doubt, in their season. Neither got we any fish all the time we lay there, but some few little ones on the shore. We found great mussels, and very fat and full of sea-pearl, but we could not eat them, for they made us all sick that did eat, as well sailors as passengers; they caused to cast and scour, but they were soon well again.

The bay is so round and circling, that before we could come to anchor we went round all the points of the compass. We could not come near the shore by three quarters of an English mile, because of shallow water, which was a great prejudice to us, for our people going on shore were forced to wade a bow shot or two in going a-land, which caused many to get colds and coughs, for it was nigh times freezing cold weather.

This day before we came to harbor, observing some not well affected to unity and concord, but gave some appearance of faction, it was thought good there should be an association and agreement that we should combine together in one body, and to submit to such government and governors as we should by common consent agree to make and choose, and set our hands to this that follows word for word."

true, indeed, the affections and love of their brethren at Leyden was cordial and entire towards them, but they had little power to help them, or themselves; and how the case stood between them and the merchants at their coming away, hath already been declared. What could now sustain them but the spirit of God and his grace?

May not and ought not the children of these fathers rightly say: "Our fathers were Englishmen which came over this great ocean, and were ready to perish in this wilderness; but they cried unto the Lord, and he heard their voice, and looked on their adversity, etc. Let them therefore praise the Lord, because he is good, and his mercies endure forever. Yea, let them which have been redeemed of the Lord, show how he hath delivered them from the hand of the oppressor. When they wandered in the desert wilderness out of the way, and found no city to dwell in, both hungry, and thirsty, their soul was overwhelmed in them. Let them confess before the Lord his loving kindness, and his wonderful works before the sons of men.

http://members.aol.com/calebj/bradford_journal9.html

CRITICAL THINKING

A. Pretend that you are part of an expedition to Mars. Write a one-page descriptive essay about your surroundings. What similarities do you find between your description and to Bradford's in his diary?

Write a one-paragraph summary of what you find.

Write a one-sentence summary.

B. What was William Bradford's view of nature?

C. An allusion is a brief, often indirect reference to a person, place, event, or artistic work which the author assumes the reader will recognize. To that end, Bradford uses many Biblical allusions. Find two examples and in a one-page illustrative essay show how Bradford uses them.

> An illustrative essay begins with a paragraph introducing the thesis and then has supportive paragraphs to support that thesis.

ENRICHMENT

A. Generally, European Americans made no effort either to live side-by-side with Native Americans or to assimilate Native Americans into their lives. Native Americans were treated as aliens and subversives. As General Sheridan observed 2 centuries later, an only good Indian was a dead Indian. Therefore, the American military employed a systematic form of genocide unparalleled in American history. History shows that early colonial efforts to create a European society to the exclusion of Native Americans resulted in an ethnic cleansing which eliminated almost the entire Native population in the early 19th century.

First, discuss the moral implications of this action. Secondly, offer an alternative solution.

B. Read J. I. Packer, *A Quest For Godliness: The Puritan Vision of the Christian Life* (Wheaton, IL: Crossway Books, Inc., 1990). Packer argues that the depth and breadth of Puritan spiritual life stands in stark contrast to the facile and deadness of modern Western Christianity. He concludes that the main difference between the Puritans and us is spiritual maturity—the Puritans had it, and we simply do not. The Puritans believed in an omnipotent God. They were not grouchy, legalistic, colorless settlers. Rather, they enjoyed life. They had a passion for righteousness; they had a passion for God. In a one-page essay, agree or disagree with Packer's thesis.

C. Edward Taylor (1642-1729) was a New England Puritan's Puritan. Taylor was a colleague of the famous Increase Mather. American critic Donald Stanford says, "Taylor seems to have been endowed with most of those qualities usually connoted by the word *puritan*. He was learned, grave, severe, stubborn, and stiff-necked. He was very, very pious. But his piety was sincere. It was fed by a long continuous spiritual experience arising, so he felt, from a mystical communion with Christ. The reality and depth of this experience is amply witnessed by his poetry."

It was his custom to write a poem ("Meditation") before each Lord's Supper. These poems are wonderful examples of spiritual experience and devotion. Some readers are embarrassed by Taylor's raw intimacy with our Lord!

I can clearly remember a day, when, as a young graduate student at Harvard University in the mid-1970s, surrounded by ivy-covered brick walls, slightly east from Sevier Hall, I stood in Harvard Yard looking at a statue of John Harvard and wondering what had gone wrong. All around me was nihilism and chaos, intellectual pretension and mendacity. Where was the beautiful simplicity and intellectual integrity of the Puritan John Harvard who had founded Harvard College in 1636? Then, to my wonder and surprise, I heard an old praise song. "We are one in the Spirit, we are one in the Lord . . ." It was coming from the Dunster House, which apparently not only had the best breakfast in the yard (i.e., Harvard Yard), but also had a thriving Christian fellowship. Yes, God was very much alive at Harvard University. These saints were the spiritual children of John Harvard, the very reason he founded this august institution. (James Stobaugh)

Meditation 1

What Love is this of thine, that Cannot bee
In thine Infinity, O Lord, Confinde,
Unless it in thy very Person see,
Infinity, and Finity Conjoyn'd?
What hath thy Godhead, as not satisfide
Marri'de our Manhood, making it its Bride?

Oh, Matchless Love! filling Heaven to the brim!
O're running it: all running o're beside
This World! Nay Overflowing Hell; wherein . . .
http://www.puritansermons.com/poetry/taylor.htm

Edward Taylor's poetry displays the influence of English metaphysical poets.

Research the metaphysical poets in England and compare and contrast their writings with Taylor's.

Native American Voice

It would be a mistake to think of Native American peoples as being one people, one nation. In fact, dozens of Native American tribes living along the eastern seaboard warred against each another.

The main Native American tribe in the Virginia area in the early 17th century was the Lenape Powhatan Tribe. By the time the English colonists had arrived, the chief of the Powhatans, Chief Powhatan, ruled a formidable 30-tribe confederacy. He allegedly controlled 128 villages with about 9,000 inhabitants. Powhatan initially opposed the English settlement at Jamestown. According to legend, he changed his policy in 1607 when he released the captured Smith. In April 1614, Pocahontas, Powhatan's daughter, married the planter John Rolfe, and afterwards Powhatan negotiated a peace agreement with his son-in-law's people.

Peace reigned until after Powhatan died in 1618. In 1622 a great war broke out between the English settlers and the Powhatan Confederacy. Initially the Powhatan Confederation very nearly destroyed the Jamestown settlement. In the long term, however, the war destroyed the Confederacy as a viable entity.

The main Native American tribe that the Pilgrims (i.e., Separatist Puritans) encountered was the Wampanoag. In 1600 the Wampanoag probably numbered 12,000 with 40 villages divided roughly between 8,000 on the mainland and another 4,000 on the offshore islands of Martha's Vineyard and Nantucket. However, epidemics swept across New England between 1614 and 1620 and devastated the Wampanoag. Thus, when the Pilgrims landed in 1620, fewer than 2,000 Wampanoag had survived.

There is no recorded Wampanoag Creation legend; however, the story below exemplifies most Native American creation legends.

BIBLICAL APPLICATION

A. Compare the following creation legend with Genesis 1-2.

B. Based on this creation text, compare Native American views of mankind with Biblical views.

Navajo Creation Legend

These stories were told to Sandoval, Hastin Tlo'tsi hee, by his grandmother, Esdzan Hosh kige. Her ancestor was Esdzan at a', the medicine woman who had the Calendar Stone in her keeping. Here are the stories of the Four Worlds that had no sun, and of the Fifth, the world we live in, which some call the Changeable World.

The First World, Ni'hodilqil, was black as black wool. It had four corners, and over these appeared four clouds. These four clouds contained within themselves the elements of the First World. They were in color, black, white, blue, and yellow.

The Black Cloud represented the Female Being or Substance. For as a child sleeps when being nursed, so life slept in the darkness of the Female Being. The White Cloud represented the Male Being or Substance. He was the Dawn, the Light-Which-Awakens, of the First World.

In the East, at the place where the Black Cloud and the White Cloud met, First Man, Atse'hastqin was formed; and with him was formed the white corn, perfect in shape, with kernels covering the whole ear. Dolionot i'ni is the name of this first seed corn, and it is also the name of the place where the Black Cloud and the White Cloud met.

The First World was small in size, a floating island in mist or water. On it there grew one tree, a pine tree, which was later brought to the present world for firewood.

Man was not, however, in his present form. The conception was of a male and a female being who were to become man and woman. The creatures of the First World are thought of as the Mist People; they had no definite form, but were to change to men, beasts, birds, and reptiles of this world.

Now on the western side of the First World, in a place that later was to become the Land of Sunset, there appeared the Blue Cloud, and opposite it there appeared the Yellow Cloud. Where they came together First Woman was formed, and with her the yellow corn. This ear of corn was also perfect. With First Woman there came the white shell and the turquoise and the yucca.

First Man stood on the eastern side of the First World. He represented the Dawn and was the Life Giver. First Woman stood opposite in the West. She represented Darkness and Death.

First Man burned a crystal for a fire. The crystal belonged to the male and was the symbol of the mind and of clear seeing. When First Man burned it, it was the mind's awakening. First Woman burned her turquoise for a fire. They saw each other's lights in the distance. When the Black Cloud and the White Cloud rose higher in the sky First Map set out to find the turquoise light. He went twice without success, and again a third time; then he broke a forked branch from his tree, and, looking through the fork, he marked the place where the light burned. And the fourth time he walked to it and found smoke coming from a home.

"Here is the home I could not find," First Man said.

First Woman answered: "Oh, it is you. I saw you walking around and I wondered why you did not come."

Again the same thing happened when the Blue Cloud and the Yellow Cloud rose higher in the sky. First Woman saw a light and she went out to find it. Three times she was unsuccessful, but the fourth time she saw the smoke and she found the home of First Man.

"I wondered what this thing could be," she said.

"I saw you walking and I wondered why you did not come to me," First Man answered.

About this time there came another person, the Great-Coyote-Who-Was-Formed-in-the-Water, and he was in the form of a male being. He told the two that he had been hatched from an egg. He knew all that was under the water and all that was in the skies. First Man placed this person ahead of himself in all things. The three began to plan what was to come to pass; and while they were thus occupied another being came to them. He also had the form of a man, but he wore a hairy coat, lined with white fur, that fell to his knees and was belted in at the waist. His name was Atse'hashke', First Angry or Coyote. He said to the three: "You believe that you were the first persons. You are mistaken. I was living when you were formed."

Then four beings came together. They were yellow in color and were called the tsts'na or wasp people. They knew the secret of shooting evil and could harm others. They were very powerful.

This made eight people.

Four more beings came. They were small in size and wore red shirts and had little black eyes. They were the naazo'zi or spider ants. They knew how to sting, and were a great people.

After these came a whole crowd of beings. Dark colored they were, with thick lips and dark, protruding eyes. They were the wolazhi'ni, the black ants. They also knew the secret of shooting evil and were powerful; but they killed each other steadily.

By this time there were many people. Then came a multitude of little creatures. They were peaceful and harmless, but the odor from them was unpleasant. They were called the wolazhi'ni nlchu nigi, meaning that which emits an odor. And after the wasps and the different ant people there came the beetles, dragonflies, bat people, the Spider Man and Woman, and the Salt Man and Woman, and others that rightfully had no definite form but were among those people who peopled the First World. And this world, being small in size, became crowded, and the people quarreled and fought among themselves, and in all ways made living very unhappy.

Because of the strife in the First World, First Man, First Woman, the Great-Coyote-Who-Was-Formed-in-the-Water, and the Coyote called First Angry, followed by all the others, climbed up from the World of Darkness and Dampness to the Second or Blue World.

They found a number of people already living there: blue birds, blue hawks, blue jays, blue herons, and all the blue-feathered beings. The powerful swallow people lived there also, and these people made the Second World unpleasant for those who had come from the First World. There was fighting and killing.

The First Four found an opening in the World of Blue Haze; and they climbed through this and led the people up into the Third or Yellow world. The bluebird was the first to reach the Third or Yellow World. After him came the First Four and all the others.

A great river crossed this land from north to south. It was the Female River. There was another river crossing it from east to West, it was the Male River. This Male River flowed through the Female River and on; and the name of this place is tqo alna'osdli, the Crossing of the waters.

There were six mountains in the Third World. In the East was Sis na' jin, the Standing Black Sash. Its ceremonial name is Yolgai'dzil, the Dawn or White Shell Mountain. In the South stood Tso'dzil, the Great Mountain, also called Mountain Tongue. Its ceremonial name is Yodolt i'zhi dzil, the Blue Bead or Turquoise Mountain. In the West stood Dook'oslid, and the meaning of this name is forgotten. Its ceremonial name is Dichi'li dzil, the Abalone Shell Mountain. In the North stood Debe'ntsa, Many Sheep Mountain. Its ceremonial name is Bash'zhini dzil, Obsidian Mountain. Then there was Dzil na'odili, the Upper Mountain. It was very sacred; and its name means also the Center Place, and the people moved around it. Its ceremonial name is Ntl'is dzil, Precious Stone or Banded Rock Mountain. There was still another mountain called Chol'i'i or Dzil na'odili choli, and it was also a sacred mountain.

There was no sun in this land, only the two rivers and the six mountains. And these rivers and mountains were not in their present form, but rather the substance of mountains and rivers as were First Man, First Woman, and the others.

Now beyond Sis na' jin, in the east, there lived the Turquoise Hermaphrodite, Ashton nutli. He was also known as the Turquoise Boy. And near this person grew the male reed. Beyond, still farther in the east, there lived a people called the Hadahuneya'nigi, the Mirage or Agate People. Still farther in the east there lived twelve beings called the Naaskiddi. And beyond the home of these beings there lived four others—the Holy Man, the Holy Woman, the Holy Boy, and the Holy Girl.

In the West there lived the White Shell Hermaphrodite or Girl, and with her was the big female reed which grew at the water's edge. It had no tassel. Beyond her in the West there lived another stone people called the Hadahunes'tqin, the Ground Heat People. Still farther on there lived another twelve beings, but these were all females. And again, in the Far West, there lived four Holy Ones.

Within this land there lived the Kisa'ni, the ancients of the Pueblo People. On the six mountains there lived the Cave Dwellers or Great Swallow People. On the mountains lived also the light and dark squirrels, chipmunks, mice, rats, the turkey people, the deer and cat people, the spider people, and the lizards and snakes. The beaver people lived along the rivers, and the frogs and turtles and all the underwater people in the water. So far all the people were similar. They had no definite form, but they had been given different names because of different characteristics.

Now the plan was to plant.

First Man called the people together. He brought forth the white corn which had been formed with him. First Woman brought the yellow corn. They laid the perfect ears side by side; then they asked one person from among the many to come and help them. The Turkey stepped forward. They asked him where he had come from, and he said that he had come from the Gray Mountain. He danced back and forth four times, then he shook his feather coat and there dropped from his clothing four kernels of corn, one gray, one blue, one black, and one red. Another person was asked to help in the plan of the planting. The Big Snake came forward. He likewise brought forth four seeds, the pumpkin, the watermelon, the cantaloupe, and the muskmelon. His plants all crawl on the ground.

They planted the seeds, and their harvest was great.

After the harvest the Turquoise Boy from the East came and visited First Woman. When First Man returned to his home he found his wife with this boy. First Woman told her husband that Ashon nutli' was of her flesh and not of his flesh. She said that she had used her own fire, the turquoise, and had ground her own yellow corn into meal. This corn she had planted and cared for herself.

Now at that time there were four chiefs: Big Snake, Mountain Lion, Otter, and Bear. And it was the custom when the black cloud rose in the morning for First Man to come out of his dwelling and speak to the people. After First Man had spoken the four chief s told them what they should do that day. They also spoke of the past and of the future. But after First Man found his wife with another he would not come out to speak to the people. The black cloud rose higher, but First Man would not leave his dwelling; neither would he eat or drink. No one spoke to the people for days. All during this time First Man remained silent, and would not touch food or water. Four times the white cloud rose. Then the four chiefs went to First Man and demanded to know why he would not speak to the people. The chiefs asked this question three times, and a fourth, before First Man would answer them.

He told them to bring him an emetic. This he took and purified himself. First Man then asked them to send the hermaphrodite to him. When he came First Man asked him if the metate and brush were his. He said that they were. First Man asked him if he could cook and prepare food like a woman, if he could weave, and brush the hair. And when he had assured First Man that he could do all manner of woman's work, First Man said: "Go and prepare food and bring it to me." After he had eaten, First Man told the four chiefs what he had seen, and what his wife had said.

At this time the Great-Coyote-Who-Was-Formed-in-the-Water came to First Man and told him to cross the river. They made a big raft and crossed at the place where the Male River followed through the Female River. And all the male beings left the female beings on the river bank; and as they rowed across the river they looked back and saw that First Woman and the female beings were laughing. They were also behaving very wickedly.

In the beginning the women did not mind being alone. They cleared and planted a small field. On the other side of the river First Man and the chiefs hunted and planted their seeds. They had a good harvest. Nadle ground the corn and cooked the food. Four seasons passed. The men continued to have plenty and were happy; but the women became lazy, and only weeds grew on their land. The women wanted fresh meat. Some of them tried to join the men and were drowned in the river.

First Woman made a plan. As the women had no way to satisfy their passions, some fashioned long narrow rocks, some used the feathers of the turkey, and some used strange plants (cactus). First Woman told them to use these things. One woman brought forth a big stone. This stone-child was later the Great Stone that rolled over the earth killing men. Another woman brought forth the Big Birds of Tsa bida'hi; and others gave birth to the giants and monsters who later destroyed many people.

On the opposite side of the river the same condition existed. The men, wishing to satisfy their passions, killed the females of mountain sheep, lion, and antelope. Lightning struck these men. When First Man learned of this he warned his men that they would all be killed. He told them that they were indulging in a dangerous practice. Then the second chief spoke: he said that life was hard and that it was a pity to see women drowned. He asked why they should not bring the women across the river and all live together again.

"Now we can see for ourselves what comes from our wrong doing," he said. "We will know how to act in the future." The three other chiefs of the animals agreed with him, so First Man told them to go and bring the women.

After the women had been brought over the river, First Man spoke: "We must be purified," he said. "Everyone must bathe. The men must dry themselves with white corn meal, and the women, with yellow."

This they did, living apart for days. After the fourth day, First Woman came and threw her right arm around her husband. She spoke to the others and said that she could see her mistakes, but with her husband's help she would henceforth lead a good life. Then all the male and female beings came and lived with each other again.

The people moved to different parts of the land. Some time passed; then First Woman became troubled by the monotony of life. She made a plan. She went to Atse'hashke, the Coyote called First Angry, and giving him the rainbow she said: "I have suffered greatly in the past. I have suffered from want of meat and corn and clothing. Many of my maidens have died. I have suffered many things. Take the rainbow and go to the place where the rivers cross. Bring me the two pretty children of Tqo holt sodi, the Water Buffalo, a boy and a girl.

The Coyote agreed to do this. He walked over the rainbow. He entered the home of the Water Buffalo and stole the two children; and these he hid in his big skin coat with the white fur lining. And when he returned he refused to take off his coat, but pulled it around himself and looked very wise. After this happened the people saw white light in the East and in the South and West and North. One of the deer people ran to the East, and returning, said that the white light was a great sheet of water. The sparrow hawk flew to the South, the great hawk to the West, and the kingfisher to the North. They returned and said that a flood was coming. The kingfisher said that the water was greater in the North, and that it was near. The flood was coming and the Earth was sinking. And all this happened because the Coyote had stolen the two children of the Water Buffalo, and only First Woman and the Coyote knew the truth.

When First Man learned of the coming of the water, he sent word to all the people, and he told them to come to the mountain called Sis na'jin. He told them to bring with them all of the seeds of the plants used for food. All living beings were to gather on the top of Sis na'jin. First Man traveled to the six sacred mountains, and, gathering earth from them, he put it in his medicine bag.

The water rose steadily.

When all the people were halfway up Sis na' jin, First Man discovered that he had forgotten his medicine bag. Now this bag contained not only the earth from the six sacred mountains, but his magic, the medicine he used to call the rain down upon the earth and to make things grow. He could not live without his medicine bag, and he wished to jump into the rising water; but the others begged him not to do this. They went to the kingfisher and asked him to dive into the water and recover the bag. This the bird did. When First Man had his medicine bag again in his possession, he breathed on it four times and thanked his people.

When they had all arrived it was found that the Turquoise Boy had brought with him the big Male Reed; and the White Shell Girl had brought with her the big Female Reed. Another person brought poison ivy; and another, cotton, which was later used for cloth. This person was the spider. First Man had with him his spruce tree which he planted on the top of Sis na'jin. He used his fox medicine to make it grow; but the spruce tree began to send out branches and to taper at the top, so First Man planted the big Male Reed. All the people blew on it, and it grew and grow until it reached the canopy of the sky. They tried to blow inside the reed, but it was solid. They asked the woodpecker to drill out the hard heart. Soon they were able to peek through the opening, but they had to blow and blow before it was large enough to climb through. They climbed up inside the big male reed, and after them the water continued to rise.

When the people reached the Fourth World, they saw that it was not a very large place. Some say that it was called the White World; but not all medicine men agree that this is so.

The last person to crawl through the reed was the turkey from Gray Mountain. His feather coat was flecked with foam, for after him came the water. And with the water came the female Water Buffalo who pushed her head through the opening in the reed. She had a great quantity of curly hair which floated on the water, and she had two horns, half black and half yellow. From the tips of the horns the lightning flashed.

First Man asked the Water Buffalo why she had come and why she had sent the flood. She said nothing. Then the Coyote drew the two babies from his coat and said that it was, perhaps, because of them.

The Turquoise Boy took a basket and filled it with turquoise. On top of the turquoise he placed the blue pollen, tha'di'thee do tlij, from the blue flowers, and the yellow pollen from the corn; and on top of these he placed the pollen from the water flags, tquel aqa'di din; and again on top of these he placed the crystal, which is river pollen. This basket he gave to the Coyote who put it between the horns of the Water Buffalo. The Coyote said that with this sacred offering he would give back the male child. He said that the male child would be known as the Black Cloud or Male Rain, and that he would bring the thunder and lightning. The female child he would keep. She would be known as the Blue, Yellow, and White Clouds or Female Rain. She would

be the gentle rain that would moisten the earth and help them to live. So he kept the female child, and he placed the male child on the sacred basket between the horns of the Water Buffalo. And the Water Buffalo disappeared, and the waters with her.

After the water sank, there appeared another person. They did not know him, and they asked him where he had come from. He told them that he was the badger, nahashch'id, and that he had been formed. First Man was not satisfied with the Fourth World. It was a small barren land; and the great water had soaked the earth and made the sowing of seeds impossible. He planted the big Female Reed and it grew up to the vaulted roof of this Fourth World. First Man sent the newcomer, the badger, up inside the reed, but before he reached the upper world water began to drip, so he returned and said that he was frightened.

At this time there came another strange being. First Man asked him where he had been formed, and he told him that he had come from the Earth itself. This was the locust. He said that it was now his turn to do something, and he offered to climb up the reed.

The locust made a headband of a little reed, and on his forehead he crossed two arrows. These arrows were dressed with yellow tail feathers. With this sacred headdress and the help of all the Holy Beings the locust climbed up to the Fifth World. He dug his way through the reed as he digs in the earth now. He then pushed through mud until he came to water. When he emerged he saw a black water bird swimming toward him. He had arrows crossed on the back of his head and big eyes.

The bird said: "What are you doing here? This is not your country." And continuing, he told the locust that unless he could make magic be would not allow him to remain. The black water bird drew an arrow from back of his head, and shoving it into his mouth drew it out his nether extremity. He inserted it underneath his body and drew it out of his mouth.

"That is nothing," said the locust. He took the arrows from his headband and pulled them both ways through his body, between his shell and his heart. The bird believed that the locust possessed great medicine, and he swam away to the East, taking the water with him. Then came the blue water bird from the South, and the yellow water bird from the West, and the white water bird from the North, and everything happened as before. The locust performed the magic with his arrows, and when the last water bird had gone he found himself sitting on land.

The locust returned to the lower world and told the people that the beings above had strong medicine, and that he had had great difficulty getting the best of them.

Now two dark clouds and two white clouds rose, and this meant that two nights and two days had passed, for there was still no sun. First Man again sent the badger to the upper world, and he returned covered with mud, terrible mud. First Man gathered chips of turquoise which he offered to the five Chiefs of the Winds who lived in the uppermost world of all. They were pleased with the gift, and they sent down the winds and dried the Fifth World.

First Man and his people saw four dark clouds and four white clouds pass, and then they sent the badger up the reed. This time when the badger returned he said that he had come out on solid earth. So First Man and First Woman led the people to the Fifth World, which some call the Many Colored Earth and some the Changeable Earth. They emerged through a lake surrounded by four mountains. The water bubbles in this lake when anyone goes near.

Now after all the people had emerged from the lower worlds, First Man and First Woman dressed the Mountain Lion with yellow, black, white, and grayish corn and placed him on one side. They dressed the Wolf with white tail feathers and placed him on the other side. They divided the people into two groups. The first group was told to choose whichever chief they wished. They made their choice, and, although they thought they had chosen the Mountain Lion, they found that they had taken the Wolf for their chief. The Mountain Lion was the chief for the other side. And these people who had the Mountain Lion for their chief turned out to be the people of the Earth. They were to plant seeds and harvest corn. The followers of the Wolf chief became the animals and birds; they turned into all the creatures that fly and crawl and run and swim.

And after all the beings were divided, and each had his own form, they went their ways.

This is the story of the Four Dark Worlds and the Fifth, the World we live in. Some medicine men tell us that there are two worlds above us; the first is the World of the Spirits of Living Things; the second is the Place of Melting into One.

http://www.earthbow.com/native/navajo/firstman.htm

CRITICAL THINKING

Normally Native People governments were *benevolent despotisms*; however, the Iroquois Confederacy made a great effort to be *democratic*. Why? Offer evidence from the following text.

Iroquois Confederacy Constitution

BACKGROUND

Another important eastern Native American representation was the Iroquois Confederacy. The Iroquois was founded in the 16th century in what is now central New York State. The original confederacy consisted of five tribes—the Mohawk, Onondaga, Cayuga, Oneida, and Seneca—and was known as the Five Nations, or the League of Five Nations. Sometime between 1715 and 1722, however, the Tuscaroras, an Iroquoian tribe originally of North Carolina, which had migrated to New York, was formally admitted to the confederacy, and the name of the league was changed to the Six Nations, or the League of Six Nations. At least 150 years before the American Colonists wrote their constitution, the Iroquois nation had a constitution. The first section of that lengthy constitution is presented below:

The Great Binding Law, Gaywnashagowa

1. I am Dekanawidah and with the Five Nations' Confederate Lords I plant the Tree of Great Peace. I plant it in your territory, Adodarhoh, and the Onondaga Nation, in the territory of you who are Firekeepers.

I name the tree the Tree of the Great Long Leaves. Under the shade of this Tree of the Great Peace we spread the soft white feathery down of the globe thistle as seats for you, Adodarhoh, and your cousin Lords.

We place you upon those seats, spread soft with the feathery down of the globe thistle, there beneath the shade of the spreading branches of the Tree of Peace. There shall you sit and watch the Council Fire of the Confederacy of the Five Nations, and all the affairs of the Five Nations shall be transacted at this place before you, Adodarhoh, and your cousin Lords, by the Confederate Lords of the Five Nations.

2. Roots have spread out from the Tree of the Great Peace, one to the north, one to the east, one to the south and one to the west. The name of these roots is The Great White Roots and their nature is Peace and Strength.

If any man or any nation outside the Five Nations shall obey the laws of the Great Peace and make known their disposition to the Lords of the Confederacy, they may trace the Roots to the Tree and if their minds are clean and they are obedient and promise to obey the wishes of the Confederate Council, they shall be welcomed to take shelter beneath the Tree of the Long Leaves.

We place at the top of the Tree of the Long Leaves an Eagle who is able to see afar. If he sees in the distance any evil approaching or any danger threatening he will at once warn the people of the Confederacy.

3. To you Adodarhoh, the Onondaga cousin Lords, I and the other Confederate Lords have entrusted the caretaking and the watching of the Five Nations Council Fire.

When there is any business to be transacted and the Confederate Council is not in session, a messenger shall be dispatched either to Adodarhoh, Hononwirehtonh or Skanawatih, Fire Keepers, or to their War Chiefs with a full statement of the case desired to be considered. Then shall Adodarhoh call his cousin (associate) Lords together and consider whether or not the case is of sufficient importance to demand the attention of the Confederate Council. If so, Adodarhoh shall dispatch messengers to summon all the Confederate Lords to assemble beneath the Tree of the Long Leaves.

When the Lords are assembled, the Council Fire shall be kindled, but not with chestnut wood, and Adodarhoh shall formally open the Council.

Then shall Adodarhoh and his cousin Lords, the Fire Keepers, announce the subject for discussion.

The Smoke of the Confederate Council Fire shall ever ascend and pierce the sky so that other nations who may be allies may see the Council Fire of the Great Peace.

Adodarhoh and his cousin Lords are entrusted with the Keeping of the Council Fire.

4. You, Adodarhoh, and your thirteen cousin Lords, shall faithfully keep the space about the Council Fire clean and you shall allow neither dust nor dirt to accumulate. I lay a Long Wing before you as a broom. As a weapon against a crawling creature I lay a staff with you so that you may thrust it away from the Council Fire. If you fail to cast it out then call the rest of the United Lords to your aid.

5. The Council of the Mohawk shall be divided into three parties as follows: Tekarihoken, Ayonhwhathah and Shadekariwade are the first party; Sharenhowaneh, Deyoenhegwenh and Oghrenghrehgowah are the second party, and Dehennakrineh, Aghstawenserenthah and Shoskoharowaneh are the third party. The third party is to listen only to the discussion of the first and second parties and if an error is made or the proceeding is irregular they are to call attention to it, and when the case is right and properly decided by the two parties they shall confirm the decision of the two parties and refer the case to the Seneca Lords for their decision. When the Seneca Lords have decided in accord with the Mohawk Lords, the case or question shall be referred to the Cayuga and Oneida Lords on the opposite side of the house.

6. I, Dekanawidah, appoint the Mohawk Lords the heads and the leaders of the Five Nations Confederacy. The Mohawk Lords are the foundation of the Great Peace and it shall, therefore, be against the Great Binding Law to pass measures in the Confederate Council after the Mohawk Lords have protested against them.

No council of the Confederate Lords shall be legal unless all the Mohawk Lords are present.

7. Whenever the Confederate Lords shall assemble for the purpose of holding a council, the Onondaga Lords shall open it by expressing their gratitude to their cousin Lords and greeting them, and they shall make an address and offer thanks to the earth where men dwell, to the streams of water, the pools, the springs and the lakes, to the maize and the fruits, to the medicinal herbs and trees, to the forest trees for their usefulness, to the animals that serve as food and give their pelts for clothing, to the great winds and the lesser winds, to the Thunderers, to the Sun, the mighty warrior, to the moon, to the messengers of the Creator who reveal his wishes and to the Great Creator who dwells in the heavens above, who gives all the things useful to men, and who is the source and the ruler of health and life.

Then shall the Onondaga Lords declare the council open.

The council shall not sit after darkness has set in.

8. The Firekeepers shall formally open and close all councils of the Confederate Lords, and they shall pass upon all matters deliberated upon by the two sides and render their decision.

Every Onondaga Lord (or his deputy) must be present at every Confederate Council and must agree with the majority without unwarrantable dissent, so that a unanimous decision may be rendered.

If Adodarhoh or any of his cousin Lords are absent from a Confederate Council, any other Firekeeper may open and close the Council, but the Firekeepers present may not give any decisions, unless the matter is of small importance.

9. All the business of the Five Nations Confederate Council shall be conducted by the two combined bodies of Confederate Lords. First the question shall be

passed upon by the Mohawk and Seneca Lords, then it shall be discussed and passed by the Oneida and Cayuga Lords. Their decisions shall then be referred to the Onondaga Lords, (Fire Keepers) for final judgement.

The same process shall obtain when a question is brought before the council by an individual or a War Chief.

10. In all cases the procedure must be as follows: when the Mohawk and Seneca Lords have unanimously agreed upon a question, they shall report their decision to the Cayuga and Oneida Lords who shall deliberate upon the question and report a unanimous decision to the Mohawk Lords. The Mohawk Lords will then report the standing of the case to the Firekeepers, who shall render a decision as they see fit in case of a disagreement by the two bodies, or confirm the decisions of the two bodies if they are identical. The Fire Keepers shall then report their decision to the Mohawk Lords who shall announce it to the open council.

11. If through any misunderstanding or obstinacy on the part of the Fire Keepers, they render a decision at variance with that of the Two Sides, the Two Sides shall reconsider the matter and if their decisions are jointly the same as before they shall report to the Fire Keepers who are then compelled to confirm their joint decision.

12. When a case comes before the Onondaga Lords (Fire Keepers) for discussion and decision, Adodarho shall introduce the matter to his comrade Lords who shall then discuss it in their two bodies. Every Onondaga Lord except Hononwiretonh shall deliberate and he shall listen only. When a unanimous decision shall have been reached by the two bodies of Fire Keepers, Adodarho shall notify Hononwiretonh of the fact when he shall confirm it. He shall refuse to confirm a decision if it is not unanimously agreed upon by both sides of the Fire Keepers.

13. No Lord shall ask a question of the body of Confederate Lords when they are discussing a case, question or proposition. He may only deliberate in a low tone with the separate body of which he is a member.

14. When the Council of the Five Nation Lords shall convene they shall appoint a speaker for the day. He shall be a Lord of either the Mohawk, Onondaga or Seneca Nation.

The next day the Council shall appoint another speaker, but the first speaker may be reappointed if there is no objection, but a speaker's term shall not be regarded more than for the day.

15. No individual or foreign nation interested in a case, question or proposition shall have any voice in the Confederate Council except to answer a question put to him or them by the speaker for the Lords.

16. If the conditions which shall arise at any future time call for an addition to or change of this law, the case shall be carefully considered and if a new beam seems necessary or beneficial, the proposed change shall be voted upon and if adopted it shall be called, "Added to the Rafters".

http://www.earthbow.com/native/navajo/firstman.htm

SUGGESTED
Weekly *Implementation*

DAY 1	DAY 2	DAY 3	DAY 4	DAY 5
Prayer journal. Review the required reading(s) *before* the assigned lesson begins. Teacher may want to discuss assigned reading(s) with students. Teacher will discuss with students the number of essays to be assigned with this lesson. They may choose two or three essays. The rest of the essays can be outlined, answered with shorter answers, or skipped. Review all readings for Lesson 1.	**Prayer journal.** Review reading(s) from next lesson. Outline essays due at the end of the week. Per teacher instructions, students may answer orally in a group setting some of the essays that are not assigned as formal essays.	**Prayer journal.** Students should write rough drafts of all assigned essays. The teacher or a peer evaluator may correct rough drafts.	**Prayer journal.** Rewrite corrected copies of essays due tomorrow.	**Prayer journal.** Essays are due. Take the Lesson 1 test. Reading ahead: No readings are necessary for Lesson 2. Students should review *Religious Affections*, Jonathan Edwards for Lesson 3. Guide: What does the word "worldview" mean? What is your worldview? What worldviews do you encounter in the world around you?

LESSON 2
WORLDVIEW FORMATION AND DISCERNMENT

BACKGROUND

If you are a committed Christian believer, you will be challenged to analyze the worldviews of individuals and institutions around you. You are inextricably tied to your culture, but that does not mean you can't be *in* this culture but not *of* this culture. Furthermore, you will be asked to explain your own worldview and to defend that worldview against all sorts of assaults. It is important that you pause and examine several worldviews that you will encounter. You also need to be able to articulate your own worldview.

Throughout this course and your educational career, you will be challenged to analyze the worldviews of many writers. You will be asked to articulate your own worldview and to defend that worldview against all sorts of assaults. William Bradford, for instance, has a worldview that is radically different from many writers you have read but which is probably similar to yours. What is Bradford's worldview? His worldview is obviously Christian Theism. For now, though, it is important that you examine several worldviews that you will encounter in literature and the arts. Afterwards, you will be able to articulate your own worldview.

What is a "worldview?" A worldview is a way that a person understands, relates to, and responds from a

You will learn to articulate your own worldview as you evaluate the veracity of other worldviews.

Reading ahead: *Religious Affections*, Edwards.
Guide Question: Why was Jonathan Edwards so effective in his preaching during the 18th century?

philosophical position that he embraces as his own. Worldview is a framework that ties everything together, that allows us to understand society, the world, and our place in it. A worldview helps us to make the critical decisions which will shape our future. A worldview colors all our decisions and all our artistic creations. In the first *Star Wars* movie (1977), for instance, Luke Skywalker clearly values a Judeo-Christian code of ethics. That does not mean that he is a believing Christian—indeed he is not—but he does uphold and fight for a moral world. Darth Vader, on the other hand, represents chaos and amoral behavior. He does whatever it takes to advance the Emperor's agenda, regardless of who he hurts or what rule he breaks. It is important that you learn to articulate your worldview so that you will be ready to discern other worldviews later.

From studying Greek history we know that there are basically two worldview roots: One originates from Aristotle and argues that the empirical world is primary. Thus, if one wants to advance knowledge, one has to learn more about the world. Another root originates with Plato who argues that the unseen world is primary. In Plato's case that meant that if one wished to understand the world, one studied the gods. In our case, we agree with Plato to the extent that we believe God—who cannot be seen or measured—is in fact more real than the world.

Both Plato and Aristotle were impacted by Socrates. Socrates was one of the most influential but mysterious figures in Western philosophy. He wrote nothing, yet he had a profound influence on someone who did: Plato. Plato carefully recorded most of his

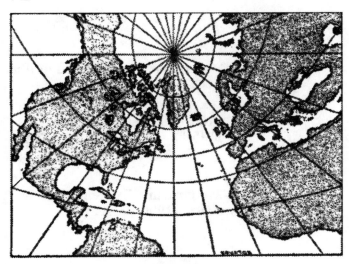

© Arttoday.com

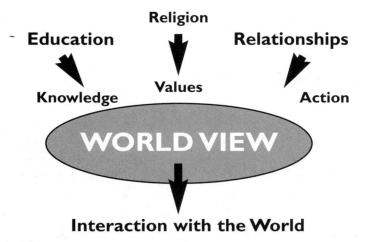

Education — Religion — Relationships

Knowledge — Values — Action

WORLD VIEW

Interaction with the World

dialogues. Unlike earlier philosophers, Socrates' main concern was with ethics. There was nothing remotely pragmatic about Socrates who was the consummate idealist. Until his day, philosophers invested most of their time explaining the natural world. In fact, the natural world often intruded into the abstract world of ideas and reality. Socrates kept both worlds completely separate. To Socrates, the natural laws governing the rotation of the earth were merely uninteresting speculation of no earthly good. Socrates was more interested in such meaty concepts as "virtue" and "justice." Taking issue with the Sophists, Socrates believed that ethics, specifically virtue, must be learned and practiced like any trade. One was not born virtuous; one developed virtue as he would a good habit. Virtue could be practiced only by experts. There was, then, nothing pragmatic about the pursuit of virtue. It was systematic; it was intentional. Virtue was acquired and maintained by open and free dialogue. For the first time, the importance of human language was advanced by a philosopher (to reappear at the end of the 20th century in Post-modern philosophy).

There was no more important philosopher in Western culture than Socrates' disciple, Plato. Plato, like Socrates, regarded ethics as the highest branch of knowledge. He stressed the intellectual basis of virtue, identifying virtue with wisdom. Plato believed that the world was made of *forms* (such as a rock) and *ideas* (such as virtue). The ability of human beings to appreciate forms made a person virtuous. Knowledge came from the gods; opinion was from man. Virtuous activity, then, was dependent upon knowledge of the forms.

To Plato, knowledge and virtue were inseparable. To Aristotle, they were unconnected. Aristotle was not on a search for absolute truth. He was not even certain it existed. Truth, beauty, and goodness were to be observed and quantified from human behavior and the senses, but they were not the legal tender of the land. Goodness in particular was not an absolute, and in Aristotle's opinion it was much abused. Goodness was an average between two absolutes. Aristotle said that mankind should strike a balance between passion and temperance, between extremes of all sorts. He said that good people should seek the "Golden Mean" defined as a course of life that was never extreme. Finally, while Plato argued that reality lay in knowledge of the gods, Aristotle argued that reality lay in empirical, measurable knowledge. To Aristotle, reality was tied to purpose and to action. For these reasons, Aristotle, became known as the father of modern science. His most enduring impact occurred in the area of metaphysics—philosophical speculation about the nature, substance, and structure of reality. It is not physics concerned with the visible or natural world. Metaphysics is concerned with explaining the non-physical world. Aristotle advanced the discussion about God, the human soul, and the nature of space and time. What makes this particularly interesting is Aristotle's penchant for delving into the metaphysical by talking about the gods in human terms. He said, "All men by nature desire to know," and it is by the senses that the gods were known—or not. Faith had nothing to do with it. In other words, Aristotle, for the first time, discussed the gods as if they were quantified entities. He spoke about them as if they were not present. The Hebrews had done this earlier (Genesis 3), but Aristotle was probably not aware of Moses' text. While some Christian thinkers such as Augustine and Aquinas employed Aristotelian logic in their discussions about God, they never speculated about His existence as Aristotle did.

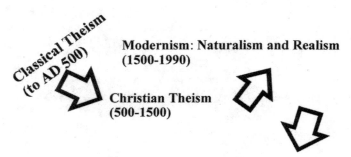

Classical Theism (to AD 500)

Christian Theism (500-1500)

Modernism: Naturalism and Realism (1500-1990)

Post-Modernism: Existentialism & Absurdism (1990-Present)

They only used Aristotle's techniques to understand more about Him.

From Aristotle vs. Plato a panoply of worldviews evolved in four main epochs.

The following are characteristics of each epoch:

Most of you have not heard of this particular worldview paradigm. It is called a cultural worldview paradigm (as contrasted to a socio-political paradigm). Both are useful. Both are accurate. However, most Americans obtain their worldviews from culture, not from scholarship and education.

Classical Theism	Pernicious gods involved in human affairs
Christian Theism	Loving God involved in human affairs
Modernism	Faith in science
Post-Modernism	Faith in experience; suspicious of science

While socio-political descriptions of worldviews are completely accurate, they are not used by American universities or the media at all. When have you hear the word "Cosmic Humanist" used on television? In a movie? Very few people use this terminology in the real world. Therefore, if Christians wish to be involved in apologetics, they must use a language that the unsaved can understand. Chesterton once lamented that Evangelical Christians are like Americans who visit France. He generalized that Americans, by and large, speak their words slower, articulate their words more carefully, and speak fewer words to complete a thought. However, what they should do, Chesterton argues, is to speak French in France! If we believers want the world to hear us, we need to relate to their language.

The four epochs above manifested seven basic worldviews. The worldviews are best discerned through works of art and of literature. The worldview of an artist/writer is a reflection of how the author expresses his views on such essential issues as *God, Man,* and *Morality*. The following seven worldviews are found in art and literature:

Christian Theism: God is personally involved with humankind. Theism argues that the universe is a purposive, divinely created entity. It argues that all human life is sacred and all persons are of equal dignity. They are, in other words, created in the image of God.

History is linear and moves toward a final goal. Nature is controlled by God and is an orderly system. Humanity is neither the center of nature nor the universe, but is the steward of creation. Righteousness will triumph in a decisive conquest of evil. Earthly life does not exhaust human existence but looks ahead to the resurrection of the dead and to a final, comprehensive judgment of humanity (adapted form Carl F. H. Henry, *Toward a Recovery of Christian Belief*). This is the only viable worldview until the Renaissance. Examples: Homer, Virgil, C. S. Lewis, A. J. Cronin, Tolkien.

Deism: God *was* present but is no longer present. The world is like a clock wound up by God many years ago, but He is now absent. The clock (i.e., the world) is present; God is absent. Still, though, Deism embraced a Judeo-Christian morality. God's absence, for instance, in no way mitigated His importance to original creation. He was also omnipotent, but not omniscient. His absence was His decision. He was in no way forced to be absent from the world. He chose to assume that role so that Socratic empiricism and rationalism could reign as sovereign king. Speculative Theism replaced revelatory biblical Theism. Once the Living God was abandoned, Jesus Christ and the Bible became cognitive orphans (Carl F. H. Henry). Examples: Ben Franklin, Thomas Jefferson.

Romanticism: Once Americans distanced themselves from the self-revealing God of the Old and New Testaments, they could not resist making further concessions to subjectivity. Romanticism, and its American version, Transcendentalism, posited that God was nature, and "it" was good. The more natural things were, the better. Nature was inherently good. Nature alone was the ultimate reality. In other words, nature was the Romantic god. Man was essentially a complex animal, too complex to be controlled by absolute, codified truth (as one would find in the Bible). Human intuition replaced the Holy Spirit. Depending upon the demands on individual lives, truth and good were relative and changing. Romanticism, however, like Deism, had not completely abandoned Judeo-Christian moral-

> Modern people conclude that history really has no meaning. . .The biblical view is that history had a beginning and will have an end and that both the beginning and the end are in God's hands. Therefore, what comes between them is invested with meaning and purpose.—from Herbert Schlossberg, *Idols For Destruction.*

ity. Truth and the good, although changing, were nonetheless relatively durable. Examples: James Fenimore Cooper, Goethe.

Naturalism: If God exists, He is pretty wimpish. Only the laws of nature have any force. God is either uninterested or downright mean. All reality was reducible to impersonal processes and energy events (Carl F. H. Henry). All life, including human life, was transient. Its final destination was death. Truth and good, therefore, were also transient. They were culture-conditioned distinctions that the human race projected upon the cosmos and upon history. (Carl F. H. Henry) This maturation, as it were, of the human race, necessitated a deliberate rejection of all transcendentally final authority. Examples: Joseph Conrad, Stephen Crane.

Realism: Akin to Naturalism is Realism. Reality is, to a Realist, a world with no purpose, no meaning, no order. Realism insists that personality has no ultimate status in the universe but is logically inconsistent when it affirms an ethically imperative social agenda congruent with universal human rights and dignity. Realism throws around such terms as "dignity" and "human rights" and "power." What Realists mean, however, is that these concepts are real when they fulfill a social agenda that enhances human dominance over the universal. Thus, Realism believes in a world where bad things happen all the time to good people. Why not? There is no God, no ontological controlling force for good. The world is a place where the only reality is that which we can experience, but it must be experience that we can measure or replicate. Certainly, pain and misery fit that category. If an experience is a unique occurrence (Example: a miracle) it is not real. Examples: Ernest Hemingway, F. Scott Fitzgerald.

Absurdism: A modern movement where there is neither a god, nor any reason to have one. Everything is disorganized, anarchy rules. There is a complete abandonment of explaining the cosmos and therefore an abandonment of being in relationship with the deity. It is not that Absurdists are unsure about who creates everything or is in control of everything. Absurdists simply do not care one way or the other. Examples: John Barth, Kurt Vonnegut, Jr.

Existentialism: The submergence of God in overwhelming data and in experience is the first step toward putting God out to die. Truth is open to debate. Everything is relative. Existentialism is a very pessimistic view. Examples: Albert Camus, Franz Kafka, and Jean Paul Sartre.

Culture Wars: The Battle for Truth

Greek Mythology

The Greeks introduced the idea that the universe is orderly, that man's senses are valid and, as a consequence, that man's proper purpose is to live his own life to the fullest.

Ionian School
(500 B.C.)

The Ionian fascination with the physical world anticipated later discussions in Western philosophy.

The Phythagoreans
(530 B.C.)

Phythagoras was the first philosopher to require some standard of behavior from his followers. One can imagine what a novel and important step this was—that a religion would require a commitment from its adherents.

The Eleatic School
(500 B.C.)

The Eleatic School argued that reality was indivisible and endless.

The Pluralists
(500 B.C.)

With no outside force in place, by chance the universe evolved from chaos to structure, and vice versa, in an eternal cycle.

The Sophists
(500 B.C.)

Ethical rules needed to be followed only when it was to one's practical advantage to do so. Goodness, morality, and ethics were a reflection of culture rather than vice versa.

Naturalism can provide no conclusive reason why radical self-interest should not be the high altar on which all principles can be advantageously sacrificed. Indeed, Naturalism can give no reason for taking reason or even itself seriously (Carl F. H. Henry, *Toward a Recovery of Christian Belief*).

Socrates
(469-399 B.C.)

For the first time, the importance of human language was advanced by a philosopher. Plato stressed the intellectual basis of virtue, identifying virtue with wisdom.

Plato
(428 B.C.-?)

"Love" to Plato was a "form" from which virtue flowed.

Aristotle
(350 B.C.-?)

Aristotle was the first agnostic. Aristotle argued that reality lay in empirical, measurable knowledge. Aristotle, for the first time discussed the gods as if they were quantified entities. He spoke about them as if they were not present.

Cynicism
(350 B.C.)

For the first time, philosophers began to talk about the individual in earnest, as if he were a subject to be studied.

Skepticism
(300 B. C.)

Skepticism maintained that human beings could know nothing of the real nature of things, and that consequently the wise person would give up trying to know anything.

Epicurianism
(300 B. C.)

The aim of human life, Epicurus claimed, was to achieve maximum pleasure with the least effort and risk.

Stoicism
(300 B.C.)

Stoicism celebrated the human spirit and became the measuring rod against which all social and religious institutions were measured.

Neoplatonism
(A.D. 50)

Neoplatonism dared to speak of a religious experience as a philosophical phenomenon

Augustine
(A.D. 354-430)

Augustine effectively articulated a theology and worldview for the Church as it journeyed into the inhospitable, post-Christian, barbarian era.

Scholasticism
(A.D. 1100-1300)

Scholasticism, with varying degrees of success, attempted to use natural human reason—in particular, the philosophy and science of Aristotle—to understand the metaphysical content of Christian revelation.

Erasmus
(1466-1536)

Erasmus, for the first time, discussed things like happiness as being centered in the self or personhood of the man or woman. Happiness was based on some narcissistic notions of self-love.

Michel de Montaigne
(1533-1592)

Montaigne reintroduced Greek skepticism to Western culture.

Frances Bacon
(1561-1626)

Bacon advanced vigorously the idea that reasoning must triumph over theology.

Thomas Hobbes
(1588-1679)

Hobbes was one of the first modern Western thinkers to provide a secular justification for political power.

Rene Descartes
(1596-1650)

After Descartes, mankind replaced God as the center of the universe in the midst of many. This was an ominous moment in Western culture.

Benedictus de Spinoza
(1732-1677)

Spinoza argued that human morality arose from self-interest.

John Locke
(1632-1704)

Locke believed in reasoning and common sense, rather than in metaphysics.

G. W. Leibniz
(1646-1716)

Leibniz believed in a God who created a world separate from His sovereignty.

George Berkeley
(1685-1753)

Berkeley called "intuition" the voice of God to mankind.

Davie Hume
(1711-1726)

Hume, for the first time in Western history, seriously suggested that there was no necessary connection between cause and effect.

Immanuel Kant
(1724-1804)

Kant argued that reality was experience. If one could not experience something with his senses, then it was not real.

Jean Jacques Rousseau
(1712-1778)

Rousseau advocated one of the first "back-to-nature" movements.

William Godwin
(1756-1836)

The notion that there were individual rights, or a codex of governing laws, was anathema to Godwin.

Soren Kierkegaard
(1813-1855)

Kiergegaard explained life in terms of logical necessity, which became a means of avoiding choice and responsibility.

G. W. F. Hegel
(1770-1831)

Truth had no application if there were not opposites warring for its reality.

Karl Marx
(1818-1883)

To the Hegelian Marx, Christianity was a fairy tale created to placate weak people.

Pierre Joseph Proudon
(1809-1865)

Proudon instituted the last serious philosophical attempt to undermine the human will as a determining factor in human decision-making.

Arthur Schopenhauer
(1788-1860)

The human will, with all its chauvinism and narcissism, was the most powerful human impulse.

Herbert Spencer
(1820-1903)

Spencer argued that in biological sciences and in the social sciences the fittest and the strongest survived

Frederich Nietzsche
(1844-1890)

Nietzsche believed that the collapse of the religious impulse has left a huge vacuum. The history of modern times is in great part the history of how that vacuum is filled.

Martin Heidegger
(1889-1976)

The meaning of the world must be discovered outside human experience.

Jean Paul Sartre
(1905-1980)

People exist in a world of their own making.

Simone De Beauvoir
(1906-1986)

Beauvoir was an advocate of "free love" and completely rejected the biblical understanding of marriage, which she saw as an oppressive institution.

John Dewey
(1859-1952)

Truth to Dewey was a reflection of circumstances and contingencies.

Bertrand Russell
(1872-1970)

If an actual event could not be quantified or repeated, then it was not real.

John Stuart Mill
(1806-1873)

To Mill, the individual and his needs were paramount.

Max Weber
(1864-1920)

The notion that God was pleased with hard work and frugal living assured a healthy maturation of society.

Ludwig Wittgenstein
(1889-1951)

If a person could not speak it, it was not real.

Richard Rorty
(1931-)

Truth to Rorty is what we all agree is truth, and what we agree is truth is more a reflection of circumstances than any absolute or objective reality outside mankind's experience.

Alfred North Whitehead
(1861-1947)

The agnostic Whitehead believed in God—if a decidedly anemic God.

Jacques Derrida
(1930-)

Derrida argued that most of us merely play language games. Every utterance is a move in a language game.

Jean Baudrillard
(1929-)

Reality to Baudrillard is not necessarily defined by human language: it is defined by the public media.

Jurgen Habermas
(1929-)

Habermas has resurrected the works of Plato and other metaphysicists and has taken philosophy away from language and communication and has taken it back to a discussion of rationality.

Viktor E. Frankl
(1905-1997)

Man was the result of a purposeless and materialistic process that did not have him in mind.

Contemporary Worldviews

A. Life is what happens to you when you're busy making other plans.–Yoko Ono

B. I don't think any of us really know why we are here.–Ray Charles

C. Animal liberation will come!–Ingrid Newkirk

D. If we had no other purpose in life, it would be good enough simply to goose
   people once in a while.–Garrison Keillor

E. The meaning of life is felt through relationship–Jonas Salk

F. To fulfill the purpose of life is to ignite the spark of divinity in us and give meaning to our lives.–Michael Jackson

G. Just chill out.–Ice-T.

WORLDVIEW REVIEW

Christian Theism. Christian Theism advances a worldview that there is an omnipotent God who has authored an inspired, authoritative work called the Bible, upon whose precepts mankind should base its society.

Deism. Deism advances a worldview that accepts the notion that there is an authoritative, inspired source from which mankind should base its society (i.e., the Bible). Likewise the Deist is certain that there was once an omnipotent God. However, once the world was created, that same omnipotent God chose to absent Himself from His creation. The world, then, is like a clock. It was once created by an intelligent process. However, now the creator is absent, leaving mankind on its own to figure out how the clock works and to go on living.

Romanticism. A natural companion to Deism was Rationalism. Rationalism (e.g., John Locke's philosophy) invited the Deist to see mankind as a "chalkboard" on which was written experience that ultimately created a personality. Thus, Rationalists/Deists were fond of speaking of "unalienable rights" or "common sense." The Romantic (in America the Romantic would be called "the Transcendentalist") took issue with Deism and Theism. To the Romantic, Nature was God. Nature—an undefined indigenous, omnipotent presence—was very good. Original sin was man's separation from Nature. In fact, the degree to which mankind returned to Nature would determine his goodness and effectiveness. Thus, a man like Henry David Thoreau lived a year on Walden Pond so that he could find his God. In *Deerslayer* by James Fenimore Cooper, the protagonist is safe while he is on a lake separated from evil mankind. Only when he participates in human society is he in trouble. The Romantic was naturally suspicious of Theism because Theism appeared to be dogmatic and close minded. The Romantics had confessions, but they had no dogma. Deism also bothered the Romantics. Romanticism emphasized the subjective; Deism emphasized the objective. In the Romantic novel *Frankenstein*, the Deist/Rationalist Dr. Frankenstein creates a monster. Dr. Frankenstein, with disastrous results, turns his back on the subjective and tries to use science to create life.

Naturalism. Naturalism was inclined to agree with Romanticism's criticism of Theism and Deism but did not believe in a benevolent Nature. In fact, Nature, to the Naturalist, was malevolent, mischievous, and unpredictable. Mankind, as it were, lost control of the universe and the person who had control did not really care much for his creation. Theism of course was absurd. How could any sane person who experienced World War I believe in a loving, living God? Deism was equally wrong. God was not absent—he was present in an unpredictable, at times evil way. Romanticism was on the right track but terribly naive. God and His creation were certainly not "good" in any sense of the word. Nature was evil. Naturalism embraced a concept of fate not dissimilar to that held by the Greeks. In Homer's *Iliad*, for instance, the characters were subject to uncontrolled fate and pernicious gods and goddesses who inflicted terrible and good things on mankind with no apparent design or reason. No, to the Naturalist, God was at best absent or wimpish; at worst, he was malevolent.

Realism. Realism was philosophically akin to Naturalism. In a sense, Naturalism was a natural companion to Realism. Realism was different from Naturalism in degree, not in substance. Realism argued that if people were honest, they would admit that God was not present at all. It there were anything worth embracing, it was reality. Realism advanced an in-your-face view of life. Realists prided themselves in "telling it like it is." They entered the cosmic arena and let the chips fall where they might. They shared the same criticisms of views that the Naturalists held.

Absurdism. Absurdism certainly believed that Realism was on track. Where Realism erred, however, was its propensity to see meaning in life. Mind you, the meaning was tied to things one could see and feel—not in things that were abstract or immutable—but the Realist still sought some meaning in this life. The Absurdist abandoned all hope of finding meaning in life and embraced a sort of nihilism. The Absurdist was convinced that everything was meaningless and absurd. The subjectivity of a Romantic was appealing to the Absurdist. However, even that implied that something was transcendent—a desire—and the Absurdist would have nothing to do with that. Billy Pilgrim, a protagonist in one of the Absurdist Kurt Vonnegut, Jr.'s novels, became "unhinged from time" and "wandered around in the cosmos." Things without meaning happen to him whose life had no meaning. Everything was absurd.

Existentialism. Existentialism stepped outside the debate of meaning altogether. Existentialists argued that the quest was futile. The only thing that mattered was subjective feeling. "Experience" was a God at whose feet the Existentialist worshiped. Romanticism was on the right track in that it invited mankind to explore subjectivity. Where it erred was when it refused to give up the deity. Naturalism was an anomaly. It was too busy arguing with the cosmos to see that reality was in human desire not in providence. The degree to which mankind was to discover and experience these desires determined the degree to which people participated in the divine.

CRITICAL THINKING

A. In a two page essay, compare the worldviews of each if the following passages.

So God created man in His own image, in the image of God.

Gatsby believed . . . tomorrow we will run faster, stretch out our arms farther . . . And one fine morning—So we beat on, boats against the current, borne back ceaselessly into the past (Fitzgerald, *The Great Gatsby*, Charles Scribner's Sons, 1925, p. 182)

For mere improvement is not redemption . . . God became man to turn creatures into sons: not simply to produce better men of the old kind but to produce a new kind of man (Lewis, *Mere Christianity*, A Touchstone Book, 1980, p. 183).

If it feels good do it!—The world is totally insane, out of control, stupid!

All my friends do it, so it must be ok.

B. Compare the worldviews represented in the next two passages. Which worldview is obviously Christian? From these descriptions what generalizations can you draw about the Virginia and Plymouth settlements?

Being thus left to our fortunes, it fortuned that within ten dayes scarce ten amongst us could either goe, or well stand, such extreame weaknes and sicknes oppressed us. And thereat none need marvaile, if they consider the cause and reason, which was this; whiles the ships stayed, our allowance was somewhat bettered, by a daily proportion of Bisket, which the sailers would pilfer to sell, give, or exchange with us, for money, Saxefras, furres, or love. But when they departed, there remained neither taverne, beere house, nor place of reliefe, but the common Kettell. Had we beene as free from all sinnes as gluttony, and drunkennesse, we might have been canonized for Saints; But our President would never have beene admitted, for ingrossing to his private, Oatmeale, Sacke, Oyle, Aquavitae, Beefe, Egges, or what not, but the Kettell; that indeed he allowed equally to be distributed, and that was halfe a pint of wheat, and as much barely boyled with water for a man a day, and this having fryed some 26 weekes in the ships hold, contained as many wormes as graines; so that we might truely call it rather so much bran then corne, our drinke was water, our lodgings Castles in the ayre: with this lodging and dyet, our extreame toile in bearing and planting Pallisadoes, so strained and bruised us, and our continuall labour in the extremities of the heat had so weakned us, as were cause sufficient to have made us as miserable in our native Countrey, or any other place in the world. . . . The new president and Martin, being little beloved, of weake judgement in dangers, and less industrie in peace, committted managing of all things abroad to Captaine Smith: who by his owne example, good words, and faire promises, set some to mow, others to binde thatch, some to build houses, others to thatch them, himselfe always bearing the greatest taske for his own share, so that in short time, he provided most of them lodgings, neglecting any for himselfe. This done, seeing the Salvages superfluitie beginne to decrease (with some of his workmen) shipped himselfe in the Shallop to search the Country for trade. The want of the language, knowledge to mannage his boat without sailes, the want of a sufficient power, (knowing the multitude of the Salvages) apparell for his men, and other necessaries, were infinite impediments, yet no discouragement.–Captain John Smith, *The General History of Virginia*, 1624.

Ch.9: Sept 6: These troubles being blowne over,

CAPTAIN JOHN SMITH.
© Arttoday.com

© Arttoday.com

and now all being compacte togeather in one shipe, they put to sea againe with a prosperous winde, which continued diverce days togeather, which was some incouragement unto them; yet according to the usuall maner many were afflicted with seasickness. And I may not omite hear a spetiall worke of Gods providence. There was a proud and very profane yonge man, one of the seamen, of a lustie, able body, which made him the more hauty; he would allway be contemning the poore people in their sicknes, and cursing them dayly with greevous execrations, and did not let to tell them, that he hoped to help to cast halfe of them over board before they came to their jurneys end, and to make merry with what they had; and if he were by any gently reproved, he would curse and swear most bitterly. But it pleased God before they came halfe seas over, to smite this yong man with a greevous disease, of which he dyed in a desperate maner, and so was him self the first that was throwne overbord. Thus his curses light on his owne head; and it was an astonishment to all his fellow, for they noted it to be the just hand of God upon him. After they had injoyed faire winds and weather for a season, they were incountred many times with crosse winds, and mette with many feirce stormes, with which the shipe was shroudly shaken, and her upper works made very leakie; and one of the maine beames in the midd ships was bowed and craked, which put them in some fear that the shipe could not be able to performe the vioage. . . . –William Bradford, *The History of Plimoth Plantation*, 1620.

BIBLICAL APPLICATION

The Puritans based their society on Old Testament law. For instance, the Connecticut Code, 1650 stated: " If any man have a stubborn and rebellious son of sufficient years and understanding . . . which will not obey the voice of his father of mother . . . but lives in sundry notorious crimes, such a son shall be put to death." Why should/should not Old Testament law have literal application to today's society?

ENRICHMENT QUESTION

Most Americans obtain their world view from the television. The following advertisements represent a particular worldview(s). What is(are) it (they)?

SUGGESTED
Weekly *Implementation*

DAY 1	DAY 2	DAY 3	DAY 4	DAY 5
Prayer journal.	**Prayer journal.**	**Prayer journal.**	**Prayer journal.**	**Prayer journal.**
Review the required reading(s) *before* the assigned lesson begins.	Review reading(s) from next lesson.	Write rough drafts of all assigned essays.	Student will re-write corrected copies of essays due tomorrow.	Essays are due.
Teacher and students will discuss essays to be assigned this week.	Outline essays that are due at the end of the week.	The teacher or a peer evaluator may correct rough drafts.		Students should take the Lesson 2 test.
The rest of the essays can be outlined, answered with shorter answers, or skipped.	Per teacher instructions, students may answer orally in a group setting some of the essays that are not assigned as formal essays.			Reading ahead: Students should review *Religious Affections*, Edwards.
Students will review all readings for Lesson 2.				Guide: Why was Jonathan Edwards so effective in his preaching during the 18th century?

LESSON 3

THE NEW LAND TO 1750: PURITANISM

Puritan Worldview

CRITICAL THINKING

You will learn about Puritan worldviews and write your own worldview in this lesson. Students should review poems by Anne Bradstreet (provided in this text) and historical information on the Puritans.

Reading ahead: *The Autobiography of Benjamin Franklin*

Guide Question: Does Anne Bradstreet typify Puritan spirituality or is she an aberration?

A. In his book *A Modell of Christian Charity* (1630), John Winthrop, first governor of the Puritan Massachusetts Bay Colony, wrote:

> The Lord will make our name a praise and glory, so that men shall say of succeeding plantations: The Lord make it like that of New England. For we must consider that we shall be like a City upon a Hill; the eyes of all people are on us.

http://www.history.hanover.edu/texts/winthmod.html

What does Winthrop mean "a City upon a Hill?" Why does/does not this statement seem a little presumptuous on his part?

B. Puritans effectively combined sound scholarship and profound spirituality. They led American society in education and science for a century. They founded most of the universities in New England. Some modern Evangelical scholars lament that this combination has been lost. Professor Mark Noll, professor at Wheaton College, argues that "the scandal of the evangelical mind is that there is not much of an evangelical mind." Noll is speaking of a comprehensive ability to think theologically across a broad spectrum of life (e.g., politics, arts, culture, and economics). Evangelicals, he argues, have a propensity for shallow analysis of complex cultural issues (See Mark A. Noll, *The Scandal of the Evangelical Mind*, Grand Rapids, MI: Eerdmans Publishing Company, 1994). This is a view held by other scholars as well. (See David F. Wells, *God in the Wasteland: The Reality of Truth in a World of Fading Dreams*, Eerdmans). "Surely the God who is rendered 'weightless' by modern culture (especially evangelical Christians) is quite different from the living God."

Do you agree with Noll and Wells?
Is there hope that born-again Christians will regain the high ground in culture and thought?

C. In American culture the concept of "hero" has changed considerably over the last 50 years.

What is a hero?

1940s
"classical" Theism

John Wayne: Do the Right Thing the Right Way.

1970s
"nostalgic" Theism

Star Wars: Do the Right Thing For the Downtrodden.

1980s
"nostalgic" Theism

Clint Eastwood: Do The Right Thing even if you have to do the Wrong Thing to Get there.

1990s
Absurdism

Toy Story Character. Do The Right Thing The Old Fashioned Way—But Toys can do it Better.

2000
Existentialism/Romanticism Revivalism

Tom Cruise: Doing the Right Thing is What is Right For Me.

How will the American hero evolve in the next 20 years?

BIBLICAL APPLICATION

In about one page you should answer biblical applications in essay form; include biblical references.

A. Describe Edwards' religious affections and explain how they are evidences of true religion.

The following is Chapter One:
PART I. CONCERNING THE NATURE OF THE AFFECTIONS AND THEIR IMPORTANCE IN RELIGION
http://www.ccel.org/e/edwards/religious_affections/religious_affections.html

1 Peter 1:8: Whom having not seen, ye love; in whom, though now ye see him not, yet believing, ye rejoice with joy unspeakable and full of glory.

In these words, the apostle represents the state of the minds of the Christians he wrote to, under the persecutions they were then the subjects of. These persecutions are what he has respect to, in the two preceding verses, when he speaks of the trial of their faith, and of their being in heaviness through manifold temptations.

Such trials are of threefold benefit to true religion. Hereby the truth of it is manifested, and it appears to be indeed true religion; they, above all other things, have a tendency to distinguish between true religion and false, and to cause the difference between them evidently to appear. Hence they are called by the name of trials, in the verse nextly preceding the text, and in innumerable other places; they try the faith and religion of professors, of what sort it is, as apparent gold is tried in the fire, and manifested, whether it be true gold or no. And the faith of true Christians being thus tried and proved to be true, is "found to praise, and honor, and glory," as in that preceding verse.

And then, these trials are of further benefit to true religion; they not only manifest the truth of it, but they make its genuine beauty and amiableness remarkably to appear. True virtue never appears so lovely, as when it is most oppressed; and the divine excellency of real Christianity, is never exhibited with such advantage, as when under the greatest trials: then it is that true faith appears much more precious than gold! And upon this account is "found to praise, and honor, and glory."

And again, another benefit that such trials are of to true religion, is, that they purify and increase it. They not only manifest it to be true, but also tend to refine it, and deliver it from those mixtures of that which is false, which encumber and impede it; that nothing may be left but that which is true. They tend to cause the amiableness of true religion to appear to the best advantage, as was before observed; and not only so, but they tend to increase its beauty, by establishing and confirming it, and making it more lively and vigorous, and purifying it from those things that obscured its luster and glory. As gold that is tried in the fire, is purged from its alloy, and all remainders of dross, and comes forth more solid and beautiful; so true faith being tried as gold is tried in the fire, becomes more precious, and thus also is "found unto praise, and honor, and glory." The apostle seems to have respect to each of these benefits, that persecutions are of to true religion, in the verse preceding the text.

And, in the text, the apostle observes how true religion operated in the Christians he wrote to, under their persecutions, whereby these benefits of persecution appeared in them; or what manner of operation of true religion, in them, it was, whereby their religion, under persecution, was manifested to be true religion, and eminently appeared in the genuine beauty and amiableness of true religion, and also appeared to be increased and purified, and so was like to be "found unto praise, and honor, and glory, at the appearing of Jesus Christ." And there were two kinds of operation, or exercise of true religion, in them, under their sufferings, that the apostle takes notice of in the text, wherein these benefits appeared.

1. Love to Christ: "Whom having not yet seen, ye love." The world was ready to wonder, what strange principle it was, that influenced them to expose themselves to so great sufferings, to forsake the things that were seen, and renounce all that was dear and pleasant, which was the object of sense. They seemed to the men of the world about them, as though they were beside themselves, and to act as though they hated themselves; there was nothing in their view, that could induce them thus to suffer, and support them under, and carry them through such trials. But although there was nothing that was seen, nothing that the world saw, or that the Christians themselves ever saw with their bodily eyes, that thus influenced and supported them, yet they had a supernatural principle of love to something unseen; they loved Jesus Christ, for they saw him spiritually whom the world saw not, and whom they themselves had never seen with bodily eyes.

2. Joy in Christ. Though their outward sufferings were very grievous, yet their inward spiritual joys were greater than their sufferings; and these supported them, and enabled them to suffer with cheerfulness.

There are two things which the apostle takes notice of in the text concerning this joy.

1. The manner in which it rises, the way in which Christ, though unseen, is the foundation of it, viz., by faith; which is the evidence of things not seen: "In whom, though now ye see him not, yet believing, ye rejoice."

2. The nature of this joy; "unspeakable and full of glory." Unspeakable in the kind of it; very different from worldly joys, and carnal delights; of a vastly more pure, sublime, and heavenly nature, being something supernatural, and truly divine, and so ineffably excellent; the sublimity and exquisite sweetness of which, there were no words to set forth. Unspeakable also in degree; it pleasing God to give them this holy joy, with a liberal hand, and in large measure, in their state of persecution.

Their joy was full of glory. Although the joy was unspeakable, and no words were sufficient to describe it, yet something might be said of it, and no words more fit to represent its excellency than these, that it was full of glory; or, as it is in the original, glorified joy. In rejoicing with this joy, their minds were filled, as it were, with a glorious brightness, and their natures exalted and perfected. It was a most worthy, noble rejoicing, that did not corrupt and debase the mind, as many carnal joys do; but did greatly beautify and dignify it; it was a prelibation of the joy of heaven, that raised their minds to a degree of heavenly blessedness; it filled their minds with the light of God's glory, and made themselves to shine with some communication of that glory.

Hence the proposition or doctrine, that I would raise from these words, is this:

DOCTRINE. True religion, in great part, consists in holy affections.

We see that the apostle, in observing and remarking the operations and exercises of religion in the Christians he wrote to, wherein their religion appeared to be true and of the right kind, when it had its greatest trial of what sort it was, being tried by persecution as gold is tried in the fire, and when their religion not only proved true, but was most pure, and cleansed from its dross and mixtures of that which was not true, and when religion appeared in them most in its genuine excellency and native beauty, and was found to praise, and honor, and glory; he singles out the religious affections of love and joy, that were then in exercise in them: these are the exercises of religion he takes notice of wherein their religion did thus appear true and pure, and in its proper glory. Here, I would, 1. Show what is intended by the affections. 2. Observe some things which make it evident, that a great part of true religion lies in the affections.

Read Jonathan Edward's sermon entitled "Sinners in the Hands of an Angry God." A portion of the sermon is included below. It is interesting that

Jonathan Edwards delivered his sermon from a written manuscript with no emotion at all! However, Edwards was more than a great preacher. He was a devoted husband and beloved dad. His family adored him. He greatly loved Mrs. Edwards. Every afternoon he and his wife would enjoy long horseback rides. Every night he would read stories to his children. In fact, he was such a dedicated father that he was ultimately fired from his church. They were bothered that he did not visit his congregation more. Think about it: the most famous evangelist of the eighteenth century fired because he did not visit Jimmy Jones or Sally Smith!

Excerpt from "Sinners in the Hands of an Angry God"

http://www.leaderu.com/cyber/books/edwards/sinners.html

The use of this awful subject may be of awakening unconverted persons in this congregation. This that you have heard is the case of every one of you that are out of Christ. That world of mercy, that lake of burning brimstone, is extended abroad under you. There is the dreadful pit of the glowing flames of the wrath of god; there is hell's wide gaping mouth open; and you have nothing to stand upon, nor any thing to take hold of. There is nothing between you and hell but the air; it is only the power and mere pleasure of God that holds you up. You probably are not sensible of this; you find you are kept out of hell but do not see the hand of God in it; but look at other things, as the good state of your bodily constitution, your care of your own life, and the means you use for your own preservation. But indeed these things are nothing; if God should withdraw His hand, they would avail no more to keep you from falling than the thin air to hold up a person that is suspended in it. Your wickedness makes you, as it were, heavy as lead and to tend downwards with great weight and pressure towards hell; and if God should let you go, you would immediately sink and swiftly descend and plunge into the bottomless gulf, and your healthy constitution, and your care and prudence, and best contrivance, and all your righteousness, would have no more influence to uphold you and keep you out of hell, than a spider's web would have to stop a falling rock. Were it not that so is the sovereign pleasure of God, the earth would not bear you one moment; for you are a burden to it; the creation groans with you; the creature is made subject to the bondage of your corruption, not willingly; the sun does not willingly shine upon you to give you light to serve sin and Satan; the earth does not willingly yield her increase to satisfy your lusts; nor is it willingly a stage for your wickedness to be acted upon; the air does not willingly serve you for breath to maintain the flame of life in your vitals while you spend your life in the service of God's enemies. "Sinners in the Hands of an Angry God," Jonathan Edwards.

B. Read the following passage from Esther Edwards' diary entitled "...The Awful Sweetness of Walking With God." Esther, by the way, had a famous son, Aaron Burr.

> Though father is usually taciturn or preoccupied—my mother will call these large words—even when he takes one of us children with him, today he discoursed to me of the awful sweetness of walking with God in Nature. He seems to feel God in the woods, the sky, and the grand sweep of the river which winds so majestically through the woody silences here. (Written in Northhampton, MA, 1741.)

> ("Esther Edwards" in James Miller, Robert O'Neal, and Robert Hayden, *The American Literary Tradition*, NY: Scott, Foresman, and Company, 1973, 36-37)

Compare and contrast the image we see of Jonathan Edwards through his sermon and the way Esther saw him. (If you are unfamiliar with writing comparison and contrast papers, refer to a writing manual.)

C. Describe your dad (or another parent or guardian) using Esther's method of description of her dad. In what ways has the Lord used your father (or another adult) in your life? Compare your dad/adult with King David, Joseph, or another dad in the Bible.

D. Have you ever been disappointed? How did you keep from being bitter? Many Christian thinkers are calling brothers and sisters to forgiveness: forgiveness helps the person wronged more than the person who committed the wrong. Find scriptural evidence that commands you to forgive those who have wronged you.

Jonathan Edwards gave his whole life to the Northhampton Church and was fired anyway. The following is his farewell sermon. Does he show any sign of bitterness?

Edwards' Farewell Sermon:

I have just now said that I have had a peculiar concern for the young people, and in so saying I did not intend to exclude you. You are in youth, and in the most early youth. Therefore I have been sensible that if those that were young had a precious opportunity for their souls" good, you who are very young had, in many respects, a peculiarly precious opportunity. And accordingly I have not neglected you. I have endeavored to do the part of a faithful shepherd, in feeding the lambs as well as the sheep. Christ did once commit the care of your souls to me as your minister; and you know, dear children, how I have instructed you, and warned you from time to time. You know how I have often called you together for that end, and some of you, sometimes, have seemed to be affected with what I have said to you. But I am afraid it has had no saving effect as to many of you, but that you remain still in an unconverted condition, without any real saving work wrought in your souls, convincing you thoroughly of your sin and misery, causing you to see the great evil of sin, and to mourn for it, and hate it above all things, and giving you a sense of the excellency of the Lord Jesus Christ, bringing you with all your hearts to cleave to him as your Savior, weaning your hearts from the world, and causing you to love God above all, and to delight in holiness more than in all the pleasant things of this earth. And I must now leave you in a miserable condition, having no interest in Christ, and so under the awful displeasure and anger of God, and in danger of going down to the pit of eternal misery. — Now I must bid you farewell. I must leave you in the hands of God. I can do no more for you than to pray for you. Only I desire you not to forget, but often think of the counsels and warnings I have given you, and the endeavors I have used, that your souls might be saved from everlasting destruction.

Dear children, I leave you in an evil world that is full of snares and temptations. God only knows what will become of you. This, the Scripture, has told us that there are but few saved, and we have abundant confirmation of it from what we see. This we see, that children die as well as others. Multitudes die before they grow up, and of those that grow up, comparatively few ever give good evidence of saving conversion to God. I pray God to pity you, and take care of you, and provide for you the best means for the good of your souls, and that God himself would undertake for you to be your heavenly Father, and the mighty Redeemer of your immortal souls. Do not neglect to pray for yourselves. Take heed you be not of the number of those who cast off fear, and restrain prayer before God. Constantly pray to God in secret, and often remember that great day when you must appear before the judgment seat of Christ, and meet your minister there, who has so often counseled and warned you.

http://www.jonathanedwards.com/sermons.htm

ENRICHMENT ACTIVITIES/PROJECTS

Write worldview statements for a popular actor (actress), for an active politician, and for a local clergyperson.

Discuss the worldviews of advertising signs along roads. Also discuss worldviews found in the local newspaper. How does a particular worldview influence the way a current event is presented?

A. Read *Evangelical Ethics*, by Professor John Jefferson Davis, Ph.D., Gordon Conwell Seminary, South Hamilton, MA. After reading Dr. Davis' book, state your position on these ethical issues: euthanasia, abortion, capital punishment, and others.

B. Summarize what Edwards says about the youth of his town in this passage from "A Faithful Narrative of the Surprising Work of God." Next, compare these youth to the youth in your church.

THE COURTSHIP OF BILL TAFT.
© Arttoday.com

Excerpt from "A Faithful Narrative of the Surprising Work of God"

The people of the country, in general, I suppose, are as sober, orderly, and good sort of people, as in any part of New England; and I believe they have been preserved the freest by far of any part of the country, from error, and variety of sects and opinions. Our being so far within the land, at a distance from sea-ports, and in a corner of the country, has doubtless been one reason why we have not been so much corrupted with vice, as most other parts. But without question, the religion and good order of the county, and purity in doctrine, has, under God, been very much owing to the great abilities, and eminent piety of my venerable and honored grandfather Stoddard. I suppose we have been the freest of any part of the land from unhappy divisions and quarrels in our ecclesiastical and religious affairs, till the late lamentable Springfield contention. (The Springfield Contention relates to the settlement of a minister there, which occasioned too warm debates between some, both pastors and people, that were for it, and others that were against it, on account of their different apprehensions about his principles, and about some steps that were taken to procure his ordination.)

Being much separated from other parts of the province and having comparatively but little intercourse with them, we have always managed our ecclesiastical affairs within ourselves. It is the way in which the country, from its infancy, has gone on, by the practical agreement of all; and the way in which our peace and good order has hitherto been maintained.

The town of Northampton is of about 82 years standing, and has now about 200 families; which mostly dwell more compactly together than any town of such a size in these parts of the country. This probably has been an occasion, that both our corruptions and reformations have been, from time to time, the more swiftly propagated from one to another through the town. Take the town in general, and so far as I can judge, they are as rational and intelligent a people as most I have been acquainted with. Many of them have been noted for religion; and particularly remarkable for their distinct knowledge in things that relate to heart religion, and Christian experience, and their great regards thereto.

I am the third minister who has been settled in the town. The Rev. Mr. Eleazer Mather, who was the first, was ordained in July, 1669. He was one whose heart was much in his work, and abundant in labors for the good of precious souls. He had the high esteem and great love for his people, and was blessed with no small success. The Rev. Mr. Stoddard who succeeded him, came first to the town the November after his death; but was not ordained till September 11, 1672, and died February 11, 1728-9. So that he continued in the work of the ministry here, from his first coming to town, near 60 years. And as he was eminent and renowned for his gifts and grace; so he was blessed, from the beginning, with extraordinary success in his ministry, in the conversion of many souls. He had five harvests, as he called them. The first was about 57 years ago; the second about 53; the third about 40; the fourth about 24; the fifth and last about 18 years ago. Some of these times were much more remarkable than others, and the ingathering of souls more plentiful. Those about 53, and 40, and 24 years ago, were much greater than either the first or the last: but in each of them, I have heard my grandfather say, the greater part of the young people in the town, seemed to be mainly concerned for their eternal salvation.

© Arttoday.com

After the last of these, came a far more degenerate time (at least among the young people), I suppose, than ever before. Mr. Stoddard, indeed, had the comfort, before he died, of seeing a time where there were no small appearances of a divine work among some, and a considerable ingathering of souls, even after I was settled with him in the ministry, which was about two years before his death; and I have reason to bless God for the great advantage I had by it. In these two years there were nearly twenty that Mr. Stoddard hoped to be savingly converted; but there was nothing of any general awakening. The greater part seemed to be at that time very insensible of the things of religion, and engaged in other cares and pursuits. Just after my grandfather's death, it seemed to be a time of extraordinary dullness in religion. Licentiousness for some years prevailed among the youth of the town; there were many of them very much addicted to night-walking, and frequenting the tavern, and lewd practices, wherein some, by their example, exceedingly corrupted others. It was their manner very frequently to get together, in conventions of both sexes for mirth and jollity, which they called frolics; and they would often spend the greater part of the night in them, without regard to any order in the families they belonged to: and indeed family government did too much fail in the town. It was become very customary with many of our young people to be indecent in their carriage at meeting, which doubtless would not have prevailed in such a degree, had it not been that my grandfather, through his great age (though he retained his powers surprisingly to the last), was not so able to observe them. There had also long prevailed in the town a spirit of contention between two parties, into which they had for many years been divided; by which they maintained a jealousy one of the other, and were prepared to oppose one another in all public affairs.

But in two or three years after Mr. Stoddard's death, there began to be a sensible amendment to these evils. The young people showed more of a disposition to hearken to counsel, and by degrees left off their frolics; they grew observably more decent in their attendance on the public worship, and there were more who manifested a religious concern than there used to be.

http://www.jonathanedwards.com/sermons.html

C. In America, religion has more or less embraced revivalism as a mode of church expansion, growth, and influence. According to historian D. E. Dieter, "Revivalism is the movement within the Christian tradition which emphasizes the appeal of religion to the emotional and affectional nature of individuals as well as to their intellectual and rational nature. It believes that vital Christianity begins with a response of the whole being to the gospel's call for repentance and spiritual rebirth by faith in Jesus Christ. This experience results in a personal relationship with God. Some have sought to make revivalism a purely American and even a predominantly frontier phenomenon." Historian Geoff Waugh writes, "Revival must of necessity make an impact on the community and this is one means by which we may distinguish it from the more usual operations of the Holy Spirit." Roy Hession notes that the outward forms of revivals do, of course, differ considerably, but the inward and permanent content of them is always the same: a new experience of conviction of sin among the saints; a new vision of the Cross and of Jesus and of redemption; a new willingness on man's part for brokenness, repentance, confession, and restitution; a joyful experience of the power of the blood of Jesus to cleanse fully from sin and restore and heal all that sin has lost and broken; a new entering into the fullness of the Holy Spirit and of His power to do His own work through His people; and a new gathering in of the lost ones to Jesus.

Research recent church history and speculate upon the form and nature of future revivalism. Will it be like the mass rallies in the past or will revivalism look a lot different?

D. Write a worldview for yourself. Use the following questions to guide you.

What is the priority of the spiritual world?

Authority: Is the Bible important to you? Do you obey God and other authority, your parents, officials of the court, etc. even when it is uncomfortable to do so?

Pleasure: What do you really enjoy doing? Does it please God?

What is the essential uniqueness of man?

Fate: What/who really determines your life? Chance? Circumstances? God?

When you write your worldview, consider these three essential questions:

A. What is the priority of the spiritual world?

B. What is the essential uniqueness of man?

C. What is the objective character of truth and goodness?— Carl F. H. Henry, *Toward a Recovery of Christian Belief*, Crossway Books, Wheaton, IL, 1990, 20.

What is the objective character of truth and goodness?

(Carl F. H. Henry, *Toward a Recovery of Christian Belief*, Wheaton, IL: Crossway Books, 1990, 20).

Justice: What are the consequences of your actions? Is there some sort of judgment? Do bad people suffer? Why do good people suffer?

SAMPLE WORLDVIEW ESSAY:

Isaac Watts' famous hymn, "When I Survey the Wondrous Cross," is the best summation of my worldview:

"When I survey the wondrous cross on which the Prince of Glory died,/My richest gain I count but loss, And pour contempt on all my pride . . ." As the theologian Dietrich Bonhoeffer mused a few weeks before his death in a Nazi prison in late World War II, so I profess: Christ is at once my boundary and my rediscovered center. In my Resurrected Lord I see the faithfulness of gracious God encountering sinful humankind.

How we need the grace of God! We are a lonely, separated, broken people desperately in need of a Savior. All humankind, good and bad alike, rich and poor, are in the wrong before God, and we all fall under God's judgment. In spite of our sincere intentions, we systematically, inevitably shatter our virtuous dreams by allowing self-interest and hostility to motivate our lives. Without the resurrected Lord at the center of our being, we are, as the Christian poet T. S. Eliot hauntingly reflects, "paralyzed force, gesture without motion." Yes, we all deserve the wrath of God. As the theologian Karl Barth explains, "The judgment of God is the righteousness of God without Jesus Christ." However, God, out of His great love for us all, gave us His Son to be our Savior. Yes, with Christ as the center of our lives, we have hope. I am unequivocal in my confession that a decision for Christ is the only way to health, happiness, wholeness, and eternal security.

"Were the whole realm of nature mine, that were a present far too small;/Love so amazing, so divine, Demands my soul, my life, my all." God's love is so amazing that He sent His only Begotten Son to die for me. Therefore, He has a right to demand all of me in return!

Likewise, I am not ambivalent in my confession that "there is neither Jew nor Greek, there is neither slave nor free person, there is neither male nor female: for you are all one in Christ Jesus (Gals. 3:28). In the areas of social justice, equality between the sexes and races, ministry to the poor and to the homeless, peace-making, the church must be prophetic. "For in as much as you helped the least of these, you helped me . . ."

Equally important is my responsibility to create and to support wholesome family life. The Christian family remains the single most important channel that God has chosen to inculcate in humankind His nurturing principles of fulfilled living. Solid, healthy Christian family life is a primary goal for my time on this earth. Recognizing the pressures of economics and time, I must nonetheless obtain the knowledge and skills necessary to keep Jesus Christ in the center of my home. (James P. Stobaugh)

Anne Bradstreet

BACKGROUND

Anne Bradstreet was born in England, married a Puritan believer, immigrated to America, and wrote some of the most engaging poetry of the 17th century. On a ship named the Arabella, Bradstreet and her husband brought their Puritan faith to America. After short stays in Salem, Charlestown, and Newtown (now Cambridge), they settled in Ipswich, outside Boston in what was then the frontier. There, Anne home schooled eight children and wrote many of the poems that were eventually published in *The Tenth Muse* (London: Stephen Bowtell, 1650) after her brother-in-law took her manuscript back with him to England and had it printed without her knowledge. The Bradstreets moved to Andover, Massachusetts, in the mid-1640s, where Anne lived until her death in 1672. Remarkably, Bradstreet wrote many poems full of literary techniques and Christian flavor, reared eight children, and helped create a new nation. Today's younger generation, who are called to create a new civilization, do well to look closely at Bradstreet's life. There is little doubt that her work was extremely difficult and exhausting. Her full time job was homemaking. She cooked meals, made clothing, and doctored her family in addition to cleaning, making household goods to use and to sell, taking care of the family's animals, maintaining a fire and even tending to the kitchen gardens. The house she maintained was a thatch-roofed structure with a dirt floor. Colonial women were often married by the age of 13 or 14. Marriage was mostly for economic benefits, not romantic situations. However, evidence suggests that Anne deeply loved her husband and saw her union as a way to be more effective for the Kingdom.

One of Bradstreet's publications
© arttoday.com

CRITICAL THINKING

Compare "Eleanor Rigby" by Paul McCartney and John Lennon with Anne Bradstreet's "Upon the Burning of Our House." Identify differences in theme, tone, plot, and use of figurative language.

Upon the Burning of Our House
Anne Bradstreet

In silent night when rest I took,
For sorrow near I did not look,
I waken'd was with thund'ring noise
And piteous shrieks of dreadful voice.
That fearful sound of fire and fire,
Let no man know is my desire.

I, starting up, the light did spy,
And to my God my heart did cry
To strengthen me in my distress

A copy of Eleanor Rigby can be obtained on the internet: http://mondaypapers.com/summerinthecity/eleanorrigby.html

And not to leave me succorless.
Then coming out beheld a space,
The flame consume my dwelling place.

And, when I could no longer look,
I blest his name
That gave and took,
That laid my good now in the dust:
Yea so it was, and so 'twas just.
It was his own: it was not mine;
Far be it that I should repine.

He might of all justly bereft,
But yet sufficient for us left.
When by the ruins oft I past,
My sorrowing eyes aside did cast,
And here and there the places spy
Where oft I sat, and long did lie.

Here stood that trunk,
And there that chest;
There lay that store I counted best:
My pleasant things in ashes lie,
And them behold no more shall I.
Under thy roof no guest shall sit,
Nor at thy table eat a bit. . .

Then straight I gin my heart to chide,
And did thy wealth on earth abide?
Didst fix thy hope on mould'ring dust,
The arm of flesh dist make thy trust?
Raise up thy thoughts above the sky
That dunghill mists away may fly.

Thou has an house on high erect,
Fram'd by that mighty Architect,
With glory richly furnished,
Stands permanent tho' this be fled.
It's purchased, and paid for too
By him who hath enough to do.

A prize so vast as is unknown,
Yet, by his gift, is made thine own.
There's wealth enough, I need no more;
Farewell my pelf, farewell my store.
The world no longer let me love,
My hope and treasure lies above.
http://eir,library.utotonto.ca/rpo/display/poet27.html

BIBLICAL APPLICATION

Compare Eleanor Rigby with the woman caught in adultery (John 8:2-11).

ENRICHMENT

A. Modern Americans accuse the Puritans of being colorless and legalistic. Typically, to be "Puritan" means "to hide one's feelings." Yet, to read Anne Bradstreet, one is struck by the power of Puritan emotion! She never hesitated to share her heart with her reader.

Choose phrases from the following poem that defy the notion that Puritans hide their feelings:

To My Dear And Loving Husband
If ever two were one, then surely we.
If ever man were lov'd by wife, then thee.
If ever wife was happy in a man,
Compare with me, ye women, if you can.
I prize thy love more than whole Mines of gold
Or all the riches that the East doth hold.
My love is such that Rivers cannot quench,
Nor ought but love from thee give recompense.
Thy love is such I can no way repay.
The heavens reward thee manifold, I pray.
Then while we live, in love let's so persevere
That when we live no more, we may live ever.
http://eirlibrary.utotonto.ca/rpo/display/poet27.html

Explore the genesis of the notion that Puritans were emotionless, colorless people. Which historian/writer first advanced that idea?

B. Do you agree or disagree with Puritan Cotton Mather's rendition of what a good school is?

A Good School deserves to be call'd, the very Salt of the Town, that hath it: And the Pastors of every Town are under peculiar obligations to make this a part of their Pastoral Care, That they may have a Good School, in their Neighbourhood. A woeful putrefaction threatens the Rising Generation; Barbarous Ignorance, and the unavoidable consequence of it, Outrageous Wickedness will make the Rising Generation Loathsome, if it have not Schools to preserve it.

One can imagine how inviolable home was to Anne Bradstreet. What allure is greater to Anne Bradstreet than her possessions and her own safety?

Is there something you simply cannot give up—even for God?

But Schools, wherein the Youth may by able Masters be Taught the Things that are necessary to qualify them for future Serviceableness, and have their Manners therewithal well-formed under a Laudable Discipline, and be over and above Well-Catechised in the principles of Religion, Those would be a Glory of our Land, and the preservatives of all other Glory. . .When the Reformation began in Europe an hundred and fourscore years ago, to Erect Schools everywhere was one principal concern of the Glorious and Heroic Reformers; and it was a common thing even for Little Villages of Twenty or Thirty Families, in the midst of all their Charges, and their Dangers, to maintain one of them. The Colonies of New England were planted on the Design of pursuing that Holy Reformation; and now the Devil cannot give a greater Blow to the Reformation among us, than by causing Schools to Languish under Discouragements. If our General Courts decline to contrive and provide Laws for the Support of Schools; or if particular Towns Employ their Wits, for Cheats to Elude the wholesome Laws; little do they consider how much they expose themselves to that Rebuke of God, Thou hast destroyed thyself, O New England.

And the first Instance of their Barbarity will be, that they will be undone for want of men, but not see and own what it was that undid them." You will therefore pardon my Freedom with you, if I Address you, in the words of Luther: "If ever there be any Considerable Blow given to the Devil's Kingdom, it must be, by Youth Excellently Educated. It is a serious Thing, a weighty Thing, and a thing that hath much of the Interest of Christ, and of Christianity in it, that Youth be well-trained up, and that Schools, and School-Masters be maintained. Learning is an unwelcome guest to the Devil, and therefore he would fain starve it out." But the Freedom with which this Address is made unto you, is not so great as the Fervour that has animated it. My Fathers and Brethren, If you have any Love to God and Christ and Posterity; let (Godly) Schools be more Encouraged (Cotton Mather).

http://www.spurgeon.org/~phil/mather/edkids.htm

FINAL PROJECT

Correct and rewrite all essays and place them in your Final Portfolio.

SUGGESTED
Weekly *Implementation*

DAY 1	DAY 2	DAY 3	DAY 4	DAY 5
Prayer journal.	**Prayer journal.**	**Prayer journal.**	**Prayer journal.**	**Prayer journal.**
Review the required reading(s) *before* the assigned lesson begins.	Review reading(s) from next lesson.	Write rough drafts of all assigned essays.	Rewrite corrected copies of essays due tomorrow.	Essays are due.
Teacher may want to discuss assigned reading(s) with students.	Outline essays due at the end of the week.	The teacher and/or a peer evaluator may correct rough drafts.		Take Lesson 3 test.
Teacher and students will decide the number of essays required for this lesson, choosing two or three essays.	Per teacher instructions, students may answer orally in a group setting some of the essays that are not assigned as formal essays.			Reading ahead: Review *The Autobiography of Benjamin Franklin*, Benjamin Franklin.
The rest of the essays can be outlined, answered with shorter answers, or skipped.				Guide: What was Franklin's faith? Was it a Christian faith or a sort of "good works" civil faith?
Review all readings for Lesson 3.				

The Autobiography of Benjamin Franklin

Benjamin Franklin

BACKGROUND

Speaking to his "Dear Son," Benjamin Franklin began what is one of the most famous autobiographies in world history. At the age of sixty-two, Franklin wrote his reminiscences for the benefit of his son William Franklin (1731-1813). The book was composed in sections, the first part dealing with Franklin's first twenty-four years. He finished this section in 1771. Then, with the end of the American Revolution, he resumed his writing in 1783. He finished it in 1789. Ironically, though, the *Autobiography* covers his life only until 1757. There is no mention, for instance, of the American Revolution. Nonetheless, full of anecdotes and wisdom, *The Autobiography of Benjamin Franklin* remains a timeless classic.

CRITICAL THINKING

A. After reading *The Autobiography of Benjamin Franklin*, determine the writing style that he employs.

B. What are the definitions of the underlined words?

Having emerged from the poverty and <u>obscurity</u> in which I was born and bred, to a state of <u>affluence</u> and some degree of reputation in the world, and having gone so far through life with a considerable share of <u>felicity</u>, the <u>conducing</u> means I made use of, which with the blessing of God so well succeeded, my <u>posterity</u> may like to know, as they may find some of them suit-

able to their own situations, and therefore fit to be imitated (Part I).

It was written in 1675, in the home-spun verse of that time and people, and addressed to those then concerned in the government there. It was in favor of liberty of conscience, and in behalf of the Baptists, Quakers, and other sectaries that had been under persecution, ascribing the Indian wars, and other distresses that had befallen the country, to that persecution, as so many judgments of God to punish so <u>heinous</u> an offense, and <u>exhorting</u> a repeal of those <u>uncharitable</u> laws (Part I).

At his table he liked to have, as often as he could, some sensible friend or neighbor to converse with, and always took care to start some <u>ingenious</u> or useful topic for <u>discourse</u>, which might tend to improve the minds of his children (Part I).

I continu'd this method some few years, but gradually left it, retaining only the habit of expressing myself in terms of modest <u>diffidence</u> (Part II).

In 1751, Dr. Thomas Bond, a particular friend of mine, conceived the idea of establishing a hospital in Philadelphia a very <u>beneficent</u> design, which has been ascrib'd to me, but was originally his), for the reception and cure of poor sick persons, whether inhabitants of the province or strangers. He was <u>zealous</u> and active in endeavoring to <u>procure</u> subscriptions for it, but the proposal being a <u>novelty</u> in America, and at first not well understood, he met with but small success (Part IV).

(http://etext.lib.virginia.edu/toc.modeng/public/
Fra2Aut.html)

BIBLICAL APPLICATION

Describe Franklin's faith journey using the following quote and other passages: "Before I enter upon my public appearance in business, it may be well to let you know the then state of my mind with regard to my principles and morals, that you may see how far those influenc'd the future events of my life. My parents had early given me religious impressions, and brought me through my childhood piously in the Dissenting way. But I was scarce fifteen, when, after doubting by turns of several points, as I found them disputed in the different books I read, I began to doubt of Revelation itself. Some books against Deism fell into my hands; they were said to be the substance of sermons preached at Boyle's Lectures. It happened that they wrought an effect on me quite contrary to what was intended by them; for the arguments of the Deists, which were quoted to be refuted, appeared to me much stronger than the refutations; in short, I soon became a thorough Deist. My arguments perverted some others, particularly Collins and Ralph; but, each of them having afterwards wrong'd me greatly without the least compunction, and recollecting Keith's conduct towards me (who was another freethinker), and my own towards Vernon and Miss Read, which at times gave me great trouble, I began to suspect that this doctrine, tho' it might be true, was not very useful."

ENRICHMENT

Was the Autobiography a "rags to riches" story or was it a self-serving, egotistical story of a man's self-absorption? Support your opinion with passages from Franklin's writings.

FINAL PROJECT

Correct and rewrite all essays and place them in your Final Portfolio.

SUGGESTED
Weekly *Implementation*

DAY 1	DAY 2	DAY 3	DAY 4	DAY 5
Prayer journal.	**Prayer journal.**	**Prayer journal.**	**Prayer journal.**	**Prayer journal.**
Review the required reading(s) *before* the assigned lesson begins. Teacher may want to discuss assigned reading(s) with students. Teacher and students will decide on the number of required essays for this lesson, choosing two or three essays. The rest of the essays can be outlined, answered with shorter answers, or skipped. Review all readings for Lesson 4.	Review reading(s) from next lesson. Outline essays due at the end of the week. Per teacher instructions, students may answer orally in a group setting some of the essays that are not assigned as formal essays.	Write rough drafts of all assigned essays. The teacher and/or a peer evaluator may correct rough drafts.	Rewrite corrected copies of essays due tomorrow.	Essays are due. Take Lesson 4 test. Reading ahead: Review poems by Phillis Wheatley; *Speech in the Virginia Convention*, Patrick Henry; *The Declaration of Independence*, Thomas Jefferson; *Letter to Her Daughter from the New White House*, Abigail Adams. Guide: In the midst of slavery and fear, how can Wheatley write with such optimism?

LESSON 5

THE REVOLUTIONARY PERIOD *1750-1800 (Part 2)*

HISTORICAL BACKGROUND

In the beginning of the 18th century, the American Colonies clearly felt isolated from England. While England was experiencing the beginning of an industrial revolution and was also dealing with the problems of being an empire, America was trying to survive on the frontier. Besides, Boston and New York were nothing like London and Birmingham. New York was located approximately 3400 miles from England's center of power, London. It was the British way to administrate the colonies in a hands-off way that would allow the colonists to have all the rights of Englishmen. Initially at least, it also seemed fiscally advantageous to the Mother county. Happy colonies were prosperous colonies, and everyone made a lot of money.

Colonial legislatures had a great deal of power including the ability to muster troops, levy taxes, and pass laws. They became accustomed to these rights and were unwilling to relinquish them when England finally decided to involve itself in colonial affairs.

By 1700, the predominating economic theory was called mercantilism. Mercantilism was an economic theory stating that colonies existed solely for the benefit of the mother country. After all, England had founded and nurtured the colonies and still provided military protection. At the very least the colonies should pay for these privileges. Mercantilism also argued that there was a limited amount of wealth and that it must be controlled by limited entities (e.g., countries). Therefore, it was important for countries like England to preserve its wealth. The most important thing, then, for Britain to do was keep its wealth in the Empire and not trade with other countries to get necessary items. Naturally, some outside trade was necessary—no one thought America could provide tea and spices, but the colonies were expected to provide agricultural items.

Meanwhile, several philosophers offered the American colonists an entirely alternative view of government. Thomas Hobbes wrote an influential book titled *Leviathan* in which he detailed the idea of the social contract, which stated that men originally formed governments because of their need for protection.

You will read and analyze: poems by Phillis Wheatley; *Speech in the Virginia Convention*, Patrick Henry; *The Declaration of Independence*, Thomas Jefferson; *Letter to Her Daughter from the New White House*, Abigail Adams.

Reading ahead: Students should read 18th and 19th century poetry and the 19th century short story "The Devil and Tom Walker," Washington Irving.

Guide Question: What are the worldview battles being waged in 18th and 19th century literature?

Hobbes had no problem with British-type representative monarchies (although personally he preferred a good old dictatorship). The pay back for all this safety was that folks gave up their rights to control the state and the right to revolt. While American colonists did not particularly want to give up natural rights in order to obtain the privilege of social safety, they nonetheless liked the idea of a "social contract." Social contracts could be made and broken.

John Locke argued there were certainly unalienable rights that even states could not take away. Thus, free people had rights with which no government should tamper. Jean Jacques Rousseau's *Social Contract* (1762) wrote that government existed only by consent of the governed. Social contracts merged with inalienable rights and consent government were a potent combination.

In any event, these views contradicted mercantilism. Eighteenth century western social philosophy and political theory were in conflict. These three political theories conspired to cause many Americans to question British hegemony over a place so distant and different from the British Isles. These ideals gave them permission to question openly British right to rule in the American colonies. Very few really questioned British right to rule, even after the beginning of the Revolutionary War. Most Americans, however, felt that they had a right, even an obligation, to determine what form that rule would take. This obviously did not sit well with the British monarchy or Parliament.

These conflicts were only the start. There were many other unresolved problems and issues. By 1700, the trans-Appalachian region of North America remained basically uninhabited by Europeans. As the British colonies became more populated, colonists began to look to the West for new opportunities. This land, however, was inhabited. Native Americans liked the land, thank you very much, and so did French trappers. While neither group really wished to build barns on it, they still considered it their land. The mercantilistic British saw raw material opportunities that could not be overlooked. Thus, an epic world contest ensued among the British and their Native American allies and the French and their Native American allies. This contest eventually led to the French and Indian War.

Professor Seymour I. Schwartz reminds us that the French and Indian War took more lives than the American Revolution. In fact, this war was the bloodiest 18th century war on North American soil. "It erased France's political influence from the continent and established English dominance east of the Mississippi and in Canada. It also set the stage for the American Revolution and the establishment of the United States of America."

Three of the major events commonly regarded as preludes to the American Revolution occurred immediately after the end of the French and Indian War: the enactment of the Sugar Act (1764), the Stamp Act (1765), and the Proclamation of 1763. The first two were designed to increase British tax revenues to pay for the costly French and Indian War. Parliament and Grenville, the prime minister, increasingly felt the colonies should at least pay a part of their debt and future protection. The American colonies did not see it that way. They saw these acts to be governmental intrusions without the consent of the governed. Americans were growing increasingly uneasy with British representative democracy that they felt did not give them enough self-government.

The final irritant was the Proclamation of 1763 that mandated that no further settlements would occur over the Appalachian Mountains. To the British, this seemed to be a just way to placate the desires and needs of their Indian allies. No argument there, and, besides it made costly forts in Ohio unnecessary. To the American colonies that constantly needed more land, though, this arbitrary limit on expansion was not merely illegal, it was immoral. The British parliament had no right to make such a law.

This was an important turning point in the American attitude because from then on, opposition was not based solely on practical politics; it increasingly became grounded on fundamental political and philosophical objections.

Another phenomenon arose in the American colonies: opposition was strong and violent. With written protests and non-violent civil disobedience, colonial legislatures challenged the right of the British to tax the territories. This strategy was entirely new. Never had a governed people systematically opposed the governmental actions of a higher authority. The commotion surrounding the Sugar Act and the Stamp Act was only the beginning.

Within a year, the issue was raised again with the implementation of the Townshend Duties.

In 1767 the English Parliament cut its own unpopular property taxes, and, to balance the budget, Prime Minister Townshend promised that he would tax the Americans to make up the difference. At American ports Townshend placed import duties on paper, lead, glass, and tea shipped from England. The money that was collected was used to pay the salaries of British colonial officials. By doing this the British tried to make these officials independent of colonial legislatures and better able to enforce British orders and laws. The use of writs of assistance was authorized, and British federal courts were established. The British, in other words, asked the Americans to pay for their own bureaucracy.

Colonial opposition to the Townshend Revenue Act was swift and powerful. Colonial nonimportation agreements sharply cut British exports to America. British political leaders soon realized that the Act was foolish, for what it really did was to establish protective tariffs against the shipment of British manufactures to the colonies. Furthermore, very little money was collected because of the nonimportation agreements. In 1770, Parliament, led by a new ministry headed by Lord North, repealed all the Townshend Revenue Act except for the tax on tea, which was kept in order to maintain the principle of the right of parliament to tax the colonies.

Americans were still angry and continued protesting. In Massachusetts in 1768 the assembly was dissolved because it didn't want to collect the Townshend Duties. In the same year in Boston a mob attacked customs officers responsible for collecting the hated tea tax. This attack led to the infamous Boston Massacre. British soldiers, ably defended by John Adams, were acquitted.

On December 16, 1773, Samuel Adams led three groups of fifty men dressed like Mohawk Indians and broke into 342 chests and threw all the tea overboard. By today's market standards they destroyed about a million-dollars worth of tea!

The Intolerable Acts were passed in 1774 to punish the colonists for the Boston Tea Party. The first was the Boston Port Bill which closed the Boston Harbor until the people of Boston paid for the tea they had throw into the harbor. It went into effect on June 1, 1774. The Administration of Justice Act became effective May 20th and did not allow British soldiers to be tried in the colonies for any crimes they might commit. This meant the soldiers could do anything they wanted since they would probably not be punished for their crimes. The Massachusetts Government Act which also took effect on May 20, 1774, restricted town meetings to one a year unless the governor approved any more.

The Massachusetts Assembly could still not meet. The governor would appoint all the officials, juries and sheriffs.

The Quebec Act was established May 20, 1774. This act extended the Canadian borders to cut some of Massachusetts, Connecticut, and Virginia.

There was also the Quartering Act that was established on March 24th. It required the colonial authorities to provide housing and supplies for the British troops.

These laws added fuel to political unrest, and by April, 1775, Britain and her colonists were very close to war.

Onto this stage and into this arena walked such great men and women as Phillis Wheatley, Patrick Henry, Thomas Jefferson, and Abigail Adams.

Phillis Wheatley

LITERARY BACKGROUND

Born in 1753 in Africa, seven-year-old Phillis Wheatley was kidnapped and sold to a prosperous Boston family, the Wheatleys. While nothing softens the horrors of slavery, the Wheatley family was very kind to her. They valued her sharp mind and taught her grammar and writing. It is clear that the Wheatley family were born-again Christians. Therefore, it is not surprising that Phillis Wheatley committed her life to Christ and came to know the Bible well. At the same time, three English Christian poets—Milton, Pope and Gray—touched her deeply and exerted a strong influence on her verse. She became a sensation in Boston in the 1760s when her

Phillis Wheatley
©Arttoday.com

poem on the death of the great evangelist George Whitefield was circulated.

Phillis Wheatley was one of the earliest African American evangelists. She argued that all men and women, regardless of race or class, were in need of salvation. To students at Harvard College, she wrote:

Students, to you 'tis given to scan the heights
Above, to traverse the ethereal space,
And mark the systems of revolving worlds.
Still more, ye sons of science ye receive
The blissful news by messengers from heav'n,
How Jesus blood for your redemption flows.
See Him with hands outstretched upon the cross;
Immense compassion in His bosom glows;
He hears revilers, nor resents their scorn:
What matchless mercy in the Son of God!
When the whole human race by sin had fall'n,
He deigned to die that they might rise again,
And share with in the sublimist skies,
Life without death, and glory without end.
Improve your privileges while they stay,
Ye pupils, and each hour redeem, that bears
Or good or bad report of you to heav'n.
Let sin, that baneful evil to the soul,
By you be shunned, nor once remit your guard;
Suppress the deadly serpent in its egg.
Ye blooming plants of human race divine,
An Ethiop tells you 'tis your greatest foe;
Its transient sweetness turns to endless pain,
And immense perdition sinks the soul.
http://darkwig.uoregon.edu/~rbear/wheatley.html

The first slaves arrive in Virginia.
©arttoday.com

By the time Phillis Wheatley wrote her poetry, slavery had existed in the American colonies for more than 160 years. In fact, the institution of slavery had existed in Western Civilization since biblical times, but the first slaves came to the Western Hemisphere in the early 1500s. However, not until 20 African slaves were brought to Jamestown, Virginia, in 1619, was slavery present in America. In fact it is not altogether clear whether the first African slaves were brought as indentured servants (to be released in seven years) or chattel slavery (never to be released). Nevertheless, it quickly became a moot point. A series of complex colonial laws made sure that Africans and their descendants were to remain in slavery for perpetuity. What came first, racism or slavery? It is hard to say, but racism was not institutionalized in America until white Americans created a language to describe American people groups. When in 1619 the first African American came to the Jamestown colony, that language was already present. Europeans from the 1200s to the early 1500s used terms such as "Negro" to refer to persons with dark-colored skin. Initially, these terms were not used to denigrate a "race" or caste, nor were they used in a genealogical sense. They were used to designate a different physical attribute. Later, "Negro" and "Mulatto" gained a negative connotation.

As white Americans learned to name minorities, a system of control arose, resulting in racism. Racism, with all its stereotyping components, evolved into the deprecating form in which it exists today. The historian David R. Roediger argues, "The idea of race, then, emerges from the ways that social meaning becomes attached to physical differences. White Europeans gave such meaning an inherent, God-given origin, and (white) Americans kept up the tradition."

"Blackness" was considered to be a disease. The rhetoric of disease was a critical component in white American racism. White Americans loved to frame their racism in scientific terms. One favorite theory was that the skin color and facial features of the black were the result of congenital leprosy. Benjamin Rush, the Father of American Psychiatry, saw black people as the greatest threat to the public health in Eighteenth Century America. Rush argued that the black skin of African Americans was the result of a form of leprosy. Contemporary racist literature authenticated these racist stereotypes and maintained them in the American language.

Most slaves were taken from West Africa. There is little doubt that Phillis Wheatley came from this area. The African American historian Benjamin Quarles described these West African people groups in the following manner:

Of the varied Old World people that entered America, none came with as wide a geographical area as the blacks. The vast majority came from the West Coast of Africa, a 3000-mile stretch extending from the Senegal River . . . to Angola . . . . These groups shared no common language . . . . Indeed, there are more than 200 distinct languages in present day Nigeria alone. There was no such thing as the "African personality" since the varied groups differed as much in their way of

West African warriors—some of whom became slaves.
© arttoday.com

life as in the physical characteristics they exhibited . . . . Whatever the type of society, the different groups of Africans all operated under well-organized social systems . . . . African societies before the coming of the Europeans were not backward and changeless . . . . (Benjamin Quarles, *Black Abolitionists*, New York: Oxford University Press, 1969, 74)

Quarles also described slave trading and the middle passage. Normally, European settlers established forts on the edge of the jungle. Africans traders, wishing to obtain the trade goods, would capture young men and women from nearby tribes and take them to the fort. The terror is unimaginable! African young people were stolen from their families and were never seen again. The slaves were kept in makeshift prisons or warehouses until their proprietor had enough to justify a shipment—about 250.

One of the most awful parts of slavery was the middle passage.

Imagine being stolen from everything familiar, from everyone you love—placed in a dark prison, perhaps raped and abused, chained side-to-side, naked, with hundreds of strangers of all ages and sexes inside the dark insides of a ship. Imagine lying in your own waste for six weeks, hearing the cries of anguish and death, smelling the results of human sin. Phillis Wheatley experienced this middle passage, and yet there seems to be no invectiveness in her writing.

The South Atlantic trade network involved several international routes. The best known of the triangular trades included the transportation of manufactured goods from Europe to Africa, where they were traded for slaves. Slaves were then transported across the Atlantic—the infamous middle passage—primarily to Brazil and the Caribbean, where they were sold. It was

not uncommon for up to one-eighth of the human cargo to die. Dead slaves were thrown overboard where schools of sharks followed the slave ships. However, profits were so vast that the loss was considered to be incidental. Often the slaves would stay in the West Indies for several weeks while they were acclimated to their new North American home.

The final leg of this triangular trade brought tropical products to Europe. In another variation, manufactured goods from colonial America were taken to West Africa; slaves were carried to the Caribbean and Southern colonies; and sugar, molasses and other goods were returned to home ports.

A basic step toward successful slave management was to implant in the slaves an identity of personal inferiority. They had to keep their places, to understand that bondage was their natural status. Thus, from the beginning, Africans understood that their resistance to white domination was a question of identity survival. Indeed, resistance seemed to be the only way to survive in the face of profound white systemic racism. It was from this root that later separatist ideology sprang.

However, Africans began to resist even before they were out of sight of Africa. Resistance became a way of life. Whether it was in the colonial South Carolina Stono Rebellion or in the Brer Rabbit stories, or in everyday work in the cotton fields, African Americans resisted. Slaves defiantly cut off the roots of the plants with their hoes, just under the ground so no one noticed. Slaves used work stoppages, self-injuries, and, especially in the first few weeks of bondage, suicide to resist white enslavement. African Americans were resisting so vigorously that at times it seemed like a white minority was under siege.

One of the cleverest ways the African Americans resisted the whites was by their maintenance of a rich culture. This pattern of behavior continued into the 20th Century. Numbers and size of African American communities affected the degree and nature of resistance, but resistance existed. A chasm grew between whites and African Americans that politics, religion, and economics would never bridge. This chasm, real or imagined, became an indelible part of the American ethos.

In summary, the dominant white community did not allow the African American community to express overtly their frustration. Therefore, the African

> Slaves resisted their captivity. In what way were the writings of Phillis Wheatley a form of resistance?

Within the context of chattel slavery, the African American community created patterns of resistance that remain today. Resistance—not accommodation, not abdication—was the behavioral outcome of three hundred years of white American prejudice.

American slave community used the folktale to express hostility toward their masters, impart wisdom to the young, and teach survival skills. In the folktale "The Tar Baby Tricks Brer Rabbit" Brer Rabbit slyly convinced his arch enemies—Fox and Bear—to throw him into the brier patch rather than into the well. Of course that was exactly what Bear and Fox did and exactly what Brer Rabbit wanted them to do. For, then, Brer Rabbit could escape through the brier patch! The African American slave community resisted slavery in every possible way. From the beginning the African Community saw itself in an adversarial role to the white community and has sought to escape into its own culture as a way to defend itself against white domination.

African American slaves stayed aloof from the white world. This was especially true in their religious life. Many African American church leaders resisted assimilation into church institutions in which whites participated. It was a fundamental way that African Americans showed their defiance. In fact, to many observers the early civil rights movement appeared to be a religious protest movement more than a political protest movement.

© Arttoday.com

(The Klan is here)... to protect the weak, the innocent, and the defenseless from the indignities ... of the lawless; to relieve the injured and oppressed; to succor the suffering and unfortunate, and especially the widows and orphans of Confederate soldiers. Second, to protect and to defend the Constitution of the United States.... Third, to aid and assist in the execution of all constitutional laws...We ... reverentially acknowledge the supremacy of the Diving Being ...we are dedicated to the Lordship of Jesus Christ.

(Barry E. Black, Imperial Wizard, Keystone Knights, Knights of the Klu, Klux Klan, "Three Keystone American," Unpublished Newsletter, Nov/Dec, 1994, P. O. Box 873, Johnston, PA 15907-0873.)

CRITICAL THINKING

A. Read the following two poems written by Phillis Wheatley. Historians have marveled at the fact that Phillis Wheatley, brought from Africa at the age of eight and enslaved nearly all her life, was able to acquire literary and scholastic acumen. Her avocation was certainly not typical of most colonial women of any race! Explore your own history texts and materials from your home and public libraries for accounts of the status of slaves and that of women in colonial America. Write a descriptive two page essay about colonial women—both white and black, colonist and Native American or slave.

B. Read the two poems below. Some critics—especially of African American descent—have been critical of Phillis Wheatley. While they respect her achievements and writing ability, they wish that she had used her talents to lead a slave revolt or to perform a Harriet Tubman-like role, at least not to extol the whites. She seemed too willing to accept

Persuasive essays should begin with a clear statement of the position you are arguing. Persuasive essays should provide facts to support the argument. Avoid sentimental opinions.

her station in life. Do you agree? State your position and defend it in a one-page persuasive essay.

On Being Brought to America From Africa

'TWAS mercy brought me from my Pagan land,
Taught my benighted soul to understand
That there's a God, that there's a Saviour too:
Once I redemption neither fought nor knew,
Some view our sable race with scornful eye,
"Their colour is a diabolic dye."
Remember, Christians, Negroes, black as Cain,
May be refin'd, and join th' angelic train.
http://darkwing.uoregon.edu/

> How could a slave who experienced or even knew about the Middle Passage describe her captivity in this way?

To His Excellency General Washington

Sir,

I have taken the freedom to address your Excellency in the enclosed poem, and entreat your acceptance, though I am not insensible of its inaccuracies. Your being appointed by the Grand Continental Congress to be Generalissimo of the armies of North America, together with the fame of your virtues, excite sensations not easy to suppress. Your generosity, therefore, I presume, will pardon the attempt. Wishing your Excellency all possible success in the great cause you are so generously engaged in. I am, Your Excellency's most obedient humble servant,
     Phillis Wheatley.

Celestial choir! enthron'd in realms of light,
Columbia's scenes of glorious toils I write.
While freedom's cause her anxious breast alarms,
She flashes dreadful in refulgent arms.
See mother earth her offspring's fate bemoan,
And nations gaze at scenes before unknown!
See the bright beams of heaven's revolving light
Involved in sorrows and the veil of night!
The goddess comes, she moves divinely fair,
Olive and laurel binds her golden hair;
Wherever shines the native of the skies,
Unnumber'd charms and recent graces rise.
Muse! bow propitious while my pen relates

How pour her armies through a thousand gates,
As when Eolus heaven's fair face deforms,
Enwrapp'd in tempest and a night of storms;
Astonish'd ocean feels the wild uproar,
The refluent surges beat the sounding shore;
Or thick as leaves in Autumn's golden reign,
Such, as so many, moves the warriors's train.
In bright array they seek the work of war,
Where high unfurl'd the ensign waves in air.
Shall I to Washington their praise recite?
Enough thou know'st them in the fields of fight.
Thee, first in peace and honours,—we demand
The grace and glory of thy martial band.
Fam'd for thy valour, for thy virtues more,
Hear every tongue thy guardian aid implore!
One century scarce perform'd its destined round,
When Gallic powers Columbia's fury found;
And so may you, whoever dares disgrace
The land of freedom's heaven-defended race!
Fix'd are the eyes of nations on the scales,
For in their hopes Columbia's arm prevails.
Anon Britannia droops the pensive head,
While round increase the rising hills of dead.
Ah! cruel blindness to Columbia's state!
Lament thy thirst of boundless power too late.
Proceed, great chief, with virtue on thy side,
Thy ev'ry action let the goddess guide.
A crown, a mansion, and a throne that shine,
With gold unfading, WASHINGTON! be thine. 1776.
http://darkwing.uoregon.edu/

ENRICHMENT

A. Research the Jamestown, VA, settlement. Contrast this settlement (1607) with the Pilgrim settlement (1620) and Puritan experiment (1630).

B. Describe how it might have felt to be a member of the Lenape Native American tribe. Your name is Mary White Feather. You are the mother of three children. Your husband is an average Native American brave. You are watching these strange people in their big ships land at Jamestown. Describe your fears and hopes.

C. Describe how you would feel if you were an Englishman named Ebenezer Davis. It is 1619. You have survived a long harrowing sea voyage and are now a settler in Jamestown. You have left your family behind in Yorkshire, England. You have never seen anything like America, much less a Lenape Native American! What are your fears and expectations?

D. Pretend you are Joe Black (your English name) to your slave owners, but you know that your real name is Lomatata (your African name). You were captured and enslaved in West Africa two years ago. You have (had?) a wife and three children in Africa. You doubt that you will ever see them again. You have spent two years working in the West Indies. Now you are being sold to new owners in Jamestown, VA. It is 1619. How do you feel? What do you think about the Native Americans?

E. Notwithstanding the somewhat fictionalized Disney version, Pocahontas was a real person. Research your history books and find out about this Native American princess!

CRITICAL THINKING

What rhetorical devices does Patrick Henry employ to persuade his audience in the following speech?

Give Me Liberty or Give Me Death

A speech delivered by Patrick Henry on
March 23, 1775

No man thinks more highly than I do of the patriotism, as well as abilities, of the very worthy gentlemen who have just addressed the House. But different men often see the same subject in different lights; and, therefore, I hope it will not be thought disrespectful to those gentlemen if, entertaining as I do opinions of a character very opposite to theirs, I shall speak forth my sentiments freely and without reserve. This is no time for ceremony. The questing before the House is one of awful moment to this country. For my own part, I consider it as nothing less than a question of freedom or slavery; and in proportion to the magnitude of the subject ought to be the freedom of the debate. It is only in this way that we can hope to arrive at truth, and fulfill

> Descriptive essays describe. Using as many details as possible, bring the idea, object, or place alive to your reader. The more precise you are, the better your essay will be. Use active voice and present tense as much as possible.

Pocahontas
© Arttoday.com

the great responsibility which we hold to God and our country. Should I keep back my opinions at such a time, through fear of giving offense, I should consider myself as guilty of treason towards my country and of an act of disloyalty toward the Majesty of Heaven, which I revere above all earthly kings.

Mr. President, it is natural to man to indulge in the illusions of hope. We are apt to shut our eyes against a painful truth, and listen to the song of that siren till she transforms us into beasts. Is this the part of wise men, engaged in a great and arduous struggle for liberty? Are we disposed to be of the number of those who, having eyes, see not, and, having ears, hear not, the things which so nearly concern their temporal salvation? For my part, whatever anguish of spirit it may cost, I am willing to know the whole truth; to know the worst, and to provide for it.

I have but one lamp by which my feet are guided, and that is the lamp of experience. I know of no way of judging of the future but by the past. And judging by the past, I wish to know what there has been in the conduct of the British ministry for the last ten years to justify those hopes with which gentlemen have been pleased to solace themselves and the House. Is it that insidious smile with which our petition has been lately received? Trust it not, sir; it will prove a snare to your feet. Suffer not yourselves to be betrayed with a kiss. Ask yourselves how this gracious reception of our petition comports with those warlike preparations which cover our waters and darken our land. Are fleets and armies necessary to a work of love and reconciliation? Have we shown ourselves so unwilling to be reconciled that force must be called in to win back our love? Let us not deceive ourselves, sir. These are the implements of war and subjugation; the last arguments to which kings resort. I ask gentlemen, sir, what means this martial array, if its purpose be not to force us to submission? Can gentlemen assign any other possible motive for it? Has Great Britain any enemy, in this quarter of the world, to call for all this accumulation of navies and armies? No, sir, she has none. They are meant for us: they can be meant for no other. They are sent over to bind and rivet upon us those chains which the British ministry have been so long forging. And what have we to oppose to them? Shall we try argument? Sir, we have been trying that for the last ten years. Have we anything new to offer upon the subject? Nothing. We have held the subject up in every light of which it is capable; but it has been all in vain. Shall we resort to entreaty and humble supplication? What terms shall we find which have not been already exhausted? Let us not, I beseech you, sir, deceive ourselves. Sir, we have done everything that could be done to avert the storm which is now coming on. We have petitioned; we have remonstrated; we have supplicated; we have prostrated ourselves before the throne, and have implored its interposition to arrest the tyrannical hands of the ministry and Parliament. Our petitions have been slighted; our remonstrances have produced additional violence and insult; our supplications have been disregarded; and we have been spurned, with contempt, from the foot of the throne! In vain, after these things, may we indulge the fond hope of peace and reconciliation. There is no longer any room for hope. If we wish to be free—if we mean to preserve inviolate those inestimable privileges for which we have been so long contending— if we mean not basely to abandon the noble struggle in which we have been so long engaged, and which we have pledged ourselves never to abandon until the glorious object of our contest shall be obtained—we must fight! I repeat it, sir, we must fight! An appeal to arms and to the God of hosts is all that is left us!

They tell us, sir, that we are weak; unable to cope with so formidable an adversary. But when shall we be stronger? Will it be the next week, or the next year? Will it be when we are totally disarmed, and when a British guard shall be stationed in every house? Shall we gather strength but irresolution and inaction? Shall we acquire the means of effectual resistance by lying supinely on our backs and hugging the delusive phantom of hope, until our enemies shall have bound us hand and foot? Sir, we are not weak if we make a proper use of those means which the God of nature hath placed in our power. The millions of people, armed in the holy cause of liberty, and in such a country as that which we possess, are invincible by any force which our enemy can send against us. Besides, sir, we shall not fight our battles alone. There is a just God who presides over the destinies of nations, and who will raise up friends to fight our battles for us. The battle, sir, is not to the strong alone; it is to the vigilant, the active, the brave. Besides, sir, we have no election. If we were base enough to desire it, it is now too late to retire from the contest. There is no retreat but in submission and slavery! Our chains are forged! Their clanking may be heard on the plains of Boston! The war is inevitable—and let it come! I repeat it, sir, let it come.

It is in vain, sir, to extenuate the matter. Gentlemen may cry, Peace, Peace—but there is no peace. The war is actually begun! The next gale that sweeps from the north will bring to our ears the clash of resounding arms! Our brethren are already in the field! Why stand we here idle? What is it that gentlemen wish? What would they have? Is life so dear, or peace so sweet, as to be purchased at the price of chains and slavery? Forbid it, Almighty God! I know not what course others may take; but as for me, give me liberty or give me death! http://libertyonline.hypermall.com/

BIBLICAL APPLICATION

To a Christian, revolution is a very knotty issue. At what point, if ever, should a Christian rebellion against authority? Read *The Declaration of Independence* below and ponder: Does Thomas Jefferson offer sufficient arguments to justify a revolution?

The Declaration of Independence of the Thirteen Colonies July 4, 1776
The unanimous Declaration of the thirteen united States of America

When in the Course of human events, it becomes necessary for one people to dissolve the political bands which have connected them with another, and to assume among the powers of the earth, the separate and equal station to which the Laws of Nature and of

Nature's God entitle them, a decent respect to the opinions of mankind requires that they should declare the causes which impel them to the separation.

We hold these truths to be self-evident, that all men are created equal, that they are endowed by their Creator with certain unalienable Rights, that among these are Life, Liberty and the pursuit of Happiness. That to secure these rights, Governments are instituted among Men, deriving their just powers from the consent of the governed, That whenever any Form of Government becomes destructive of these ends, it is the Right of the People to alter or to abolish it, and to institute new Government, laying its foundation on such principles and organizing its powers in such form, as to them shall seem most likely to effect their Safety and Happiness. Prudence, indeed, will dictate that Governments long established should not be changed for light and transient causes; and accordingly all experience hath shewn, that mankind are more disposed to suffer, while evils are sufferable, than to right themselves by abolishing the forms to which they are accustomed. But when a long train of abuses and usurpations, pursuing invariably the same Object evinces a design to reduce them under absolute Despotism, it is their right, it is their duty, to throw off such Government, and to provide new Guards for their future security. Such has been the patient sufferance of these Colonies; and such is now the necessity which constrains them to alter their former Systems of Government. The history of the present King of Great Britain [George III] is a history of repeated injuries and usurpations, all having in direct object the establishment of an absolute Tyranny over these States. To prove this, let Facts be submitted to a candid world.

He has refused his Assent to Laws, the most wholesome and necessary for the public good.

He has forbidden his Governors to pass Laws of immediate and pressing importance, unless suspended in their operation till his Assent should be obtained; and when so suspended, he has utterly neglected to attend to them.

He has refused to pass other Laws for the accommodation of large districts of people, unless those people would relinquish the right of Representation in the Legislature, a right inestimable to them and formidable to tyrants only.

He has called together legislative bodies at places unusual, uncomfortable, and distant from the depository of their public Records, for the sole purpose of fatiguing them into compliance with his measures.

He has dissolved Representative Houses repeatedly, for opposing with manly firmness his invasions on the rights of the people.

He has refused for a long time, after such dissolutions, to cause others to be elected; whereby the Legislative powers, incapable of Annihilation, have returned to the People at large for their exercise; the State remaining in the mean time exposed to all the dangers of invasion from without, and convulsions within.

He has endeavoured to prevent the population of these States; for that purpose obstructing the Laws for Naturalization of Foreigners; refusing to pass others to encourage their migrations hither, and raising the conditions of new Appropriations of Lands.

He has obstructed the Administration of Justice, by refusing his Assent to Laws for establishing Judiciary powers.

He has made Judges dependent on his Will alone, for the tenure of their offices, and the amount and payment of their salaries.

He has erected a multitude of New Offices, and sent hither swarms of Officers to harass our people, and eat out their substance.

He has kept among us, in times of peace, Standing Armies without the consent of our legislatures.

He has affected to render the Military independent of and superior to the Civil power.

He has combined with others to subject us to a jurisdiction foreign to our constitution and unacknowledged by our laws; giving his Assent to their Acts of pretended Legislation:

For Quartering large bodies of armed troops among us:

For protecting them, by a mock Trial, from punishment for any Murders which they should commit on the Inhabitants of these States:

For cutting off our Trade with all parts of the world:

For imposing Taxes on us without our Consent:

For depriving us, in many cases, of the benefits of Trial by Jury:

For transporting us beyond Seas to be tried for pretended offences:

For abolishing the free System of English Laws in a neighbouring Province, establishing therein an Arbitrary government, and enlarging its Boundaries so as to render it at once an example and fit instrument for introducing the same absolute rule into these Colonies:

For taking away our Charters, abolishing our most valuable Laws, and altering fundamentally the Forms of our Governments:

For suspending our own Legislatures, and

declaring themselves invested with power to legislate for us in all cases whatsoever.

He has abdicated Government here, by declaring us out of his Protection and waging War against us.

He has plundered our seas, ravaged our Coasts, burnt our towns, and destroyed the lives of our people.

He is at this time transporting large Armies of foreign Mercenaries to compleat the works of death, desolation and tyranny, already begun with circumstances of Cruelty and perfidy scarcely paralleled in the most barbarous ages, and totally unworthy the Head of a civilized nation.

He has constrained our fellow Citizens taken Captive on the high Seas to bear Arms against their Country, to become the executioners of their friends and Brethren, or to fall themselves by their Hands.

He has excited domestic insurrections amongst us, and has endeavoured to bring on the inhabitants of our frontiers, the merciless Indian Savages, whose known rule of warfare, is an undistinguished destruction of all ages, sexes and conditions.

In every stage of these Oppressions We have Petitioned for Redress in the most humble terms: Our repeated Petitions have been answered only by repeated injury. A Prince whose character is thus marked by every act which may define a Tyrant, is unfit to be the ruler of a free people.

Nor have We been wanting in attentions to our British brethren. We have warned them from time to time of attempts by their legislature to extend an unwarrantable jurisdiction over us. We have reminded them of the circumstances of our emigration and settlement here. We have appealed to their native justice and magnanimity, and we have conjured them by the ties of our common kindred to disavow these usurpations, which would inevitably interrupt our connections and correspondence. They too have been deaf to the voice of justice and of consanguinity. We must, therefore, acquiesce in the necessity, which denounces our Separation, and hold them, as we hold the rest of mankind, Enemies in War, in Peace Friends.

We, therefore, the Representatives of the united States of America, in General Congress, Assembled, appealing to the Supreme Judge of the world for the rectitude of our intentions, do, in the Name, and by the Authority of the good People of these Colonies, solemnly publish and declare, That these United Colonies are, and of Right ought to be Free and Independent States; that they are Absolved from all Allegiance to the British Crown, and that all political connection between them and the State of Great Britain, is and ought to be totally dissolved; and that as Free and Independent States, they have full Power to levy War, conclude Peace, contract Alliances, establish Commerce, and to do all other Acts and Things which Independent States may of right do. And for the support of this Declaration, with a firm reliance on the protection of divine Providence, we mutually pledge to each other our Lives, our Fortunes and our sacred Honor.

http://www.law.indiana.edu/unlawdocs/declaration.html

ENRICHMENT

Such men and women as Phillis Wheatley, Patrick Henry, Thomas Jefferson, and Abigail Adams were critical to this Revolutionary period. Does history make people, or do people make history? In other words, were these famous Americans the product of their age, or did they actually create the events that unfolded in their age?

Consider the following letter by Abigail Adams as you think about this issue:

Letter to Her Daughter
Abigail Adams

Abigail Adams, wife of the second president of the United States, watched the first battle of the American Revolution from her front porch and lived to see the nation secure under a new president. In 1800 she wrote the following letter to her daughter from the White House:

Washington, November 21, 1800

My Dear Child,

I arrived here on Sunday last, and without meeting with any accident worth noticing, except losing ourselves when we left Baltimore, and going eight or nine miles on the Frederick road, by which means we were obliged to go the other eight through woods, where we wandered two hours without finding a guide or the path. Fortunately, a straggling black came up with us, and we engaged him as a guide to extricate us out of our difficulty. But woods are all you see from Baltimore until you reach the city, which is only so in name. Here and there is a small cot, without a glass window, interspersed amongst the forests, through which you travel miles without seeing any human being. In the city there are buildings enough, if they were compact and finished, to accommodate Congress and those attached to it: but as they are, and scattered as they are, I see no great comfort for them. The river, which runs up to Alexandria, is in full view of my window, and I see the vessels as they pass and repass. The house is upon a grand and superb scale, requiring about thirty servants to attend and keep the apartments in proper order, and perform the ordinary business of the house and stables: an establishment very well proportioned to the President's salary. The light in the apartments from the kitchen to parlours and chambers, is a tax indeed; daily agues, is another very cheering comfort. To assist us in this great castle, and render less attendance necessary, bells are wholly wanting, not one single one being hung through the whole house, and promises are all you can obtain. This is so great an inconvenience that I know not what to do, or how to do. The ladies from Georgetown and in the city have many of them visited me. Yesterday I returned fifteen visits,—but such a place as Georgetown appears,—why our Milton is beautiful. But no comparisons; if they will put me up some bells, and let me have wood enough to keep fires, I design to be pleased. I could content myself almost anywhere three months; but surrounded with forest, can you believe that wood is not to be had, because people cannot be found to cut and cart it? Briesler entered into a contract with a man to supply him with wood; a small part, a few cords only, has he been able to get. Most of that was expended to dry the walls of the house before we came in, and yesterday the man told him it was impossible for him to procure it to be cut and carted. He has had recourse to coals; but we cannot get grates made and set. We have indeed come into a new country.

You must keep all this to yourself, and when asked how I like it, say that I write you the situation is beautiful, which is true. The house is made habitable, but there is not a single apartment finished, and all within-inside, except the plastering, has been done since Briesler came. We have not the least fence-yard, or other convenience, without, and the great unfinished audience room I make a drying-room of, to hang up the clothes in. The principal stairs are not up, and will not be this winter. Six chambers are made comfortable; two are occupied by the President and Mr. Shaw; two lower rooms, one for a common parlor and one for a levee room. Upstairs there is the oval room, which is designed for the drafting-room, and has the crimson furniture in it. It is a very handsome room now, but when completed, wilt be beautiful. If the twelve years, in which this place has been considered as the future seat of government, had been improved, as they would have been if in New England, very

many of the present inconveniences would have been removed. It is a beautiful spot, capable of every improvement, and the more I view it, the more I am delighted with it. Since I sat down to write, I have been called down to a servant from Mount Vernon, with a billet from Major Custis, and a haunch of venison, and a kind, congratulatory letter from Mrs. Lewis, upon my arrival in the city, with Mrs. Washington's love, inviting me to Mount Vernon, where, health permitting, I will go, before I leave this place. Two articles are much distressed for: the one is bells, but the more important one is wood. Yet you cannot see wood for the trees. No arrangement has been made, but by promises never performed, to supply the newcomers with fuel. Of the promises, Briesler had received his full share. He had procured nine cords of wood: between six and seven of that was kindly burnt up to dry the walls of the house, which ought to have been done by the commissioners, but which, if left to them, would have remained undone to this day. Congress poured in, but shiver, shiver. No wood-cutters nor carters to be had at any rate. We are now indebted to a Pennsylvania waggon to bring us, through the first clerk in the Treasury Office, one cord and a half of wood, which is all we have for this house, where twelve fires are constantly required and where, we are told, the roads will soon be so bad that it cannot be drawn. Briesler procured two hundred bushels of coal, or we must have suffered. This is the situation of almost every other person. The public officers have sent to Philadelphia for wood cutters and wagons.

The vessel which has my clothes and other matters is not arrived. The ladies are impatient for a drawing-room: I have no looking-glasses, but dwarfs, for this house; not a twentieth part lamps enough to light it. Many things were stolen, many are broken by the removal; amongst the number, my tea-china is more than half missing. Georgetown affords nothing. My rooms are very pleasant and warm, whilst the doors of the hall are closed.

You can scarce believe that here, in this wilderness-city, I should find myself so occupied as it is. My visitors—some of them come three or four miles. The return of one of them is the work of one day. Most of the ladies reside in Georgetown, or in scattered parts of the city, at two and three miles' distance. We have all been very well as yet; if we can by any means get wood, we shall not let our fires go out, but it is at a price indeed; from four dollars it has risen to nine. Some say it will fall, but there must be more industry than is to be found here to bring half enough to the market for the

consumption of the inhabitants.
http://www.whitehousehistory.org/

POINTS TO PONDER:

During the 18th century, literature and the arts—in other words, popular culture—began to move away from the personalized, travelogue advertisements of their adventures written by John Smith and others. American culture began to develop into a style and worldview all its own. There was, as you have seen, a culture war—even then! The war was between the secularism of a John Smith and the piety of a William Bradford. Although there is no evidence that these two contemporaries met, they were nonetheless involved in a culture war. Ultimately the worldview of John Smith won. Puritanism and its Christian Theism gave way in the 18th century to the subtle deism of Thomas Paine. In the Christian Theistic world of the Puritan, God was intimately involved in the affairs of man. In a Deistic world, God, the watchmaker, supposedly created a perfect world and then retreated, allowing people to work out their own fate. Humanity was in charge. Or so it thought . . .

SUGGESTED
Weekly *Implementation*

DAY 1	DAY 2	DAY 3	DAY 4	DAY 5
Prayer journal. Review the required reading(s) *before* the assigned lesson begins. Teacher may want to discuss assigned reading(s) with students. Teacher and students will discuss the number of essays to be required for this lesson, choosing two or three essays. The rest of the essays can be outlined, answered with shorter answers, or skipped. Review all readings for Lesson 5.	**Prayer journal.** Review reading(s) from next lesson. Outline essays due at the end of the week. Per teacher instructions, students may answer orally in a group setting some of the essays that are not assigned as formal essays.	**Prayer journal.** Write rough drafts of all assigned essays. The teacher and/or a peer evaluator may correct rough drafts.	**Prayer journal.** Rewrite corrected copies of essays due tomorrow.	**Prayer journal.** Essays are due. Take Lesson 5 test. Reading ahead: Students should review 18th and 19th century poetry and the 19th century short story "The Devil and Tom Walker," Washington Irving. Guide: What are the worldview battles being waged in 18th and 19th literature?

A Growing Nation

BACKGROUND

In 1800, for the first time in history, an elected government replaced an entirely different ideological party. Granted, there were no political parties as we know them today in 1800. Nonetheless, it is remarkable and a credit to the American civilization that two candidates could vigorously debate issues and remain friends and colleagues after one is elected.

If unity prevailed nationally, disunity grew among the states. Namely, there was the growing struggle over slavery expansion. As long as the United States was confined to the eastern seaboard and southern and northern states had approximately the same representation in Congress, slavery was only a moral issue. With the acquisition of the Louisiana Purchase all that changed. The Missouri Compromise of 1820 tried to answer the problem of slavery expansion by stating that slavery was to be confined to the area south of the Missouri border (Missouri was a slave state). Of course, the problem was not solved, only postponed.

However, the real changes in America from 1800-1840 (and beyond) were in the social realm. This era was a time for extension of the American nation and, above all, of the American ethos. The advent of steam travel and railroad transportation profoundly changed American life. A trip from Philadelphia, PA, to Pittsburgh, PA, for instance, could take two months in 1820. By 1835 it would take two days.

At the same time, steamboats replaced rafts on the Mississippi and sharply reduced the price of Mississippi commerce. The Erie Canal, the most successful private project constructed during the era, enabled efficient western grain producers to ship their produce east and therefore encouraged western expansion.

As radical as transportation changes were, the changes in worldview were doubly radical. In one generation, America moved from orthodox Christian Theism to pagan Romanticism/ Transcendentalism.

You will analyze: "Thanatopsis," William Cullen Bryant and the short stories "The Devil and Tom Walker" and "The Legend of Sleepy Hollow," Washington Irving.

Reading Ahead: Students should review the poem "The Raven" and the short stories "Fall of the House of Usher" and "The Tell Tale Heart," both by Edgar Allan Poe.

Guide Question: What makes Poe's short stories so perfect?

William Cullen Bryant

BACKGROUND

William Cullen Bryant (1794-1878) was born in Massachusetts in a rural area. The rural motif was to dominate most of his poetry. He was a child-prodigy: when he was only 17, he wrote his most famous poem "Thanatopsis."

CRITICAL THINKING

After reading and pondering the following poem, offer several examples of figurative language and discuss how Bryant uses them to advance the purposes of his poem.

Thanatopsis

To him who in the love of Nature holds
Communion with her visible forms, she speaks
A various language; for his gayer hours
She has a voice of gladness, and a smile
And eloquence of beauty, and she glides
Into his darker musings, with a mild
And healing sympathy, that steals away

Their sharpness, ere he is aware. When thoughts
Of the last bitter hour come like a blight
Over thy spirit, and sad images
Of the stern agony, and shroud, and pall,
And breathless darkness, and the narrow house,
Make thee to shudder, and grow sick at heart;—
Go forth, under the open sky, and list
To Nature's teachings, while from all around—
Earth and her waters, and the depths of air—
Comes a still voice—Yet a few days, and thee
The all-beholding sun shall see no more
In all his course; nor yet in the cold ground,
Where thy pale form was laid, with many tears,
Nor in the embrace of ocean, shall exist
Thy image. Earth, that nourished thee, shall claim
Thy growth, to be resolved to earth again,
And, lost each human trace, surrendering up
Thine individual being, shalt thou go
To mix forever with the elements,
To be a brother to the insensible rock
And to the sluggish clod, which the rude swain
Turns with his share, and treads upon. The oak
Shall send his roots abroad, and pierce thy mould.

Yet not to thine eternal resting-place
Shalt thou retire alone, nor couldst thou wish
Couch more magnificent. Thou shalt lie down
With patriarchs of the infant world—with kings,
The powerful of the earth—the wise, the good,
Fair forms, and hoary seers of ages past,
All in one mighty sepulchre. The hills
Rock-ribbed and ancient as the sun,—the vales
Stretching in pensive quietness between;
The venerable woods—rivers that move
In majesty, and the complaining brooks
That make the meadows green; and, poured round all
Old Ocean's gray and melancholy waste,—
Are but the solemn decorations all
Of the great tomb of man. The golden sun,
The planets, all the infinite host of heaven,
Are shining on the sad abodes of death,
Through the still lapse of ages. All that tread
The globe are but a handful to the tribes
That slumber in its bosom.—Take the wings
Of morning, pierce the Barcan wilderness,
Or lose thyself in the continuous woods
Where rolls the Oregon, and hears no sound,
Save his own dashings—yet the dead are there:
And millions in those solitudes, since first
The flight of years began, have laid them down
In their last sleep—the dead reign there alone.

So shalt thou rest, and what if thou withdraw
In silence from the living, and no friend
Take note of thy departure? All that breathe
Will share thy destiny. The gay will laugh
When thou art gone, the solemn brood of care
Plod on, and each one as before will chase
His favorite phantom; yet all these shall leave
Their mirth and their employments, and shall come
And make their bed with thee. As the long train
Of ages glide away, the sons of men,
The youth in life's green spring, and he who goes
In the full strength of years, matron and maid,
The speechless babe, and the gray-headed man—
Shall one by one be gathered to thy side,
By those, who in their turn shall follow them.

So live, that when thy summons comes to join
The innumerable caravan, which moves
To that mysterious realm, where each shall take
His chamber in the silent halls of death,
Thou go not, like the quarry-slave at night,
Scourged to his dungeon, but, sustained and soothed
By an unfaltering trust, approach thy grave,
Like one who wraps the drapery of his couch
About him, and lies down to pleasant dreams.
www.bartleby.com/42/746.html

BIBLICAL APPLICATION

Bryant hid "Thanatopsis" for many years because he
was afraid it would offend his Christian hearers. Why
do you think he was/was not justified in his fears?

Washington Irving

BACKGROUND

WASHINGTON IRVING.
© Arttoday.com

Irving was one of the
first really popular
American writers. A
prolific if mediocre
writer, Irving was read
by people all over the
world. He was the
John Grisham of his
day. Irving (1783—
1859) is remembered
today for having writ-
ten *Rip Van Winkle* and
*The Legend of Sleepy
Hollow.* In these stories,

as well as in *Knickerbocker's History of New York*, Irving celebrated the folkways of New York's Dutch settlers. Notice unusual instances of punctuation and sentence structure in his writing.

CRITICAL THINKING

As you read "The Devil and Tom Walker" below, consider these critical thinking, biblical application, and enrichment questions:

A. In "The Devil and Tom Walker" Irving uses an extensive vocabulary. Define the following words and use them in separate sentences.

    melancholy parsimonious
  propitiatory ostentatious superfluous

B. The use of these difficult words makes his short story more humorous. How?

C. Find the sentence in the conclusion of the short story where Tom makes an ironic statement.

D. What is the meaning of the Woodman's scoring of the trees in "The Devil and Tom Walker?" What do the trees symbolize?

E. As Tom ages, he becomes "a violent churchgoer." Is Tom's conversion genuine? Offer evidence to support your answer.

F. Hyperbole is a figure of speech in which exaggeration of fact is used in order to produce humor. Give an example of hyperbole in "The Devil and Tom Walker." What purpose does hyperbole serve in this short story?

G. The theme of this book—selling one's soul to the devil—is a common theme in world literature. Offer at least one other example and compare that example to this short story.

H. Make notes on the unusual punctuation and sentence structure you find in Irving's writing.

> *Dramatic irony* is a literary device whereby a character inadvertently speaks the truth, foreshadowing tragic events of which he is unaware.

BIBLICAL APPLICATION

A. Write an expository essay describing two or three biblical characters who compromised their faith for fame, fortune, or other reasons.

B. Create a modern version of "The Devil and Tom Walker." Your short story should be about five to ten pages.

ENRICHMENT

A. Compare and contrast Irving's short story with Goethe's *Faust*.

B. Critic Harold Bloom in *The Western Canon* laments the propensity for other critics to discuss worldview in literary works. He argues that suggesting that literary works have a worldview cheapens their artistic value. Is it possible to read literature as if it does not have a worldview? Why do you agree or disagree with Bloom?

C. Compare "Sleepy Hollow" by Washington Irving with "The Devil and Tom Walker."

The Devil and Tom Walker

A few miles from Boston, in Massachusetts, there is a deep inlet winding several miles into the interior of the country from Charles Bay, and terminating in a thickly wooded swamp, or morass. On one side of this inlet is a beautiful dark grove; on the opposite side the land rises abruptly from the water's edge, into a high ridge on which grow a few scattered oaks of great age and immense size. Under one of these gigantic trees, according to old stories, there was a great amount of treasure buried by Kidd the pirate. The inlet allowed a facility to bring the money in a boat secretly and at night to the very foot of the hill. The elevation of the place permitted a good look out to be kept that no one was at hand, while the remarkable trees formed good landmarks by which the place might easily be found again. The old stories add, moreover, that the devil presided at the hiding of the money, and took it under his guardianship; but this, it is well known, he always does with buried treasure, particularly when it has been ill gotten. Be that as it may, Kidd never returned to recover his wealth; being shortly after seized at Boston, sent out to England, and there hanged for a pirate.

About the year 1727, just at the time when earthquakes were prevalent in New England, and shook many tall sinners down upon their knees, there lived near this place a meagre miserly fellow of the name of Tom Walker. He had a wife as miserly as himself; they were so miserly that they even conspired to cheat each other. Whatever the woman could lay hands on she hid away: a hen could not cackle but she was on the alert to secure the new-laid egg. Her husband was continually prying about to detect her secret hoards, and many and fierce were the conflicts that took place about what ought to have been common property. They lived in a forlorn looking house that stood alone and had an air of starvation. A few straggling savin trees, emblems of sterility, grew near it; no smoke ever curled from its chimney; no traveller stopped at its door. A miserable horse, whose ribs were as articulate as the bars of a gridiron, stalked about a field where a thin carpet of moss, scarcely covering the ragged beds of pudding stone, tantalized and balked his hunger; and sometimes he would lean his head over the fence, look piteously at the passer by, and seem to petition deliverance from this land of famine. The house and its inmates had altogether a bad name. Tom's wife was a tall termagant, fierce of temper, loud of tongue, and strong of arm. Her voice was often heard in wordy warfare with her husband; and his face sometimes showed signs that their conflicts were not confined to words. No one ventured, however, to interfere between them; the lonely wayfarer shrunk within himself at the horrid clamour and clapper clawing; eyed the den of discord askance, and hurried on his way, rejoicing, if a bachelor, in his celibacy.

One day that Tom Walker had been to a distant part of the neighbourhood, he took what he considered a short cut homewards through the swamp. Like most short cuts, it was an ill chosen route. The swamp was thickly grown with great gloomy pines and hemlocks, some of them ninety feet high; which made it dark at noonday, and a retreat for all the owls of the neighborhood. It was full of pits and quagmires, partly covered with weeds and mosses; where the green surface often betrayed the traveler into a gulf of black smothering mud; there were also dark and stagnant pools, the abodes of the tadpole, the bull-frog, and the water snake, and where trunks of pines and hemlocks lay half drowned, half rotting, looking like alligators, sleeping in the mire.

Tom had long been picking his way cautiously through this treacherous forest; stepping from tuft to tuft of rushes and roots which afforded precarious footholds among deep sloughs; or pacing carefully, like a cat, along the prostrate trunks of trees; startled now and then by the sudden screaming of the bittern, or the quacking of a wild duck, rising on the wing from some solitary pool. At length he arrived at a piece of firm ground, which ran out like a peninsula into the deep bosom of the swamp. It had been one of the strong holds of the Indians during their wars with the first colonists. Here they had thrown up a kind of fort which they had looked upon as almost impregnable, and had used as a place of refuge for their squaws and children. Nothing remained of the Indian fort but a few embankments gradually sinking to the level of the surrounding earth, and already overgrown in part by oaks and other forest trees, the foliage of which formed a contrast to the dark pines and hemlocks of the swamp.

It was late in the dusk of evening that Tom Walker reached the old fort, and he paused there for a while to rest himself. Anyone but he would have felt unwilling to linger in this lonely melancholy place, for the common people had a bad opinion of it from the stories handed down from the time of the Indian wars; when it was asserted that the savages held incantations here and made sacrifices to the evil spirit. Tom Walker, however, was not a man to be troubled with any fears of the kind.

He reposed himself for some time on the trunk of a fallen hemlock, listening to the boding cry of the tree toad, and delving with his walking staff into a mound of black mold at his feet. As he turned up the soil unconsciously, his staff struck against something hard. He raked it out of the vegetable mold, and lo! a cloven skull with an Indian tomahawk buried deep in it, lay before him. The rust on the weapon showed the time that had elapsed since this death blow had been given. It was a dreary memento of the fierce struggle that had taken place in this last foothold of the Indian warriors.

"Humph!" said Tom Walker, as he gave the skull a kick to shake the dirt from it.

"Let that skull alone!" said a gruff voice.

Tom lifted up his eyes and beheld a great black man, seated directly opposite him on the stump of a tree. He was exceedingly surprised, having neither seen nor heard any one approach, and he was still more perplexed on observing, as well as the gathering gloom would permit, that the stranger was neither Negro nor Indian. It is true, he was dressed in a rude, half Indian garb, and had a red belt or sash swathed round his body, but his face was neither black nor copper color, but swarthy and dingy and begrimed with soot, as if he had been accustomed to toil among fires and forges. He had a shock of coarse black hair that stood out from his head in all directions; and bore an axe on his shoulder.

He scowled for a moment at Tom with a pair of great red eyes.

"What are you doing in my grounds?" said the black man, with a hoarse growling voice.

"Your grounds?" said Tom, with a sneer; "no more your grounds than mine: they belong to Deacon Peabody."

"Deacon Peabody be d——d," said the stranger, "as I flatter myself he will be, if he does not look more to his own sins and less to his neighbour's. Look yonder, and see how Deacon Peabody is faring."

Tom looked in the direction that the stranger pointed, and beheld one of the great trees, fair and flourishing without, but rotten at the core, and saw that it had been nearly hewn through, so that the first high wind was likely to below it down. On the bark of the tree was scored the name of Deacon Peabody. He now looked round and found most of the tall trees marked with the name of some great men of the colony, and all more or less scored by the axe. The one on which he had been seated, and which had evidently just been hewn down, bore the name of Crowninshield; and he recollected a mighty rich man of that name, who made a vulgar display of wealth, which it was whispered he had acquired by buccaneering.

"He's just ready for burning!" said the black man, with a growl of triumph. "You see I am likely to have a good stock of firewood for winter."

"But what right have you," said Tom, "to cut down Deacon Peabody's timber?"

"The right of prior claim," said the other. "This woodland belonged to me long before one of your white faced race put foot upon the soil."

"And pray, who are you, if I may be so bold?" said Tom.

"Oh, I go by various names. I am the Wild Huntsman in some countries; the Black Miner in others. In this neighborhood I am known by the name of the Black Woodsman. I am he to whom the red men devoted this spot, and now and then roasted a white man by way of sweet smelling sacrifice. Since the red men have been exterminated by you white savages, I amuse myself by presiding at the persecutions of Quakers and Anabaptists; I am the great patron and prompter of slave dealers, and the grand master of the Salem witches."

"The upshot of all which is, that, if I mistake not," said Tom, sturdily, "you are he commonly called Old Scratch."

"The same at your service!" replied the black man, with a half civil nod.

Such was the opening of this interview, according to the old story, though it has almost too familiar an air to be credited. One would think that to meet with such a singular personage in this wild lonely place would have shaken any man's nerves: but Tom was a hard-minded fellow, not easily daunted, and he had lived so long with a termagant wife, that he did not even fear the devil.

It is said that after this commencement, they had a long and earnest conversation together, as Tom returned homewards. The black man told him of great sums of money which had been buried by Kidd the pirate, under the oak trees on the high ridge not far from the morass. All these were under his command and protected by his power, so that none could find them but such as propitiated his favor. These he offered to place within Tom Walker's reach, having conceived an especial kindness for him: but they were to be had only on certain conditions. What these conditions were, may easily be surmised, though Tom never disclosed them publicly. They must have been very hard, for he required time to think of them, and he was not a man to stick at trifles where money was in view. When they had reached the edge of the swamp the stranger paused.

"What proof have I that all you have been telling me is true?" said Tom.

"There is my signature," said the black man, pressing his finger on Tom's forehead. So saying, he turned off among the thickets of the swamp, and seemed, as Tom said, to go down, down, down, into the earth, until nothing but his head and shoulders could be seen, and so on until he totally disappeared.

When Tom reached home he found the black print of a finger burnt, as it were, into his forehead, which nothing could obliterate.

The first news his wife had to tell him was the sudden death of Absalom Crowninshield the rich buccaneer. It was announced in the papers with the usual flourish that "a great man had fallen in Israel."

Tom recollected the tree which his black friend had just hewn down, and which was ready for burning. "Let the freebooter roast," said Tom, "who cares!" He now felt convinced that all he had heard and seen was no illusion.

He was not prone to let his wife into his confidence; but as this was an uneasy secret, he willingly shared it with her. All her avarice was awakened at the mention of hidden gold, and she urged her husband to comply with the black man's terms and secure what would make them wealthy for life. However Tom might have felt disposed to sell himself to the devil, he was determined not to do so to oblige his wife; so he flatly refused out of the mere spirit of contradiction. Many and bitter were the quarrels they had on the subject, but the more she talked the more resolute was Tom not to be damned to please her. At length she determined to drive the bargain on her own account, and if she succeeded, to keep all the gain to herself.

Being of the same fearless temper as her husband, she set off for the old Indian fort towards the close of a summer's day. She was many hours absent. When she came back she was reserved and sullen in her replies. She spoke something of a black man whom she had met about twilight, hewing at the root of a tall tree. He was sulky, however, and would not come to terms; she was to go again with a propitiatory offering, but what it was she forbore to say.

The next evening she set off again for the swamp, with her apron heavily laden. Tom waited and waited for her, but in vain: midnight came, but she did not make her appearance; morning, noon, night returned, but still she did not come. Tom now grew uneasy for her safety; especially as he found she had carried off in her apron the silver teapot and spoons and every portable article of value. Another night elapsed, another morning came; but no wife. In a word, she was never heard of more.

What was her real fate nobody knows, in consequence of so many pretending to know. It is one of those facts that have become confounded by a variety of historians. Some asserted that she lost her way among the tangled mazes of the swamp and sunk into some pit or slough; others, more uncharitable, hinted that she had eloped with the household booty, and made off to some other province; while others assert that the tempter had decoyed her into a dismal quagmire on top of which her hat was found lying. In confirmation of this, it was said a great black man with an axe on his shoulder was seen late that very evening coming out of the swamp, carrying a bundle tied in a check apron, with an air of surly triumph.

The most current and probable story, however, observes that Tom Walker grew so anxious about the fate of his wife and his property that he sat out at length to seek them both at the Indian fort. During a long summer's afternoon he searched about the gloomy place, but no wife was to be seen. He called her name repeatedly, but she was no where to be heard. The bittern alone responded to his voice, as he flew screaming by; or the bull-frog croaked dolefully from a neighboring pool. At length, it is said, just in the brown hour of twilight, when the owls began to hoot and the bats to flit about; his attention was attracted by the clamor of carrion crows that were hovering about a cypress tree. He looked and beheld a bundle tied in a check apron and hanging in the branches of the tree; with a great vulture perched hard by, as if keeping watch upon it. He leaped with joy, for he recognized his wife's apron, and supposed it to contain the household valuables.

"Let us get hold of the property," said he, consolingly to himself, "and we will endeavor to do without the woman."

As he scrambled up the tree the vulture spread its wide wings, and sailed off screaming into the deep shadows of the forest. Tom seized the check apron, but, woeful sight! found nothing but a heart and liver tied up in it.

Such, according to the most authentic old story, was all that was to be found of Tom's wife. She had probably attempted to deal with the black man as she had been accustomed to deal with her husband; but though a female scold is generally considered a match for the devil, yet in this instance she appears to have had the worst of it. She must have died game however; for it is said Tom noticed many prints of cloven feet deeply stamped about the tree, and several handful of hair, that looked as if they had been plucked from the coarse black shock of the woodsman.

Tom knew his wife's prowess by experience. He shrugged his shoulders as he looked at the signs of a fierce clapper clawing. "Egad," said he to himself, "Old Scratch must have had a tough time of it!"

Tom consoled himself for the loss of his property with the loss of his wife; for he was a man of fortitude. He even felt something like gratitude towards the black woodsman, who he considered had done him a kindness. He sought, therefore, to cultivate a farther acquaintance with him, but for some time without success; the old black legs played shy, for whatever people may think, he is not always to be had for calling for; he knows how to play his cards when pretty sure of his game.

At length, it is said, when delay had whetted Tom's eagerness to the quick, and prepared him to agree to any thing rather than not gain the promised treasure, he met the black man one evening in his usual woodman dress, with his axe on his shoulder, sauntering along the edge of the swamp, and humming a tune. He affected to receive Tom's advance with great indifference, made brief replies, and went on humming his tune.

By degrees, however, Tom brought him to business, and they began to haggle about the terms on which the former was to have the pirate's treasure. There was one condition which need not be mentioned, being generally understood in all cases where the devil grants favors; but there were others about which, though of less importance, he was inflexibly obstinate. He insisted that the money found through his means should be employed in his service. He proposed, therefore, that Tom should employ it in the black traffic; that is to say, that he should fit out a slave ship. This, however, Tom resolutely refused; he was bad enough in all conscience; but the devil himself could not tempt him to turn slave dealer.

Finding Tom so squeamish on this point, he did not insist upon it, but proposed instead that he should turn usurer; the devil being extremely anxious for the increase of usurers, looking upon them as his peculiar people.

To this no objections were made, for it was just to Tom's taste.

"You shall open a broker's shop in Boston next month," said the black man.

"I'll do it tomorrow, if you wish," said Tom Walker.

"You shall lend money at two per cent a month."

"Egad, I'll charge four!" replied Tom Walker.

"You shall extort bonds, foreclose mortgages, drive the merchant to bankruptcy—"

"I'll drive him to the d——l," cried Tom Walker, eagerly.

"You are the usurer for my money!" said the black legs, with delight. "When will you want the rhino?"

"This very night."

"Done!" said the devil.

"Done!" said Tom Walker. So they shook hands, and struck a bargain.

A few days' time saw Tom Walker seated behind his desk in a counting house in Boston. His reputation for a ready moneyed man, who would lend money out for a good consideration, soon spread abroad. Every body remembers the days of Governor Belcher, when money was particularly scarce. It was a time of paper credit. The country had been deluged with government bills; the famous Land Bank had been established; there had been a rage for speculating; the people had run mad with schemes for new settlements; for building cities in the wilderness; land jobbers went about with maps of grants, and townships, and Eldorados, lying nobody knew where, but which every body was ready to purchase. In a word, the great speculating fever which breaks out every now and then in the country, had raged to an alarming degree, and every body was dreaming of making sudden fortunes from nothing. As usual the fever had subsided; the dream had gone off, and the imaginary fortunes with it; the patients were left in doleful plight, and the whole country resounded with the consequent cry of "hard times."

At this propitious time of public distress did Tom Walker set up as a usurer in Boston. His door was soon thronged by customers. The needy and the adventurous; the gambling speculator; the dreaming land jobber; the thriftless tradesman; the merchant with cracked credit; in short, every one driven to raise money by desperate means and desperate sacrifices, hurried to Tom Walker.

Thus Tom was the universal friend of the needy, and he acted like a "friend in need;" that is to say, he always exacted good pay and good security. In proportion to the distress of the applicant was the hardness of his terms. He accumulated bonds and mortgages; gradually squeezed his customers closer and closer; and sent them at length, dry as a sponge from his door.

In this way he made money hand over hand; becme a rich and mighty man, and exalted his cocked hat upon change. He built himself, as usual, a vast house, out of ostentation; but left the greater part of it unfinished and unfurnished out of parsimony. He even set up a carriage in the fullness of his vain glory, though he nearly starved the horses which drew it; and as the ungreased wheels groaned and screeched on the axle trees, you would have thought you heard the souls of the poor debtors he was squeezing.

As Tom waxed old, however, he grew thoughtful. Having secured the good things of this world, he began to feel anxious about those of the next. He thought with regret on the bargain he had made with his black friend, and set his wits to work to cheat him out of the conditions. He became, therefore, all of a sudden, a violent church goer. He prayed loudly and strenuously as if heaven were to be taken by force of lungs. Indeed, one might always tell when he had sinned most during the week, by the clamor of his Sunday devotion. The quiet Christians, who had been modestly and steadfastly traveling Zionward, were struck with self reproach at seeing themselves so suddenly outstripped in their career by this new-made convert. Tom was as rigid in religious, as in money matters; he was a stern supervisor and censurer of his neighbors, and seemed to think every sin entered up to their account became a credit on his own side of the page. He even talked of the expediency of reviving the persecution of Quakers and Anabaptists. In a word, Tom's zeal became as notorious as his riches.

Still, in spite of all this strenuous attention to forms, Tom had a lurking dread that the devil, after all, would have his due. That he might not be taken unawares, therefore, it is said he always carried a small Bible in his coat pocket. He had also a great folio Bible on his counting house desk, and would frequently be found reading it when people called on business; on such occasions he would lay his green spectacles on the book, to mark the place, while he turned round to drive some usurious bargain.

Some say that Tom grew a little crack brained in his old days, and that fancying his end approaching, he had his horse new shod, saddled and bridled, and buried with his feet uppermost; because he supposed that at the last day the world would be turned upside down; in which case he should find his horse standing ready for mounting, and he was determined at the worst to give his old friend a run for it. This, however, is probably a mere old wives fable. If he really did take such a precaution it was totally superfluous; at least so says the authentic old legend which closes his story in the following manner.

On one hot afternoon in the dog days, just as a terrible black thunder gust was coming up, Tom sat in his counting house in his white linen cap and India silk morning gown. He was on the point of foreclosing a mortgage, by which he would complete the ruin of an unlucky land speculator for whom he had professed the greatest friendship. The poor land jobber begged him to grant a few months indulgence. Tom had grown testy and irritated and refused another day.

"My family will be ruined and brought upon the parish," said the land jobber. "Charity begins at home," replied Tom, "I must take care of myself in these hard times."

"You have made so much money out of me," said the speculator.

Tom lost his patience and his piety "The devil take me," said he, "if I have made a farthing!"

Just then there were three loud knocks at the street door. He stepped out to see who was there. A black man was holding a black horse which neighed and stamped with impatience.

"Tom, you're come for!" said the black fellow, gruffly. Tom shrunk back, but too late. He had left his little Bible at the bottom of his coat pocket, and his big Bible on the desk buried under the mortgage he was about to foreclose: never was sinner taken more unawares. The black man whisked him like a child astride the horse and away he galloped in the midst of a thunder storm. The clerks stuck their pens behind their ears and stared after him from the windows. Away went Tom Walker, dashing down the streets; his white cap bobbing up and down; his morning gown fluttering in the wind, and his steed striking fire out of the pavement at every bound. When the clerks turned to look for the black man he had disappeared.

Tom Walker never returned to foreclose the mortgage. A countryman who lived on the borders of the swamp, reported that in the height of the thunder gust he had heard a great clattering of hoofs and a howling along the road, and that when he ran to the window he just caught sight of a figure, such as I have described, on a horse that galloped like mad across the fields, over the hills and down into the black hemlock swamp towards the old Indian fort; and that shortly after a thunderbolt fell in that direction which seemed to set the whole forest in a blaze.

The good people of Boston shook their heads and shrugged their shoulders, but had been so much accustomed to witches and goblins and tricks of the devil in all kinds of shapes from the first settlement of the colony, that they were not so much horror struck as might have been expected. Trustees were appointed to take charge of Tom's effects. There was nothing, however, to administer upon. On searching his coffers all his bonds and mortgages were found reduced to cinders. In place of gold and silver his iron chest was filled with chips and shavings; two skeletons lay in his stable instead of his half starved horses, and the very next day his great house took fire and was burnt to the ground.

Such was the end of Tom Walker and his ill gotten wealth. Let all griping money brokers lay this story to heart. The truth of it is not to be doubted. The very hole under the oak trees, from whence he dug Kidd's money is to be seen to this day; and the neighboring swamp and old Indian fort is often haunted in stormy nights by a figure on horseback, in a morning gown and white cap, which is doubtless the troubled spirit of the usurer. In fact, the story has resolved itself into a proverb, and is the origin of that popular saying, prevalent throughout New England, of "The Devil and Tom Walker."

http://classiclit.about.com/library/bl-etexts/ wirving/bl-wirving-devil.htm

The Legend of Sleepy Hollow

A pleasing land of drowsy head it was,
Of dreams that wave before the half-shut eye;
And of gay castles in the clouds that pass,
Forever flushing round a summer sky.
—Castle of Indolence.

In the bosom of one of those spacious coves which indent the eastern shore of the Hudson, at that broad expansion of the river denominated by the ancient Dutch navigators the Tappan Zee, and where they always prudently shortened sail and implored the protection of St. Nicholas when they crossed, there lies a small market town or rural port, which by some is called Greensburgh, but which is more generally and properly known by the name of Tarry Town. This name was given, we are told, in former days, by the good housewives of the adjacent country, from the inveterate propensity of their husbands to linger about the village tavern on market days. Be that as it may, I do not vouch for the fact, but merely advert to it, for the sake of being precise and authentic. Not far from this village, perhaps about two miles, there is a little valley or rather lap of land among high hills, which is one of the quietest places in the whole world. A small brook glides through it, with just murmur enough to lull one to repose; and the occasional whistle of a quail or tapping of a woodpecker is almost the only sound that ever breaks in upon the uniform tranquillity.

I recollect that, when a stripling, my first exploit in squirrel shooting was in a grove of tall walnut trees that shades one side of the valley. I had wandered into it at noontime, when all nature is peculiarly quiet, and was startled by the roar of my own gun, as it broke the Sabbath stillness around and was prolonged and reverberated by the angry echoes. If ever I should wish for a retreat whither I might steal from the world and its distractions, and dream quietly away the remnant of a troubled life, I know of none more promising than this little valley.

From the listless repose of the place, and the peculiar character of its inhabitants, who are descendants from the original Dutch settlers, this sequestered glen has long been known by the name of Sleepy Hollow, and its rustic lads are called the Sleepy Hollow Boys throughout all the neighboring country. A drowsy, dreamy influence seems to hang over the land, and to pervade the very atmosphere. Some say that the place was bewitched by a High German doctor, during the early days of the settlement; others, that an old Indian chief, the prophet or wizard of his tribe, held his powwows there before the country was discovered by Master Hendrick Hudson. Certain it is, the place still continues under the sway of some witching power that holds a spell over the minds of the good people, causing them to walk in a continual reverie. They are given to all kinds of marvelous beliefs; are subject to trances and visions, and frequently see strange sights, and hear music and voices in the air. The whole neighborhood abounds with local tales, haunted spots, and twilight superstitions; stars shoot and meteors glare oftener across the valley than in any other part of the country, and the nightmare, with her whole ninefold, seems to make it the favorite scene of her gambols.

The dominant spirit, however, that haunts this enchanted region, and seems to be commander-in-chief of all the powers of the air, is the apparition of a figure on horseback, without a head. It is said by some to be the ghost of a Hessian trooper, whose head had been carried away by a cannon ball in some nameless battle during the Revolutionary War, and who is ever and anon seen by the country folk hurrying along in the gloom of night, as if on the wings of the wind. His haunts are not confined to the valley, but extend at times to the adjacent roads, and especially to the vicinity of a church at no great distance. Indeed, certain of the most authentic historians of those parts, who have been careful in collecting and collating the floating facts concerning this specter, allege that the body of the trooper having been buried in the churchyard, the ghost rides forth to the scene of battle in nightly quest of his head, and that the rushing speed with which he sometimes passes along the Hollow, like a midnight blast, is owing to his being belated, and in a hurry to get back to the churchyard before daybreak.

Such is the general purport of this legendary superstition, which has furnished materials for many a wild story in that region of shadows; and the specter is known at all the country firesides, by the name of the Headless Horseman of Sleepy Hollow.

It is remarkable that the visionary propensity I have mentioned is not confined to the native inhabitants of the valley, but is unconsciously imbibed by every one who resides there for a time. However wide awake they may have been before they entered that sleepy region, they are sure, in a little time, to inhale the witching influence of the air, and begin to grow imaginative, to dream dreams, and see apparitions.

I mention this peaceful spot with all possible laud for it is in such little retired Dutch valleys, found here and there embosomed in the great State of New York, that population, manners, and customs remain fixed, while the great torrent of migration and improvement, which is making such incessant changes in other parts of this restless country, sweeps by them unobserved. They are like those little nooks of still water, which border a rapid stream, where we may see the straw and bubble riding quietly at anchor, or slowly revolving in their mimic harbor, undisturbed by the rush of the passing current. Though many years have elapsed since I trod the drowsy shades of Sleepy Hollow, yet I question whether I should not still find the same trees and the same families vegetating in its sheltered bosom.

In this byplace of nature there abode, in a remote period of American history, that is to say, some thirty years since, a worthy wight of the name of Ichabod Crane, who sojourned, or, as he expressed it, "tarried," in Sleepy Hollow, for the purpose of instructing the children of the vicinity. He was a native of Connecticut, a State which supplies the Union with pioneers for the mind as well as for the forest, and sends forth yearly its legions of frontier woodmen and country schoolmasters. The cognomen of Crane was not inapplicable to his person. He was tall, but exceedingly lank, with narrow shoulders, long arms and legs, hands that dangled a mile out of his sleeves, feet that might have served for shovels, and his whole frame most loosely hung together. His head was small, and flat at top, with huge ears, large green glassy eyes, and a long snipe nose, so that it looked like a weather cock perched upon his spindle neck to tell which way the wind blew. To see him striding along the profile of a hill on a windy day, with his clothes bagging and fluttering about him, one might have mistaken him for the genius of famine descending upon the earth, or some scarecrow eloped from a cornfield.

His schoolhouse was a low building of one large room, rudely constructed of logs; the windows partly glazed, and partly patched with leaves of old copybooks. It was most ingeniously secured at vacant hours, by a withe twisted in the handle of the door, and stakes set against the window shutters; so that though a thief might get in with perfect ease, he would find some embarrassment in getting out, an idea most probably borrowed by the architect, Yost Van Houten, from the mystery of an eel pot. The schoolhouse stood in a rather lonely but pleasant situation, just at the foot of a woody hill, with a brook running close by, and a formidable birch tree growing at one end of it. From hence the low murmur of his pupils' voices, conning over their lessons, might be heard in a drowsy summer's day, like the hum of a beehive; interrupted now and then by the authoritative voice of the master, in the tone of menace or command, or, peradventure, by the appalling sound of the birch, as he urged some tardy loiterer along the flowery path of knowledge. Truth to say, he was a conscientious man, and ever bore in mind the golden maxim, "Spare the rod and spoil the child." Ichabod Crane's scholars certainly were not spoiled.

I would not have it imagined, however, that he was one of those cruel potentates of the school who joy in the smart of their subjects; on the contrary, he administered justice with discrimination rather than severity; taking the burden off the backs of the weak, and laying it on those of the strong. Your mere puny stripling, that winced at the least flourish of the rod, was passed by with indulgence; but the claims of justice were satisfied by inflicting a double portion on some little tough wrong headed, broad-skirted Dutch urchin, who sulked and swelled and grew dogged and sullen beneath the birch. All this he called "doing his duty by their parents;" and he never inflicted a chastisement without following it by the assurance, so consolatory to the smarting urchin, that "he would remember it and thank him for it the longest day he had to live."

When school hours were over, he was even the companion and playmate of the larger boys; and on holiday afternoons would convoy some of the smaller ones home, who happened to have pretty sisters, or good housewives for mothers, noted for the comforts of the cupboard. Indeed, it behooved him to keep on good terms with his pupils. The revenue arising from his school was small, and would have been scarcely sufficient to furnish him with daily bread, for he was a huge feeder, and, though lank, had the dilating powers of an anaconda; but to help out his maintenance, he was, according to country custom in those parts, boarded and lodged at the houses of the farmers whose children he instructed. With these he lived successively a week at a time, thus going the rounds of the neighborhood, with all his worldly effects tied up in a cotton handkerchief.

That all this might not be too onerous on the purses of his rustic patrons, who are apt to considered the costs of schooling a grievous burden, and schoolmasters as mere drones he had various ways of rendering himself both useful and agreeable. He assisted the farmers occasionally in the lighter labors of their farms, helped to make hay, mended the fences, took the horses to water, drove the cows from pasture, and cut wood for the winter fire. He laid aside, too, all the dominant dignity and absolute sway with which he lorded it in his little empire, the school, and became wonderfully gentle and ingratiating. He found favor in the eyes of the mothers by petting the children, particularly the youngest; and like the lion bold, which whilom so magnanimously the lamb did hold, he would sit with a child on one knee, and rock a cradle with his foot for whole hours together.

In addition to his other vocations, he was the singing master of the neighborhood, and picked up many bright shillings by instructing the young folks in psalmody. It was a matter of no little vanity to him on Sundays, to take his station in front of the church gallery, with a band of chosen singers; where, in his own mind, he completely carried away the palm from the parson. Certain it is, his voice resounded far above all the rest of the congregation; and there are peculiar quavers still to be heard in that church, and which may even be heard half a mile off, quite to the opposite side of the mill pond, on a still Sunday morning, which are said to be legitimately descended from the nose of Ichabod Crane. Thus, by divers little makeshifts, in that ingenious way which is commonly denominated "by hook and by crook," the worthy pedagogue got on tolerably enough, and was thought, by all who understood nothing of the labor of headwork, to have a wonderfully easy life of it.

The schoolmaster is generally a man of some importance in the female circle of a rural neighborhood; being considered a kind of idle, gentlemanlike personage, of vastly superior taste and accomplishments to the rough country swains, and, indeed, inferior in learning only to the parson. His appearance, therefore, is apt to occasion some little stir at the tea table of a farmhouse, and the addition of a supernumerary dish of cakes or sweetmeats, or, peradventure, the parade of a silver teapot. Our man of letters, therefore, was peculiarly happy in the smiles of all the country damsels. How he would figure among them in the churchyard, between services on Sundays; gathering grapes for them from the wild vines that overran the surrounding trees; reciting for their amusement all the epitaphs on the tombstones; or sauntering, with a whole bevy of them, along the banks of the adjacent mill pond; while the more bashful country bumpkins hung sheepishly back, envying his superior elegance and address.

From his half-itinerant life, also, he was a kind of traveling gazette, carrying the whole budget of local gossip from house to house, so that his appearance was always greeted with satisfaction. He was, moreover, esteemed by the women as a man of great erudition, for he had read several books quite through, and was a perfect master of Cotton Mather's "History of New England Witchcraft," in which, by the way, he most firmly and potently believed.

He was, in fact, an odd mixture of small shrewdness and simple credulity. His appetite for the marvelous, and his powers of digesting it, were equally extraordinary; and both had been increased by his residence in this spell-bound region. No tale was too gross or monstrous for his capacious swallow. It was often his

delight, after his school was dismissed in the afternoon, to stretch himself on the rich bed of clover bordering the little brook that whimpered by his schoolhouse, and there con over old Mather's direful tales, until the gathering dusk of evening made the printed page a mere mist before his eyes. Then, as he wended his way by swamp and stream and awful woodland, to the farmhouse where he happened to be quartered, every sound of nature, at that witching hour, fluttered his excited imagination, the moan of the whip-poor-will from the hillside, the boding cry of the tree toad, that harbinger of storm, the dreary hooting of the screech owl, to the sudden rustling in the thicket of birds frightened from their roost. The fireflies, too, which sparkled most vividly in the darkest places, now and then startled him, as one of uncommon brightness would stream across his path; and if, by chance, a huge blockhead of a beetle came winging his blundering flight against him, the poor varlet was ready to give up the ghost, with the idea that he was struck with a witch's token. His only resource on such occasions, either to drown thought or drive away evil spirits, was to sing psalm tunes and the good people of Sleepy Hollow, as they sat by their doors of an evening, were often filled with awe at hearing his nasal melody, "in linked sweetness long drawn out," floating from the distant hill, or along the dusky road.

Another of his sources of fearful pleasure was to pass long winter evenings with the old Dutch wives, as they sat spinning by the fire, with a row of apples roasting and spluttering along the hearth, and listen to their marvelous tales of ghosts and goblins, and haunted fields, and haunted brooks, and haunted bridges, and haunted houses, and particularly of the headless horseman, or Galloping Hessian of the Hollow, as they sometimes called him. He would delight them equally by his anecdotes of witchcraft, and of the direful omens and portentous sights and sounds in the air, which prevailed in the earlier times of Connecticut; and would frighten them woefully with speculations upon comets and shooting stars; and with the alarming fact that the world did absolutely turn round, and that they were half the time topsy-turvy!

But if there was a pleasure in all this, while snugly cuddling in the chimney corner of a chamber that was all of a ruddy glow from the crackling wood fire, and where, of course, no specter dared to show its face, it was dearly purchased by the terrors of his subsequent walk homewards. What fearful shapes and shadows beset his path, amidst the dim and ghastly glare of a snowy night! With what wistful look did he eye every trembling ray of light streaming across the waste fields from some distant window! How often was he appalled by some shrub covered with snow, which, like a sheeted specter, beset his very path! How often did he shrink with curdling awe at the sound of his own steps on the frosty crust beneath his feet; and dread to look over his shoulder, lest he should behold some uncouth being tramping close behind him! and how often was he thrown into complete dismay by some rushing blast, howling among the trees, in the idea that it was the Galloping Hessian on one of his nightly scourings!

All these, however, were mere terrors of the night, phantoms of the mind that walk in darkness; and though he had seen many specters in his time, and been more than once beset by Satan in divers shapes, in his lonely perambulations, yet daylight put an end to all these evils; and he would have passed a pleasant life of it, in despite of the Devil and all his works, if his path had not been crossed by a being that causes more perplexity to mortal man than ghosts, goblins, and the whole race of witches put together, and that was—a woman.

Among the musical disciples who assembled, one evening in each week, to receive his instructions in psalmody, was Katrina Van Tassel, the daughter and only child of a substantial Dutch farmer. She was a booming lass of fresh eighteen; plump as a partridge; ripe and melting and rosy-cheeked as one of her father's peaches, and universally famed, not merely for her beauty, but her vast expectations. She was withal a little of a coquette, as might be perceived even in her dress, which was a mixture of ancient and modern fashions, as most suited to set of her charms. She wore the ornaments of pure yellow gold, which her great-great-grandmother had brought over from Saar dam; the tempting stomacher of the olden time, and withal a provokingly short petticoat, to display the prettiest foot and ankle in the country round.

Ichabod Crane had a soft and foolish heart towards the sex; and it is not to be wondered at, that so tempting a morsel soon found favor in his eyes, more especially after he had visited her in her paternal mansion. Old Baltus Van Tassel was a perfect picture of a thriving, contented, liberal-hearted farmer. He seldom, it is true, sent either his eyes or his thoughts beyond the boundaries of his own farm; but within those everything was snug, happy and well-conditioned. He was satisfied with his wealth, but not proud of it; and piqued himself upon the hearty abundance, rather than the style in which he lived. His stronghold was situated on the banks of the Hudson, in one of those green, shel-

tered, fertile nooks in which the Dutch farmers are so fond of nestling. A great elm tree spread its broad branches over it, at the foot of which bubbled up a spring of the softest and sweetest water, in a little well formed of a barrel; and then stole sparkling away through the grass, to a neighboring brook, that babbled along among alders and dwarf willows. Hard by the farmhouse was a vast barn, that might have served for a church; every window and crevice of which seemed bursting forth with the treasures of the farm; the flail was busily resounding within it from morning to night; swallows and martins skimmed twittering about the eaves; an rows of pigeons, some with one eye turned up, as if watching the weather, some with their heads under their wings or buried in their bosoms, and others swelling, and cooing, and bowing about their dames, were enjoying the sunshine on the roof. Sleek unwieldy porkers were grunting in the repose and abundance of their pens, from whence sallied forth, now and then, troops of sucking pigs, as if to snuff the air. A stately squadron of snowy geese were riding in an adjoining pond, convoying whole fleets of ducks; regiments of turkeys were gobbling through the farmyard, and Guinea fowls fretting about it, like ill-tempered housewives, with their peevish, discontented cry. Before the barn door strutted the gallant cock, that pattern of a husband, a warrior and a fine gentleman, clapping his burnished wings and crowing in the pride and gladness of his heart, sometimes tearing up the earth with his feet, and then generously calling his ever-hungry family of wives and children to enjoy the rich morsel which he had discovered.

The pedagogue's mouth watered as he looked upon this sumptuous promise of luxurious winter fare. In his devouring mind's eye, he pictured to himself every roasting pig running about with a pudding in his belly, and an apple in his mouth; the pigeons were snugly put to bed in a comfortable pie, and tucked in with a coverlet of crust; the geese were swimming in their own gravy; and the ducks pairing cosily in dishes, like snug married couples, with a decent competency of onion sauce. In the porkers he saw carved out the future sleek side of bacon, and juicy relishing ham; not a turkey but he beheld daintily trussed up, with its gizzard under its wing, and, peradventure, a necklace of savory sausages; and even bright chanticleer himself lay sprawling on his back, in a side dish, with uplifted claws, as if craving that quarter which his chivalrous spirit disdained to ask while living.

As the enraptured Ichabod fancied all this, and as he rolled his great green eyes over the fat meadow lands, the rich fields of wheat, of rye, of buckwheat, and Indian corn, and the orchards burdened with ruddy fruit, which surrounded the warm tenement of Van Tassel, his heart yearned after the damsel who was to inherit these domains, and his imagination expanded with the idea, how they might be readily turned into cash, and the money invested in immense tracts of wild land, and shingle palaces in the wilderness. Nay, his busy fancy already realized his hopes, and presented to him the blooming Katrina, with a whole family of children, mounted on the top of a wagon loaded with household trumpery, with pots and kettles dangling beneath; and he beheld himself bestriding a pacing mare, with a colt at her heels, setting out for Kentucky, Tennessee, or the Lord knows where!

When he entered the house, the conquest of his heart was complete. It was one of those spacious farmhouses, with high ridged but lowly sloping roofs, built in the style handed down from the first Dutch settlers; the low projecting eaves forming a piazza along the front, capable of being closed up in bad weather. Under this were hung flails, harness, various utensils of husbandry, and nets for fishing in the neighboring river. Benches were built along the sides for summer use; and a great spinning wheel at one end, and a churn at the other, showed the various uses to which this important porch might be devoted. From this piazza the wondering Ichabod entered the hall, which formed the center of the mansion, and the place of usual residence. Here rows of resplendent pewter, ranged on a long dresser, dazzled his eyes. In one corner stood a huge bag of wool, ready to be spun; in another, a quantity of linsey-woolsey just from the loom; ears of Indian corn, and strings of dried apples and peaches, hung in gay festoons along the walls, mingled with the gaud of red pep-

© Arttoday.com

pers; and a door left ajar gave him a peep into the best parlor, where the claw-footed chairs and dark mahogany tables shone like mirrors; andirons, with their accompanying shovel and tongs, glistened from their covert of asparagus tops; mock-oranges and conch-shells decorated the mantelpiece; strings of various colored birds eggs were suspended above it; a great ostrich egg was hung from the center of the room, and a corner cupboard, knowingly left open, displayed immense treasures of old silver and well-mended china.

From the moment Ichabod laid his eyes upon these regions of delight, the peace of his mind was at an end, and his only study was how to gain the affections of the peerless daughter of Van Tassel. In this enterprise, however, he had more real difficulties than generally fell to the lot of a knight-errant of yore, who seldom had anything but giants, enchanters, fiery dragons, and such like easily conquered adversaries, to contend with and had to make his way merely through gates of iron and brass, and walls of adamant to the castle keep, where the lady of his heart was confined; all which he achieved as easily as a man would carve his way to the center of a Christmas pie; and then the lady gave him her hand as a matter of course. Ichabod, on the contrary, had to win his way to the heart of a country coquette, beset with a labyrinth of whims and caprices, which were forever presenting new difficulties and impediments; and he had to encounter a host of fearful adversaries of real flesh and blood, the numerous rustic admirers, who beset every portal to her heart, keeping a watchful and angry eye upon each other, but ready to fly out in the common cause against any new competitor.

Among these, the most formidable was a burly, roaring, roistering blade, of the name of Abraham, or, according to the Dutch abbreviation, Brom Van Brunt, the hero of the country round which rang with his feats of strength and hardihood. He was broad-shouldered and double-jointed, with short curly black hair, and a bluff but not unpleasant countenance, having a mingled air of fun and arrogance. From his Herculean frame and great powers of limb he had received the nickname of Brom Bones, by which he was universally known. He was famed for great knowledge and skill in horsemanship, being as dexterous on horseback as a Tartar. He was foremost at all races and cock fights; and, with the ascendancy which bodily strength always acquires in rustic life, was the umpire in all disputes, setting his hat on one side, and giving his decisions with an air and tone that admitted of no gainsay or appeal. He was always ready for either a fight or a frolic; but had more mischief than ill-will in his composition; and with all his overbearing roughness, there was a strong dash of waggish good humor at bottom. He had three or four boon companions, who regarded him as their model, and at the head of whom he scoured the country, attending every scene of feud or merriment for miles round. In cold weather he was distinguished by a fur cap, surmounted with a flaunting fox's tail; and when the folks at a country gathering descried this well-known crest at a distance, whisking about among a squad of hard riders, they always stood by for a squall. Sometimes his crew would be heard dashing along past the farmhouses at midnight, with whoop and halloo, like a troop of Don Cossacks; and the old dames, startled out of their sleep, would listen for a moment till the hurry-scurry had clattered by, and then exclaim, "Ay, there goes Brom Bones and his gang!" The neighbors looked upon him with a mixture of awe, admiration, and goodwill; and, when any madcap prank or rustic brawl occurred in the vicinity, always shook their heads, and warranted Brom Bones was at the bottom of it.

This rantipole hero had for some time singled out the blooming Katrina for the object of his uncouth gallantries, and though his amorous toyings were something like the gentle caresses and endearments of a bear, yet it was whispered that she did not altogether discourage his hopes. Certain it is, his advances were signals for rival candidates to retire, who felt no inclination to cross a lion in his amours; insomuch, that when his horse was seen tied to Van Tassel's paling, on a Sunday night, a sure sign that his master was courting, or, as it is termed, "sparking," within, all other suitors passed by in despair, and carried the war into other quarters.

Such was the formidable rival with whom Ichabod Crane had to contend, and, considering, all things, a stouter man than he would have shrunk from the competition, and a wiser man would have despaired. He had, however, a happy mixture of pliability and perseverance in his nature; he was in form and spirit like a supple-jack yielding, but tough; though he bent, he never broke; and though he bowed beneath the slightest pressure, yet, the moment it was away—jerk!—he was as erect, and carried his head as high as ever.

To have taken the field openly against his rival would have been madness; for he was not a man to be thwarted in his amours, any more than that stormy lover, Achilles. Ichabod, therefore, made his advances in a quiet and gently insinuating manner. Under cover of his character of singing-master, he made frequent visits at the farmhouse; not that he had anything to apprehend from the meddlesome interference of parents, which is so often a stumbling-block in the path of lovers. Balt Van Tassel was an easy indulgent soul; he loved his daughter better even than his pipe, and, like a reasonable man and an excellent father, let her have her way in everything. His notable little wife, too, had enough to do to attend to her housekeeping and manage her poultry; for, as she sagely observed, ducks and geese are foolish things, and must be looked after, but girls can take care of themselves. Thus, while the busy dame bustled about the house, or plied her spinning-wheel at one end of the piazza, honest Balt would sit smoking his evening pipe at the other, watching the achievements of a little wooden warrior, who, armed with a sword in each hand, was most valiantly fighting the wind on the pinnacle of the barn. In the mean time, Ichabod would carry on his suit with the daughter by the side of the spring under the great elm, or sauntering along in the twilight, that hour so favorable to the lover's eloquence.

I profess not to know how women's hearts are wooed and won. To me they have always been matters of riddle and admiration. Some seem to have but one vulnerable point, or door of access; while others have a thousand avenues, and may be captured in a thousand different ways. It is a great triumph of skill to gain the former, but a still greater proof of generalship to maintain possession of the latter, for man must battle for his fortress at every door and window. He who wins a thousand common hearts is therefore entitled to some renown; but he who keeps undisputed sway over the heart of a coquette is indeed a hero. Certain it is, this was not the case with the redoubtable Brom Bones; and from the moment Ichabod Crane made his advances, the interests of the former evidently declined: his horse was no longer seen tied to the palings on Sunday nights, and a deadly feud gradually arose between him and the preceptor of Sleepy Hollow.

Brom, who had a degree of rough chivalry in his nature, would fain have carried matters to open warfare and have settled their pretensions to the lady, according to the mode of those most concise and simple reasoners, the knights—errant of yore—by single combat; but Ichabod was too conscious of the superior might of his adversary to enter the lists against him; he had overheard a boast of Bones, that he would "double the schoolmaster up, and lay him on a shelf of his own schoolhouse;" and he was too wary to give him an opportunity. There was something extremely provoking, in this obstinately pacific system; it left Brom no alternative but to draw upon the funds of rustic waggery in his disposition, and to play off boorish practical jokes upon his rival. Ichabod became the object of whimsical persecution to Bones and his gang of rough riders. They harried his hitherto peaceful domains, smoked out his singing-school by stopping up the chimney, broke into the schoolhouse at night, in spite of its formidable fastenings of withe and window stakes, and turned everything topsy-turvy, so that the poor schoolmaster began to think all the witches in the country held their meetings there. But what was still more annoying, Brom took all Opportunities of turning him into ridicule in presence of his mistress, and had a scoundrel dog whom he taught to whine in the most ludicrous manner, and introduced as a rival of Ichabod's, to instruct her in psalmody.

In this way matters went on for some time, without producing any material effect on the relative situations of the contending powers. On a fine autumnal afternoon, Ichabod, in pensive mood, sat enthroned on the lofty stool from whence he usually watched all the concerns of his little literary realm. In his hand he swayed a ferule, that scepter of despotic power; the birch of justice reposed on three nails behind the throne, a constant terror to evil doers, while on the desk before him might be seen sundry contraband articles and prohibited weapons, detected upon the persons of idle urchins, such as half-munched apples, popguns, whirligigs, flycages, and whole legions of rampant little paper gamecocks. Apparently there had been some appalling act of justice recently inflicted, for his scholars were all busily intent upon their books, or slyly whispering behind them with one eye kept upon the master; and a kind of buzzing stillness reigned throughout the schoolroom. It was suddenly interrupted by the appearance of a Negro in tow-cloth jacket and trousers, a round-crowned fragment of a hat, like the cap of Mercury, and mounted on the back of a ragged, wild, half-broken colt, which he managed with a rope by way of halter. He came clattering up to the school door with an invitation to Ichabod to attend a merry-making or "quilting-frolic," to be held that evening at Mynheer Van Tassel's; and having, delivered his message with that air of importance and effort at fine language which a Negro is apt to display on petty embassies of the kind, he dashed over the brook, and was seen scampering away up the Hollow, full of the importance and hurry of his mission.

All was now bustle and hubbub in the late quiet schoolroom. The scholars were hurried through their lessons without stopping at trifles; those who were nimble skipped over half with impunity, and those who were tardy had a smart application now and then in the rear, to quicken their speed or help them over a tall word. Books were flung aside without being put away on the shelves, inkstands were overturned, benches thrown down, and the whole school was turned loose an hour before the usual time, bursting forth like a legion of young imps, yelping and racketing about the green in joy at their early emancipation.

The gallant Ichabod now spent at least an extra half hour at his toilet, brushing and furbishing up his best, and indeed only suit of rusty black, and arranging his locks by a bit of broken looking-glass that hung up in the schoolhouse. That he might make his appearance before his mistress in the true style of a cavalier, he borrowed a horse from the farmer with whom he was domiciliated, a choleric old Dutchman of the name of Hans Van Ripper, and, thus gallantly mounted, issued forth like a knight-errant in quest of adventures. But it is meet I should, in the true spirit of romantic story, give some account of the looks and equipments of my hero and his steed. The animal he bestrode was a broken-down plow-horse, that had outlived almost everything but its viciousness. He was gaunt and shagged, with a ewe neck, and a head like a hammer; his rusty mane and tail were tangled and knotted with burs; one eye had lost its pupil, and was glaring and spectral, but the other had the gleam of a genuine devil in it. Still he must have had fire and mettle in his day, if we may judge from the name he bore of Gunpowder. He had, in fact, been a favorite steed of his master's, the choleric Van Ripper, who was a furious rider, and had infused, very probably, some of his own spirit into the animal; for, old and broken-down as he looked, there was more of the lurking devil in him than in any young filly in the country.

Ichabod was a suitable figure for such a steed. He rode with short stirrups, which brought his knees nearly up to the pommel of the saddle; his sharp elbows stuck out like grasshoppers'; he carried his whip perpendicularly in his hand, like a scepter, and as his horse jogged on, the motion of his arms was not unlike the flapping of a pair of wings. A small wool hat rested on the top of his nose, for so his scanty strip of forehead might be called, and the skirts of his black coat fluttered out almost to the horse's tail. Such was the appearance of Ichabod and his steed as they shambled out of the gate of Hans Van Ripper, and it was altogether such an apparition as is seldom to be met with in broad daylight.

It was, as I have said, a fine autumnal day; the sky was clear and serene, and nature wore that rich and golden livery which we always associate with the idea of abundance. The forests had put on their sober brown and yellow, while some trees of the tenderer kind had been nipped by the frosts into brilliant dyes of orange, purple, and scarlet. Streaming files of wild ducks began to make their appearance high in the air; the bark of the squirrel might be heard from the groves of beech and hickory-nuts, and the pensive whistle of the quail at intervals from the neighboring stubble field.

The small birds were taking their farewell banquets. In the fullness of their revelry, they fluttered, chirping and frolicking from bush to bush, and tree to tree, capricious from the very profusion and variety around them. There was the honest cockrobin, the favorite game of stripling sportsmen, with its loud querulous note; and the twittering blackbirds flying in sable clouds, and the golden-winged woodpecker with his crimson crest, his broad black gorget, and splendid plumage; and the cedar-bird, with its red tipped wings and yellow-tipped tail and its little monteiro cap of feathers; and the blue jay, that noisy coxcomb, in his gay light blue coat and white underclothes, screaming and chattering, nodding and bobbing and bowing, and pretending to be on good terms with every songster of the grove.

As Ichabod jogged slowly on his way, his eye, ever open to every symptom of culinary abundance, ranged with delight over the treasures of jolly autumn. On all sides he beheld vast store of apples: some hanging in oppressive opulence on the trees; some gathered into baskets and barrels for the market; others heaped up in rich piles for the cider-press. Farther on he beheld great fields of Indian corn, with its golden ears peeping from their leafy coverts, and holding out the promise of cakes and hasty-pudding; and the yellow pumpkins lying beneath them, turning up their fair round bellies to the sun, and giving ample prospects of the most luxurious of pies; and anon he passed the fragrant buckwheat fields breathing the odor of the beehive, and as he beheld them, soft anticipations stole over his mind of dainty slap-jacks, well buttered, and garnished with honey or treacle, by the delicate little dimpled hand of Katrina Van Tassel.

Thus feeding his mind with many sweet thoughts and "sugared suppositions," he journeyed along the sides of a range of hills which look out upon some of the goodliest scenes of the mighty Hudson. The sun gradually wheeled his broad disk down in the west. The wide bosom of the Tappan Zee lay motionless and glassy, excepting that here and there a gentle undulation waved and prolonged the blue shallow of the distant mountain. A few amber clouds floated in the sky, without a breath of air to move them. The horizon was of a fine golden tint, changing gradually into a pure apple green, and from that into the deep blue of the mid-heaven. A slanting ray lingered on the woody crests of the precipices that overhung some parts of the river, giving greater depth to the dark gray and purple of their rocky sides. A sloop was loitering in the distance, dropping slowly down with the tide, her sail hanging uselessly against the mast; and as the reflection of the sky gleamed along the still water, it seemed as if the vessel was suspended in the air.

It was toward evening that Ichabod arrived at the castle of the Heer Van Tassel, which he found thronged with the pride and flower of the adjacent country Old farmers, a spare leathern-faced race, in homespun coats and breeches, blue stockings, huge shoes, and magnificent pewter buckles. Their brisk, withered little dames, in close crimped caps, long waisted short-gowns, homespun petticoats, with scissors and pin-cushions, and gay calico pockets hanging on the outside. Buxom lasses, almost as antiquated as their mothers, excepting where a straw hat, a fine ribbon, or perhaps a white frock, gave symptoms of city innovation. The sons, in short square-skirted coats, with rows of stupendous brass buttons, and their hair generally queued in the fashion of the times, especially if they could procure an eel skin for the purpose, it being esteemed throughout the country as a potent nourisher and strengthener of the hair.

Brom Bones, however, was the hero of the scene, having come to the gathering on his favorite steed Daredevil, a creature, like himself, full of mettle and mischief, and which no one but himself could manage. He was, in fact, noted for preferring vicious animals, given to all kinds of tricks which kept the rider in constant risk of his neck, for he held a tractable, well-broken horse as unworthy of a lad of spirit.

Fain would I pause to dwell upon the world of charms that burst upon the enraptured gaze of my hero, as he entered the state parlor of Van Tassel's mansion. Not those of the bevy of buxom lasses, with their luxurious display of red and white; but the ample charms of a genuine Dutch country tea-table, in the sumptuous time of autumn. Such heaped up platters of cakes of various and almost indescribable kinds, known only to experienced Dutch housewives! There was the doughty doughnut, the tender olykoek, and the crisp and crumbling cruller; sweet cakes and short cakes, ginger cakes and honey cakes, and the whole family of cakes. And then there were apple pies, and peach pies, and pumpkin pies; besides slices of ham and smoked beef; and moreover delectable dishes of preserved plums, and peaches, and pears, and quinces; not to mention broiled shad and roasted chickens; together with bowls of milk and cream, all mingled higgledy-pig-glely, pretty much as I have enumerated them, with the motherly teapot sending up its clouds of vapor from the midst—Heaven bless the mark! I want breath and time to discuss this banquet as it deserves, and am too eager to get on with my story. Happily, Ichabod Crane was not in so great a hurry as his historian, but did ample justice to every dainty.

He was a kind and thankful creature, whose heart dilated in proportion as his skin was filled with good cheer, and whose spirits rose with eating, as some men's do with drink. He could not help, too, rolling his large eyes round him as he ate, and chuckling with the possi-bility that he might one day be lord of all this scene of almost unimaginable luxury and splendor. Then, he thought, how soon he'd turn his back upon the old schoolhouse; snap his fingers in the face of Hans Van Ripper, and every other niggardly patron, and kick any itinerant pedagogue out of doors that should dare to call him comrade!

Old Baltus Van Tassel moved about among his guests with a face dilated with content and good humor, round and jolly as the harvest moon. His hospitable attentions were brief, but expressive, being confined to a shake of the hand, a slap on the shoulder, a loud laugh, and a pressing invitation to "fall to, and help themselves."

And now the sound of the music from the common room, or hall, summoned to the dance. The musician was an old gray-headed Negro, who had been the itin-erant orchestra of the neighborhood for more than half a century. His instrument was as old and battered as himself. The greater part of the time he scraped on two or three strings, accompanying every movement of the bow with a motion of the head; bowing almost to the ground, and stamping with his foot whenever a fresh couple were to start.

Ichabod prided himself upon his dancing as much as upon his vocal powers. Not a limb, not a fibre about him was idle; and to have seen his loosely hung frame in full motion, and clattering about the room, you would have thought St. Vitus himself, that blessed patron of the dance, was figuring before you in person. He was the admiration of all the Negroes; who, having gath-ered, of all ages and sizes, from the farm and the neigh-borhood, stood forming a pyramid of shining black faces at every door and window; gazing with delight at the scene; rolling their white eye-balls, and showing grinning rows of ivory from ear to ear. How could the flogger of urchins be otherwise than animated and joy-

ous? The lady of his heart was his partner in the dance, and smiling graciously in reply to all his amorous oglings; while Brom Bones, sorely smitten with love and jealousy, sat brooding by himself in one corner.

When the dance was at an end, Ichabod was attracted to a knot of the sager folks, who, with Old Van Tassel, sat smoking at one end of the piazza, gos-siping over former times, and drawing out long stories about the war.

This neighborhood, at the time of which I am speaking, was one of those highly favored places which abound with chronicle and great men. The British and American line had run near it during the war; it had, therefore, been the scene of marauding and infested with refugees, cow-boys, and all kinds of border chivalry. Just sufficient time had elapsed to enable each story-teller to dress up his tale with a little becoming fiction, and, in the indistinctness of his recollection, to make himself the hero of every exploit.

There was the story of Doffue Martling, a large blue-bearded Dutchman, who had nearly taken a British frigate with an old iron nine-pounder from a mud breastwork, only that his gun burst at the sixth discharge. And there was an old gentleman who shall be nameless, being too rich a mynheer to be lightly mentioned, who, in the battle of White Plains, being an excellent master of defense, parried a musket-ball with a small-sword, insomuch that he absolutely felt it whiz round the blade, and glance off at the hilt; in proof of which he was ready at any time to show the sword, with the hilt a little bent. There were several more that had been equally great in the field, not one of whom but was persuaded that he had a considerable hand in bringing the war to a happy termination.

But all these were nothing to the tales of ghosts and apparitions that succeeded. The neighborhood is rich in legendary treasures of the kind. Local tales and super-stitions thrive best in these sheltered, long settled retreats; but are trampled under foot by the shifting throng that forms the population of most of our country places. Besides, there is no encouragement for ghosts in most of our villages, for they have scarcely had time to finish their first nap and turn themselves in their graves, before their surviving friends have traveled away from the neighborhood; so that when they turn out at night to walk their rounds, they have no acquain-tance left to call upon. This is perhaps the reason why we so seldom hear of ghosts except in our long-estab-lished Dutch communities.

The immediate cause, however, of the prevalence of supernatural stories in these parts, was doubtless owing to the vicinity of Sleepy Hollow. There was a contagion in the very air that blew from that haunted region; it breathed forth an atmosphere of dreams and fancies infecting all the land. Several of the Sleepy Hollow people were present at Van Tassel's, and, as usual, were doling out their wild and wonderful legends. Many dismal tales were told about funeral trains, and mourning cries and wailings heard and seen about the great tree where the unfortunate Major Andre was taken, and which stood in the neighborhood. Some mention was made also of the woman in white, that haunted the dark glen at Raven Rock, and was often heard to shriek on winter nights before a storm, having perished there in the snow. The chief part of the stories, however, turned upon the favorite spectre of Sleepy Hollow, the Headless Horseman, who had been heard several times of late, patrolling the country; and, it was said, tethered his horse nightly among the graves in the churchyard.

The sequestered situation of this church seems always to have made it a favorite haunt of troubled spirits. It stands on a knoll, surrounded by locust, trees and lofty elms, from among which its decent, whitewashed walls shine modestly forth, like Christian purity beaming through the shades of retirement. A gentle slope descends from it to a silver sheet of water, bordered by high trees, between which, peeps may be caught at the blue hills of the Hudson. To look upon its grass-grown yard, where the sunbeams seem to sleep so quietly, one would think that there at least the dead might rest in peace. On one side of the church extends a wide woody dell, along which raves a large brook among broken rocks and trunks of fallen trees. Over a deep black part of the stream, not far from the church, was formerly thrown a wooden bridge; the road that led to it, and the bridge itself, were thickly shaded by overhanging trees, which cast a gloom about it, even in the daytime; but occasioned a fearful darkness at night. Such was one of the favorite haunts of the Headless Horseman, and the place where he was most frequently encountered. The tale was told of old Brouwer, a most heretical disbeliever in ghosts, how he met the Horseman returning from his foray into Sleepy Hollow, and was obliged to get up behind him; how they galloped over bush and brake, over hill and swamp, until they reached the bridge; when the Horseman suddenly turned into a skeleton, threw old Brouwer into the brook, and sprang away over the tree-tops with a clap of thunder.

This story was immediately matched by a thrice marvelous adventure of Brom Bones, who made light of the Galloping Hessian as an arrant jockey. He affirmed that on returning one night from the neighboring village of Sing Sing, he had been overtaken by this midnight trooper; that he had offered to race with him for a bowl of punch, and should have won it too, for Daredevil beat the goblin horse all hollow, but just as they came to the church bridge, the Hessian bolted, and vanished in a flash of fire.

All these tales, told in that drowsy undertone with which men talk in the dark, the countenances of the listeners only now and then receiving a casual gleam from the glare of a pipe, sank deep in the mind of Ichabod. He repaid them in kind with large extracts from his invaluable author, Cotton Mather, and added many marvelous events that had taken place in his native State of Connecticut, and fearful sights which he had seen in his nightly walks about Sleepy Hollow.

The revel now gradually broke up. The old farmers gathered together their families in their wagons, and were heard for some time rattling along the hollow roads, and over the distant hills. Some of the damsels mounted on pillions behind their favorite swains, and their light-hearted laughter, mingling with the clatter of hoofs, echoed along the silent woodlands, sounding fainter and fainter, until they gradually died away, — and the late scene of noise and frolic was all silent and deserted. Ichabod only lingered behind, according to the custom of country lovers, to have a tete-a-tete with the heiress; fully convinced that he was now on the high road to success. What passed at this interview I will not pretend to say, for in fact I do not know. Something, however, I fear me, must have gone wrong, for he certainly sallied forth, after no very great interval, with an air quite desolate and chapfallen. Oh, these women! these women! Could that girl have been playing off any of her coquettish tricks? Was her encouragement of the poor pedagogue all a mere sham to secure her conquest of his rival? Heaven only knows, not I! Let it suffice to say, Ichabod stole forth with the air of one who had been sacking a henroost, rather than a fair lady's heart. Without looking to the right or left to notice the scene of rural wealth, on which he had so often gloated, he went straight to the stable, and with several hearty cuffs and kicks roused his steed most uncourteously from the comfortable quarters in which he was soundly sleeping, dreaming of mountains of corn and oats, and whole valleys of timothy and clover.

It was the very witching time of night that Ichabod, heavy hearted and crest-fallen, pursued his travels homewards, along the sides of the lofty hills which rise above Tarry Town, and which he had traversed so cheerily in the afternoon. The hour was as dismal as himself. Far below him the Tappan Zee spread its dusky and indistinct waste of waters, with here and there the tall mast of a sloop, riding quietly at anchor under the land. In the dead hush of midnight, he could even hear the barking of the watchdog from the opposite shore of the Hudson; but it was so vague and faint as only to give an idea of his distance from this faithful companion of man. Now and then, too, the long-drawn crowing of a cock, accidentally awakened, would sound far, far off, from some farmhouse away among the hills—but it was like a dreaming sound in his ear. No signs of life occurred near him, but occasionally the melancholy chirp of a cricket, or perhaps the guttural twang of a bull-frog from a neighboring marsh, as if sleeping uncomfortably and turning suddenly in his bed.

All the stories of ghosts and goblins that he had heard in the afternoon now came crowding upon his recollection. The night grew darker and darker; the stars seemed to sink deeper in the sky, and driving clouds occasionally hid them from his sight. He had never felt so lonely and dismal. He was, moreover, approaching the very place where many of the scenes of the ghost stories had been laid. In the center of the road stood an enormous tulip-tree, which towered like a giant above all the other trees of the neighborhood, and formed a kind of landmark. Its limbs were gnarled and fantastic, large enough to form trunks for ordinary trees, twisting down almost to the earth, and rising again into the air. It was connected with the tragical story of the unfortunate Andre, who had been taken prisoner hard by; and was universally known by the name of Major Andre's tree. The common people regarded it with a mixture of respect and superstition, partly out of sympathy for the fate of its ill-starred namesake, and partly from the tales of strange sights, and doleful lamentations, told concerning it.

As Ichabod approached this fearful tree, he began to whistle; he thought his whistle was answered; it was but a blast sweeping sharply through the dry branches. As he approached a little nearer, he thought he saw something white, hanging in the midst of the tree: he paused, and ceased whistling but, on looking more narrowly, perceived that it was a place where the tree had been scathed by lightning, and the white wood laid bare. Suddenly he heard a groan—his teeth chattered, and his knees smote against the saddle: it was but the rubbing of one huge bough upon another, as they were swayed about by the breeze. He passed the tree in safety, but new perils lay before him.

About two hundred yards from the tree, a small brook crossed the road, and ran into a marshy and thickly-wooded glen, known by the name of Wiley's Swamp. A few rough logs, laid side by side, served for a bridge over this stream. On that side of the road where the brook entered the wood, a group of oaks and chestnuts, matted thick with wild grape-vines, threw a cavernous gloom over it. To pass this bridge was the severest trial. It was at this identical spot that the unfortunate Andre was captured, and under the covert of those chestnuts and vines were the sturdy yeomen concealed who surprised him. This has ever since been considered a haunted stream, and fearful are the feelings of the school-boy who has to pass it alone after dark.

As he approached the stream, his heart began to thump; he summoned up, however, all his resolution, gave his horse half a score of kicks in the ribs, and attempted to dash briskly across the bridge; but instead of starting forward, the perverse old animal made a lateral movement, and ran broadside against the fence. Ichabod, whose fears increased with the delay, jerked the reins on the other side, and kicked lustily with the contrary foot: it was all in vain; his steed started, it is true, but it was only to plunge to the opposite side of the road into a thicket of brambles and alder-bushes. The schoolmaster now bestowed both whip and heel upon the starveling ribs of old Gunpowder, who dashed forward, snuffling and snorting, but came to a stand just by the bridge, with a suddenness that had nearly sent his rider sprawling over his head. Just at this moment a plashy tramp by the side of the bridge caught the sensitive ear of Ichabod. In the dark shadow of the grove, on the margin of the brook, he beheld something huge, misshapen and towering. It stirred not, but seemed gathered up in the gloom, like some gigantic monster ready to spring upon the traveller.

The hair of the affrighted pedagogue rose upon his

© Arttoday.com

head with terror. What was to be done? To turn and fly was now too late; and besides, what chance was there of escaping ghost or goblin, if such it was, which could ride upon the wings of the wind? Summoning up, therefore, a show of courage, he demanded in stammering accents, "Who are you?" He received no reply. He repeated his demand in a still more agitated voice. Still there was no answer. Once more he cudgelled the sides of the inflexible Gunpowder, and, shutting his eyes, broke forth with involuntary fervor into a psalm tune. Just then the shadowy object of alarm put itself in motion, and with a scramble and a bound stood at once in the middle of the road. Though the night was dark and dismal, yet the form of the unknown might now in some degree be ascertained. He appeared to be a horseman of large dimensions, and mounted on a black horse of powerful frame. He made no offer of molestation or sociability, but kept aloof on one side of the road, jogging along on the blind side of old Gunpowder, who had now got over his fright and waywardness.

Ichabod, who had no relish for this strange midnight companion, and bethought himself of the adventure of Brom Bones with the Galloping Hessian, now quickened his steed in hopes of leaving him behind. The stranger, however, quickened his horse to an equal pace. Ichabod pulled up, and fell into a walk, thinking to lag behind—the other did the same. His heart began to sink within him; he endeavored to resume his psalm tune, but his parched tongue clove to the roof of his mouth, and he could not utter a stave. There was something in the moody and dogged silence of this pertinacious companion that was mysterious and appalling. It was soon fearfully accounted for. On mounting a rising ground, which brought the figure of his fellow-traveler in relief against the sky, gigantic in height, and muffled in a cloak, Ichabod was horror-struck on perceiving that he was headless! but his horror was still more increased on observing that the head, which should have rested on his shoulders, was carried before him on the pommel of his saddle! His terror rose to desperation; he rained a shower of kicks and blows upon Gunpowder, hoping by a sudden movement to give his companion the slip; but the specter started full jump with him. Away, then, they dashed through thick and thin; stones flying and sparks flashing at every bound. Ichabod's flimsy garments fluttered in the air, as he stretched his long lank body away over his horse's head, in the eagerness of his flight.

They had now reached the road which turns off to Sleepy Hollow; but Gunpowder, who seemed possessed with a demon, instead of keeping up it, made an opposite turn, and plunged headlong down hill to the left. This road leads through a sandy hollow shaded by trees for about a quarter of a mile, where it crosses the bridge famous in goblin story; and just beyond swells the green knoll on which stands the whitewashed church.

As yet the panic of the steed had given his unskillful rider an apparent advantage in the chase, but just as he had got half way through the hollow, the girths of the saddle gave way, and he felt it slipping from under him. He seized it by the pommel, and endeavored to hold it firm, but in vain; and had just time to save himself by clasping old Gunpowder round the neck, when the saddle fell to the earth, and he heard it trampled under foot by his pursuer. For a moment the terror of Hans Van Ripper's wrath passed across his mind—for it was his Sunday saddle; but this was no time for petty fears; the goblin was hard on his haunches; and (unskillful rider that he was!) he had much ado to maintain his seat; sometimes slipping on one side, sometimes on another, and sometimes jolted on the high ridge of his horse's backbone, with a violence that he verily feared would cleave him asunder.

An opening, in the trees now cheered him with the hopes that the church bridge was at hand. The wavering reflection of a silver star in the bosom of the brook told him that he was not mistaken. He saw the walls of the church dimly glaring under the trees beyond. He recollected the place where Brom Bones' ghostly competitor had disappeared. "If I can but reach that bridge," thought Ichabod, "I am safe." Just then he heard the black steed panting and blowing close behind him; he even fancied that he felt his hot breath. Another convulsive kick in the ribs, and old Gunpowder sprang upon the bridge; he thundered over the resounding planks; he gained the opposite side; and now Ichabod cast a look behind to see if his pursuer should vanish, according to rule, in a flash of fire and brimstone. Just then he saw the goblin rising in his stirrups, and in the very act of hurling his head at him. Ichabod endeavored to dodge the horrible missile, but too late. It encountered his cranium with a tremendous crash—he was tumbled headlong into the dust, and Gunpowder, the black steed, and the goblin rider, passed by like a whirlwind.

The next morning the old horse was found without his saddle, and with the bridle under his feet, soberly cropping the grass at his master's gate. Ichabod did not make his appearance at breakfast; dinner-hour came, but no Ichabod. The boys assembled at the schoolhouse, and strolled idly about the banks of the brook; but no schoolmaster. Hans Van Ripper now began to

During the 18ᵗʰ century, literature and the arts—in other words, popular culture—began to move away from the personalized, travelogue advertisements of their adventures written by John Smith and others. American culture began to develop into a style and worldview all its own. There was, as you have seen, a culture war—even then! The war was between the secularism of a John Smith and the piety of a William Bradford. Although there is no evidence that these two contemporaries met, they were nonetheless involved in a culture war. Ultimately the worldview of John Smith won. Puritanism and its Christian Theism gave way in the 18ᵗʰ century to the subtle Deism of Thomas Paine. In the Christian Theistic world of the Puritan, God was intimately involved in the affairs of man. In a Deistic world, God, the watchmaker, supposedly created a perfect world and then retreated allowing people to work out their own fate: humanity was in charge. Or so it thought . . .

feel some uneasiness about the fate of poor Ichabod, and his saddle. An inquiry was set on foot, and after diligent investigation they came upon his traces. In one part of the road leading to the church was found the saddle trampled in the dirt; the tracks of horses' hoofs deeply dented in the road, and evidently at furious speed, were traced to the bridge, beyond which, on the bank of a broad part of the brook, where the water ran deep and black, was found the hat of the unfortunate Ichabod, and close beside it a shattered pumpkin.

The brook was searched, but the body of the schoolmaster was not to be discovered. Hans Van Ripper as executor of his estate, examined the bundle which contained all his worldly effects. They consisted of two shirts and a half; two stocks for the neck; a pair or two of worsted stockings; an old pair of corduroy small-clothes; a rusty razor; a book of psalm tunes full of dog's-ears; and a broken pitch-pipe. As to the books and furniture of the schoolhouse, they belonged to the community, excepting Cotton Mather's <u>History of Witchcraft</u>, a <u>New England Almanac</u>, and book of dreams and fortune-telling; in which last was a sheet of foolscap much scribbled and blotted in several fruitless attempts to make a copy of verses in honor of the heiress of Van Tassel. These magic books and the poetic scrawl were forthwith consigned to the flames by Hans Van Ripper; who, from that time forward, determined to send his children no more to school; observing that he never knew any good come of this same reading and writing. Whatever money the schoolmaster possessed, and he had received his quarter's pay but a day or two before, he must have had about his person at the time of his disappearance.

The mysterious event caused much speculation at the church on the following Sunday. Knots of gazers and gossips were collected in the churchyard, at the bridge, and at the spot where the hat and pumpkin had been found. The stories of Brouwer, of Bones, and a

whole budget of others were called to mind; and when they had diligently considered them all, and compared them with the symptoms of the present case, they shook their heads, and came to the conclusion chat Ichabod had been carried off by the Galloping Hessian. As he was a bachelor, and in nobody's debt, nobody troubled his head any more about him; the school was removed to a different quarter of the Hollow, and another pedagogue reigned in his stead.

It is true, an old farmer, who had been down to New York on a visit several years after, and from whom this account of the ghostly adventure was received, brought home the intelligence that Ichabod Crane was still alive; that he had left the neighborhood partly through fear of the goblin and Hans Van Ripper, and partly in mortification at having been suddenly dismissed by the heiress; that he had changed his quarters to a distant part of the country; had kept school and studied law at the same time; had been admitted to the bar; turned politician; electioneered; written for the newspapers; and finally had been made a justice of the ten pound court. Brom Bones, too, who, shortly after

his rival's disappearance conducted the blooming Katrina in triumph to the altar, was observed to look exceedingly knowing whenever the story of Ichabod was related, and always burst into a hearty laugh at the mention of the pumpkin; which led some to suspect that he knew more about the matter than he chose to tell.

The old country wives, however, who are the best judges of these matters, maintain to this day that Ichabod was spirited away by supernatural means; and it is a favorite story often told about the neighborhood round the winter evening fire. The bridge became more than ever an object of superstitious awe; and that may be the reason why the road has been altered of late years, so as to approach the church by the border of the mill pond. The schoolhouse being deserted soon fell to decay, and was reported to be haunted by the ghost of the unfortunate pedagogue and the plough-boy, loitering homeward of a still summer evening, has often fancied his voice at a distance, chanting a melancholy psalm tune among the tranquil solitudes of Sleepy Hollow.

http://www.angeltowns.com/members/shortstories/index.html

FINAL PROJECT

Correct and rewrite all essays and place them in your Final Portfolio.

SUGGESTED
Weekly *Implementation*

DAY 1	DAY 2	DAY 3	DAY 4	DAY 5
Prayer journal. Students review the required reading(s) before the assigned lesson begins. Teacher may want to discuss assigned reading(s) with students. Teacher and students will decide on the number of required essays for this lesson, choosing two or three essays. The rest of the essays can be outlined, answered with shorter answers, or skipped. Students will review all readings for Lesson 6.	**Prayer journal.** Students should review reading(s) from next lesson. Students should outline essays due at the end of the week. Per teacher instructions, students may answer orally in a group setting some of the essays that are not assigned as formal essays.	**Prayer journal.** Students should write rough drafts of all assigned essays. The teacher and/or a peer evaluator may correct rough drafts.	**Prayer journal.** Student will re-write corrected copies of essays due tomorrow.	**Prayer journal.** Essays are due. Students should take the Lesson 6 test. Reading Ahead: Students should review the poem "The Raven," and the short stories "Fall of the House of Usher" and "The Tell Tale Heart" both by Edgar Allan Poe. Guide: What makes Poe's short stories so perfect?

Edgar Allan Poe

Edgar Allan Poe

© Arttoday.com

Edgar Allan Poe, the greatest American short story writer, invented the modern detective story. His poetry, too, was extraordinary. In fact, Poe was perhaps the first and greatest poet America produced. In Poe's poems, as in his tales, his characters were tortured by nameless fears and longings. Today Poe is acclaimed as one of America's greatest writers, but in his own unhappy lifetime he knew little but failure. Struggling with ill-health, and later drug and alcoholic addiction, Poe was a broken man. The untimely death of his young wife was the last blow. It broke his heart and perhaps drove him mad.

BACKGROUND

Edgar Allan Poe was a romantic eccentric. He was a disturbed man, but his short stories were some of the best ever written. Poe wrote four types of short stories:

A. Strange: use of the supernatural; symbolic fantasies of the human condition; (e.g., "The Fall of the House of Usher" and "Tell Tale Heart").

B. Exaggerated: heightening of one aspect of a character (e.g., "The Man Who Was Used Up").

C. Detective fiction: (e.g., "The Purloined Letter").

D. Descriptive: (e.g., "The Landscape Garden")

You will analyze: the poem "The Raven" and the short stories "Fall of the House of Usher" and "The Tell Tale Heart," both by Edgar Allan Poe.

Read Ahead: *The Scarlet Letter* and "The Birthmark," Nathaniel Hawthorne.

Guide Question: What romantic themes emerge in Hawthorne's novel *The Scarlet Letter* and the short story "The Birthmark?"

CRITICAL THINKING

As you read the following poem and short stories, prepare to answer these questions in essay form:

A. Part of Poe's genius is his ability to create mood by the use of connotative language (language that suggests more than the words explicitly express). Write an essay describing how this literary technique is employed by Poe in "The Raven" and in "The Fall of the House of Usher."

B. Write a characterization of Roderick Usher.

C. Though what structure does Poe identifies the Usher family? Why? How does he do this? Use copious evidence from the text.

D. How does first-person narration enhance Poe's purposes to scare his readers? Who is the narrator? Is he reliable? Why or why not?

E. Find the narrator's description of Roderick's picture. Define foreshadowing and show how this scene foreshadows future events.

ENRICHMENT

Read the "Tell Tale Heart" by Edgar Allan Poe and compare it to "The Fall of the House of Usher."

Characterization is a technique that a writer employs to reveal his character to his audience. How do we meet the main character? Do we see into his mind? What do others think of him?

BIBLICAL APPLICATION

A. The problem of evil for Christians is a real one. Explore the biblical understanding of evil and create a theology.

B. One problem with the romantic worldview is the weak image of God. This presages the later naturalistic view that rejects an omnipotent God altogether. God, to the romantic, is unable to overcome the power of nature and the human will. There is a moral vision, but it is mitigated by sentimental notions about nature. Using the Bible as your main resource, critique this worldview.

C. Christian teacher Thomas Merton, in an essay entitled "A Devout Meditation in Memory of Adolf Eichmann" (a Nazi leader who implemented the Holocaust) challenges modern man to rethink sanity. "One of the most disturbing facts," Merton begins, "that came out in the Eichmann trial was that a psychiatrist examined him and pronounced him perfectly sane." The fact is, given our world, we can no longer assume that because a person is "sane" or "adjusted" he/she is OK. Merton reminds us that such people can be well adjusted even in hell itself! Merton says, "The whole concept of sanity in a society where spiritual values have lost their meaning is itself meaningless." In light of biblical discussions of human depravity—especially as they appear in the book of Romans—write an essay reflecting on the accuracy of Merton's statement.

FINAL PROJECT

Correct and rewrite all essays and place them in your Final Portfolio.

The Raven

National Park Service
http://www.nps.gov/
edal/index.htm

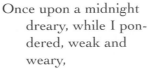

Once upon a midnight
    dreary, while I pon-
    dered, weak and
    weary,
Over many a quaint and
    curious volume of forgotten lore,
While I nodded, nearly napping, suddenly there came
    a tapping,
As of some one gently rapping, rapping at my cham-
    ber door.
"'Tis some visitor," I muttered, "tapping at my cham-
    ber door—
Only this, and nothing more."
Ah, distinctly I remember it was in the bleak
    December,
And each separate dying ember wrought its ghost
    upon the floor.
Eagerly I wished the morrow; vainlyI had sought to
    borrow
From my books surcease of sorrow—sorrow for the
    lost Lenore—
For the rare and radiant maiden whom the angels
    name Lenore—
Nameless here for evermore.

And the silken sad uncertain rustling of each purple
    curtain
Thrilled me—filled me with fantastic terrors never felt
    before;
So that now, to still the beating of my heart, I stood
    repeating,
"'Tis some visitor entreating entrance at my chamber
    door—
Some late visitor entreating entrance at my chamber
    door;—
This it is, and nothing more."

Presently my soul grew stronger; hesitating then no
    longer,
"Sir," said I, "or Madam, truly your forgiveness I
    implore;
But the fact is I was napping, and so gently you came
    rapping,
And so faintly you came tapping, tapping at my cham-
    ber door,

That I scarce was sure I heard you"—here I opened
   wide the door;—
Darkness there, and nothing more.

Deep into that darkness peering, long I stood there
   wondering, fearing,
Doubting, dreaming dreams no mortals ever dared to
   dream before;
But the silence was unbroken, and the stillness gave
   no token,
And the only word there spoken was the whispered
   word, "Lenore!"
This I whispered, and an echo murmured back the
   word, "Lenore!"—
Merely this, and nothing more.

Back into the chamber turning, all my soul within me
   burning,
Soon again I heard a tapping somewhat louder than
   before.
"Surely," said I, "surely that is something at my window lattice:
Let me see, then, what the threat is, and this mystery
   explore—
Let my heart be still a moment and this mystery
   explore;—
'Tis the wind and nothing more."

Open here I flung the shutter, when, with many a flirt
   and flutter,
In there stepped a stately raven of the saintly days of
   yore;
Not the least obeisance made he; not a minute stopped
   or stayed he;
But, with mien of lord or lady, perched above my
   chamber door—
Perched upon a bust of Pallas just above my chamber
   door—
Perched, and sat, and nothing more.

Then this ebony bird beguiling my sad fancy into
   smiling,
By the grave and stern decorum of the countenance it
   wore.
"Though thy crest be shorn and shaven, thou," I said,
   "art sure no craven,
Ghastly grim and ancient raven wandering from the
   Nightly shore—
Tell me what thy lordly name is on the Night's
   Plutonian shore!"
Quoth the Raven, "Nevermore."

Much I marvelled this ungainly fowl to hear discourse
   so plainly,
Though its answer little meaning—little relevancy
   bore;
For we cannot help agreeing that no living human
   being
Ever yet was blest with seeing bird above his chamber
   door—
Bird or beast upon the sculptured bust above his
   chamber door,
With such name as "Nevermore."

But the raven, sitting lonely on the placid bust, spoke
   only
That one word, as if his soul in that one word he did
   outpour.
Nothing further then he uttered—not a feather then
   he fluttered—
Till I scarcely more than muttered, "other friends have
   flown before—
On the morrow he will leave me, as my hopes have
   flown before."
Then the bird said, "Nevermore."

Startled at the stillness broken by reply so aptly spo-
   ken,
"Doubtless," said I, "what it utters is its only stock and
   store,
Caught from some unhappy master whom unmerciful
   Disaster
Followed fast and followed faster till his songs one
   burden bore—
Till the dirges of his Hope that melancholy burden
   bore
Of 'Never—nevermore'."

But the Raven still beguiling all my fancy into smiling,
Straight I wheeled a cushioned seat in front of bird,
   and bust and door;
Then upon the velvet sinking, I betook myself to
   linking
Fancy unto fancy, thinking what this ominous bird of
   yore—
What this grim, ungainly, ghastly, gaunt and ominous
   bird of yore
Meant in croaking "Nevermore."

This I sat engaged in guessing, but no syllable
        expressing
To the fowl whose fiery eyes now burned into my
        bosom's core;
This and more I sat divining, with my head at ease
        reclining
On the cushion's velvet lining that the lamplight
        gloated o'er,
But whose velvet violet lining with the lamplight
        gloating o'er,
She shall press, ah, nevermore!

Then methought the air grew denser, perfumed from
        an unseen censer
Swung by Seraphim whose footfalls tinkled on the
        tufted floor.
"Wretch," I cried, "thy God hath lent thee—by these
        angels he hath sent thee
Respite—respite and nepenthe, from thy memories of
        Lenore!
Quaff, oh quaff this kind nepenthe and forget this lost
        Lenore!"
Quoth the Raven, "Nevermore."

"Prophet!" said I, "thing of evil!—prophet still, if bird
        or devil!—
Whether Tempter sent, or whether tempest tossed
        thee here ashore,
Desolate yet all undaunted, on this desert land
        enchanted—
On this home by horror haunted—tell me truly, I
        implore—
Is there—is there balm in Gilead?—tell me—tell me, I
        implore!"
Quoth the Raven, "Nevermore."

"Prophet!" said I, "thing of evil—prophet still, if bird
        or devil!
By that Heaven that bends above us—by that God we
        both adore—
Tell this soul with sorrow laden if, within the distant
        Aidenn,
It shall clasp a sainted maiden whom the angels name
        Lenore—
Clasp a rare and radiant maiden whom the angels
        name Lenore."
Quoth the Raven, "Nevermore."

"Be that word our sign in parting, bird or fiend," I
        shrieked, upstarting—

"Get thee back into the tempest and the Night's
        Plutonian shore!
Leave no black plume as a token of that lie thy soul
        hath spoken!
Leave my loneliness unbroken!—quit the bust above
        my door!
Take thy beak from out my heart, and take thy form
        from off my door!"
Quoth the Raven, "Nevermore."

And the Raven, never flitting, still is sitting, still is
        sitting
On the pallid bust of Pallas just above my chamber
        door;
And his eyes have all the seeming of a demon's that is
        dreaming,
And the lamplight o'er him streaming throws his
        shadow on the floor;
And my soul from out that shadow that lies floating on
        the floor
Shall be lifted—nevermore!

"I had gone so far as the conception of a Raven—the bird of ill omen—monotonously repeating the one word, "Nevermore," at the conclusion of each stanza, in a poem of melancholy tone, and in length about one hundred lines. Now, never losing sight of the object supremeness, or perfection, at all points, I asked myself, "Of all melancholy topics, what, according to the universal understanding of mankind, is the most melancholy?" Death was the obvious reply. "And when," I said, is the most melancholy of topics most poetical?" From what I have already explained at some length, the answer, here also, is obvious, "When it most closely allies itself to beauty: the death, then, of a beautiful woman is, unquestionably, the most poetical topic in the world—and equally is it beyond doubt that the lips best suited for such a topic are those of a bereaved lover."

From Edgar Allan Poe's "The Philosophy of Composition," which was first published in *Graham's Magazine*, April, 1846.

The Fall of the House of Usher

During the whole of a dull, dark, and soundless day in the autumn of the year, when the clouds hung oppressively low in the heavens, had been passing alone, on horseback, through a singularly dreary tract of country; and at length found myself, as the shades of the evening drew on, within view of the melancholy House of Usher. I know not how it was—but, with the first glimpse of the building, a sense of insufferable gloom pervaded my spirit. I say insufferable; for the feeling was unrelieved by any of that half-pleasurable, because poetic, sentiment, with which the mind usually receives even the sternest natural images of the desolate or terrible. I looked upon the scene before me—upon the mere house, and the simple landscape features of the domain—upon the bleak walls—upon the vacant eye-like windows—upon a few rank sedges—and upon a few white trunks of decayed trees—with an utter depression of soul which I can compare to no earthly sensation more properly than to the after-dream of the reveler upon opium—the bitter lapse into everyday life—the hideous dropping off of the veil. There was an iciness, a sinking, a sickening of the heart—an unredeemed dreariness of thought which no goading of the imagination could torture into aught of the sublime. What was it—I paused to think—what was it that so unnerved me in the contemplation of the House of Usher? It was a mystery all insoluble; nor could I grapple with the shadowy fancies that crowded upon me as I pondered. I was forced to fall back upon the unsatisfactory conclusion, that while, beyond doubt, there are combinations of very simple natural objects which have the power of thus affecting us, still the analysis of this power lies among considerations beyond our depth.

It was possible, I reflected, that a mere different arrangement of the particulars of the scene, of the details of the picture, would be sufficient to modify, or perhaps to annihilate its capacity for sorrowful impression; and, acting upon this idea, I reined my horse to the precipitous brink of a black and lurid tarn that lay in unruffled luster by the dwelling, and gazed down—but with a shudder even more thrilling than before—upon the remodeled and inverted images of the gray sedge, and the ghastly tree-stems, and the vacant and eye-like windows.

Nevertheless, in this mansion of gloom I now proposed to myself a sojourn of some weeks. Its proprietor, Roderick Usher, had been one of my boon companions in boyhood; but many years had elapsed since our last meeting. A letter, however, had lately reached me in a distant part of the country—a letter from him—which, in its wildly importunate nature, had admitted of no other than a personal reply. The MS. gave evidence of nervous agitation. The writer spoke of acute bodily illness—of a mental disorder which oppressed him—and of an earnest desire to see me, as his best, and indeed his only personal friend, with a view of attempting, by the cheerfulness of my society, some alleviation of his malady. It was the manner in which all this, and much more, was said—it the apparent heart that went with his request—which allowed me no room for hesitation; and I accordingly obeyed forthwith what I still considered a very singular summons.

Although, as boys, we had been even intimate associates, yet I really knew little of my friend. His reserve had been always excessive and habitual. I was aware, however, that his very ancient family had been noted, time out of mind, for a peculiar sensibility of temperament, displaying itself, through long ages, in many

works of exalted art, and manifested, of late, in repeated deeds of munificent yet unobtrusive charity, as well as in a passionate devotion to the intricacies, perhaps even more than to the orthodox and easily recognizable beauties, of musical science. I had learned, too, the very remarkable fact, that the stem of the Usher race, all time-honored as it was, had put forth, at no period, any enduring branch; in other words, that the entire family lay in the direct line of descent, and had always, with very trifling and very temporary variation, so lain. It was this deficiency, I considered, while running over in thought the perfect keeping of the character of the premises with the accredited character of the people, and while speculating upon the possible influence which the one, in the long lapse of centuries, might have exercised upon the other—it was this deficiency, perhaps, of collateral issue, and the consequent undeviating transmission, from sire to son, of the patrimony with the name, which had, at length, so identified the two as to merge the original title of the estate in the quaint and equivocal appellation of the "House of

Usher"—an appellation which seemed to include, in the minds of the peasantry who used it, both the family and the family mansion.

I have said that the sole effect of my somewhat childish experiment—that of looking down within the tarn—had been to deepen the first singular impression. There can be no doubt that the consciousness of the rapid increase of my superstition—for why should I not so term it?—served mainly to accelerate the increase itself. Such, I have long known, is the paradoxical law of all sentiments having terror as a basis. And it might have been for this reason only, that, when I again uplifted my eyes to the house itself, from its image in the pool, there grew in my mind a strange fancy—a fancy so ridiculous, indeed, that I but mention it to show the vivid force of the sensations which oppressed me. I had so worked upon my imagination as really to believe that about the whole mansion and domain there hung an atmosphere peculiar to themselves and their immediate vicinity-an atmosphere which had no affinity with the air of heaven, but which had reeked up from the decayed trees, and the gray wall, and the silent tarn—a pestilent and mystic vapor, dull, sluggish, faintly discernible, and leaden-hued. Shaking off from my spirit what must have been a dream, I scanned more narrowly the real aspect of the building. Its principal feature seemed to be that of an excessive antiquity. The discoloration of ages had been great. Minute fungi overspread the whole exterior, hanging in a fine tangled web-work from the eaves. Yet all this was apart from any extraordinary dilapidation. No portion of the masonry had fallen; and there appeared to be a wild inconsistency between its still perfect adaptation of parts, and the crumbling condition of the individual stones. In this there was much that reminded me of the specious totality of old wood-work which has rotted for long years in some neglected vault, with no disturbance from the breath of the external air. Beyond this indication of extensive decay, however, the fabric gave little token of instability. Perhaps the eye of a scrutinizing observer might have discovered a barely perceptible fissure, which, extending from the roof of the building in front, made its way down the wall in a zigzag direction, until it became lost in the sullen waters of the tarn.

Noticing these things, I rode over a short causeway to the house. A servant in waiting took my horse, and I entered the Gothic archway of the hall. A valet, of stealthy step, thence conducted me, in silence, through many dark and intricate passages in my progress to the studio of his master. Much that I encountered on the way contributed, I know not how, to heighten the vague sentiments of which I have already spoken. While the objects around me—while the carvings of the ceilings, the somber tapestries of the walls, the ebon blackness of the floors, and the phantasmagoric armorial trophies which rattled as I strode, were but matters to which, or to such as which, I had been accustomed from my infancy—while I hesitated not to acknowledge how familiar was all this—I still wondered to find how unfamiliar were the fancies which ordinary images were stirring up. On one of the staircases, I met the physician of the family. His countenance, I thought, wore a mingled expression of low cunning and perplexity. He accosted me with trepidation and passed on. The valet now threw open a door and ushered me into the presence of his master. The room in which I found myself was very large and lofty. The windows were long, narrow, and pointed, and at so vast a distance from the black oaken floor as to be altogether inaccessible from within. Feeble gleams of encrimsoned light made their way through the trellised panes, and served to render sufficiently distinct the more prominent objects around the eye, however, struggled in vain to reach the remoter angles of the chamber, or the recesses of the vaulted and fretted ceiling. Dark draperies hung upon the walls. The general furniture was profuse, comfortless, antique, and tattered. Many books and musical instruments lay scattered about, but failed to give any vitality to the scene. I felt that I breathed an atmosphere of sorrow. An air of stern, deep, and irredeemable gloom hung over and pervaded all.

Upon my entrance, Usher arose from a sofa on which he had been lying at full length, and greeted me with a vivacious warmth which had much in it, I at first thought, of an overdone cordiality—of the constrained effort of the ennui man of the world. A glance, however, at his countenance, convinced me of his perfect sincerity. We sat down; and for some moments, while he spoke not, I gazed upon him with a feeling half of pity, half of awe. Surely, man had never before so terribly altered, in so brief a period, as had Roderick Usher! It was with difficulty that I could bring myself to admit the identity of the wan being before me with the companion of my early boyhood. Yet the character of his face had been at all times remarkable. A cadaverousness of complexion; an eye large, liquid, and luminous beyond comparison; lips somewhat thin and very pallid, but of a surpassingly beautiful curve; a nose of a delicate Hebrew model, but with a breadth of nostril unusual in similar formations; a finely molded chin, speaking, in its want of prominence, of a want of moral energy; hair of a more than web-like softness and tenuity; these features, with an inordinate expansion above the regions of the temple, made up altogether a countenance not easily to be forgotten. And now in the mere exaggeration of the prevailing character of these features, and of the expression they were wont to convey, lay so much of change that I doubted to whom I spoke. The now ghastly pallor of the skin, and the now miraculous luster of the eye, above all things startled and even awed me. The silken hair, too, had been suffered to grow all unheeded, and as, in its wild gossamer texture, it floated rather than fell about the face, I could not, even with effort, connect its Arabesque expression with any idea of simple humanity.

In the manner of my friend I was at once struck with an incoherence—an inconsistency; and I soon found this to arise from a series of feeble and futile struggles to overcome an habitual trepidancy—an excessive nervous agitation. For something of this nature I had indeed been prepared, no less by his letter, than by reminiscences of certain boyish traits, and by conclusions deduced from his peculiar physical conformation and temperament. His action was alternately vivacious and sullen. His voice varied rapidly from a tremulous indecision (when the animal spirits seemed utterly in abeyance) to that species of energetic concision—that abrupt, weighty, unhurried, and hollow-sounding enunciation—that leaden, self-balanced and perfectly modulated guttural utterance, which may be observed in the lost drunkard, or the irreclaimable eater of opium, during the periods of his most intense excitement.

It was thus that he spoke of the object of my visit, of his earnest desire to see me, and of the solace he expected me to afford him. He entered, at some length, into what he conceived to be the nature of his malady. It was, he said, a constitutional and a family evil, and one for which he despaired to find a remedy—a mere nervous affection, he immediately added, which would undoubtedly soon pass off. It displayed itself in a host of unnatural sensations. Some of these, as he detailed them, interested and bewildered me; although, perhaps, the terms, and the general manner of the narration had their weight. He suffered much from a morbid acuteness of the senses; the most insipid food was alone endurable; he could wear only garments of certain texture; the odors of all flowers were oppressive; his eyes were tortured by even a faint light; and there were but peculiar sounds, and these from stringed instruments, which did not inspire him with horror. To an anomalous species of terror I found him a bounden slave. "I shall perish," said he, "I must perish in this deplorable folly.

Thus, thus, and not otherwise, shall I be lost. I dread the events of the future, not in themselves, but in their results. I shudder at the thought of any, even the most trivial, incident, which may operate upon this intolerable agitation of soul. I have, indeed, no abhorrence of danger, except in its absolute effect—in terror. In this unnerved, in this pitiable condition—I feel that the period will sooner or later arrive when I must abandon life and reason together, in some struggle with the grim phantasm, FEAR." I learned, moreover, at intervals, and through broken and equivocal hints, another singular feature of his mental condition. He was enchained by certain superstitious impressions in regard to the dwelling which he tenanted, and whence, for many years, he had never ventured forth—in regard to an influence whose supposititious force was conveyed in terms too shadowy here to be re-stated—an influence which some peculiarities in the mere form and substance of his family mansion, had, by dint of long sufferance, he said, obtained over his spirit-an effect which the physique of the gray walls and turrets, and of the dim tarn into which they all looked down, had, at length, brought about upon the morale of his existence.

He admitted, however, although with hesitation, that much of the peculiar gloom which thus afflicted him could be traced to a more natural and far more palpable origin—to the severe and long-continued illness—indeed to the evidently approaching dissolution of a tenderly beloved sister—his sole companion for long years—his last and only relative on earth. "Her decease," he said, with a bitterness which I can never forget, "would leave him (him the hopeless and the frail) the last of the ancient race of the Ushers." While he spoke, the lady Madeline (for so was she called) passed slowly through a remote portion of the apartment, and, without having noticed my presence, disappeared. I regarded her with an utter astonishment not unmingled with dread—and yet I found it impossible to account for such feelings. A sensation of stupor oppressed me, as my eyes followed her retreating steps. When a door, at length, closed upon her, my glance sought instinctively and eagerly the countenance of the brother—but he had buried his face in his hands, and I could only perceive that a far more than ordinary wanness had overspread the emaciated fingers through which trickled many passionate tears. The disease of the lady Madeline had long baffled the skill of her physicians. A settled apathy, a gradual wasting away of the person, and frequent although transient affections of a partially cataleptical character, were the unusual diagnosis. Hitherto she had steadily borne up against the pressure of her malady, and had not betaken herself finally to bed; but, on the closing in of the evening of my arrival at the house, she succumbed (as her brother told me at night with inexpressible agitation) to the prostrating power of the destroyer; and I learned that the glimpse I had obtained of her person would thus probably be the last I should obtain—that the lady, at least while living, would be seen by me no more.

For several days ensuing, her name was unmentioned by either Usher or myself: and during this period I was busied in earnest endeavors to alleviate the melancholy of my friend. We painted and read together; or I listened, as if in a dream, to the wild improvisations of his speaking guitar. And thus, as a closer and still intimacy admitted me more unreservedly into the recesses of his spirit, the more bitterly did I perceive the futility of all attempt at cheering a mind from which darkness, as if an inherent positive quality, poured forth upon all objects of the moral and physical universe, in one unceasing radiation of gloom.

I shall ever bear about me a memory of the many solemn hours I thus spent alone with the master of the House of Usher. Yet I should fail in any attempt to convey an idea of the exact character of the studies, or of the occupations, in which he involved me, or led me the way. An excited and highly distempered ideality threw a sulphurous luster over all. His long improvised dirges will ring forever in my cars. Among other things, I hold painfully in mind a certain singular perversion and amplification of the wild air of the last waltz of Von Weber. From the paintings over which his elaborate fancy brooded, and which grew, touch by touch, into vaguenesses at which I shuddered the more thrillingly, because I shuddered knowing not why; from these paintings (vivid as their images now are before me) I would in vain endeavor to educe more than a small portion which should lie within the compass of merely written words. By the utter simplicity, by the nakedness of his designs, he arrested and overawed attention. If ever mortal painted an idea, that mortal was Roderick Usher. For me at least—in the circumstances then surrounding me—there arose out of the pure abstractions which the hypochondriac contrived to throw upon his canvas, an intensity of intolerable awe, no shadow of which felt I ever yet in the contemplation of the certainly glowing yet too concrete reveries of Fuseli.

One of the phantasmagoric conceptions of my friend, partaking not so rigidly of the spirit of abstraction, may be shadowed forth, although feebly, in words. A small picture presented the interior of an immensely long and rectangular vault or tunnel, with low walls, smooth, white, and without interruption or device. Certain accessory points of the design served well to convey the idea that this excavation lay at an exceeding depth below the surface of the earth. No outlet was observed in any portion of its vast extent, and no torch, or other artificial source of light was discernible; yet a flood of intense rays rolled throughout, and bathed the whole in a ghastly and inappropriate splendor.

I have just spoken of that morbid condition of the auditory nerve which rendered all music intolerable to the sufferer, with the exception of certain effects of stringed instruments. It was, perhaps, the narrow limits to which he thus confined himself upon the guitar, which gave birth, in great measure, to the fantastic character of his performances. But the fervid facility of his impromptus could not be so accounted for. They must have been, and were, in the notes, as well as in the words of his wild fantasias (for he not unfrequently accompanied himself with rhymed verbal improvisations), the result of that intense mental collectedness and concentration to which I have previously alluded as observable only in particular moments of the highest artificial excitement. The words of one of these rhapsodies I have easily remembered. I was, perhaps, the more forcibly impressed with it, as he gave it, because, in the under or mystic current of its meaning, I fancied that I perceived, and for the first time, a full consciousness on the part of Usher, of the tottering of his lofty reason upon her throne. The verses, which were entitled "The Haunted Palace," ran very nearly, if not accurately, thus:

I.

In the greenest of our valleys,
By good angels tenanted,
Once fair and stately palace—
Radiant palace—reared its head.
In the monarch Thought's dominion—
It stood there!
Never seraph spread a pinion
Over fabric half so fair.

II.

Banners yellow, glorious, golden,
On its roof did float and flow;
(This—all this—was in the olden
Time long ago)
And every gentle air that dallied,
In that sweet day,
Along the ramparts plumed and pallid,
A winged odor went away.

III.

Wanderers in that happy valley
Through two luminous windows saw
Spirits moving musically
To a lute's well-tuned law,
Round about a throne, where sitting
(Porphyrogene!)
In state his glory well befitting,
The ruler of the realm was seen.

IV.

And all with pearl and ruby glowing
Was the fair palace door,
Through which came flowing, flowing, flowing
And sparkling evermore,
A troop of Echoes whose sweet duty
Was but to sing,
In voices of surpassing beauty,
The wit and wisdom of their king.

V.

But evil things, in robes of sorrow,
Assailed the monarch's high estate;
(Ah, let us mourn, for never morrow
Shall dawn upon him, desolate!)
And, round about his home, the glory
That blushed and bloomed
Is but a dim-remembered story
Of the old time entombed.

VI.

And travelers now within that valley,
Through the red-litten windows, see
Vast forms that move fantastically
To a discordant melody;
While, like a rapid ghastly river,
Through the pale door,
A hideous throng rush out forever,
And laugh—but smile no more.

I well remember that suggestions arising from this ballad led us into a train of thought wherein there became manifest an opinion of Usher's which I mention not so much on account of its novelty (for other men have thought thus) as on account of the pertinacity with which he maintained it. This opinion, in its general form, was that of the sentience of all vegetable things. But, in his disordered fancy the idea had assumed a more daring character, and trespassed, under certain conditions, upon the kingdom of inorganization. I lack words to express the full extent, or the earnest abandon of his persuasion. The belief, however, was connected (as I have previously hinted) with the gray stones of the home of his forefathers. The conditions of the sentience had been here, he imagined, fulfilled in the method of collocation of these stones—in the order of their arrangement, as well as in that of the many fungi which overspread them, and of the decayed trees which stood around—above all, in the long undisturbed endurance of this arrangement, and in its reduplication in the still waters of the tarn. Its evidence—the evidence of the sentience—was to be seen, he said, (and I here started as he spoke,) in the gradual yet certain condensation of an atmosphere of their own about the waters and the walls. The result was discoverable, he added, in that silent, yet importunate and terrible influence which for centuries had molded the destinies of his family, and which made him what I now saw him—what he was. Such opinions need no comment, and I will make none.

Our books—the books which, for years, had formed no small portion of the mental existence of the invalid—were, as might be supposed, in strict keeping with this character of phantasm. We pored together over such works as the Ververt et Chartreuse of Gresset; the Belphegor of Machiavelli; the Heaven and Hell of Swedenborg; the Subterranean Voyage of Nicholas Klimm by Holberg; the Chiromancy of Robert Flud, of Jean D'Indagine, and of De la Chambre; the Journey into the Blue Distance of Tieck; and the City of the Sun of Campanella. One favorite volume was a small octavo edition of the Directorium Inquisitorum, by the Dominican Eymeric de Gironne; and there were passages in Pomponius Mela, about the old African Satyrs over which Usher would sit dreaming for hours. His chief delight, however, was found in the perusal of an exceedingly rare and curious book in quarto Gothic—the manual of a forgotten church—the Vigilae Mortuorum secundum Chorum Ecclesiae Maguntinae. I could not help thinking of the wild ritual of this work, and of its probable influence upon the hypochondriac, when, one evening, having informed me abruptly that the lady Madeline was no more, he stated his intention of preserving her corpse for a fortnight (previously to its final interment) in one of the numerous vaults within the main walls of the building. The worldly reason, however, assigned for this singular proceeding, was one which I did not feel at liberty to dispute. The brother had been led to his resolution (so he told me) by consideration of the unusual character of the malady of the deceased, of certain obtrusive and eager inquiries on the part of her medical men, and of the remote and exposed situation of the burial-ground of the family. I will not deny that when I called to mind the sinister countenance of the person whom I met upon the stair case, on the day of my arrival at the house, I had no desire to oppose what I regarded as at best but a harmless, and by no means an unnatural, precaution. At the request of Usher, I personally aided him in the arrangements for the temporary entombment. The body having been encoffined, we two alone bore it to its rest. The vault in which we placed it (and which had been so long unopened that our torches, half smothered in its oppressive atmosphere, gave us little opportunity for investigation) was small, damp, and entirely without means of admission for light; lying, at great depth, immediately beneath that portion of the building in which was my own sleeping apartment. It had been used, apparently, in remote feudal times, for the worst purposes of a donjon-keep, and, in later days, as a place of deposit for powder, or some other highly combustible substance, as a portion of its floor, and the whole interior of a long archway through which we reached it, were carefully sheathed with copper. The door, of massive iron, had been, also, similarly protected. Its immense weight caused an unusually sharp grating sound, as it moved upon its hinges.

Having deposited our mournful burden upon tressels within this region of horror, we partially turned aside the yet unscrewed lid of the coffin, and looked upon the face of the tenant. A striking similitude between the brother and sister now first arrested my attention; and Usher, divining, perhaps, my thoughts, murmured out some few words from which I learned that the deceased and himself had been twins, and that sympathies of a scarcely intelligible nature had always existed between them. Our glances, however, rested not long upon the dead—for we could not regard her unawed. The disease which had thus entombed the lady in the maturity of youth, had left, as usual in all maladies of a strictly cataleptical character, the mockery of a faint blush upon the bosom and the face, and that suspiciously lingering smile upon the lip which is so terrible in death. We replaced and screwed down the lid, and, having secured the door of iron, made our way, with toll, into the scarcely less gloomy apartments of the upper portion of the house.

And now, some days of bitter grief having elapsed, an observable change came over the features of the mental disorder of my friend. His ordinary manner had vanished. His ordinary occupations were neglected or forgotten. He roamed from chamber to chamber with hurried, unequal, and objectless step. The pallor of his countenance had assumed, if possible, a more ghastly hue—but the luminousness of his eye had utterly gone out. The once occasional huskiness of his tone was heard no more; and a tremulous quaver, as if of extreme terror, habitually characterized his utterance. There were times, indeed, when I thought his unceasingly agitated mind was laboring with some oppressive secret, to divulge which he struggled for the necessary outrage. At times, again, I was obliged to resolve all into the mere inexplicable vagaries of madness, for I beheld him gazing upon vacancy for long hours, in an attitude of the profoundest attention, as if listening to some imaginary sound. It was no wonder that his condition terrified, that it infected me. I felt creeping upon me, by slow yet certain degrees, the wild influences of his own fantastic yet impressive superstitions. It was, especially, upon retiring to bed late in the night of the seventh or eighth day after the placing of the lady Madeline within the donjon, that I experienced the full power of such feelings.

Sleep came not near my couch—while the hours waned and waned away. I struggled to reason off the nervousness which had dominion over me. I endeavored to believe that much, if not all of what I felt, was due to the bewildering influence of the gloomy furniture of the room—of the dark and tattered draperies, which, tortured into motion by the breath of a rising tempest, swayed fitfully to and fro upon the walls, and rustled uneasily about the decorations of the bed. But my efforts were fruitless. An irrepressible tremor gradually pervaded my frame; and, at length, there sat upon my very heart an incubus of utterly causeless alarm. Shaking this off with a gasp and a struggle, I uplifted myself upon the pillows, and, peering earnestly within the intense darkness of the chamber, hearkened—I know not why, except that an instinctive spirit prompted me—to certain low and indefinite sounds which came, through the pauses of the storm, at long intervals, I knew not whence. Overpowered by an intense sentiment of horror, unaccountable yet unendurable, I threw on my clothes with haste (for I felt that I should sleep no more during the night), and endeavored to arouse myself from the pitiable condition into which I had fallen, by pacing rapidly to and fro through the apartment.

I had taken but few turns in this manner, when a

light step on an adjoining staircase arrested my attention. I presently recognized it as that of Usher. In an instant afterward he rapped, with a gentle touch, at my door, and entered, bearing a lamp. His countenance was, as usual, cadaverously wan—but, moreover, there was a species of mad hilarity in his eyes—an evidently restrained hysteria in his whole demeanor. His air appalled me—but anything was preferable to the solitude which I had so long endured, and I even welcomed his presence as a relief.

"And you have not seen it?" he said abruptly, after having stared about him for some moments in silence—"you have not then seen it?—but, stay! you shall." Thus speaking, and having carefully shaded his lamp, he hurried to one of the casements, and threw it freely open to the storm.

The impetuous fury of the entering gust nearly lifted us from our feet. It was, indeed, a tempestuous yet sternly beautiful night, and one wildly singular in its terror and its beauty. A whirlwind had apparently collected its force in our vicinity; for there were frequent and violent alterations in the direction of the wind; and the exceeding density of the clouds (which hung so low as to press upon the turrets of the house) did not prevent our perceiving the life-like velocity with which they flew careering from all points against each other, without passing away into the distance. I say that even their exceeding density did not prevent our perceiving this—yet we had no glimpse of the moon or stars—nor was there any flashing forth of the lightning. But the under surfaces of the huge masses of agitated vapor, as well as all terrestrial objects immediately around us, were glowing in the unnatural light of a faintly luminous and distinctly visible gaseous exhalation which hung about and enshrouded the mansion.

"You must not—you shall not behold this!" said I, shudderingly, to Usher, as I led him, with a gentle violence, from the window to a seat. "These appearances, which bewilder you, are merely electrical phenomena not uncommon—or it may be that they have their ghastly origin in the rank miasma of the tarn. Let us close this casement; the air is chilling and dangerous to your frame. Here is one of your favorite romances. I will read, and you shall listen; and so we will pass away this terrible night together."

The antique volume which I had taken up was the "Mad Trist" of Sir Launcelot Canning; but I had called it a favorite of Usher's more in sad jest than in earnest; for, in truth, there is little in its uncouth and unimaginative prolixity which could have had interest for the lofty and spiritual ideality of my friend. It was, how-

ever, the only book immediately at hand; and I indulged a vague hope that the excitement which now agitated the hypochondriac, might find relief (for the history of mental disorder is full of similar anomalies) even in the extremeness of the folly which I should read. Could I have judged, indeed, by the wild over-strained air of vivacity with which he hearkened, or apparently hearkened, to the words of the tale, I might well have congratulated myself upon the success of my design. I had arrived at that well-known portion of the story where Ethelred, the hero of the Trist, having sought in vain for peaceable admission into the dwelling of the hermit, proceeds to make good an entrance by force. Here, it will be remembered, the words of the narrative run thus: "And Ethelred, who was by nature of a doughty heart, and who was now mighty withal, on account of the powerfulness of the wine which he had drunken, waited no longer to hold parley with the hermit, who, in sooth, was of an obstinate and maliceful turn, but, feeling the rain upon his shoulders, and fearing the rising of the tempest, uplifted his mace outright, and, with blows, made quickly room in the plankings of the door for his gauntleted hand; and now pulling there-with sturdily, he so cracked, and ripped, and tore all asunder, that the noise of the dry and hollow-sounding wood alarmed and reverberated throughout the forest.

At the termination of this sentence I started, and for a moment, paused; for it appeared to me (although I at once concluded that my excited fancy had deceived me)—it appeared to me that, from some very remote portion of the mansion, there came, indistinctly, to my ears, what might have been, in its exact similarity of character, the echo (but a stifled and dull one certainly) of the very cracking and ripping sound which Sir Launcelot had so particularly described.

It was, beyond doubt, the coincidence alone which had arrested my attention; for, amid the rattling of the sashes of the casements, and the ordinary commingled noises of the still increasing storm, the sound, in itself, had nothing, surely, which should have interested or disturbed me. I continued the story:

"But the good champion Ethelred, now entering within the door, was sore enraged and amazed to perceive no signal of the maliceful hermit; but, in the stead thereof, a dragon of a scaly and prodigious demeanor, and of a fiery tongue, which sate in guard before a palace of gold, with a floor of silver; and upon the wall there hung a shield of shining brass with this legend enwritten—Who entereth herein, a conqueror hath bin; Who slayeth the dragon, the shield he shall win; And Ethelred uplifted his mace, and struck upon the head of the dragon, which fell before him, and gave up his pasty breath, with a shriek so horrid and harsh, and withal so piercing, that Ethelred had fain to close his ears with his hands against the dreadful noise of it, the like whereof was never before heard."

Here again I paused abruptly, and now with a feeling of wild amazement—for there could be no doubt whatever that, in this instance, I did actually hear (although from what direction it proceeded I found it impossible to say) a low and apparently distant, but harsh, protracted, and most unusual screaming or grating sound—the exact counterpart of what my fancy had already conjured up for the dragon's unnatural shriek as described by the romancer.

Oppressed, as I certainly was, upon the occurrence of the second and most extraordinary coincidence, by a thousand conflicting sensations, in which wonder and extreme terror were predominant, I still retained sufficient presence of mind to avoid exciting, by any observation, the sensitive nervousness of my companion. I was by no means certain that he had noticed the sounds in question; although, assuredly, a strange alteration had, during the last few minutes, taken place in his demeanor. From a position fronting my own, he had gradually brought round his chair, so as to sit with his face to the door of the chamber; and thus I could but partially perceive his features, although I saw that his lips trembled as if he were murmuring inaudibly. His head had dropped upon his breast—yet I knew that he was not asleep, from the wide and rigid opening of the eye as I caught a glance of it in profile. The motion of his body, too, was at variance with this idea—for he rocked from side to side with a gentle yet constant and uniform sway. Having rapidly taken notice of all this, I resumed the narrative of Sir Launcelot, which thus proceeded: "And now, the champion, having escaped from the terrible fury of the dragon, bethinking himself of the brazen shield, and of the breaking up of the enchantment which was upon it, removed the carcass from out of the way before him, and approached valorously over the silver pavement of the castle to where the shield was upon the wall; which in sooth tarried not for his full coming, but fell down at his feet upon the silver floor, with a mighty great and terrible ringing sound."

No sooner had these syllables passed my lips, than—as if a shield of brass had indeed, at the moment, fallen heavily upon a floor of silver became aware of a distinct, hollow, metallic, and clangorous, yet appar-

ently muffled reverberation. Completely unnerved, I leaped to my feet; but the measured rocking movement of Usher was undisturbed. I rushed to the chair in which he sat. His eyes were bent fixedly before him, and throughout his whole countenance there reigned a stony rigidity. But, as I placed my hand upon his shoulder, there came a strong shudder over his whole person; a sickly smile quivered about his lips; and I saw that he spoke in a low, hurried, and gibbering murmur, as if unconscious of my presence. Bending closely over him, I at length drank in the hideous import of his words.

"Not hear it?—yes, I hear it, and have heard it. Long—long—long—many minutes, many hours, many days, have I heard it—yet I dared not—oh, pity me, miserable wretch that I am!—I dared not—I dared not speak! We have put her living in the tomb! Said I not that my senses were acute? I now tell you that I heard her first feeble movements in the hollow coffin. I heard them—many, many days ago—yet I dared not—I dared not speak! And now—to-night—Ethelred—ha! ha!—the breaking of the hermit's door, and the death-cry of the dragon, and the clangor of the shield!—say, rather, the rending of her coffin, and the grating of the iron hinges of her prison, and her struggles within the coppered archway of the vault! Oh whither shall I fly? Will she not be here anon? Is she not hurrying to upbraid me for my haste? Have I not heard her footstep on the stair? Do I not distinguish that heavy and horrible beating of her heart? MADMAN!" here he sprang furiously to his feet, and shrieked out his syllables, as if in the effort he were giving up his soul—"MADMAN! I TELL YOU THAT SHE NOW STANDS WITHOUT THE DOOR!"

As if in the superhuman energy of his utterance there had been found the potency of a spell—the huge antique panels to which the speaker pointed, threw slowly back, upon the instant, ponderous and ebony jaws. It was the work of the rushing gust—but then without those doors there DID stand the lofty and enshrouded figure of the lady Madeline of Usher. There was blood upon her white robes, and the evidence of some bitter struggle upon every portion of her emaciated frame. For a moment she remained trembling and reeling to and fro upon the threshold, then, with a low moaning cry, fell heavily inward upon the person of her brother, and in her violent and now final death-agonies, bore him to the floor a corpse, and a victim to the terrors he had anticipated.

From that chamber, and from that mansion, I fled aghast. The storm was still abroad in all its wrath as I found myself crossing the old causeway. Suddenly there shot along the path a wild light, and I turned to see whence a gleam so unusual could have issued; for the vast house and its shadows were alone behind me. The radiance was that of the full, setting, and blood-red moon which now shone vividly through that once barely-discernible fissure of which I have before spoken as extending from the roof of the building, in a zigzag direction, to the base. While I gazed, this fissure rapidly widened—there came a fierce breath of the whirlwind—the entire orb of the satellite burst at once upon my sight—my brain reeled as I saw the mighty walls rushing asunder—there was a long tumultuous shouting sound like the voice of a thousand waters— and the deep and dank tarn at my feet closed sullenly and silently over the fragments of the "HOUSE OF USHER."

http://www.angeltowns.com/members/shortstories/index.html

The Tell Tale Heart

Edgar Allan Poe

TRUE! nervous, very, very dreadfully nervous I had been and am; but why WILL you say that I am mad? The disease had sharpened my senses, not destroyed, not dulled them. Above all was the sense of hearing acute. I heard all things in the heaven and in the earth. I heard many things in hell. How then am I mad? Hearken! and observe how healthily, how calmly, I can tell you the whole story.

It is impossible to say how first the idea entered my brain, but, once conceived, it haunted me day and night. Object there was none. Passion there was none. I loved the old man. He had never wronged me. He had never given me insult. For his gold I had no desire. I think it was his eye! Yes, it was this! One of his eyes resembled that of a vulture—a pale blue eye with a film over it. Whenever it fell upon me my blood ran cold, and so by degrees, very gradually, I made up my mind to take the life of the old man, and thus rid myself of the eye for ever.

Now this is the point. You fancy me mad. Madmen know nothing. But you should have seen me. You should have seen how wisely I proceeded—with what caution—with what foresight, with what dissimulation, I went to work! I was never kinder to the old man than during the whole week before I killed him. And every night about midnight I turned the latch of his door and opened it oh, so gently! And then, when I had made an opening sufficient for my head, I put in a dark lantern all closed, closed so that no light shone out, and then I thrust in my head. Oh, you would have laughed to see how cunningly I thrust it in! I moved it slowly, very, very slowly, so that I might not disturb the old man's sleep. It took me an hour to place my whole head within the opening so far that I could see him as he lay upon his bed. Ha! would a madman have been so wise as this? And then when my head was well in the room I undid the lantern cautiously—oh, so cautiously—cautiously (for the hinges creaked), I undid it just so much that a single thin ray fell upon the vulture eye. And this I did for seven long nights, every night just at midnight, but I found the eye always closed, and so it was impossible to do the work, for it was not the old man who vexed me but his Evil Eye. And every morning, when the day broke, I went boldly into the chamber and spoke courageously to him, calling him by name in a hearty tone, and inquiring how he had passed the night. So you see he would have been a very profound old man, indeed, to suspect that every night, just at twelve, I looked in upon him while he slept.

Upon the eighth night I was more than usually cautious in opening the door. A watch's minute hand moves more quickly than did mine. Never before that night had I felt the extent of my own powers, of my sagacity. I could scarcely contain my feelings of triumph. To think that there I was opening the door little by little, and he not even to dream of my secret deeds or thoughts. I fairly chuckled at the idea, and perhaps he heard me, for he moved on the bed suddenly as if startled. Now you may think that I drew back—but no. His room was as black as pitch with the thick darkness (for the shutters were close fastened through fear of robbers), and so I knew that he could not see the opening of the door, and I kept pushing it on steadily, steadily.

I had my head in, and was about to open the lantern, when my thumb slipped upon the tin fastening, and the old man sprang up in the bed, crying out, "Who's there?"

I kept quite still and said nothing. For a whole hour I did not move a muscle, and in the meantime I did not hear him lie down. He was still sitting up in the bed, listening; just as I have done night after night hearkening to the death watches in the wall.

Presently, I heard a slight groan, and I knew it was the groan of mortal terror. It was not a groan of pain or of grief—oh, no! It was the low stifled sound that arises from the bottom of the soul when overcharged with awe. I knew the sound well. Many a night, just at midnight, when all the world slept, it has welled up from my own bosom, deepening, with its dreadful echo, the terrors that distracted me. I say I knew it well. I knew what the old man felt, and pitied him although I chuckled at heart. I knew that he had been lying awake ever since the first slight noise when he had turned in the bed. His fears had been ever since growing upon him. He had been trying to fancy them causeless, but could not. He had been saying to himself, "It is nothing but the wind in the chimney, it is only a mouse crossing the floor," or, "It is merely a cricket which has made a single chirp." Yes he has been trying to comfort himself with these suppositions; but he had found all in vain. ALL IN VAIN, because Death in approaching him had stalked with his black shadow before him and enveloped the victim. And it was the mournful influence of the unperceived shadow that caused him to feel, although he neither saw nor heard, to feel the presence of my head within the room.

When I had waited a long time very patiently without hearing him lie down, I resolved to open a little—a very, very little crevice in the lantern. So I opened it—you cannot imagine how stealthily, stealthily—until at length a single dim ray like the thread of the spider shot out from the crevice and fell upon the vulture eye.

It was open, wide, wide open, and I grew furious as I gazed upon it. I saw it with perfect distinctness—all a dull blue with a hideous veil over it that chilled the very marrow in my bones, but I could see nothing else of the old man's face or person, for I had directed the ray as if by instinct precisely upon the damned spot.

And now have I not told you that what you mistake for madness is but over-acuteness of the senses? now, I say, there came to my ears a low, dull, quick sound, such as a watch makes when enveloped in cotton. I knew that sound well too. It was the beating of the old man's heart. It increased my fury as the beating of a drum stimulates the soldier into courage.

But even yet I refrained and kept still. I scarcely breathed. I held the lantern motionless. I tried how steadily I could maintain the ray upon the eye. Meantime the hellish tattoo of the heart increased. It grew quicker and quicker, and louder and louder, every instant. The old man's terror must have been extreme! It grew louder, I say, louder every moment!—do you mark me well? I have told you that I am nervous: so I am. And now at the dead hour of the night, amid the dreadful silence of that old house, so strange a noise as this excited me to uncontrollable terror. Yet, for some minutes longer I refrained and stood still. But the beating grew louder, louder! I thought the heart must burst. And now a new anxiety seized me—the sound would be heard by a neighbour! The old man's hour had come! With a loud yell, I threw open the lantern and leaped into the room. He shrieked once—once only. In an instant I dragged him to the floor, and pulled the heavy bed over him. I then smiled gaily, to find the deed so far done. But for many minutes the heart beat on with a muffled sound. This, however, did not vex me; it would not be heard through the wall. At length it ceased. The old man was dead. I removed the bed and examined the corpse. Yes, he was stone, stone dead. I placed my hand upon the heart and held it there many minutes. There was no pulsation. He was stone dead. His eye would trouble me no more.

If still you think me mad, you will think so no longer when I describe the wise precautions I took for the concealment of the body. The night waned, and I worked hastily, but in silence.

I took up three planks from the flooring of the chamber, and deposited all between the scantlings. I then replaced the boards so cleverly so cunningly, that no human eye—not even his—could have detected anything wrong. There was nothing to wash out—no stain of any kind—no blood-spot whatever. I had been too wary for that.

When I had made an end of these labors, it was four o'clock—still dark as midnight. As the bell sounded the hour, there came a knocking at the street door. I went down to open it with a light heart, for what had I now to fear? There entered three men, who introduced themselves, with perfect suavity, as officers of the police. A shriek had been heard by a neighbour during the night; suspicion of foul play had been aroused; information had been lodged at the police office, and they (the officers) had been deputed to search the premises.

I smiled,—for what had I to fear? I bade the gentlemen welcome. The shriek, I said, was my own in a dream. The old man, I mentioned, was absent in the country. I took my visitors all over the house. I bade them search—search well. I led them, at length, to his chamber. I showed them his treasures, secure, undisturbed. In the enthusiasm of my confidence, I brought chairs into the room, and desired them here to rest from their fatigues, while I myself, in the wild audacity of my perfect triumph, placed my own seat upon the very spot beneath which reposed the corpse of the victim.

The officers were satisfied. My MANNER had convinced them. I was singularly at ease. They sat and while I answered cheerily, they chatted of familiar things. But, ere long, I felt myself getting pale and wished them gone. My head ached, and I fancied a ringing in my ears; but still they sat, and still chatted. The ringing became more distinct: I talked more freely to get rid of the feeling: but it continued and gained definitiveness—until, at length, I found that the noise was NOT within my ears.

No doubt I now grew VERY pale; but I talked more fluently, and with a heightened voice. Yet the sound increased—and what could I do? It was A LOW, DULL, QUICK SOUND—MUCH SUCH A SOUND AS A WATCH MAKES WHEN ENVELOPED IN COTTON. I gasped for breath, and yet the officers heard it not. I talked more quickly, more vehemently but the noise steadily increased. I arose and argued about trifles, in a high key and with violent gesticulations; but the noise steadily increased. Why WOULD they not be gone? I paced the floor to and fro with heavy strides, as if excited to fury by the observations of the men, but the noise steadily increased. O God! what COULD I do? I foamed—I raved—I swore! I swung the chair upon which I had

been sitting, and grated it upon the boards, but the noise arose over all and continually increased. It grew louder—louder—louder! And still the men chatted pleasantly , and smiled. Was it possible they heard not? Almighty God!—no, no? They heard!—they suspected!—they KNEW!—they were making a mockery of my horror!—this I thought, and this I think. But anything was better than this agony! Anything was more tolerable than this derision! I could bear those hypocritical smiles no longer! I felt that I must scream or die!—and now—again—hark! louder! louder! louder! LOUDER!—

"Villains!" I shrieked, "dissemble no more! I admit the deed!—tear up the planks!—here, here!—it is the beating of his hideous heart!"
http://www.angeltowns.com/members/shortstories/index.html

SUGGESTED
Weekly *Implementation*

DAY 1	DAY 2	DAY 3	DAY 4	DAY 5
Prayer journal. Review the required reading(s) *before* the assigned lesson begins. Teacher may want to discuss assigned reading(s) with students. Teacher and students will decide on the number of required essays for this lesson, choosing two or three essays. The rest of the essays can be outlined, answered with shorter answers, or skipped. Review all readings for Lesson 7.	**Prayer journal.** Review reading(s) from next lesson. Outline essays due at the end of the week. Per teacher instructions, students may answer orally in a group setting some of the essays that are not assigned as formal essays.	**Prayer journal.** Write rough drafts of all assigned essays. The teacher and/or a peer evaluator may correct rough drafts.	**Prayer journal.** Rewrite corrected copies of essays due tomorrow.	**Prayer journal.** Essays are due. Take Lesson 7 test. Reading ahead: Students should review *The Scarlet Letter* and "The Birthmark," Nathaniel Hawthorne. Guide: What romantic themes emerge in Hawthorne's novel *The Scarlet Letter* and the short story "The Birthmark?"

LESSON 8

ROMANTICISM: NEW ENGLAND RENAISSANCE, 1840-1855
(Part 1)

Romanticism/ Transcendentalism

BACKGROUND

Romanticism is a worldview in philosophy and literature that argues for a higher reality than that found in tactile experience or in a higher kind of knowledge than that achieved by human reason. Romanticism celebrates the subjective and the unusual. For our purposes, Transcendentalism is the American version of Romanticism. Transcendentalism as an artistic and intellectual moment was localized in New England. Thus, this period is called the New England Renaissance.

The Scarlet Letter
Nathaniel Hawthorne (1850)

BACKGROUND

The Scarlet Letter is based on a true incident. In 1697 the Rev. John Cotton, pastor of Plymouth, MA, Church, was fired from his job for committing adultery. Nearly 150 years later Hawthorne wrote a story with a similar plot. This novel, however, represents both a literary

> **You will analyze:** *The Scarlet Letter* and "The Birthmark," Nathaniel Hawthorne.
>
> **Reading ahead:** Poems by Henry Wadsworth Longfellow, Oliver Wendell Holmes, James Russell Lowell, John Greenleaf Whittier, and Emily Dickinson.
>
> **Guide Question:** What moral vision do these poets present?

milestone and a worldview milestone. First, *The Scarlet Letter* is perhaps the best American romantic novel ever written. Secondly, this is the final American novel, many believe, that has a moral vision. In short, *The Scarlet Letter* is the last American Christian Theistic novel of superior quality that was to appear for 150 years. In *The Scarlet Letter* Hawthorne unapologetically presents a character who takes responsibility for her sin and, as a result, is extolled and admired by her community. Hester Prynne and Arthur Dimmesdale are correctly punished by God for their sin. They grow stronger—not weaker—for their felicity and fidelity. This American novel is one of the last critically acclaimed for such a stance. By contrast, Hawthorne's contemporary, Herman Melville, wrote *Billy Budd* where the protagonist, Billy Budd, is "redeemed" by

Elements of Romanticism/ Transcendentalism	Frontier is a vast expanse; it represents freedom, innocence, and opportunity.
Writing Techniques	1. Appeals to imagination; use of the "willing suspension of disbelief." 2. Stress on emotion and imagination rather than reason; optimism, geniality. 3. Subjectivity in form and meaning. 4. Prefers a remote setting in time and space. 5. Prefers exotic and improbable plots. 6. Prefers aberrant characterization. 7. Form rises out of content, non-formal. 8. Prefers individualized, subjective writing.

some sort of self-actualization. The preacher in *Billy Budd* is a wimpish, amoral character who, on the last night of Billy Budd's life, abandoned his attempt to lead Billy Budd to a saving relationship with Christ because Billy Budd appeared to be saved already by his good works. On the other hand, Arthur Dimmesdale, the pastor in *The Scarlet Letter*, sinned grievously but at the end of the novel was nonetheless "redeemed" by honest confession of sin. He may be the last American literary character who is.

ABOUT THE AUTHOR

© Arttoday.com

Born in Salem, Massachusetts, in 1804, Nathaniel Hawthorne later graduated from Bowdoin College, in Brunswick, Maine. Hawthorne wrote *The Scarlet Letter*, a historical romance of 17th century Boston, as one reliving his own historical past. Hawthorne's first relative came to Salem in 1630 "a soldier, legislator, judge, and Puritan." The next ancestor was a Salem witch trial judge. Hawthorne's father was a sea captain who died when his only son was four. Hawthorne, in this and later books, explored his own past. Hester Prynne, Chillingsworth, and Dimmesdale are truly contemporary characters. *The Scarlet Letter* remains as modern, as dramatic, as passionate, and as moving as if it were written yesterday.

Other Notable Works: *Twice-Told Tales* (1837) and *The House of the Seven Gables* (1851)

Romanticism is a literary and artistic movement that arose in the middle of the 19th century. Romanticism as a worldview was a reaction to the perceived rigidity of Puritanism on one hand, and to the chauvinistic elements of Rationalism on the other. Romanticism and the American version called Transcendentalism placed the individual center stage and celebrated human emotion, intuition, subjectivity, and freedom. Romanticism naturally, then, preferred an unsoiled nature to human civilization.

Hawthorne House
Salem, MA
© Arttoday.com

SUGGESTED VOCABULARY WORDS

As you read the assigned prose, poetry, and novels, make vocabulary cards. On one side put the word you do not know. On the other side put the definition of the word and a sentence with the word used in it. Read 35-50 pages per night (200 pages per week). At the same time, create 3x5 vocabulary cards. You should use five new words in each essay you write. The following are vocabulary works in *The Scarlet Letter*. Find more as you read the novel.

II	ignominy
III	heterogeneous
	iniquity
VIII	imperious
XII	dauntless
	forlorn
	odious
	efficacious
XIII	expiation
	scurrilous
XIX	misanthropy
XX	effluence
	choleric
XXI	vicissitude

CRITICAL THINKING

A. In *The Scarlet Letter*, as he did in most of his books, Hawthorne combined historical truth with imaginative detail to create an allegory. An allegory

Sophia Peabody Hawthorne

is a narrative in which characters, action, and sometimes setting represent abstract concepts or moral qualities. What moral qualities are represented by Arthur? Hester? Roger? Write an illustrative essay describing the moral qualities each character represents.

B. *The Scarlet Letter* was one of the last books in American literature that had a Theistic moral vision. Although Hawthorne never hinted that Prynne's punishment was unjust, he seemed far more disturbed by Dimmesdale's deception and Chillingsworth's evil ways. In a two-page essay, using this book as a metaphor for the tensions existing in American society c. 1850, discuss these tensions and evidence from the text. Who is the victim in this book?

C. A recent television commercial argued, "Doesn't everyone deserve a second chance?" Why do you agree or disagree with this statement? Why does this book offend or not offend your sense of justice?

D. Pretend that Hester Prynne lived in City Anywhere, USA. How would she be treated at a public school? At the grocery story? At your church? Defend your answer.

E. Many scholars find evidence that Nathaniel Hawthorne was a believer. While there were evidences of Transcendentalism in his writings, Hawthorne admired and advanced the Puritan Theistic vision. The ambivalence in his writing may have been from his Transcendalist/Universalist wife Sophia Peabody Hawthorne and his friends who no doubt influenced him. In an essay, offer evidence from the *The Scarlet Letter* and other writings that indicates or does not indicate this influence.

F. Give a characterization of Hester. What sort of woman is she? She could have run away with Arthur. Why doesn't she?

G. Pearl functions as a *foil* (a character whose primary purpose is to develop the main character). Give evidence of this purpose.

© Arttoday.com

H. In another essay, compare the use of a foil in this book with another foil in another piece of literature.

I. Compare Pearl to a foil in your favorite movie (e.g. the way Aubrey is used in the movie *Chariots of Fire*).

BIBLICAL APPLICATION

A. Contrast the way Hester's community handles her adultery and the way Jesus dealt with the adulterous woman who was brought to Him (John 8). Also, contrast the way Hester handled her sin and the way the adulterous woman handled her sin.

B. While we many agree that Hester's community was somewhat rough on her, are we willing to say that she and her partner in adultery should not have been punished? Do a Bible study on the whole topics of *sin*, *repentance*, and *restoration*. Start in Matthew 18.

Begin Bible study with prayer and a fervent request that God guide your study. Then, using a concordance, check the topic or key words for textual references. Next, check related topics by following cross references. Let the text guide you: avoid following your own agenda or perceived need.

ENRICHMENT

A. Do you really think there were witches in Salem? Defend your answer.

B. *The Scarlet Letter* was a critical success but not a best seller. In American society, so structured around entertainment, one wonders if Hawthorne would be able to find a publisher. In his book *Amusing Ourselves to Death* Neil Postman argues that television is transforming our culture into one vast arena for show business (p. 80). Television is the highest order of abstract thinking and consistently undermines critical thinking (p.41). The message has become the medium. What do you think? Read Postman or use other material and write an essay explaining how our culture has been transformed by television and the entertainment industry.

C. Compare and contrast Hester Prynne in *The Scarlet Letter* and Phoebe Pyncheon in *House of the Seven Gables*.

BACKGROUND

After an initial period of anonymity during his so-called solitary years from 1825 to 1837 and a time of very little literary success, Nathaniel Hawthorne finally achieved a reputation as a gifted author. His short story "The Birthmark" was one of the best fruits from this time. Some critics described Hawthorne as writing a "dense spiritual autobiography" when he wrote stories like "The Birthmark." Use your critical thinking skills to determine what you think.

The Birthmark

Nathaniel Hawthorne

In the latter part of the last century, there lived a man of science—an eminent proficient in every branch of natural philosophy—who, not long before our story opens, had made experience of a spiritual affinity, more attractive than any chemical one. He had left his laboratory to the care of an assistant, cleared his fine countenance from the furnace smoke, washed the stain of acids from his fingers, and persuaded a beautiful woman to become his wife. In those days, when the comparatively recent discovery of electricity, and other kindred mysteries of nature, seemed to open paths into the region of miracle, it was not unusual for the love of science to rival the love of woman, in its depth and absorbing energy. The higher intellect, the imagination, the spirit, and even the heart, might all find their congenial aliment in pursuits which, as some of their ardent votaries believed, would ascend from one step of powerful intelligence to another, until the philosopher should lay his hand on the secret of creative force, and perhaps make new worlds for himself. We know not whether Aylmer possessed this degree of faith in man's ultimate control over nature. He had devoted himself, however, too unreservedly to scientific studies, ever to be weaned from them by any second passion. His love for his young wife might prove the stronger of the two; but it could only be by intertwining itself with his love of science, and uniting the strength of the latter to its own.

Such a union accordingly took place, and was attended with truly remarkable consequences, and a deeply impressive moral. One day, very soon after their marriage, Aylmer sat gazing at his wife, with a trouble in his countenance that grew stronger, until he spoke.

"Georgiana," said he, "has it never occurred to you that the mark upon your cheek might be removed?"

"No, indeed, said she, smiling; but perceiving the seriousness of his manner, she blushed deeply. "To tell you the truth, it has been so often called a charm, that I was simple enough to imagine it might be so."

"Ah, upon another face, perhaps it might," replied her husband. "But never on yours! No, dearest Georgiana, you came so nearly perfect from the hand of Nature, that this slightest possible defect—which we hesitate whether to term a defect or a beauty—shocks me, as being the visible mark of earthly imperfection."

"Shocks you, my husband!" cried Georgiana, deeply hurt; at first reddening with momentary anger, but then bursting into tears. "Then why did you take me from my mother's side? You cannot love what shocks you!"

To explain this conversation, it must be mentioned, that, in the center of Georgiana's left cheek, there was a singular mark, deeply interwoven, as it were, with the texture and substance of her face. In the usual state of her complexion—a healthy, though delicate bloom—the mark wore a tint of deeper crimson, which imperfectly defined its shape amid the surrounding rosiness. When she blushed, it gradually became more indistinct, and finally vanished amid the triumphant rush of blood, that bathed the whole cheek with its brilliant glow. But, if any shifting emotion caused her to turn pale, there was the mark again, a crimson stain upon the snow, in what Aylmer sometimes deemed an almost fearful distinctness. Its shape bore not a little similarity to the human hand, though of the smallest pigmy size. Georgiana's lovers were wont to say, that some fairy, at her birth hour, had laid her tiny hand upon the infant's cheek, and left this impress there, in token of the magic endowments that were to give her such sway over all hearts. Many a desperate swain would have risked life for the privilege of pressing his lips to the mysterious hand. It must not be concealed, however, that the impression wrought by this fairy sign—manual varied exceedingly, according to the difference of temperament in the beholders. Some fastidious persons—but they were exclusively of her own sex—affirmed that the Bloody Hand, as they chose to call it, quite destroyed the effect of Georgiana's beauty, and rendered her countenance even hideous. But it would be as reasonable to say, that one of those small blue stains, which sometimes occur in the purest statuary marble, would convert the Eve of Powers to a monster. Masculine observers, if the birthmark did not heighten their admiration, contented themselves with wishing it away, that the world might possess one living specimen of ideal loveliness, without the semblance of a flaw. After his marriage—for he thought little or nothing of the matter before—Aylmer discovered that this was the case with himself.

Had she been less beautiful—if Envy's self could have found aught else to sneer at—he might have felt his affection heightened by the prettiness of this mimic hand, now vaguely portrayed, now lost, now stealing forth again, and glimmering to and fro with every pulse of emotion that throbbed within her heart. But, seeing her otherwise so perfect, he found this one defect grow more and more intolerable, with every moment of their united lives. It was the fatal flaw of humanity, which Nature, in one shape or another, stamps ineffaceably on all her productions, either to imply that they are temporary and finite, or that their perfection must be wrought by toil and pain. The Crimson Hand expressed the ineludible gripe, in which mortality clutches the highest and purest of earthly mold, degrading them into kindred with the lowest, and even with the very brutes, like whom their visible frames return to dust. In this manner, selecting it as the symbol of his wife's liability to sin, sorrow, decay, and death, Aylmer's somber imagination was not long in rendering the birthmark a frightful object, causing him more trouble and horror than ever Georgiana's beauty, whether of soul or sense, had given him delight.

At all the seasons which should have been their happiest, he invariably, and without intending it—nay, in spite of a purpose to the contrary—reverted to this one disastrous topic. Trifling as it at first appeared, it so connected itself with innumerable trains of thought, and modes of feeling, that it became the central point of all. With the morning twilight, Aylmer opened his eyes upon his wife's face, and recognized the symbol of imperfection; and when they sat together at the evening hearth, his eyes wandered stealthily to her cheek, and beheld, flickering with the blaze of the wood fire, the spectral Hand that wrote mortality where he would fain have worshiped.

Georgiana soon learned to shudder at his gaze. It needed but a glance, with the peculiar expression that his face often wore, to change the roses of her cheek into a death-like paleness, amid which the Crimson Hand was brought strongly out, like a bas-relief of ruby on the whitest marble.

Late, one night, when the lights were growing dim, so as hardly to betray the stain on the poor wife's cheek, she herself, for the first time, voluntarily took up the subject.

"Do you remember, my dear Aylmer," said she, with a feeble attempt at a smile—"have you any recollection of a dream, last night, about this odious Hand?"

"None! None whatever!" replied Aylmer, starting; but then he added in a dry, cold tone, affected for the sake of concealing the real depth of his emotion: "I might well dream of it; for, before I fell asleep, it had taken a pretty firm hold of my fancy."

"And you did dream of it," continued Georgiana, hastily; for she dreaded lest a gush of tears should interrupt what she had to say—"A terrible dream! I wonder that you can forget it. Is it possible to forget this one expression? 'It is in her heart now—we must have it out!' Reflect, my husband; for by all means I would have you recall that dream."

The mind is in a sad state, when Sleep cannot confine her specters within the dim region of her sway, but suffers them to break forth, affrighting this actual life with secrets that perchance belong to a deeper one. Aylmer now remembered his dream. He had fancied himself, with his servant Aminadab, attempting an operation for the removal of the birthmark. But the deeper went the knife, the deeper sank the Hand, until at length its tiny grasp appeared to have caught hold of Georgiana's heart; whence, however, her husband was inexorably resolved to cut or wrench it away.

When the dream had shaped itself perfectly in his memory, Aylmer sat in his wife's presence with a guilty feeling. Truth often finds its way to the mind close-muffled in robes of sleep, and then speaks with uncompromising directness of matters in regard to which we practice an unconscious self-deception, during our waking moments. Until now, he had not been aware of the tyrannizing influence acquired by one idea over his mind, and of the lengths which he might find in his heart to go, for the sake of giving himself peace.

"Aylmer," resumed Georgiana, solemnly, "I know not what may be the cost to both of us, to rid me of this fatal birthmark. Perhaps its removal may cause cureless deformity. Or, it may be, the stain goes as deep as life itself. Again, do we know that there is a possibility, on any terms, of unclasping the firm gripe of this little Hand, which was laid upon me before I came into the world?"

"Dearest Georgiana, I have spent much thought upon the subject," hastily interrupted Aylmer—"I am convinced of the perfect practicability of its removal."

"If there be the remotest possibility of it," continued Georgiana, "let the attempt be made, at whatever risk. Danger is nothing to me; for life—while this hateful mark makes me the object of your horror and disgust—life is a burthen which I would fling down with joy. Either remove this dreadful Hand, or take my wretched life! You have deep science! All the world bears witness of it. You have achieved great wonders! Cannot you remove this little, little mark, which I cover with the tips of two small fingers! Is this beyond your power, for the sake of your own peace, and to save your poor wife from madness?"

"Noblest, dearest, tenderest wife!" cried Aylmer, rapturously. "Doubt not my power. I have already given this matter the deepest thought—thought which might almost have enlightened me to create a being less perfect than yourself. Georgiana, you have led me deeper than ever into the heart of science. I feel myself fully competent to render this dear cheek as faultless as its fellow; and then, most beloved, what will be my triumph, when I shall have corrected what Nature left imperfect, in her fairest work! Even Pygmalion, when his sculptured woman assumed life, felt not greater ecstasy than mine will be."

"It is resolved, then," said Georgiana, faintly smiling—"And, Aylmer, spare me not, though you should find the birthmark take refuge in my heart at last."

Her husband tenderly kissed her cheek—her right cheek—not that which bore the impress of the Crimson Hand.

The next day, Aylmer apprized his wife of a plan that he had formed, whereby he might have opportunity for the intense thought and constant watchfulness which the proposed operation would require; while Georgiana, likewise, would enjoy the perfect repose essential to its success. They were to seclude themselves in the extensive apartments occupied by Aylmer as a laboratory, and where, during his toilsome youth, he had made discoveries in the elemental powers of Nature, that had roused the admiration of all the learned societies in Europe. Seated calmly in this laboratory, the pale philosopher had investigated the secrets of the highest cloud-region, and of the profoundest mines; he had satisfied himself of the causes that kindled and kept alive the fires of the volcano; and had explained the mystery of fountains, and how it is that they gush forth, some so bright and pure, and others with such rich medicinal virtues, from the dark bosom of the earth. Here, too, at an earlier period, he had studied the wonders of the human frame, and attempted to fathom the very process by which Nature assimilates all her precious influences from earth and air, and from the spiritual world, to create and foster Man, her masterpiece. The latter pursuit, however, Aylmer had long laid aside, in unwilling recognition of the truth, against which all seekers sooner or later stumble, that our great creative Mother, while she amuses us with apparently working in the broadest sunshine, is yet severely careful to keep her own secrets, and, in spite of her pretended openness, shows us nothing but results. She permits us indeed to mar, but seldom to mend, and, like a jealous patentee, on no account to make. Now, however, Aylmer resumed these half-forgotten investigations; not, of course, with such hopes or wishes as first suggested them; but because they involved much physiological truth, and lay in the path of his proposed scheme for the treatment of Georgiana.

As he led her over the threshold of the laboratory, Georgiana was cold and tremulous. Aylmer looked cheerfully into her face, with intent to reassure her, but was so startled with the intense glow of the birthmark upon the whiteness of her cheek, that he could not restrain a strong convulsive shudder. His wife fainted.

"Aminadab! Aminadab!" shouted Aylmer, stamping violently on the floor. Forthwith, there issued from an inner apartment a man of low stature, but bulky frame, with shaggy hair hanging about his visage, which was grimed with the vapors of the furnace. This personage had been Aylmer's under-worker during his whole scientific career, and was admirably fitted for that office by his great mechanical readiness, and the skill with which, while incapable of comprehending a single principle, he executed all the practical details of his master's experiments. With his vast strength, his shaggy hair, his smoky aspect, and the indescribable earthiness that encrusted him, he seemed to represent man's physical nature; while Aylmer's slender figure, and pale, intellectual face, were no less apt a type of the spiritual element.

"Throw open the door of the boudoir, Aminadab," said Aylmer, "and burn a pastille."

"Yes, master," answered Aminadab, looking intently at the lifeless form of Georgiana; and then he muttered to himself: "If she were my wife, I'd never part with that birthmark."

When Georgiana recovered consciousness, she found herself breathing an atmosphere of penetrating fragrance, the gentle potency of which had recalled her from her deathlike faintness. The scene around her looked like enchantment. Aylmer had converted those smoky, dingy, somber rooms, where he had spent his brightest years in recondite pursuits, into a series of beautiful apartments, not unfit to be the secluded abode of a lovely woman. The walls were hung with gorgeous curtains, which imparted the combination of grandeur and grace, that no other species of adornment can achieve; and as they fell from the ceiling to the floor, their rich and ponderous folds, concealing all angles and straight lines, appeared to shut in the scene from infinite space. For aught Georgiana knew, it might be a pavilion among the clouds. And Aylmer, excluding the sunshine, which would have interfered with his chemical processes, had supplied its place with perfumed lamps, emitting flames of various hue, but all uniting in a soft, empurpled radiance. He now knelt by his wife's side, watching her earnestly, but without alarm; for he was confident in his science, and felt that he could draw a magic circle round her, within which no evil might intrude.

"Where am I? Ah, I remember!" said Georgiana, faintly; and she placed her hand over her cheek, to hide the terrible mark from her husband's eyes.

"Fear not, dearest!" exclaimed he. "Do not shrink from me! Believe me, Georgiana, I even rejoice in this single imperfection, since it will be such a rapture to remove it."

"Oh, spare me!" sadly replied his wife. "Pray do not look at it again. I never can forget that convulsive shudder."

In order to soothe Georgiana, and, as it were, to release her mind from the burthen of actual things, Aylmer now put in practice some of the light and playful secrets which science had taught him among its profounder lore. Airy figures, absolutely bodiless ideas, and forms of unsubstantial beauty, came and danced before her, imprinting their momentary footsteps on beams of light. Though she had some indistinct idea of the method of these optical phenomena, still the illusion was almost perfect enough to warrant the belief that her husband possessed sway over the spiritual world. Then again, when she felt a wish to look forth from her seclusion, immediately, as if her thoughts were answered, the procession of external existence flitted across a screen. The scenery and the figures of actual life were perfectly represented, but with that bewitching, yet indescribable difference, which always makes a picture, an image, or a shadow, so much more attractive than the original. When wearied of this, Aylmer bade her cast her eyes upon a vessel, containing a quantity of earth. She did so, with little interest at first, but was soon startled, to perceive the germ of a plant, shooting upward from the soil. Then came the slender stalk—the leaves gradually unfolded themselves—and amid them was a perfect and lovely flower.

"It is magical!" cried Georgiana, "I dare not touch it."

"Nay, pluck it," answered Aylmer, "pluck it, and inhale its brief perfume while you may. The flower will wither in a few moments, and leave nothing save its brown seed-vessels but thence may be perpetuated a race as ephemeral as itself." But Georgiana had no sooner touched the flower than the whole plant suffered a blight, its leaves turning coal-black, as if by the agency of fire.

"There was too powerful a stimulus," said Aylmer thoughtfully.

To make up for this abortive experiment, he proposed to take her portrait by a scientific process of his own invention. It was to be effected by rays of light striking upon a polished plate of metal. Georgiana assented—but, on looking at the result, was affrighted to find the features of the portrait blurred and indefinable; while the minute figure of a hand appeared where the cheek should have been. Aylmer snatched the metallic plate, and threw it into a jar of corrosive acid.

Soon, however, he forgot these mortifying failures. In the intervals of study and chemical experiment, he came to her, flushed and exhausted, but seemed invigorated by her presence, and spoke in glowing language of the resources of his art. He gave a history of the long dynasty of the Alchemists, who spent so many ages in a quest of the universal solvent, by which the Golden Principle might be elicited from all things vile and base. Aylmer appeared to believe, that, by the plainest scientific logic, it was altogether within the limits of possibility to discover this long-sought medium; but, he added, a philosopher who should go deep enough to acquire the power, would attain too lofty a wisdom to stoop to the exercise of it. Not less singular were his opinions in regard to the Elixir Vitae. He more than intimated, that it was at his option to concoct a liquid that should prolong life for years—perhaps interminably—but that it would produce a discord in nature, which all the world, and chiefly the quaffer of the immortal nostrum, would find cause to curse.

"Aylmer, are you in earnest?" asked Georgiana, looking at him with amazement and fear; "it is terrible to possess such power, or even to dream of possessing it."

"Oh, do not tremble, my love!" said her husband, "I would not wrong either you or myself, by working such inharmonious effects upon our lives. But I would have you consider how trifling, in comparison, is the skill requisite to remove this little Hand." At the mention of the birthmark, Georgiana, as usual, shrank, as if a red-hot iron had touched her cheek.

Again Aylmer applied himself to his labors. She could hear his voice in the distant furnace-room, giving directions to Aminadab, whose harsh, uncouth, misshapen tones were audible in response, more like the grunt or growl of a brute than human speech. After hours of absence, Aylmer reappeared, and proposed that she should now examine his cabinet of chemical products, and natural treasures of the earth. Among the former, he showed her a small vial, in which, he remarked, was contained a gentle yet most powerful fragrance, capable of impregnating all the breezes that blow across a kingdom. They were of inestimable value, the contents of that little vial; and, as he said so, he threw some of the perfume into the air, and filled the room with piercing and invigorating delight.

"And what is this?" asked Georgiana, pointing to a small crystal globe, containing a gold-colored liquid. "It is so beautiful to the eye, that I could imagine it the Elixir of Life."

"In one sense it is," replied Aylmer, "or rather the Elixir of Immortality. It is the most precious poison that ever was concocted in this world. By its aid, I could

apportion the lifetime of any mortal at whom you might point your finger. The strength of the dose would determine whether he were to linger out years, or drop dead in the midst of a breath. No king, on his guarded throne, could keep his life, if I, in my private station, should deem that the welfare of millions justified me in depriving him of it."

"Why do you keep such a terrific drug?" inquired Georgiana in horror.

"Do not mistrust me, dearest!" said her husband, smiling; "its virtuous potency is yet greater than its harmful one. But, see! Here is a powerful cosmetic. With a few drops of this, in a vase of water, freckles may be washed away as easily as the hands are cleansed. A stronger infusion would take the blood out of the cheek, and leave the rosiest beauty a pale ghost."

"Is it with this lotion that you intend to bathe my cheek?" asked Georgiana, anxiously.

"Oh, no!" hastily replied her husband, "this is merely superficial. Your case demands a remedy that shall go deeper."

In his interviews with Georgiana, Aylmer generally made minute inquiries as to her sensations, and whether the confinement of the rooms, and the temperature of the atmosphere, agreed with her. These questions had such a particular drift, that Georgiana began to conjecture that she was already subjected to certain physical influences, either breathed in with the fragrant air, or taken with her food. She fancied, likewise—but it might be altogether fancy—that there was a stirring up of her system: a strange, indefinite sensation creeping through her veins, and tingling, half-painfully, half-pleasurably, at her heart. Still, whenever she dared to look into the mirror, there she beheld herself, pale as a white rose, and with the crimson birthmark stamped upon her cheek. Not even Aylmer now hated it so much as she.

To dispel the tedium of the hours which her husband found it necessary to devote to the processes of combination and analysis, Georgiana turned over the volumes of his scientific library. In many dark old tomes, she met with chapters full of romance and poetry. They were the works of the philosophers of the middle ages, such as Albertus Magnus, Cornelius Agrippa, Paracelsus, and the famous friar who created the prophetic Brazen Head. All these antique naturalists stood in advance of their centuries, yet were imbued with some of their credulity, and therefore were believed, and perhaps imagined themselves, to have acquired from the investigation of nature a power above nature, and from physics a sway over the spiritual world. Hardly less curious and imaginative were the early volumes of the Transactions of the Royal Society, in which the members, knowing little of the limits of natural possibility, were continually recording wonders, or proposing methods whereby wonders might be wrought.

But, to Georgiana, the most engrossing volume was a large folio from her husband's own hand, in which he had recorded every experiment of his scientific career, with its original aim, the methods adopted for its development, and its final success or failure, with the circumstances to which either event was attributable. The book, in truth, was both the history and emblem of his ardent, ambitious, imaginative, yet practical and laborious, life. He handled physical details, as if there were nothing beyond them; yet spiritualized them all, and redeemed himself from materialism, by his strong and eager aspiration toward the infinite. In his grasp, the veriest clod of earth assumed a soul. Georgiana, as she read, reverenced Aylmer, and loved him more profoundly than ever, but with a less entire dependence on his judgment than heretofore. Much as he had accomplished, she could not but observe that his most splendid successes were almost invariably failures, if compared with the ideal at which he aimed. His brightest diamonds were the merest pebbles, and felt to be so by himself, in comparison with the inestimable gems which lay hidden beyond his reach. The volume, rich with achievements that had won renown for its author, was yet as melancholy a record as ever mortal hand had penned. It was the sad confession, and continual exemplification, of the short-comings of the composite man—the spirit burthened with clay and working in matter; and of the despair that assails the higher nature, at finding itself so miserably thwarted by the earthly part. Perhaps every man of genius, in whatever sphere, might recognize the image of his own experience in Aylmer's journal.

So deeply did these reflections affect Georgiana, that she laid her face upon the open volume, and burst into tears. In this situation she was found by her husband.

"It is dangerous to read in a sorcerer's books," said he, with a smile, though his countenance was uneasy and displeased. "Georgiana, there are pages in that volume, which I can scarcely glance over and keep my senses. Take heed lest it prove as detrimental to you!"

"It has made me worship you more than ever," said she.

"Ah! wait for this one success," rejoined he, "then worship me if you will. I shall deem myself hardly

unworthy of it. But, come! I have sought you for the luxury of your voice. Sing to me, dearest!"

So she poured out the liquid music of her voice to quench the thirst of his spirit. He then took his leave, with a boyish exuberance of gaiety, assuring her that her seclusion would endure but a little longer, and that the result was already certain. Scarcely had he departed, when Georgiana felt irresistibly impelled to follow him. She had forgotten to inform Aylmer of a symptom, which, for two or three hours past, had begun to excite her attention. It was a sensation in the fatal birthmark, not painful, but which induced a restlessness throughout her system. Hastening after her husband, she intruded, for the first time, into the laboratory.

The first thing that struck her eye was the furnace, that hot and feverish worker, with the intense glow of its fire, which, by the quantities of soot clustered above it, seemed to have been burning for ages. There was a distilling apparatus in full operation. Around the room were retorts, tubes, cylinders, crucibles, and other apparatus of chemical research. An electrical machine stood ready for immediate use. The atmosphere felt oppressively close, and was tainted with gaseous odors, which had been tormented forth by the processes of science. The severe and homely simplicity of the apartment, with its naked walls and brick pavement, looked strange, accustomed as Georgiana had become to the fantastic elegance of her boudoir. But what chiefly, indeed almost solely, drew her attention, was the aspect of Aylmer himself.

He was pale as death, anxious, and absorbed, and hung over the furnace as if it depended upon his utmost watchfulness whether the liquid, which it was distilling, should be the draught of immortal happiness or misery. How different from the sanguine and joyous mien that he had assumed for Georgiana's encouragement!

"Carefully now, Aminadab! Carefully, thou human machine! Carefully, thou man of clay!" muttered Aylmer, more to himself than his assistant. "Now, if there be a thought too much or too little, it is all over!"

"Hoh! Hoh!" mumbled Aminadab—"look, master, look!"

Aylmer raised his eyes hastily, and at first reddened, then grew paler than ever, on beholding Georgiana. He rushed towards her, and seized her arm with a gripe that left the print of his fingers upon it.

"Why do you come hither? Have you no trust in your husband?" cried he impetuously. "Would you throw the blight of that fatal birthmark over my labors? It is not well done. Go, prying woman, go!"

"Nay, Aylmer," said Georgiana, with the firmness of which she possessed no stinted endowment, "it is not you that have a right to complain. You mistrust your wife! You have concealed the anxiety with which you watch the development of this experiment. Think not so unworthily of me, my husband! Tell me all the risk we run and fear not that I shall shrink, for my share in it is far less than your own!"

"No, no, Georgiana!" said Aylmer impatiently, "it must not be."

"I submit," replied she calmly. "And, Aylmer, I shall quaff whatever drought you bring me; but it will be on the same principle that would induce me to take a dose of poison, if offered by your hand."

"My noble wife," said Aylmer, deeply moved, "I knew not the height and depth of your nature, until now. Nothing shall be concealed. Know, then, that this Crimson Hand, superficial as it seems, has clutched its grasp into your being, with a strength of which I had no previous conception. I have already administered agents powerful enough to do aught except to change your entire physical system. Only one thing remains to be tried. If that fail us, we are ruined!"

"Why did you hesitate to tell me this?" asked she.

"Because, Georgiana," said Aylmer, in a low voice, "there is danger!"

"Danger? There is but one danger—that this horrible stigma shall be left upon my cheek!" cried Georgiana. "Remove it! remove it!—whatever be the cost—or we shall both go mad!"

"Heaven knows, your words are too true," said Aylmer, sadly. "And now, dearest, return to your boudoir. In a little while, all will be tested."

He conducted her back, and took leave of her with a solemn tenderness, which spoke far more than his words how much was now at stake. After his departure, Georgiana became wrapped in musings. She considered the character of Aylmer, and did it completer justice than at any previous moment. Her heart exulted, while it trembled, at his honorable love, so pure and lofty that it would accept nothing less than perfection, nor miserably make itself contented with an earthlier nature than he had dreamed of. She felt how much more precious was such a sentiment, than that meaner kind which would have borne with the imperfection for her sake, and have been guilty of treason to holy love, by degrading its perfect idea to the level of the actual. And, with her whole spirit, she prayed, that, for a single moment, she might satisfy his highest and deepest conception. Longer than one moment, she well knew, it could not be; for his spirit was ever on the march—ever ascending—and each instant required something that was beyond the scope of the instant before.

The sound of her husband's footsteps aroused her. He bore a crystal goblet, containing a liquor colorless as water, but bright enough to be the drought of immortality. Aylmer was pale; but it seemed rather the consequence of a highly wrought state of mind, and tension of spirit, than of fear or doubt.

"The concoction of the drought has been perfect," said he, in answer to Georgiana's look. "Unless all my science have deceived me, it cannot fail."

"Save on your account, my dearest Aylmer," observed his wife, "I might wish to put off this birthmark of mortality by relinquishing mortality itself, in preference to any other mode. Life is but a sad possession to those who have attained precisely the degree of moral advancement at which I stand. Were I weaker and blinder, it might be happiness. Were I stronger, it might be endured hopefully. But, being what I find myself, methinks I am of all mortals the most fit to die."

"You are fit for heaven without tasting death!" replied her husband. "But why do we speak of dying? The drought cannot fail. Behold its effect upon this plant!"

On the window-seat there stood a geranium, diseased with yellow blotches, which had overspread all its leaves. Aylmer poured a small quantity of the liquid upon the soil in which it grew. In a little time, when the roots of the plant had taken up the moisture, the unsightly blotches began to be extinguished in a living verdure.

"There needed no proof," said Georgiana, quietly. "Give me the goblet. I joyfully stake all upon your word."

"Drink, then, thou lofty creature!" exclaimed Aylmer, with fervid admiration. "There is no taint of imperfection on thy spirit. Thy sensible frame, too, shall soon be all perfect!"

She quaffed the liquid, and returned the goblet to his hand.

"It is grateful," said she, with a placid smile. "Methinks it is like water from a heavenly fountain; for it contains I know not what of unobtrusive fragrance and deliciousness. It allays a feverish thirst, that had parched me for many days. Now, dearest, let me sleep. My earthly senses are closing over my spirit, like the leaves around the heart of a rose, at sunset."

She spoke the last words with a gentle reluctance, as if it required almost more energy than she could command to pronounce the faint and lingering syllables. Scarcely had they loitered through her lips, ere she was lost in slumber. Aylmer sat by her side, watching her aspect with the emotions proper to a man, the whole value of whose existence was involved in the process now to be tested. Mingled with this mood, however, was the philosophic investigation, characteristic of the man of science. Not the minutest symptom escaped him. A heightened flush of the cheek—a slight irregularity of breath—a quiver of the eyelid—a hardly perceptible tremor through the frame—such were the details which, as the moments passed, he wrote down in his folio volume. Intense thought had set its stamp upon every previous page of that volume; but the thoughts of years were all concentrated upon the last.

While thus employed, he failed not to gaze often at the fatal Hand, and not without a shudder. Yet once, by a strange and unaccountable impulse, he pressed it with his lips. His spirit recoiled, however, in the very act, and Georgiana, out of the midst of her deep sleep, moved uneasily and murmured, as if in remonstrance. Again, Aylmer resumed his watch. Nor was it without avail. The Crimson Hand, which at first had been strongly visible upon the marble paleness of Georgiana's cheek now grew more faintly outlined. She remained not less pale than ever; but the birthmark, with every breath that came and went, lost somewhat of its former distinctness. Its presence had been awful; its departure was more awful still. Watch the stain of the rainbow fading out of the sky; and you will know how that mysterious symbol passed away.

"By Heaven, it is well-nigh gone!" said Aylmer to himself, in almost irrepressible ecstasy. "I can scarcely trace it now. Success! Success! And now it is like the faintest rose-color. The slightest flush of blood across her cheek would overcome it. But she is so pale!"

He drew aside the window-curtain, and suffered the light of natural day to fall into the room, and rest upon her cheek. At the same time, he heard a gross, hoarse chuckle, which he had long known as his servant Aminadab's expression of delight.

"Ah, clod! Ah, earthly mass!" cried Aylmer, laughing in a sort of frenzy. "You have served me well! Master and Spirit—Earth and Heaven—have both done their part in this! Laugh, thing of the senses! You have earned the right to laugh."

These exclamations broke Georgiana's sleep. She slowly unclosed her eyes, and gazed into the mirror, which her husband had arranged for that purpose. A faint smile flitted over her lips, when she recognized how barely perceptible was now that Crimson Hand, which had once blazed forth with such disastrous brilliancy as to scare away all their happiness. But then her eyes sought Aylmer's face, with a trouble and anxiety that he could by no means account for.

"My poor Aylmer!" murmured she.

"Poor? Nay, richest! Happiest! Most favored!" exclaimed he. "My peerless bride, it is successful! You are perfect!"

"My poor Aylmer!" she repeated, with a more than human tenderness. "You have aimed loftily! You have done nobly! Do not repent, that, with so high and pure a feeling, you have rejected the best the earth could offer. Aylmer—dearest Aylmer, I am dying!"

Alas, it was too true! The fatal Hand had grappled with the mystery of life, and was the bond by which an angelic spirit kept itself in union with a mortal frame. As the last crimson tint of the birthmark—that sole token of human imperfection—faded from her cheek, the parting breath of the now perfect woman passed into the atmosphere, and her soul, lingering a moment near her husband, took its heavenward flight. Then a hoarse, chuckling laugh was heard again! Thus ever does the gross Fatality of Earth exult in its invariable triumph over the immortal essence, which, in this dim sphere of half-development, demands the completeness of a higher state. Yet, had Aylmer reached a profounder wisdom, he need not thus have flung away the happiness, which would have woven his mortal life of the self-same texture with the celestial. The momentary circumstance was too strong for him; he failed to look beyond the shadowy scope of Time, and living once for all in Eternity, to find the perfect Future in the present. http://www.angeltowns.com/members/shortstories/index.html

CRITICAL THINKING

A. As stated previously, Hawthorne flirted with Transcendentalism/ Romanticism but never left his theistic romanticism. Find examples of theistic romanticism in "The Birthmark."

B. Aylmer was a character who represents a modern nineteenth century scientist. Hawthorne was one of the earliest writers to point out the limits of science. Others include Mary Shelley, *Frankenstein*, and Robert Louis Stevenson, *Dr. Jekyl and Mr. Hyde*. In his book *The Age of Evolution*, George Gaylord Simpson argues that science (especially evolution) can suggest that "man is the result of a purposeless and materialistic process that did not have him in mind . . . the universe . . . lacked any purpose or plan . . . (this) has the inevitable corollary that the workings of the universe cannot provide any automatic, universal, eternal or absolute criteria of right or wrong." With all his heart Hawthorne believed that science could become a "god." What Hawthorne understood was how science related to knowledge (epistemology). He understood the danger of Transcendentalism or any other worldview that replaced Christianity. With the disestablishment of Christianity, western society has wrestled with epistemology for the past several hundred years. If materialism is one's metaphysics, then scientism becomes one's dominant epistemology. Science became the way to know anything that was to be known. Do you share Hawthorne's fear of the power of science? Why or why not?

C. How can Aylmer love both science and Georgiana? Are these loves mutually contradictory?

D. What basic differences are there between Aylmer's worldview and Transcendentalism?

E. In the final analysis, Aylmer's attempts to perfect Georgiana are doomed to failure. Why?

F. This story is an allegory. What moral quality is represented by Aylmer? By Georgiana? Aminadab? In a two-page essay, describe how Hawthorne sets up this allegory.

BIBLICAL APPLICATION

Pretend you are Aylmer's pastor. He has come to you to seek advice about his wife's physical flaw. How do you respond?

ENRICHMENT

A. Compare the theme(s) of this short story with the theme(s) of Mary Shelley's *Frankenstein*.

B. Compare and contrast Aylmer and Chillingsworth (*The Scarlet Letter*).

C. One of the places that science has failed us is in the area of the origins of man. In his book *Darwin on Trial* Phillip E. Johnson skillfully argues that Evolution—specifically natural selection—is a tautology. A tautology is a way of saying the same thing twice. Natural selection predicts that the fittest organisms will produce the most offspring, and it defines the fittest organisms as the ones that produce the most offspring! Can you find other tautologies in modern science?

FINAL PROJECT

Correct and rewrite all essays and place them in your Final Portfolio.

SUGGESTED
Weekly *Implementation*

DAY 1	DAY 2	DAY 3	DAY 4	DAY 5
Prayer journal.	**Prayer journal.**	**Prayer journal.**	**Prayer journal.**	**Prayer journal.**
Review the required reading(s) *before* the assigned lesson begins.	Review reading(s) from next lesson.	Write rough drafts of all assigned essays.	Rewrite corrected copies of essays due tomorrow.	Essays are due.
Teacher may want to discuss assigned reading(s) with students.	Outline essays due at the end of the week.	The teacher and/or a peer evaluator may correct rough drafts.		Take the Lesson 8 test.
Teacher and students will decide on the number or required essays for this lesson, choosing two or three essays.	Per teacher instructions, students may answer orally in a group setting some of the essays that are not assigned as formal essays.			Reading ahead: Review poems by Henry Wadsworth Longfellow, Oliver Wendell Holmes, James Russell Lowell, John Greenleaf Whittier, and Emily Dickenson.
The rest of the essays can be outlined, answered with shorter answers, or skipped.				Guide: What moral vision do these poets present?
Students will review all readings for Lesson 8.				

ROMANTICISM: NEW ENGLAND RENAISSANCE, *1840-1855 (Part 2)*

As you read this lesson's literary selections, prepare to answer the following questions:

CRITICAL THINKING

A. Find examples of Romanticism in each poem.

B. Give an example of satire in "The Biglow Papers" and discuss its purpose.

C. What is Holmes' view of heaven?

D. Longfellow was popular among ordinary people but mostly criticized by scholars. People loved the very thing that critics disliked: the predictable narrative enclosed in tiresome rimes. Agree or disagree with the critics.

E. What is so modern about Dickinson's poetry?

FINAL PROJECT:

Correct and rewrite all essays and place them in your Final Portfolio.

You will analyze: poems by Henry Wadsworth Longfellow, Oliver Wendell Holmes, James Russell Lowell, John Greenleaf Whittier, and Emily Dickinson.

Reading Ahead: Poems by Ralph Waldo Emerson.

Guide Question: In what ways are Emerson's poems religious?

understood and full of rime and meter. Above all, though, Longfellow wrote with optimism and hope uncharacteristic of the post-Civil War.

Paul Revere's Ride

Listen my children and you shall hear
Of the midnight ride of Paul Revere,
On the eighteenth of April, in Seventy-five;
Hardly a man is now alive
Who remembers that famous day and year.

He said to his friend, "If the British march
By land or sea from the town tonight,
Hang a lantern aloft in the belfry arch
Of the North Church tower as a signal light,

Henry Wadsworth Longfellow

© Arttoday.com

Probably the best loved of American poets is Henry Wadsworth Longfellow. Many of his lines are as familiar to us as rhymes from Mother Goose or the words of nursery songs learned in early childhood. Longfellow wrote on archetypal themes which appeal to all kinds of people. His poems are easily

© Arttoday.com

One if by land, and two if by sea;
And I on the opposite shore will be,
Ready to ride and spread the alarm
Through every Middlesex village and farm,
For the country folk to be up and to arm."

Then he said "Good-night!" and with muffled oar
Silently rowed to the Charlestown shore,
Just as the moon rose over the bay,
Where swinging wide at her moorings lay
The Somerset, British man-of-war;
A phantom ship, with each mast and spar
Across the moon like a prison bar,
And a huge black hulk, that was magnified
By its own reflection in the tide.

Meanwhile, his friend through alley and street
Wanders and watches, with eager ears,
Till in the silence around him he hears
The muster of men at the barrack door,
The sound of arms, and the tramp of feet,
And the measured tread of the grenadiers,
Marching down to their boats on the shore.

Then he climbed the tower of the Old North Church,
By the wooden stairs, with stealthy tread,
To the belfry chamber overhead,
And startled the pigeons from their perch
On the sombre rafters, that round him made
Masses and moving shapes of shade,
By the trembling ladder, steep and tall,
To the highest window in the wall,
Where he paused to listen and look down
A moment on the roofs of the town
And the moonlight flowing over all.

Beneath, in the churchyard, lay the dead,
In their night encampment on the hill,
Wrapped in silence so deep and still
That he could hear, like a sentinel's tread,
The watchful night-wind, as it went
Creeping along from tent to tent,
And seeming to whisper, "All is well!"
A moment only he feels the spell
Of the place and the hour, and the secret dread
Of the lonely belfry and the dead;
For suddenly all his thoughts are bent
On a shadowy something far away,
Where the river widens to meet the bay,
A line of black that bends and floats
On the rising tide like a bridge of boats.

Meanwhile, impatient to mount and ride,
Booted and spurred, with a heavy stride
On the opposite shore walked Paul Revere.
Now he patted his horse's side,
Now he gazed at the landscape far and near,
Then, impetuous, stamped the earth,
And turned and tightened his saddle girth;
But mostly he watched with eager search
The belfry tower of the Old North Church,
As it rose above the graves on the hill,
Lonely and spectral and sombre and still.
And lo! as he looks, on the belfry's height
A glimmer, and then a gleam of light!
He springs to the saddle, the bridle he turns,
But lingers and gazes, till full on his sight
A second lamp in the belfry burns.

A hurry of hoofs in a village street,
A shape in the moonlight, a bulk in the dark,
And beneath, from the pebbles, in passing, a spark
Struck out by a steed flying fearless and fleet;
That was all! And yet, through the gloom and the
    light,
The fate of a nation was riding that night;
And the spark struck out by that steed, in his flight,
Kindled the land into flame with its heat.

© Arttoday.com

© Arttoday.com

He has left the village and mounted the steep,
And beneath him, tranquil and broad and deep,
Is the Mystic, meeting the ocean tides;
And under the alders that skirt its edge,
Now soft on the sand, now loud on the ledge,
Is heard the tramp of his steed as he rides.

It was twelve by the village clock
When he crossed the bridge into Medford town.
He heard the crowing of the cock,
And the barking of the farmer's dog,
And felt the damp of the river fog,
That rises after the sun goes down.

It was one by the village clock,
When he galloped into Lexington.
He saw the gilded weathercock
Swim in the moonlight as he passed,
And the meeting-house windows, black and bare,
Gaze at him with a spectral glare,
As if they already stood aghast
At the bloody work they would look upon.

It was two by the village clock,
When he came to the bridge in Concord town.
He heard the bleating of the flock,

And the twitter of birds among the trees,
And felt the breath of the morning breeze
Blowing over the meadow brown.
And one was safe and asleep in his bed
Who at the bridge would be first to fall,
Who that day would be lying dead,
Pierced by a British musket ball.

You know the rest. In the books you have read
How the British Regulars fired and fled,
How the farmers gave them ball for ball,
From behind each fence and farmyard wall,
Chasing the redcoats down the lane,
Then crossing the fields to emerge again
Under the trees at the turn of the road,
And only pausing to fire and load.

So through the night rode Paul Revere;
And so through the night went his cry of alarm
To every Middlesex village and farm,
A cry of defiance, and not of fear,
A voice in the darkness, a knock at the door,
And a word that shall echo for evermore!
For, borne on the night-wind of the Past,
Through all our history, to the last,
In the hour of darkness and peril and need,
The people will waken and listen to hear
The hurrying hoof-beats of that steed,
And the midnight message of Paul Revere.
http://eserver.org/poetry/paul_revere.html

Oliver Wendell Holmes

Oliver Wendell Holmes (1809-1894) was born in Cambridge, Massachusetts, August 29, 1809, and educated at Harvard College. After graduation, he entered the Law School but soon gave up law for medicine. From 1847 to 1882 he was a professor of anatomy and physiology in the Harvard Medical School. He died in Boston, October 7, 1894. Holmes's reputation as a scientist was overshadowed by his reputation as a poet.

The Chambered Nautilus

THIS is the ship of pearl, which, poets feign,
Sails the unshadowed main, —
The venturous bark that flings
On the sweet summer wind its purpled wings
In gulfs enchanted, where the siren sings,
And coral reefs lie bare,
Where the cold sea-maids rise to sun their streaming hair.

Its webs of living gauze no more unfurl;
Wrecked is the ship of pearl!
And every chambered cell,
Where its dim dreaming life was wont to dwell,
As the frail tenant shaped his growing shell,
Before thee lies revealed, —
Its irised ceiling rent, its sunless crypt unsealed!

Year after year beheld the silent toil
That spread his lustrous coil;
Still, as the spiral grew,
He left the past year's dwelling for the new,
Stole with soft step its shining archway through,
Built up its idle door,
Stretched in his last-found home, and knew the old no more.

Thanks for the heavenly message brought by thee,
Child of the wandering sea,
Cast from her lap, forlorn!
From thy dead lips a clearer note is born
Than ever Triton blew from wreathèd horn!
While on mine ear it rings,
Through the deep caves of thought I hear a voice that sings:

Build thee more stately mansions, O my soul,
As the swift seasons roll!
Leave thy low-vaulted past!
Let each new temple, nobler than the last,
Shut thee from heaven with a dome more vast,
Till thou at length art free,
Leaving thine outgrown shell by life's unresting sea!
http://stellar-one.com/poems/

The Last Leaf

I SAW him once before,
As he passed by the door;
And again
The pavement stones resound,
As he totters o'er the ground
With his cane.

They say that in his prime,
Ere the pruning-knife of Time
Cut him down,
Not a better man was found
By the Crier on his round
Through the town.

But now he walks the streets,
And he looks at all he meets
Sad and wan;
And shakes his feeble head,
That it seems as if he said,
"They are gone."

The mossy marbles rest
On the lips that he has prest
In their bloom;
And the names he loved to hear
Have been carved for many a year
On the tomb.

My grandmamma has said —
Poor old lady, she is dead
Long ago —
That he had a Roman nose,
And his cheek was like a rose
In the snow.

But now his nose is thin,
And it rests upon his chin
Like a staff;
And a crook is in his back,
And a melancholy crack
In his laugh.

I know it is a sin
For me to sit and grin
At him here;

But the old three-cornered hat,
And the breeches and all that,
Are so queer!

And if I should live to be
The last leaf upon the tree
In the spring,
Let them smile, as I do now,

At the old forsaken bough
Where I cling.
http://stellar-one.com/poems/

James Russell Lowell

JAMES RUSSELL LOWELL.

James Russell Lowell (1819-1891) was born at Cambridge, Massachusetts, the son of a Unitarian minister. Educated at Harvard College, he tried the law, but soon gave it up for literature. In 1857 he became the first editor of the *Atlantic Monthly* and after 1864, he collaborated with Charles Eliot Norton in the editorship of the *North American Review*.

Selections from the Biglow Papers

What Mr. Robinson Thinks
GUVENER B. is a sensible man;
He stays to his home an' looks arter his folks;
He draws his furrer ez straight ez he can,
An' into nobody's tater-patch pokes;
But John P.
Robinson he
Sez he wunt vote fer Guvener B.

My! aint it terrible? Wut shall we du?
We can't never choose him o' course,—thet's flat;
Guess we shall hev to come round, (don't you?)
An' go in fer thunder an' guns, an' all that;
Fer John P.
Robinson he
Sez he wunt vote fer Guvener B.

Gineral C. is a dreffle smart man;
He's ben on all sides thet give places or pelf;
But consistency still wuz a part of his plan,—

He's been true to one party,—an' thet is himself;
So John P.
Robinson he
Sez he shall vote fer Gineral C.

Gineral C. he goes in fer the war;
He don't vally principle morn'n an old cud;
Wut did God make us raytional creeturs fer,
But glory an' gunpowder, plunder an' blood?
So John P.
Robinson he
Sez he shall vote fer Gineral C.

We were gittin' on nicely up here to our village,
With good old idees o' wut's right an' wut aint,
We kind o' thought Christ went agin war an' pillage,
An' thet eppyletts worn't the best mark of a saint;
But John P.
Robinson he
Sez this kind o' thing's an exploded idee.

The side of our country must ollers be took,
An' Presidunt Polk, you know, he is our country.
An' the angel thet writes all our sins in a book
Puts the debit to him, an' to us the per contry;
An' John P.
Robinson he
Sez this is his view o' the thing to a T.

Parson Wilbur he calls all these argimunts lies;
Sez they're nothin, on airth but jest fee, faw, fum:
An' thet all this big talk of our destinies
Is half on it ign'ance, an' t'other half rum;
But John P.
Robinson he
Sez it aint no sech thing; an', of course, so must we.

Parson Wilbur sez he never heerd in his life
Thet th' Apostles rigged out in their swaller-tail coats,
An' marched round in front of a drum an' a fife,
To git some on 'em office, an' some on 'em votes;
But John P.
Robinson he
Sez they didn't know everythin' down in Judee.

Wal, it's a marcy we've gut folks to tell us
The rights an' the wrongs o' these matters, I vow,
God sends country lawyers, an' other wise fellers,
To start the world's team wen it gits in a slough;
Fer John P.
Robinson he
Sez the world'll go right, ef he hollers out Gee!
http://www.4literature.net/James_Russell_Lowell/Selections_from_The_Biglow_Papers/2.html

John Greenleaf Whittier

JOHN GREENLEAF WHITTIER.

John Greenleaf Whittier (1807-1892), also a New Englander, was an abolitionist, too.

The Barefoot Boy

Blessings on thee, little man,
Barefoot boy, with cheek of tan!
With thy turned-up pantaloons,
And thy merry whistled tunes;
With thy red lip, redder still
Kissed by strawberries on the hill;
With the sunshine on thy face,
Through thy torn brim's jaunty grace;
From my heart I give thee joy, —
I was once a barefoot boy!
Prince thou art, — the grown-up man
Only is republican.
Let the million-dollared ride!
Barefoot, trudging at his side,
Thou hast more than he can buy
In the reach of ear and eye, —
Outward sunshine, inward joy:
Blessings on thee, barefoot boy!

Oh for boyhood's painless play,
Sleep that wakes in laughing day,
Health that mocks the doctor's rules,
Knowledge never learned of schools,
Of the wild bee's morning chase,
Of the wild-flower's time and place,
Flight of fowl and habitude
Of the tenants of the wood;
How the tortoise bears his shell,
How the woodchuck digs his cell,
And the ground-mole sinks his well;
How the robin feeds her young,
How the oriole's nest is hung;
Where the whitest lilies blow,
Where the freshest berries grow,
Where the ground-nut trails its vine,
Where the wood-grape's clusters shine;
Of the black wasp's cunning way,
Mason of his walls of clay,
And the architectural plans
Of gray hornet artisans!

For, eschewing books and tasks,
Nature answers all he asks;
Hand in hand with her he walks,
Face to face with her he talks,
Part and parcel of her joy, —
Blessings on the barefoot boy!

Oh for boyhood's time of June,
Crowding years in one brief moon,
When all things I heard or saw,
Me, their master, waited for.
I was rich in flowers and trees,
Humming-birds and honey-bees;
For my sport the squirrel played,
Plied the snouted mole his spade;
For my taste the blackberry cone
Purpled over hedge and stone;
Laughed the brook for my delight
Through the day and through the night,
Whispering at the garden wall,
Talked with me from fall to fall;
Mine the sand-rimmed pickerel pond,
Mine the walnut slopes beyond,
Mine, on bending orchard trees,
Apples of Hesperides!
Still as my horizon grew,
Larger grew my riches too;
All the world I saw or knew
Seemed a complex Chinese toy,
Fashioned for a barefoot boy!
Oh for festal dainties spread,
Like my bowl of milk and bread;
Pewter spoon and bowl of wood,
On the door-stone, gray and rude!
O'er me, like a regal tent,
Cloudy-ribbed, the sunset bent,
Purple-curtained, fringed with gold,
Looped in many a wind-swung fold;
While for music came the play
Of the pied frogs' orchestra;
And, to light the noisy choir,
Lit the fly his lamp of fire.
I was monarch: pomp and joy
Waited on the barefoot boy!

Cheerily, then, my little man,
Live and laugh, as boyhood can!
Though the flinty slopes be hard,
Stubble-speared the new-mown sward,
Every morn shall lead thee through
Fresh baptisms of the dew;

Every evening from thy feet
Shall the cool wind kiss the heat:
All too soon these feet must hide
In the prison cells of pride,
Lose the freedom of the sod,
Like a colt's for work be shod,
Made to treat the mills of toil,
Up and down in ceaseless moil:
Happy if their track be found
Never on forbidden ground;
Happy if they sink not in
Quick and treacherous sands of sin.
Ah! that thou couldst know thy joy,
Ere it passes, barefoot boy!
http://eir.library.utoronto.ca/rpo/display/poem2296.html

Emily Dickinson

© Arttoday.com

Emily Dickinson, "the belle of Amherst," is almost as famous for her mysteriously secluded life as for her poetry, which ranks her with Walt Whitman as one of the most gifted poets in modern American literature. In fact, she and Whitman introduced "Realism in poetry." She never married, and after age 30 she became a recluse. Some scholars believe that this was her response to the narrow literary establishment of her time, which expected female writers to limit their subjects to home life and romance. Dickinson, on the other hand, preferred images of real life.

Of Dickinson's 1700 plus poems, only 10 were published in her lifetime, and those without her permission. After her death, however, her sister found and published the body of her work. Dickinson wrote from a Romantic worldview in a decidedly modern way.

Emancipation

No rack can torture me,
My soul's at liberty
Behind this mortal bone
There knits a bolder one
You cannot prick with saw, Nor rend with scymitar.
Two bodies therefore be;
Bind one, and one will flee.
The eagle of his nest
No easier divest
And gain the sky,
Than mayest thou,
Except thyself may be
Thine enemy;
Captivity is consciousness,
So's liberty.
http://www.classicreader.com/read.php/sid.4bookid.10
　　87/sec.112/

I'm nobody! Who are you?

I'm nobody! Who are you?
Are you nobody, too?
Then there 's a pair of us—don't tell!
They 'd banish us, you know.
How dreary to be somebody!
How public, like a frog
To tell your name the livelong day
To an admiring bog!
http://www.classicreader.com/read.php/sid.1bookid.11
　　24/sec.3/

SUGGESTED
Weekly *Implementation*

DAY 1	DAY 2	DAY 3	DAY 4	DAY 5
Prayer journal.	**Prayer journal.**	**Prayer journal.**	**Prayer journal.**	**Prayer journal.**
Review the required reading(s) *before* the assigned lesson begins.	Review reading(s) from next lesson.	Write rough drafts of all assigned essays.	Rewrite corrected copies of essays due tomorrow.	Essays are due.
Teacher may want to discuss assigned reading(s) with students.	Outline essays due at the end of the week.	The teacher and/or a peer evaluator may correct rough drafts.		Take Lesson 9 test.
Teacher and students will decide on the number of required essays for this lesson, choosing two or three essays.	Per teacher instructions, students may answer orally in a group setting some of the essays that are not assigned as formal essays.			Reading ahead: Review poems by Ralph Waldo Emerson.
The rest of the essays can be outlined, answered with shorter answers, or skipped.				Guide: In what ways are Emerson's poems religious?
Review all readings for Lesson 9.				

LESSON 10

ROMANTICISM: NEW ENGLAND RENAISSANCE, *1840-1855 (Part 3)*

Ralph Waldo Emerson

BACKGROUND

Ralph Waldo Emerson
© Arttoday.com

Ralph Waldo Emerson represents well the transition from Puritanism to Transcendentalism. Though closely related to European Romanticism, Transcendentalism is a philosophical movement that has a peculiarly American flavor. Both Romanticism and Transcendentalism celebrate individualism and subjectivity. Both argue that intuition is more important than stated fact. Two of the most famous European Romantics were Goethe and Beethoven. Two of the most famous American Transcendentalists were Emerson and Thoreau.

CRITICAL THINKING

A. Research Transcendentalism and the effect it had on American thought.

B. Explain why Romanticism/Transcendentalism flourished in America during the 1960s, as it did in the 1830s.

C. The last six lines of "The Snowstorm" contain a description of the events of the next morning. In a

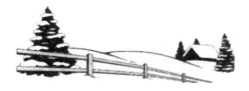

Students will analyze: poems by Ralph Waldo Emerson.

Read Ahead: *Walden*, Henry David Thoreau.

Guide Question: Is this novel a charming reflection on nature or a vitriolic diatribe against the Protestant ethic?

short essay determine what Emerson is saying. What is his worldview? Which does the author consider the true artist? Support your conclusions with references from the poem.

The Snow Storm

Announced by all the trumpets of the sky,
Arrives the snow, and, driving o'er the fields,
Seems nowhere to alight: the whited air
Hides hills and woods, the river, and the heaven,
And veils the farm-house at the garden's end.
The sled and traveller stopped, the courier's feet
Delayed, all friends shut out, the housemates sit
Around the radiant fireplace, enclosed
In a tumultuous privacy of storm.

Come see the north wind's masonry.
Out of an unseen quarry evermore
Furnished with tile, the fierce artificer
Curves his white bastions with projected roof
Round every windware stake, or tree, or door.
Speeding, the myriad-handed, his wild work
So fanciful, so savage, nought cares he
For number or proportion. Mockingly,
On coop or kennel he hangs Parian wreaths;

A swan-like form invests the hidden thorn;
Fills up the farmer's lane from wall to wall,
Maugre the farmer's sighs; and at the gate
A tapering turret overtops the work.
And when his hours are numbered, and the world
Is all his own, retiring, as he were not,
Leaves, when the sun appears, astonished Art

To mimic in slow structures, stone by stone,
Built in an age, the mad wind's night-work,
The frolic architecture of the snow.
http://www.americanpoems.com/poets/emerson/11997

D. In Emerson's poem "Days," why is the day scornful? Write an essay explaining at whom the scorn is directed.

Days

DAUGHTERS of Time, the hypocritic Days,
Muffled and dumb like barefoot dervishes,
And marching single in an endless file,
Bring diadems and fagots in their hands.
To each they offer gifts after his will,
Bread, kingdoms, stars, and sky that holds them all.
I, in my pleached garden, watched the pomp,
Forgot my morning wishes, hastily
Took a few herbs and apples, and the Day
Turned and departed silent. I, too late,
Under her solemn fillet saw the scorn.
http://www.americanpoems.com/poets/emerson/7169

E. Based on "The Rhodora," what is Emerson's idea of a god? Emerson could not accept the idea of a God separate from man and nature; in other words, Emerson was not a Christian believer. Yet, in his own way, he was a deeply religious person. How is this revealed in the last four lines of the poem "The Rhodora"? Using the "The Snow Storm" and "Days" and other Emerson writings, list phrases that illustrate how Emerson was "religious."

The Rhodora

IN May, when sea-winds pierced our solitudes,
I found the fresh Rhodora in the woods,
Spreading its leafless blooms in a damp nook,
To please the desert and the sluggish brook.
The purple petals, fallen in the pool,

Made the black water with their beauty gay;
Here might the red-bird come his plumes to cool,
And court the flower that cheapens his array.
Rhodora! if the sages ask thee why
This charm is wasted on the earth and sky,
Tell them, dear, that if eyes were made for seeing,
Then Beauty is its own excuse for being:

Why thou wert there, O rival of the rose!
I never thought to ask, I never knew:
But, in my simple ignorance, suppose
The self-same Power that brought me there brought you.
http://www.vcu.edu/engweb/transcendentalism/authors/
emerson/poems/rhodora.html

ENRICHMENT

A. Give several evidences of Transcendentalism from these poems. Defend your answer in a 2 page essay.

B. Compare the poetry of Ralph Waldo Emerson with that of another New England poet, Anne Bradstreet. Read four or five essays that Emerson wrote and compare and contrast the themes of these essays with his poetry.

BIBLICAL APPLICATION

A. Puritans saw the world in terms of individual sin and of principalities and powers. They always saw themselves as being part of a larger, more important cosmological story. They knew, without a doubt, that every knee would bow, every tongue confess. With the rise of Lockian (i.e., John Locke) rationalism and its emphasis on individual rights, supported so vigorously by such men as Thomas Jefferson, Americans privatized their faith and morality. Morality was defined according to each individual preference, and Americans avoided static moral biblical structures. For the first time in American thought, man's agendas were more important than the Word of God. Theism was still everywhere present in America, but for the first time morality was loosed from its biblical moorings—with disastrous results. *Agree or disagree with this assessment.*

B. At the same time that Emerson was writing, the well-attended revivals led by Charles Finney were being held in upstate New York. In fact, this revival had a greater impact than Emerson's essays and poetry on American society. *Write a one page report on this revival.*

C. Transcendentalism is a sad commentary on the failure of American Puritanism. By the end of the 17th Century, Puritanism was declining because of a lack of conversions and disrespect for authority. As a result of this demise, American society lost a strong sense of community. Some thinkers, such as sociologist Peter Berger, argue that one feature of modern America has been the loss of mediating institutions so that American is now full of increasingly atomistic individuals. This variety is maintained by a powerful state, with no buffers between government and people. Berger also argues that we Americans have lost all sense of community. Puritans rarely talked about themselves—they just lived their lives in the community of the Lord. Contemporary Americans talk about community so much because they experience it so little in their lives. The 17th and 18th Century Church ceased to be a mediating institution as it was in Puritan New England. As a result, Christianity lost credibility as a viable institution and Transcendentalism arose. *Agree or disagree with this statement in an essay and offer evidence to support your answer.*

D. In what way is the following statement about Jesus by the Transcendentalist/ Romantic Emerson inconsistent with a Christian Theistic worldview? "An immense progress in natural and religious knowledge has been made since his death. Even his genius cannot quicken all that stark nonsense about the blessed and the damned. Yet in the 'Life of Christ' I have thought him a Christian Plato; so rich and great was his philosophy. Is it possible the intellect should be so inconsistent with itself? It is

singular also that the bishop's morality should sometimes trip, as in his explanation of false witness."

E. Born in 1803, Emerson began his working life as a Unitarian preacher. Early widowhood plunged him into a crisis of faith (already weakened by Unitarian Universalism), and he resigned his ministry in 1832. He abandoned any semblance of Theism. In Nature alone Emerson found comfort and direction, but he had an ambivalent viewpoint towards nature. Emerson loved and respected Nature and considered it all-powerful and reverent. His faith ultimately strayed into pantheistic nature-worship. Pantheism argues that god is alive everywhere—in animate and inanimate objects alike. There is nothing new under the sun! Emerson's pantheism was very common in the Bible. In the Old Testament BAAL worship (attacked by Elijah) was very similar to Emerson's Transcendentalism. Compare and contrast the BAAL worship that such men as Joshua and Elijah fought so vigorously with the Nature worship that Transcendentalism advanced. Use the following passages as a guide for your discussion. Refute Emerson's worldview by advancing the truth as you find it in the Bible.

The texts below are from *Nature* (1836).

The Lie: Direct revelation comes to man through nature.

The foregoing generations beheld God face to face; we, through their eyes. Why should not we also enjoy an original relation to the universe? Why should not we have . . . a religion by revelation to us, and not the history of theirs? Embosomed for a season in nature, whose floods of life stream around and through us, and invite us by the powers they supply, to action. . .?

The Lie: "God" exists everywhere—but especially in Nature.

One might think the atmosphere was made transparent with this design, to give man, in the heavenly bodies, the perpetual presence of the sublime. . . If the stars should appear one night in a thousand years, how would men believe and adore; and preserve for many generations the remembrance of the City of God which had been shown! But all natural objects make a kindred impression, when the mind is open to their influence. . . .Nature says, he is my creature . . .

The Lie: Nature unifies us all.

A leaf, a drop, a crystal, a moment of time is related to the whole, and partakes of the perfection of the whole. Each particle is a microcosm, and faithfully renders the likeness of the world. . . . So intimate is this Unity, that, it is easily seen, it lies under the undermost garment of nature, and betrays its source in the Universal Spirit. . . .

F. Find instances in the Bible where Nature is controlled by God.

FINAL PROJECT

Correct and rewrite all essays and place them in your Final Portfolio.

SUGGESTED
Weekly *Implementation*

DAY 1	DAY 2	DAY 3	DAY 4	DAY 5
Prayer journal. Review the required reading(s) *before* the assigned lesson begins. Teacher may want to discuss assigned reading(s) with students. Teacher and students will decide on the number of required essays for this lesson, choosing two or three essays. The rest of the essays can be outlined, answered with shorter answers, or skipped. Review all readings for Lesson 10.	**Prayer journal.** Review reading(s) from next lesson. Outline essays due at the end of the week. Per teacher instructions, students may answer orally in a group setting some of the essays that are not assigned as formal essays.	**Prayer journal.** Write rough drafts of all assigned essays. The teacher and/or a peer evaluator may correct rough drafts.	**Prayer journal.** Rewrite corrected copies of essays due tomorrow.	**Prayer journal.** Essays are due. Take the Lesson 10 test. Reading ahead: Review *Walden*, Henry David Thoreau. Guide: Is this novel a charming reflection on nature or a vitriolic diatribe against the Protestant ethic?

ROMANTICISM: NEW ENGLAND RENAISSANCE, 1840-1855 (Part 4)

Age of Reform

BACKGROUND

America experienced an unprecedented reform movement from 1840-1855. At the center of this movement were New Englanders, notably Ralph Waldo Emerson and Henry David Thoreau.

Purporting that people are basically good is at the core of the Romanticism/Transcendentalism movement. American optimism that was spawned in American Romanticism/Transcendentalism demanded that all individuals should be afforded the same rights and privileges. That, combined with a growing Romantic worldview arguing that mankind is basically good if society will only leave him alone, ushered in an age of optimistic reform unparalleled in American history until the 1960s.

The clearest manifestation of this unbridled optimism was the clamor for more voting rights and, subsequently, more participation in the political process. If Americans were to vote in ever increasing numbers, then they should know how to read and to write. Thus, public education expanded considerably. The public school system became common throughout the northern part of the country. However, in other parts of the country the battle for public education continued for years, only to be resolved in the 1920s.

This early clamor was only the beginning. Americans dared to dream that society could be perfect. They reached for utopia. Women's rights, abolition, public education, and temperance all were part of this great surge of civil faith in the American experiment.

An influential social movement that emerged during this period was the opposition to the sale and use of alcohol—the temperance movement. It stemmed from a variety of concerns and motives: biblical beliefs, the cost of alcohol abuse in the work place, and the suffering that families experienced at the hands of heavy drinkers. In 1826 Boston ministers organized the Society for the Promotion of Temperance. Seven years later, in Philadelphia, the Society organized a national convention, which formed the American Temperance

> **You will analyze:** *Walden*, Henry David Thoreau.
>
> **Reading Ahead:** *Billy Budd*, Herman Melville.
>
> **Guide Question:** In what way is Billy Budd a Christ-like figure? In what way does this book mark the end of Christian orthodoxy in American literature?

Union. The Union called for the renunciation of all alcoholic beverages. By 1855 thirteen states had done so, although the laws were subsequently challenged in court. They survived only in northern New England, but between 1830 and 1860 the temperance movement significantly reduced Americans' per capita consumption of alcohol.

Other reformers addressed the problems of prisons and care for the insane. Efforts were made to turn insane asylums and prisons, which stressed punishment, into penitentiaries, where the guilty and infirm could undergo rehabilitation.

What has been called "the first American penitentiary, if not the first one in the world," was established in Philadelphia in 1790 in the Walnut Street Jail, a building formerly operated as a city jail. The cell blocks constructed in the Walnut Street Jail, pursuant to the law of 1790, introduced in permanent fashion the structural pattern of outside cells with a central corridor, the chief architectural feature of the Pennsylvania system of prison construction. Here, for the first time in prison history, the use of imprisonment through solitary confinement as the usual method of stopping crime was permanently established.

In Massachusetts, Dorothea Dix led a struggle to improve conditions for insane persons who were kept confined in deplorable conditions. The southern United States escaped many of these reforms, but they could not escape Dorothea Dix. After winning improvements in Massachusetts, she took her campaign to the South, where nine states established hospitals for the insane between 1845 and 1852.

Perhaps the most radical changes occurred in women's rights. Other social reforms brought many women to a realization of their own unjust position in society. Women were not permitted to vote, and their education in the 17th and 18th centuries was limited largely to reading, writing and sewing.

As the Princeton historian James McPherson explains, the economic transformation of northern society from exclusively agrarian interests to a growing industrial base took men away from the home and elevated women to leadership in the home. For better or for worse, fathers ceased to be present in the home in the same way that they once were. Middle class marriages became partnerships. Women lived longer and had more leisure time. All these changes conspired to offer women more rights (McPherson, *Battle Cry of Freedom*).

By the 1840s a group of American women emerged who would forge the first women's rights movement. Foremost in this distinguished group was Elizabeth Cady Stanton. In 1848 Cady Stanton and Lucretia Mott, another women's rights advocate, organized a women's rights convention—the first in the history of the world—at Seneca Falls, New York. Delegates drew up a declaration demanding equality with men before the law, the right to vote, and equal opportunities in education and employment (Quoted from American Archives of Public Address).

Another reform movement whose impact far surpassed its small membership was the slavery abolition movement. William Lloyd Garrison was one of the main leaders. Abolitionism was of two main types: One group argued for radical and immediate abolition of slavery; other groups argued for a more gradual abolition policy. In any event, this group influenced politicians and policy makers and in many ways hastened the coming of the Civil War.

Finally, this early 19th century generation that so closely resembled the later generation of the 1960s, dabbled in utopia, or a perfect society. In 1516 an Englishman named Sir Thomas More coined the word *utopia* when he wrote his book by the same name. Between 1840 and 1850 Americans founded 40 utopian communities. These early attempts at perfections were founded on the notion that mankind could be perfect if it lived in a cooperative—not competitive—community. Ralph Waldo Emerson was a member of this community. One notable attempt to live this life was the Brook Farm experiment in communal living which was both scandalous and revolutionary. The founder George Ripley described Brook Farm:

Our objectives, as you know, are to insure a more natural union between intellectual and manual labor than now exists; to combine the thinker and the worker, as far as possible, in the same individual; to guarantee the highest mental freedom, by proving all with labor, adapted to their tastes and talents, and securing to them the fruits of their industry; to do away with the necessity of menial services, by opening the benefits of education and the profits of labor to all; and thus to prepare a society of liberal, intelligent and cultivated persons, whose relations with each other would permit a more simple and wholesome life than can be led amidst the pressure of our competitive institutions. http://www.vcu.edu/engweb/transcendentalism/ideas/letter.html#ripley2

Founded in 1841, Brook Farm only existed for a few years, but more than anything else, it represented the hope and optimism of this age of reform. It was in this era that Henry David Thoreau wrote *Walden*.

Henry David Thoreau

© Arttoday.com

Henry David Thoreau was born in 1817 to an ordinary family in Concord, Massachusetts, and lived most of his life in the Northeast. He was the third child of a small businessman named John Thoreau and his sanguine, talkative wife, Cynthia Dunbar Thoreau. In 1828 his parents sent him to Concord Academy where he impressed his teachers and so was permitted to prepare for college. Upon graduating from the academy, he entered Harvard in 1833. Graduating in the middle ranks of the class of 1837, he searched for a teaching job and secured one in Concord at his old grammar school. He was not successful at these jobs until he embraced the Romanticism of his good friend Ralph Waldo Emerson and started writing verse. In 1845 the certifiable eccentric Henry David Thoreau leased some land owned by his friend and mentor, Ralph Waldo Emerson on Walden Pond near Concord, Massachusetts, and lived in a cabin on it for two years, two months, and two days. While there Thoreau wrote one of the most memorable, if egocentric, journal/novels in American literature.

CRITICAL THINKING

The poet Ezra Pound said that Thoreau wrote *Walden* as the "first intellectual reaction to mere approach of industrialization: Thoreau tried to see how little he need bother about other humanity."

Agree or disagree with the theory behind this statement.

BIBLICAL APPLICATION

In his concluding chapter Thoreau reflects on death. What does he conclude and does it parallel biblical teachings?

ENRICHMENT

A. Thoreau extols hard work while doing very little of it. Is he a sensitive observer of nature, a lazy over-educated snob hanging out doing nothing for a year, or — ?

B. Why was this book so popular in the 1960s?

FINAL PROJECT

Correct and rewrite all essays and place them in your Final Portfolio.

SUGGESTED
Weekly *Implementation*

DAY 1	DAY 2	DAY 3	DAY 4	DAY 5
Prayer journal.	**Prayer journal.**	**Prayer journal.**	**Prayer journal.**	**Prayer journal.**
Review the required reading(s) *before* the assigned lesson begins.	Review reading(s) from next lesson.	Write rough drafts of all assigned essays.	Rewrite corrected copies of essays due tomorrow.	Essays are due.
Teacher may want to discuss assigned reading(s) with students.	Outline essays due at the end of the week.	The teacher and/or a peer evaluator may correct rough drafts.		Take Lesson 11 test.
Teacher and students will decide on the required essays for this lesson, choosing two or three essays.	Per teacher instructions, students may answer orally in a group setting some of the essays that are not assigned as formal essays.			Reading ahead: Review *Billy Budd*, Herman Melville. Guide: In what way is Billy Budd a Christ-like figure? In what way does this book mark the end of Christian orthodoxy in American literature?
The rest of the essays can be outlined, answered with shorter answers, or skipped.				
Review all readings for Lesson 11.				

LESSON 12

ROMANTICISM: NEW ENGLAND RENAISSANCE *1840-1855* (Part 5)

Billy Budd
Herman Melville (1891)

BACKGROUND

This extraordinary novel is the story of a young man assailed by uncontrollable forces. Billy Budd finds himself restricted by forces beyond his control. In this world an omnipotent God is absent. Welcome to the New World!

ABOUT THE AUTHOR

© Arttoday.com

Herman Melville, born on August 19, 1819, was part of a radically changing world. Within his lifetime the population of the United States increased four hundred percent. Travel time from New York to Boston decreased from five days to eight hours. The generation that lived in the middle period of American history, in most respects, experienced more changes than any American generation—including our own. Melville's books struggle to make sense of all these changes. He was a very talented writer, but in his heart, he was a sailor. Melville spent almost twenty years traveling the South Seas. In microcosm Melville represents the quintessential nineteenth century American.

Written during the last years of Melville's life, *Billy Budd* is concerned with the welfare of man in a hostile, naturalistic world. The safe, ordered, theistic world of Anne Bradstreet has disappeared from American literature.

You will analyze: the romantic/naturalistic novel *Billy Budd*, by Herman Melville.

Read ahead: Review "Oh Captain! My Captain!" Walt Whitman; Negro Spirituals; "The Gettysburg Address," Abraham Lincoln; and "Surrender Speech," Chief Joseph.

Guide Questions: Is Whitman a Romantic? What were the purposes of the Negro Spirituals?

Other Notable Works
Typee (1846)
Moby Dick (1851)

SUGGESTED VOCABULARY WORDS

I   motley
    retinue
    genial
    decorum
III deference
    appellation
VIII felonious
    comely
IX   clandestine
XV   immured

CRITICAL THINKING

A. *Billy Budd* is a tragedy. There are two concepts of tragedy—the classic and the modern. Aristotle defines the classic tragedy as "imitation of an action that is serious." The tragic hero must have a tragic flaw, and he must recognize the reason for his downfall. The modern concept of tragedy can be found in the ideas of Arthur Miller who wrote *The Crucible* and *The Death of a Salesman*. The audience witnesses a tragedy when the characters are unable to achieve happiness or when the characters are misunderstood. In what way is *Billy Budd* a modern tragedy? What does this show about the way American society is changing?

B. How does David Hume's philosophy (see Lesson 2 and other sources) conflict with a Theistic/biblical worldview?

C. Give at least two examples of symbolism in this book.

D. Melville intentionally rejects Judeo-Christian notions of sin and depravity. Thus, Claggart is described as being depraved in a Platonic way. Plato defined depravity as "a depravity according to nature." Why would Melville reject a biblical understanding of sin and go to a classical definition?

E. In *Billy Budd* the setting helps to reveal character and to shape events. Give evidence for this statement.

F. How does Melville create his characters?

G. In what way is *Billy Budd* autobiographical?

BIBLICAL APPLICATION

A. Melville (who was a transitional romantic) and contemporary romantic writers tried to embrace the best of both cosmological worlds. They believed in God, although they diluted His person and substance with natural science; they also believed in human ingenuity and subjectivity. It was very hard to balance both these worldviews at the same time. Research another theist named Ahab (1 Kings) who also struggled to be a theist and a pagan—at the same time.

B. Billy Budd is obviously a Christ-like figure. Find evidence to support this idea from the book. Compare and contrast Melville's view with the New Testament account of Christ's crucifixion.

C. Billy is "saved" the night before he dies—but not through Christ. In fact, the chaplain, who presumably represents the Christian view of salvation, listens to Billy and finds his strength through this event—much like the disciples listened to Christ at the Last Supper. This time, however, Billy saves the pastor! The Romantic saves the theist! This is the first time in American literature that this switch in roles happens, and it does not bode well for future literature. Find evidence in the book to support this switch in roles. Find Scripture to show a way to discuss salvation with an unbeliever.

ENRICHMENT

A. Melville can neither believe, nor be comfortable in his unbelief. What a marvelous description of modern man. In his book *God in the Wasteland: The Reality of Truth in a World of Fading Dreams*, David F. Wells is convinced that since the middle of the last century human society has embraced "an ironic recapitulation of the

> Setting is defined as the time, place, and general milieu in which a piece of fiction occurs.

" Next instant, the luckless mate was whisked bodily into the air "
—*Page 190*

© Arttoday.com

first dislocation in which God's creatures replaced their Creator and exiled Him from His own world" (p. 14). Find examples of this development in *Billy Budd*. Agree or disagree with Wells' statement and find examples both in this book and contemporary life that support or refute this statement.

B. Two quintessential questions our culture raises by its nature and development are *what is truth?* and *what can we believe?* Our culture doesn't know the answer. It never has. The Puritans knew that. They looked beyond themselves. They looked to God, but from this point in American literature we enter a wasteland. After humorist Mark Twain wrote his satire and early Realism, American writers lost confidence in a single truth and came to the conclusion that truth is unattainable. Today we hold to a plurality of truths, and the *tolerance* of them is now a *virtue*. Truth, to our secular world, is discovered in this pluralistic struggle. Using *Billy Budd* as evidence, discuss how Melville is advocating a plurality of truth.

C. Write a *report* on early nineteenth century whaling and other commercial enterprises related to the sea.

D. In a two-page essay, discuss how Melville is poking fun at his friend Ralph Waldo Emerson and other Romantics in his essay "I and my Chimney."

I and My Chimney

http://www.online-literature.com/melville/160

I and my chimney, two grey-headed old smokers, reside in the country. We are, I may say, old settlers here; particularly my old chimney, which settles more and more every day.

Though I always say, *I and My Chimney*, as Cardinal Wolsey used to say, "*I and My King,*" yet this egotistic way of speaking, wherein I take precedence of my chimney, is hereby borne out by the facts; in everything, except the above phrase, my chimney taking precedence of me.

Within thirty feet of the turf-sided road, my chimney—a huge, corpulent old Harry VIII of a chimney—rises full in front of me and all my possessions. Standing well up a hillside, my chimney, like Lord Rosse's monster telescope, swung vertical to hit the meridian moon, is the first object to greet the approaching traveler's eye, nor is it the last which the sun salutes. My chimney, too,

is before me in receiving the first-fruits of the seasons. The snow is on its head ere on my hat; and every spring, as in a hollow beech tree, the first swallows build their nests in it.

But it is within doors that the pre-eminence of my chimney is most manifest. When in the rear room, set apart for that object, I stand to receive my guests (who, by the way call more, I suspect, to see my chimney than me) I then stand, not so much before, as, strictly speaking, behind my chimney, which is, indeed, the true host. Not that I demur. In the presence of my betters, I hope I know my place.

From this habitual precedence of my chimney over me, some even think that I have got into a sad rearward way altogether; in short, from standing behind my old-fashioned chimney so much, I have got to be quite behind the age too, as well as running behindhand in everything else. But to tell the truth, I never was a very forward old fellow, nor what my farming neighbors call a forehanded one. Indeed, those rumors about my behindhandedness are so far correct, that I have an odd sauntering way with me sometimes of going about with my hands behind my back. As for my belonging to the rear-guard in general, certain it is, I bring up the rear of my chimney—which, by the way, is this moment before me—and that, too, both in fancy and fact. In brief, my chimney is my superior; my superior, too, in that humbly bowing over with shovel and tongs, I much minister to it; yet never does it minister, or incline over to me; but, if anything, in its settlings, rather leans the other way.

My chimney is grand seignior here—the one great domineering object, not more of the landscape, than of the house; all the rest of which house, in each architectural arrangement, as may shortly appear, is, in the most marked manner, accommodated, not to my wants, but to my chimney's, which, among other things, has the center of the house to himself, leaving but the odd holes and corners to me.

But I and my chimney must explain; and as we are both rather obese, we may have to expatiate. In those houses which are strictly double houses—that is, where the hall is in the middle—the fireplaces usually are on opposite sides; so that while one member of the household is warming himself at a fire built into a recess of the north wall, say another member, the former's own brother, perhaps, may be holding his feet to the blaze before a hearth in the south wall—the two thus fairly sitting back to back. Is this well? Be it put to any man who has a proper fraternal feeling. Has it not a sort of sulky appearance? But very probably this style of chimney building originated with some architect afflicted with a quarrelsome family. Then again, almost every modem fireplace has its separate flue—separate throughout, from hearth to chimney-top. At least such an arrangement is deemed desirable. Does not this look egotistical, selfish? But still more, all these separate flues, instead of having independent masonry establishments of their own, or instead of being grouped together in one federal stock in the middle of the house—instead of this, I say, each flue is surreptitiously honey-combed into the walls; so that these last are here and there, or indeed almost anywhere, treacherously hollow, and, in consequence, more or less weak. Of course, the main reason of this style of chimney building is to economize room. In cities, where lots are sold by the inch, small space is to spare for a chimney constructed on magnanimous principles; and, as with most thin men, who are generally tall, so with such houses, what is lacking in breadth, must be made up in height. This remark holds true even with regard to many very stylish abodes, built by the most stylish of gentlemen. And yet, when that stylish gentleman, Louis le Grand of France, would build a palace for his lady, friend, Madame de Maintenon, he built it but one story high—in fact in the cottage style. But then, how uncommonly quadrangular, spacious, and broad—horizontal acres, not vertical ones. Such is the palace, which, in all its one-storied magnificence of Languedoc marble, in the garden of Versailles, still remains to this day. Any man can buy a square foot of land and plant a liberty-pole on it; but it takes a king to set apart whole acres for a grand triannon.

But nowadays it is different; and furthermore, what originated in a necessity has been mounted into a vaunt. In towns there is large rivalry in building tall houses. If one gentleman builds his house four stories high, and another gentleman comes next door and builds five stories high, then the former, not to be looked down upon that way, immediately sends for his architect and claps a fifth and a sixth story on top of his previous four. And, not till the gentleman has achieved his aspiration, not till he has stolen over the way by twilight and observed how his sixth story soars beyond his neighbor's fifth—not till then does he retire to his rest with satisfaction.

Such folks, it seems to me, need mountains for neighbors, to take this emulous conceit of soaring out of them.

If, considering that mine is a very wide house, and by no means lofty, aught in the above may appear like interested pleading, as if I did but fold myself about in the cloak of a general proposition, cunningly to tickle my individual vanity beneath it, such misconception must vanish upon my frankly conceding, that land adjoining my alder swamp was sold last month for ten dollars an acre, and thought a rash purchase at that; so that for wide houses hereabouts there is plenty of room, and cheap. Indeed so cheap—dirt cheap—is the soil, that our elms thrust out their roots in it, and hang their great boughs over it, in the most lavish and reckless way. Almost all our crops, too, are sown broadcast, even peas and turnips. A farmer among us, who should go about his twenty-acre field, poking his finger into it here and there, and dropping down a mustard seed, would be thought a penurious, narrow-minded husbandman. The dandelions in the river-meadows, and the forget-me-nots along the mountain roads, you see at once they are put to no economy in space. Some seasons, too, our rye comes up here and there a spear, sole and single like a church-spire. It doesn't care to crowd itself where it knows there is such a deal of room. The world is wide, the world is all before us, says the rye. Weeds, too, it is amazing how they spread. No such thing as arresting them—some of our pastures being a sort of Alsatia for the weeds. As for the grass, every spring it is like Kossuth's rising of what he calls the peoples. Mountains, too, a regular camp-meeting of them. For the same reason, the same all-sufficiency of room, our shadows march and countermarch, going through their various drills and masterly evolutions, like the old imperial guard on the Champs de Mars. As for the hills, especially where the roads cross them the supervisors of our various towns have given notice to all concerned, that they can come and dig them down and cart them off, and never a cent to pay, no more than for the privilege of picking blackberries. The stranger who is buried here, what liberal-hearted landed proprietor among us grudges him six feet of rocky pasture? Nevertheless, cheap, after all, as our land is, and much as it is trodden under foot, I, for one, am proud of it for what it bears; and chiefly for its three great lions—the Great Oak, Ogg Mountain, and my chimney.

Most houses, here, are but one and a half stories high; few exceed two. That in which I and my chimney dwell, is in width nearly twice its height, from sill to eaves—which accounts for the magnitude of its main content—besides showing that in this house, as in this country at large, there is abundance of space, and to spare, for both of us.

The frame of the old house is of wood—which but the more sets forth the solidity of the chimney, which is of brick. And as the great wrought nails, binding the clapboards, are unknown in these degenerate days, so are the huge bricks in the chimney walls. The architect of the chimney must have had the pyramid of Cheops before him; for, after that famous structure, it seems modeled, only its rate of decrease towards the summit is considerably less, and it is truncated. From the exact middle of the mansion it soars from the cellar, right up through each successive floor, till, four feet square, it breaks water from the ridge-pole of the roof, like an anvil-headed whale, through the crest of a billow. Most people, though, liken it, in that part, to a razed observatory, masoned up.

The reason for its peculiar appearance above the roof touches upon rather delicate ground. How shall I reveal that, forasmuch as many years ago the original gable roof of the old house had become very leaky, a temporary proprietor hired a band of woodmen, with their huge, cross-cut saws, and went to sawing the old gable roof clean off. Off it went, with all its birds' nests, and dormer windows. It was replaced with a modern roof, more fit for a railway wood-house than an old country gentleman's abode. This operation—razeeing the structure some fifteen feet—was, in effect upon the chimney, something like the falling of the great spring tides. It left uncommon low water all about the chimney—to abate which appearance, the same person now proceeds to slice fifteen feet off the chimney itself, actually beheading my royal old chimney—a regicidal act, which, were it not for the palliating fact that he was a poulterer by trade, and, therefore, hardened to such neck-wringings, should send that former proprietor down to posterity in the same cart with Cromwell.

Owing to its pyramidal shape, the reduction of the chimney inordinately widened its razed summit. Inordinately, I say, but only in the estimation of such as have no eye to the picturesque. What care I, if, unaware that my chimney, as a free citizen of this free land, stands upon an independent basis of its own, people passing it, wonder how such a brick-kiln, as they call it, is supported upon mere joists and rafters? What care I? I will give a traveler a cup of switchel, if he want it; but am I bound to supply him with a sweet taste? Men of cultivated minds see, in my old house and chimney, a goodly old elephant-and-castle.

All feeling hearts will sympathize with me in what I am now about to add. The surgical operation, above referred to, necessarily brought into the open air a part of the chimney previously under cover, and intended to remain so, and, therefore, not built of what are called weather-bricks. In consequence, the chimney, though of a vigorous constitution, suffered not a little, from so naked an exposure; and, unable to acclimate itself, ere long began to fail—showing blotchy symptoms akin to those in measles. Whereupon travelers, passing my way, would wag their heads, laughing; "See that wax nose—how it melts off!" But what cared I? The same travelers would travel across the sea to view Kenilworth peeling away, and for a very good reason: that of all artists of the picturesque, decay wears the palm—I would say, the ivy. In fact, I've often thought that the proper place for my old chimney is ivied old England.

In vain my wife—with what probable ulterior intent will, ere long, appear—solemnly warned me, that unless something were done, and speedily, we should be burnt to the ground, owing to the holes crumbling through the aforesaid blotchy parts, where the chimney joined the roof. "Wife," said I, "far better that my house should burn down, than that my chimney should be pulled down, though but a few feet. They call it a wax nose; very good; not for me to tweak the nose of my superior." But at last the man who has a mortgage on the house dropped me a note, reminding me that, if my chimney was allowed to stand in that invalid condition, my policy of insurance would be void. This was a sort of hint not to be neglected. All the world over, the picturesque yields to the pocketesque. The mortgagor cared not, but the mortgagee did.

So another operation was performed. The wax nose was taken off, and a new one fitted on. Unfortunately for the expression—being put up by a squint-eyed mason, who, at the time, had a bad stitch in the same side—the new nose stands a little awry, in the same direction.

Of one thing, however, I am proud. The horizontal dimensions of the new part are unreduced.

Large as the chimney appears upon the roof, that is nothing to its spaciousness below. At its base in the cellar, it is precisely twelve feet square; and hence covers precisely one hundred and forty-four superficial feet. What an appropriation of terra firma for a chimney, and what a huge load for this earth! In fact, it was only because I and my chimney formed no part of his ancient burden, that that stout peddler, Atlas of old, was enabled to stand up so bravely under his pack. The dimensions given may, perhaps, seem fabulous. But, like those stones at Gilgal, which Joshua set up for a memorial of having passed over Jordan, does not my chimney remain, even unto this day?

Very often I go down into my cellar, and attentively survey that vast square of masonry. I stand long, and ponder over, and wonder at it. It has a druidical look, away down in the umbrageous cellar there whose numerous vaulted passages, and far glens of gloom, resemble the dark, damp depths of primeval woods. So strongly did this conceit steal over me, so deeply was I penetrated with wonder at the chimney, that one day—when I was a little out of my mind, I now think—getting a spade from the garden, I set to work, digging round the foundation, especially at the corners thereof, obscurely prompted by dreams of striking upon some old, earthen-worn memorial of that by-gone day, when, into all this gloom, the light of heaven entered, as the masons laid the foundation-stones, peradventure sweltering under an August sun, or pelted by a March storm. Plying my blunted spade, how vexed was I by that ungracious interruption of a neighbor who, calling to see me upon some business, and being informed that I was below said I need not be troubled to come up, but he would go down to me; and so, without ceremony, and without my having been forewarned, suddenly discovered me, digging in my cellar.

"Gold digging, sir?"

"Nay, sir," answered I, starting, "I was merely—ahem!—merely—I say I was merely digging-round my chimney."

"Ah, loosening the soil, to make it grow. Your chimney, sir, you regard as too small, I suppose; needing further development, especially at the top?"

"Sir!" said I, throwing down the spade, "do not be personal. I and my chimney—"

"Personal?"

"Sir, I look upon this chimney less as a pile of masonry than as a personage. It is the king of the house. I am but a suffered and inferior subject." In fact, I would permit no gibes to be cast at either myself or my chimney; and never again did my visitor refer to it in my hearing, without coupling some compliment with the mention. It well deserves a respectful consideration. There it stands, solitary and alone—not a council—of ten flues, but, like his sacred majesty of Russia, a unit of an autocrat.

Even to me, its dimensions, at times, seem incredible. It does not look so big—no, not even in the cellar. By the mere eye, its magnitude can be but imperfectly comprehended, because only one side can be received at one time; and said side can only present twelve feet, linear measure. But then, each other side also is twelve feet long; and the whole obviously forms a square and twelve times twelve is one hundred and forty-four. And so, an adequate conception of the magnitude of this chimney is only to be got at by a sort of process in the higher mathematics by a method somewhat akin to those whereby the surprising distances of fixed stars are computed.

It need hardly be said, that the walls of my house are entirely free from fireplaces. These all congregate in the middle—in the one grand central chimney, upon all four sides of which are hearths—two tiers of hearths—so that when, in the various chambers, my family and guests are warming themselves of a cold winter's night, just before retiring, then, though at the time they may not be thinking so, all their faces mutually look towards each other, yea, all their feet point to one center; and, when they go to sleep in their beds, they all sleep round one warm chimney, like so many Iroquois Indians, in the woods, round their one heap of embers. And just as the Indians' fire serves, not only to keep them comfortable, but also to keep off wolves, and other savage monsters, so my chimney, by its obvious smoke at top, keeps off prowling burglars from the towns—for what burglar or murderer would dare break into an abode from whose chimney issues such a continual smoke—betokening that if the inmates are not stirring, at least fires are, and in case of an alarm, candles may readily be lighted, to say nothing of muskets.

But stately as is the chimney—yea, grand high altar as it is, right worthy for the celebration of high mass before the Pope of Rome, and all his cardinals—yet what is there perfect in this world? Caius Julius Caesar, had he not been so inordinately great, they say that Brutus, Cassius, Antony, and the rest, had been greater. My chimney, were it not so mighty in its magnitude, my chambers had been larger. How often has my wife ruefully told me, that my chimney, like the English aristocracy, casts a contracting shade all round it. She avers that endless domestic inconveniences arise—more particularly from the chimney's stubborn central locality. The grand objection with her is, that it stands midway in the place where a fine entrance-hall ought to be. In truth, there is no hall whatever to the house—nothing but a sort of square landing-place, as you enter from the wide front door. A roomy enough landing-place, I admit, but not attaining to the dignity of a hall. Now, as the front door is precisely in the middle of the front of the house, inwards it faces the chimney. In fact, the opposite wall of the landing-place is formed solely by the chimney; and hence—owing to the gradual tapering of the chimney—is a little less than twelve feet in width. Climbing the chimney in this part, is the principal staircase—which, by three abrupt turns, and three minor landing-places, mounts to the second floor, where, over the front door, runs a sort of narrow gallery, something less than twelve feet long, leading to chambers on either hand. This gallery, of course, is railed; and so, looking down upon the stairs, and all those landing-places together, with the main one at bottom, resembles not a little a balcony for musicians, in some jolly old abode, in times Elizabethan. Shall I tell a weakness? I cherish the cobwebs there, and many a time arrest Biddy in the act of brushing them with her broom, and have many a quarrel with my wife and daughters about it.

Now the ceiling, so to speak, of the place where you enter the house, that ceiling is, in fact, the ceiling of the second floor, not the first. The two floors are made one here; so that ascending this turning stairs, you seem going up into a kind of soaring tower, or lighthouse. At the second landing, midway up the chimney, is a mysterious door, entering to a mysterious closet; and here I keep mysterious cordials, of a choice, mysterious flavor, made so by the constant nurturing and subtle ripening of the chimney's gentle heat, distilled through that warm mass of masonry. Better for wines is it than voyages to the Indias; my chimney itself a tropic. A chair by my chimney in a November day is as good for an invalid as a long season spent in Cuba. Often I think how grapes might ripen against my chimney. How my wife's geraniums bud there! Bud in December. Her eggs, too—can't keep them near the chimney, an account of the hatching. Ah, a warm heart has my chimney.

How often my wife was at me about that projected grand entrance-hall of hers, which was to be knocked clean through the chimney, from one end of the house to the other, and astonish all guests by its generous amplitude. "But, wife," said I, "the chimney—consider the chimney: if you demolish the foundation, what is to support the superstructure?" "Oh, that will rest on the second floor." The truth is, women know next to nothing about the realities of architecture. However, my wife still talked of running her entries and partitions. She spent many long nights elaborating her plans; in imagination building her boasted hall through the chimney, as though its high mightiness were a mere spear of sorrel-top. At last, I gently reminded her that, little as she might fancy it, the chimney was a fact—a sober, substantial fact, which, in all her plannings, it would be well to take into full consideration. But this was not of much avail. And here, respectfully craving her permission, I must say a few words about this enterprising wife of mine. Though in years nearly old as myself, in spirit she is young as my little sorrel mare, Trigger, that threw me last fall. What is extraordinary, though she comes of a rheumatic family, she is straight as a pine, never has any aches; while for me with the sciatica, I am sometimes as crippled up as any old apple-tree. But she has not so much as a toothache. As for her hearing—let me enter the house in my dusty boots, and she away up in the attic. And for her sight—Biddy, the housemaid, tells other people's housemaids, that her mistress will spy a spot on the dresser straight through the pewter platter, put up on purpose to hide it. Her faculties are alert as her limbs and her senses. No danger of my spouse dying of torpor. The longest night in the year I've known her lie awake, planning her campaign for the morrow. She is a natural projector. The maxim, "Whatever is, is right," is not hers. Her maxim is, Whatever is, is wrong; and what is more, must be altered; and what is still more, must be altered right away. Dreadful maxim for the wife of a dozy old dreamer like me, who dote on seventh days as days of rest, and out of a sabbatical horror of industry, will, on a week day, go out of my road a quarter of a mile, to avoid the sight of a man at work.

That matches are made in heaven, may be, but my wife would have been just the wife for Peter the Great, or Peter the Piper. How she would have set in order that huge littered empire of the one, and with indefatigable painstaking picked the peck of pickled peppers for the other.

But the most wonderful thing is, my wife never thinks of her end. Her youthful incredulity, as to the plain theory, and still plainer fact of death, hardly seems Christian. Advanced in years, as she knows she must be, my wife seems to think that she is to teem on, and be inexhaustible forever. She doesn't believe in old age. At that strange promise in the plain of Mamre, my old wife, unlike old Abraham's, would not have jeeringly laughed within herself. Judge how to me, who, sitting in the comfortable shadow of my chimney, smoking my comfortable pipe, with ashes not unwelcome at my feet, and ashes not unwelcome all but in my mouth; and who am thus in a comfortable sort of not unwelcome, though, indeed, ashy enough way, reminded of the ultimate exhaustion even of the most fiery life; judge how to me this unwarrantable vitality in my wife must come, sometimes, it is true, with a moral and a calm, but oftener with a breeze and a ruffle.

If the doctrine be true, that in wedlock contraries attract, by how cogent a fatality must I have been drawn to my wife! While spicily impatient of present and past, like a glass of ginger-beer she overflows with her schemes; and, with like energy as she puts down her foot, puts down her preserves and her pickles, and lives with them in a continual future; or ever full of expectations both from time and space, is ever restless for newspapers, and ravenous for letters. Content with the years that are gone, taking no thought for the morrow, and looking for no new thing from any person or quarter whatever, I have not a single scheme or expectation on earth, save in unequal resistance of the undue encroachment of hers.

Old myself, I take to oldness in things; for that cause mainly loving old Montague, and old cheese, and old wine; and eschewing young people, hot rolls, new books, and early potatoes and very fond of my old claw-footed chair, and old club-footed Deacon White, my neighbor, and that still nigher old neighbor, my betwisted old grape-vine, that of a summer evening leans in his elbow for cosy company at my window-sill, while I, within doors, lean over mine to meet his; and above all, high above all, am fond of my high-mantled old chimney. But she, out of the infatuate juvenility of hers, takes to nothing but newness; for that cause mainly, loving new cider in autumn, and in spring, as if she were own daughter of Nebuchadnezzar, fairly raving after all sorts of salads and spinages, and more particularly green cucumbers (though all the time nature rebukes such unsuitable young hankerings in so elderly a person, by never permitting such things to agree with her), and has an itch after recently- discovered fine prospects (so no graveyard be in the background), and also after Sweden-borganism, and the Spirit Rapping philosophy, with other new views, alike in things natural and unnatural; and immortally hopeful, is forever making new flower-beds even on the north side of the house where the bleak mountain wind would scarce allow the wiry weed called hard-hack to gain a thorough footing; and on the road-

side sets out mere pipe-stems of young elms; though there is no hope of any shade from them, except over the ruins of her great granddaughter's gravestones; and won't wear caps, but plaits her gray hair; and takes the Ladies' Magazine for the fashions; and always buys her new almanac a month before the new year; and rises at dawn; and to the warmest sunset turns a cold shoulder; and still goes on at odd hours with her new course of history, and her French, and her music; and likes a young company; and offers to ride young colts; and sets out young suckers in the orchard; and has a spite against my elbowed old grape-vine, and my club-footed old neighbor, and my claw-footed old chair, and above all, high above all, would fain persecute, until death, my high-mantled old chimney. By what perverse magic, I a thousand times think, does such a very autumnal old lady have such a very vernal young soul? When I would remonstrate at times, she spins round on me with, "Oh, don't you grumble, old man (she always calls me old man), it's I, young I, that keep you from stagnating." Well, I suppose it is so. Yea, after all, these things are well ordered. My wife, as one of her poor relations, good soul, intimates, is the salt of the earth, and none the less the salt of my sea, which otherwise were unwholesome. She is its monsoon, too, blowing a brisk gale over it, in the one steady direction of my chimney.

Not insensible of her superior energies, my wife has frequently made me propositions to take upon herself all the responsibilities of my affairs. She is desirous that, domestically, I should abdicate; that, renouncing further rule, like the venerable Charles V, I should retire into some sort of monastery. But indeed, the chimney excepted, I have little authority to lay down. By my wife's ingenious application of the principle that certain things belong of right to female jurisdiction, I find myself, through my easy compliances, insensibly stripped by degrees of one masculine prerogative after another. In a dream I go about my fields, a sort of lazy, happy-go-lucky, good-for-nothing, loafing old Lear. Only by some sudden revelation am I reminded who is over me; as year before last, one day seeing in one corner of the premises fresh deposits of mysterious boards and timbers, the oddity of the incident at length begat serious meditation. "Wife," said I, "whose boards and timbers are those I see near the orchard there? Do you know anything about them, wife? Who put them there? You know I do not like the neighbors to use my land that way, they should ask permission first."

She regarded me with a pitying smile.

"Why, old man, don't you know I am building a new barn? Didn't you know that, old man?"

This is the poor old lady who was accusing me of tyrannizing over her.

To return now to the chimney. Upon being assured of the futility of her proposed hall, so long as the obstacle remained, for a time my wife was for a modified project. But I could never exactly comprehend it. As far as I could see through it, it seemed to involve the general idea of a sort of irregular archway, or elbowed tunnel, which was to penetrate the chimney at some convenient point under the staircase, and carefully avoiding dangerous contact with the fireplaces, and particularly steering clear of the great interior flue, was to conduct the enterprising traveler from the front door all the way into the dining-room in the remote rear of the mansion. Doubtless it was a bold stroke of genius, that plan of hers, and so was Nero's when he schemed his grand canal through the Isthmus of Corinth. Nor will I take oath, that, had her project been accomplished, then, by help of lights hung at judicious intervals through the tunnel, some Belzoni or other might have succeeded in future ages in penetrating through the masonry, and actually emerging into the dining-room, and once there, it would have been inhospitable treatment of such a traveler to have denied him a recruiting meal.

But my bustling wife did not restrict her objections, nor in the end confine her proposed alterations to the first floor. Her ambition was of the mounting order. She ascended with her schemes to the second floor, and so to the attic. Perhaps there was some small ground for her discontent with things as they were. The truth is, there was no regular passage-way up-stairs or down, unless we again except that little orchestra-gallery before mentioned. And all this was owing to the chimney, which my gamesome spouse seemed despitefully to regard as the bully of the house. On all its four sides, nearly all the chambers sidled up to the chimney for the benefit of a fireplace. The chimney would not go to them; they must needs go to it. The consequence was, almost every room, like a philosophical system, was in itself an entry, or passage-way to other rooms, and systems of rooms—a whole suite of entries, in fact. Going through the house, you seem to be forever going somewhere, and getting nowhere. It is like losing one's self in the woods; round and round the chimney you go, and if you arrive at all, it is just where you started, and so you begin again, and again get nowhere. Indeed—though I say it not in the way of faultfinding at all—never was there so labyrinthine an abode. Guests will tarry with me several weeks and every now and then, be anew astonished at some unforseen apartment.

The puzzling nature of the mansion, resulting from the chimney, is peculiarly noticeable in the dining-room, which has no less than nine doors, opening in all directions, and into all sorts of places. A stranger for the first time entering this dining-room, and naturally taking no special heed at which door he entered, will, upon rising to depart, commit the strangest blunders. Such, for instance, as opening the first door that comes handy, and finding himself stealing up-stairs by the back passage. Shutting that he will proceed to another, and be aghast at the cellar yawning at his feet. Trying a third, he surprises the housemaid at her work. In the end, no more relying on his own unaided efforts, he procures a trusty guide in some passing person, and in good time successfully emerges. Perhaps as curious a blunder as any, was that of a certain stylish young gentleman, a great exquisite, in whose judicious eyes my daughter Anna had found especial favor. He called upon the young lady one evening, and found her alone in the dining-room at her needlework. He stayed rather late; and after abundance of superfine discourse, all the while retaining his hat and cane, made his profuse adieus, and with repeated graceful bows proceeded to depart, after fashion of courtiers from the Queen, and by so doing, opening a door at random, with one hand placed behind, very effectually succeeded in backing himself into a dark pantry, where be carefully shut himself up, wondering there was no light in the entry. After several strange noises as of a cat among the crockery, he reappeared through the same door, looking uncommonly crestfallen, and, with a deeply embarrassed air, requested my daughter to designate at which of the nine he should find exit. When the mischievous Anna told me the story, she said it was surprising how unaffected and matter-of-fact the young gentleman's manner was after his reappearance. He was more candid than ever, to be sure; having inadvertently thrust his white kids into an open drawer of Havana sugar, under the impression, probably, that being what they call "a sweet fellow," his route might possibly lie in that direction.

Another inconvenience resulting from the chimney is, the bewilderment of a guest in gaining his chamber, many strange doors lying between him and it. To direct him by finger-posts would look rather queer; and just as queer in him to be knocking at every door on his route, like London's city guest, the king, at Temple-Bar.

Now, of all these things and many, many more, my family continually complained. At last my wife came out with her sweeping proposition—in toto to abolish the chimney.

"What!" said I, "abolish the chimney? To take out

the backbone of anything, wife, is a hazardous affair. Spines out of backs, and chimneys out of houses, are not to be taken like frosted lead pipes from the ground. Besides," added I, "the chimney is the one grand permanence of this abode. If undisturbed by innovators, then in future ages, when all the house shall have crumbled from it, this chimney will still survive—a Bunker Hill monument. No, no, wife, I can't abolish my backbone."

So said I then. But who is sure of himself, especially an old man, with both wife and daughters ever at his elbow and ear? In time, I was persuaded to think a little better of it; in short, to take the matter into preliminary consideration. At length it came to pass that a master-mason—a rough sort of architect—one Mr. Scribe, was summoned to a conference. I formally introduced him to my chimney. A previous introduction from my wife had introduced him to myself. He had been not a little employed by that lady, in preparing plans and estimates for some of her extensive operations in drainage. Having, with much ado, exhorted from my spouse the promise that she would leave us to an unmolested survey, I began by leading Mr. Scribe down to the root of the matter, in the cellar. Lamp in hand, I descended; for though up-stairs it was noon, below it was night.

We seemed in the pyramids; and I, with one hand holding my lamp over head, and with the other pointing out, in the obscurity, the hoar mass of the chimney, seemed some Arab guide, showing the cobwebbed mausoleum of the great god Apis.

"This is a most remarkable structure, sir," said the master-mason, after long contemplating it in silence, "a most remarkable structure, sir."

"Yes," said I complacently, "every one says so."

"But large as it appears above the roof, I would not have inferred the magnitude of this foundation, sir," eyeing it critically.

Then taking out his rule, he measured it.

"Twelve feet square; one hundred and forty-four square feet! Sir, this house would appear to have been built simply for the accommodation of your chimney."

"Yes, my chimney and me. Tell me candidly, now," I added, "would you have such a famous chimney abolished?"

"I wouldn't have it in a house of mine, sir, for a gift," was the reply. "It's a losing affair altogether, sir. Do you know, sir, that in retaining this chimney, you are losing, not only one hundred and forty-four square feet of good ground, but likewise a considerable interest upon a considerable principal?"

"How?"

"Look, sir!" said he, taking a bit of red chalk from his pocket, and figuring against a whitewashed wall, "twenty times eight is so and so; then forty-two times thirty—nine is so and so—ain't it, sir? Well, add those together, and subtract this here, then that makes so and so," still chalking away.

To be brief, after no small ciphering, Mr. Scribe informed me that my chimney contained, I am ashamed to say how many thousand and odd valuable bricks.

"No more," said I fidgeting. "Pray now, let us have a look above."

In that upper zone we made two more circumnavigations for the first and second floors. That done, we stood together at the foot of the stairway by the front door; my hand upon the knob, and Mr. Scribe hat in hand.

"Well, sir," said he, a sort of feeling his way, and, to help himself, fumbling with his hat, "well, sir, I think it can be done."

"What, pray, Mr. Scribe; *what* can be done?"

"Your chimney, sir; it can without rashness be removed, I think."

"I will think of it, too, Mr. Scribe" said I, turning the knob and bowing him towards the open space without, "I will *think* of it, sir; it demands consideration; much obliged to ye; good morning, Mr. Scribe."

"It is all arranged, then," cried my wife with great glee, bursting from the nighest room.

"When will they begin?" demanded my daughter Julia.

"To-morrow?" asked Anna.

"Patience, patience, my dears," said I, "such a big chimney is not to be abolished in a minute."

Next morning it began again.

"You remember the chimney," said my wife.

"Wife," said I, "it is never out of my house and never out of my mind."

"But when is Mr. Scribe to begin to pull it down?" asked Anna.

"Not to-day, Anna," said I.

"*When*, then?" demanded Julia, in alarm.

Now, if this chimney of mine was, for size, a sort of belfry, for ding-donging at me about it, my wife and daughters were a sort of bells, always chiming together, or taking up each other's melodies at every pause, my wife the key-clapper of all. A very sweet ringing, and pealing, and chiming, I confess; but then, the most silvery of bells may, sometimes, dismally toll, as well as merrily play. And as touching the subject in question, it became so now. Perceiving a strange relapse of opposition in me, wife and daughters began a soft and dirge-like, melancholy tolling over it.

At length my wife, getting much excited, declared to me, with pointed finger, that so long as that chimney stood, she should regard it as the monument of what she called my broken pledge. But finding this did not answer, the next day, she gave me to understand that either she or the chimney must quit the house.

Finding matters coming to such a pass, I and my pipe philosophized over them awhile, and finally concluded between us, that little as our hearts went with the plan, yet for peace' sake, I might write out the chimney's death-warrant, and, while my hand was in, scratch a note to Mr. Scribe.

Considering that I, and my chimney, and my pipe, from having been so much together, were three great cronies, the facility with which my pipe consented to a project so fatal to the goodliest of our trio; or rather, the way in which I and my pipe, in secret, conspired together, as it were, against our unsuspicious old comrade—this may seem rather strange, if not suggestive of sad reflections upon us two. But, indeed, we, sons of clay, that is my pipe and I, are no better than the rest. Far from us, indeed, to have volunteered the betrayal of our crony. We are of a peaceable nature, too. But that love of peace it was which made us false to a mutual friend, as soon as his cause demanded a vigorous vindication. But, I rejoice to add, that better and braver thoughts soon returned, as will now briefly be set forth.

To my note, Mr. Scribe replied in person.

Once more we made a survey, mainly now with a view to a pecuniary estimate.

"I will do it for five hundred dollars," said Mr. Scribe at last, again hat in hand.

"Very well, Mr. Scribe, I will think of it," replied I, again bowing him to the door.

Not unvexed by this, for the second time, unexpected response, again he withdrew, and from my wife, and daughters again burst the old exclamations. The truth is, resolved how I would, at the last pinch I and my chimney could not be parted.

"So Holofernes will have his way, never mind whose heart breaks for it" said my wife next morning, at breakfast, in that half-didactic, half-reproachful way of hers, which is harder to bear than her most energetic assault. Holofernes, too, is with her a pet name for any fell domestic despot. So, whenever, against her most ambitious innovations, those which saw me quite across the grain, I, as in the present instance, stand with however little steadfastness on the defense, she is sure to call me Holofernes, and ten to one takes the first oppor-

tunity to read aloud, with a suppressed emphasis, of an evening, the first newspaper paragraph about some tyrannic day-laborer, who, after being for many years the Caligula of his family, ends by beating his long-suffering spouse to death, with a garret door wrenched off its hinges, and then, pitching his little innocents out of the window, suicidally turns inward towards the broken wall scored with the butcher's and baker's bills, and so rushes headlong to his dreadful account.

Nevertheless, for a few days, not a little to my surprise, I heard no further reproaches. An intense calm pervaded my wife, but beneath which, as in the sea, there was no knowing what portentous movements might be going on. She frequently went abroad, and in a direction which I thought not unsuspicious; namely, in the direction of New Petra, a griffin-like house of wood and stucco, in the highest style of ornamental art, graced with four chimneys in the form of erect dragons spouting smoke from their nostrils; the elegant modern residence of Mr. Scribe, which he had built for the purpose of a standing advertisement, not more of his taste as an architect, than his solidity as a master-mason.

At last, smoking my pipe one morning, I heard a rap at the door, and my wife, with an air unusually quiet for her brought me a note. As I have no correspondents except Solomon, with whom in his sentiments, at least, I entirely correspond, the note occasioned me some little surprise, which was not dismissed upon reading the following:—

NEW PETRA, April 1st. Sir—During my last examination of your chimney, possibly you may have noted that I frequently applied my rule to it in a manner apparently unnecessary. Possibly, also, at the same time, you might have observed in me more or less of perplexity, to which, however, I refrained from giving any verbal expression. I now feel it obligatory upon me to inform you of what was then but a dim suspicion, and as such would have been unwise to give utterance to, but which now, from various subsequent calculations assuming no little probability, it may be important that you should not remain in further ignorance of. It is my solemn duty to warn you, sir, that there is architectural cause to conjecture that somewhere concealed in your chimney is a reserved space, hermetically closed, in short, a secret chamber, or rather closet. How long it has been there, it is for me impossible to say. What it contains is hid, with itself, in darkness. But

probably a secret closet would not have been contrived except for some extraordinary object, whether for the concealment of treasure, or for what other purpose, may be left to those better acquainted with the history of the house to guess. But enough: in making this disclosure, sir, my conscience is eased. Whatever step you choose to take upon it, is of course a matter of indifference to me; though, I confess, as respects the character of the closet, I cannot but share in a natural curiosity. Trusting that you may be guided aright, in determining whether it is Christian-like knowingly to reside in a house, hidden in which is a secret closet, I remain, with much respect, Yours very humbly,
HIRAM SCRIBE.

My first thought upon reading this note was, not of the alleged mystery of manner to which, at the outset, it alluded-for none such had I at all observed in the master-mason during his surveys — but of my late kinsman, Captain Julian Dacres, long a ship-master and merchant in the Indian trade, who, about thirty years ago, and at the ripe age of ninety, died a bachelor, and in this very house, which he had built. He was supposed to have retired into this country with a large fortune. But to the general surprise, after being at great cost in building himself this mansion, he settled down into a sedate, reserved and inexpensive old age, which by the neighbors was thought all the better for his heirs: but lo! upon opening the will, his property was found to consist but of the house and grounds, and some ten thousand dollars in stocks; but the place, being found heavily mortgaged, was in consequence sold. Gossip had its day, and left the grass quietly to creep over the captain's grave, where he still slumbers in a privacy as unmolested as if the billows of the Indian Ocean, instead of the billows of inland verdure, rolled over him. Still, I remembered long ago, hearing strange solutions whispered by the country people for the mystery involving his will, and, by reflex, himself; and that, too, as well in conscience as purse. But people who could circulate the report (which they did), that Captain Julian Dacres had, in his day, been a Borneo pirate, surely were not worthy of credence in their collateral notions. It is queer what wild whimsies of rumors will, like toadstools, spring up about any eccentric stranger, who settling down among a rustic population, keeps quietly to himself. With some, inoffensiveness would seem a prime cause of offense. But what chiefly had led me to scout at these rumors, particularly as referring to concealed treasure, was the circumstance, that the stranger (the same who razed the roof and the chimney) into whose hands the estate had passed on my kinsman's death, was of that sort of character, that had there been the least ground for those reports, he would speedily have tested them, by tearing down and rummaging the walls.

Nevertheless, the note of Mr. Scribe, so strangely recalling the memory of my kinsman, very naturally chimed in with what had been mysterious, or at least unexplained, about him; vague flashings of ingots united in my mind with vague gleamings of skulls. But the first cool thought soon dismissed such chimeras; and, with a calm smile, I turned towards my wife, who, meantime, had been sitting nearby, impatient enough, I dare say, to know who could have taken it into his head to write me a letter.

"Well, old man," said she, "who is it from, and what is it about?"

"Read it, wife," said I, handing it.

Read it she did, and then — such an explosion! I will not pretend to describe her emotions, or repeat her expressions. Enough that my daughters were quickly called in to share the excitement. Although they had never dreamed of such a revelation as Mr. Scribe's; yet upon the first suggestion they instinctively saw the extreme likelihood of it. In corroboration, they cited first my kinsman, and second, my chimney; alleging that the profound mystery involving the former, and the equally profound masonry involving the latter, though both acknowledged facts, were alike preposterous on any other supposition than the secret closet.

But all this time I was quietly thinking to myself: Could it be hidden from me that my credulity in this instance would operate very favorably to a certain plan of theirs? How to get to the secret closet, or how to have any certainty about it at all, without making such fell work with my chimney as to render its set destruction superfluous? That my wife wished to get rid of the chimney, it needed no reflection to show; and that Mr. Scribe, for all his pretended disinterestedness, was not opposed to pocketing five hundred dollars by the operation, seemed equally evident. That my wife had, in secret, laid heads together with Mr. Scribe, I at present refrain from affirming. But when I consider her enmity against my chimney, and the steadiness with which at the last she is wont to carry out her schemes, if by hook or crook she can, especially after having been once baffled, why, I scarcely knew at what step of hers to be surprised.

Of one thing only was I resolved, that I and my chimney should not budge.

In vain all protests. Next morning I went out into the road, where I had noticed a diabolical-looking old gander, that for its doughty exploits in the way of scratching into forbidden enclosures, had been rewarded by its master with a portentous, four-pronged, wooden decoration, in the shape of a collar of the Order of the Garotte. This gander I cornered and rummaging out its stiffest quill, plucked it, took it home, and making a stiff pen, inscribed the following stiff note:

CHIMNEY SIDE, April 2. MR. SCRIBE
Sir:-For your conjecture, we return you our joint thanks and compliments, and beg leave to assure you, that we shall remain, Very faithfully, The same, I AND MY CHIMNEY.

Of course, for this epistle we had to endure some pretty sharp raps. But having at last explicitly understood from me that Mr. Scribe's note had not altered my mind one jot, my wife, to move me, among other things said, that if she remembered aright, there was a statute placing the keeping in private of secret closets on the same unlawful footing with the keeping of gunpowder. But it had no effect.

A few days after, my spouse changed her key.

It was nearly midnight, and all were in bed but ourselves, who sat up, one in each chimney corner; she, needles in hand, indefatigably knitting a sock; I, pipe in mouth, indolently weaving my vapors. It was one of the first of the chill nights in autumn. There was a fire on the hearth, burning low. The air without was torpid and heavy; the wood, by an oversight, of the sort called soggy.

"Do look at the chimney," she began; "can't you see that something must be in it?"

"Yes, wife. Truly there is smoke in the chimney, as in Mr. Scribe's note."

"Smoke? Yes, indeed, and in my eyes, too. How you two wicked old sinners do smoke!—this wicked old chimney and you."

"Wife," said I, "I and my chimney like to have a quiet smoke together, it is true, but we don't like to be called names."

"Now, dear old man," said she, softening down, and a little shifting the subject, "when you think of that old kinsman of yours, you *know* there must be a secret closet in this chimney."

"Secret ash-hole, wife, why don't you have it? Yes, I dare say there is a secret ash-hole in the chimney; for where do all the ashes go to that drop down the queer hole yonder?"

"I know where they go to; I've been there almost as many times as the cat."

"What devil, wife, prompted you to crawl into the ash-hole? Don't you know that St. Dunstan's devil emerged from the ash-hole? You will get your death one of these days, exploring all about as you do. But supposing there be a secret closet, what then?"

"What then? why what should be in a secret closet but—"

"Dry bones, wife," broke in I with a puff, while the sociable old chimney broke in with another.

"There again! Oh, how this wretched old chimney smokes," wiping her eyes with her handkerchief. "I've no doubt the reason it smokes so is, because that secret closet interferes with the flue. Do see, too, how the jambs here keep settling; and it's down hill all the way from the door to this hearth. This horrid old chimney will fall on our heads yet; depend upon it, old man."

"Yes, wife, I do depend on it; yes indeed, I place every dependence on my chimney. As for its settling, I like it. I, too, am settling, you know, in my gait. I and my chimney are settling together, and shall keep settling, too, till, as in a great feather-bed, we shall both have settled away clean out of sight. But this secret oven; I mean, secret closet of yours, wife; where exactly do you suppose that secret closet is? "

"That is for Mr. Scribe to say."

"But suppose he cannot say exactly; what, then?"

"Why then he can prove, I am sure, that it must be somewhere or other in this horrid old chimney."

"And if he can't prove that; what, then?"

"Why then, old man," with a stately air, "I shall say little more about it."

"Agreed, wife," returned I, knocking my pipe-bowl against the jamb, "and now, to-morrow, I will for a third time send for Mr. Scribe. Wife, the sciatica takes me; be so good as to put this pipe on the mantel."

"If you get the step-ladder for me, I will. This shocking old chimney, this abominable old-fashioned old chimney's mantels are so high, I can't reach them."

No opportunity, however trivial, was overlooked for a subordinate fling at the pile.

Here, by way of introduction, it should be mentioned, that besides the fireplaces all round it, the chimney was, in the most haphazard way, excavated on each floor for certain curious out-of-the-way cupboards and closets, of all sorts and sizes, clinging here and there, like nests in the crotches of some old oak. On the second floor these closets were by far the most irregular and numerous. And yet this should hardly have been so, since the theory of the chimney was, that it pyramidically diminished as it ascended. The abridgment of its square on the roof was obvious enough; and it was supposed that the reduction must be methodically graduated from bottom to top.

"Mr. Scribe," said I when, the next day, with an eager aspect, that individual again came, "my object in sending for you this morning is, not to arrange for the demolition of my chimney, nor to have any particular conversation about it, but simply to allow you every reasonable facility for verifying, if you can, the conjecture communicated in your note."

Though in secret not a little crestfallen, it may be, by my phlegmatic reception, so different from what he had looked for; with much apparent alacrity he commenced the survey; throwing open the cupboards on the first floor, and peering into the closets on the second; measuring one within, and then comparing that measurement with the measurement without. Removing the fireboards, he would gaze up the flues. But no sign of the hidden work yet. Now, on the second floor the rooms were the most rambling conceivable. They, as it were, dovetailed into each other. They were of all shapes; not one mathematically square room among them all—a peculiarity which by the master-mason had not been unobserved. With a significant, not to say portentous expression, he took a circuit of the chimney, measuring the area of each room around it; then going down stairs, and out of doors, he measured the entire ground area; then compared the sum total of the areas of all the rooms on the second floor with the ground area; then, returning to me in no small excitement, announced that there was a difference of no less than two hundred and odd square feet—room enough, in all conscience, for a secret closet.

"But, Mr. Scribe," said I, stroking my chin, "have you allowed for the walls, both main and sectional? They take up some space, you know."

"Ah, I had forgotten that," tapping his forehead; "but," still ciphering on his paper, "that will not make up the deficiency."

"But, Mr. Scribe, have you allowed for the recesses of so many fireplaces on a floor, and for the fire-walls, and the flues; in short, Mr. Scribe, have you allowed for the legitimate chimney itself—some one hundred and forty-four square feet or thereabouts, Mr. Scribe?"

"How unaccountable. That slipped my mind, too."

"Did it, indeed, Mr. Scribe?"

He faltered a little, and burst forth with, "But we must now allow one hundred and forty-four square feet for the legitimate chimney. My position is, that within those undue limits the secret closet is contained."

I eyed him in silence a moment; then spoke:

"Your survey is concluded, Mr. Scribe; be so good now as to lay your finger upon the exact part of the chimney wall where you believe this secret closet to be; or would a witch-hazel wand assist you, Mr. Scribe?"

"No, Sir, but a crowbar would," he, with temper, rejoined.

Here, now, thought I to myself, the cat leaps out of the bag. I looked at him with a calm glance, under which he seemed somewhat uneasy. More than ever now I suspected a plot. I remembered what my wife had said about abiding by the decision of Mr. Scribe. In a bland way, I resolved to buy up the decision of Mr. Scribe.

"Sir," said I, "really, I am much obliged to you for this survey. It has quite set my mind at rest. And no doubt you, too, Mr. Scribe, must feel much relieved. Sir," I added, "you have made three visits to the chimney. With a business man, time is money. Here are fifty dollars, Mr. Scribe. Nay, take it. You have earned it. Your opinion is worth it. And by the way,"—as he modestly received the money—"have you any objections to give me a—a—little certificate—something, say, like a steamboat certificate, certifying that you, a competent surveyor, have surveyed my chimney, and found no reason to believe any unsoundness; in short, any—any secret closet in it. Would you be so kind, Mr. Scribe?"

"But, but, sir," stammered he with honest hesitation."

"Here, here are pen and paper," said I, with entire assurance.

Enough.

That evening I had the certificate framed and hung over the dining-room fireplace, trusting that the continual sight of it would forever put at rest at once the dreams and stratagems of my household.

But, no. Inveterately bent upon the extirpation of that noble old chimney, still to this day my wife goes about it, with my daughter Anna's geological hammer, tapping the wall all over, and then holding her ear against it, as I have seen the physicians of life insurance companies tap a man's chest, and then incline over for the echo. Sometimes of nights she almost frightens one, going about on this phantom errand, and still following the sepulchral response of the chimney, round and round, as if it were leading her to the threshold of the secret closet.

"How hollow it sounds," she will hollowly cry. "Yes, I declare," with an emphatic tap, "there is a secret closet here. Here, in this very spot. Hark! How hollow!"

"Psha! wife, of course it is hollow. Who ever heard

of a solid chimney?" But nothing avails. And my daughters take after, not me, but their mother.

Sometimes all three abandon the theory of the secret closet and return to the genuine ground of attack—the unsightliness of so cumbrous a pile, with comments upon the great addition of room to be gained by its demolition, and the fine effect of the projected grand hall, and the convenience resulting from the collateral running in one direction and another of their various partitions. Not more ruthlessly did the Three Powers partition away poor Poland, than my wife and daughters would fain partition away my chimney. But seeing that, despite all, I and my chimney still smoke our pipes, my wife reoccupies the ground of the secret closet, enlarging upon what wonders are there, and what a shame it is, not to seek it out and explore it.

"Wife," said I, upon one of these occasions, "why speak more of that secret closet, when there before you hangs contrary testimony of a master mason, elected by yourself to decide. Besides, even if there were a secret closet, secret it should remain, and secret it shall. Yes, wife, here for once I must say my say. Infinite sad mischief has resulted from the profane bursting open of secret recesses. Though standing in the heart of this house, though hitherto we have all nestled about it, unsuspicious of aught hidden within, this chimney may or may not have a secret closet. But if it have, it is my kinsman's. To break into that wall, would be to break into his breast. And that wall-breaking wish of Momus I account the wish of a churchrobbing gossip and knave. Yes, wife, a vile eavesdropping varlet was Momus."

"Moses? Mumps? Stuff with your mumps and Moses?"

The truth is, my wife, like all the rest of the world, cares not a fig for philosophical jabber. In dearth of other philosophical companionship, I and my chimney have to smoke and philosophize together. And sitting up so late as we do at it, a mighty smoke it is that we two smoky old philosophers make.

But my spouse, who likes the smoke of my tobacco as little as she does that of the soot, carries on her war against both. I live in continual dread lest, like the golden bowl, the pipes of me and my chimney shall yet be broken. To stay that mad project of my wife's, naught answers. Or, rather, she herself is incessantly answering, incessantly besetting me with her terrible alacrity for improvement, which is a softer name for destruction. Scarce a day I do not find her with her tape-measure, measuring for her grand hall, while Anna holds a yardstick on one side, and Julia looks approvingly on from the other. Mysterious intimations appear in the nearest village paper, signed "Claude," to the effect that a certain structure, standing on a certain hill, is a sad blemish to an otherwise lovely landscape. Anonymous letters arrive, threatening me with I know not what, unless I remove my chimney. Is it my wife, too, or who, that sets up the neighbors to badgering me on the same subject, and hinting to me that my chimney, like a huge elm, absorbs all moisture from my garden? At night, also, my wife will start as from sleep, professing to hear ghostly noises from the secret closet. Assailed on all sides, and in all ways, small peace have I and my chimney.

Were it not for the baggage, we would together pack up and remove from the country.

What narrow escapes have been ours! Once I found in a drawer a whole portfolio of plans and estimates. Another time, upon returning after a day's absence, I discovered my wife standing before the chimney in earnest conversation with a person whom I at once recognized as a meddlesome architectural reformer, who, because he had no gift for putting up anything was ever intent upon pulling them down; in various parts of the country having prevailed upon half-witted old folks to destroy their old-fashioned houses, particularly the chimneys.

But worst of all was, that time I unexpectedly returned at early morning from a visit to the city, and upon approaching the house, narrowly escaped three brickbats which fell, from high aloft, at my feet. Glancing up, what was my horror to see three savages, in blue jean overalls in the very act of commencing the long-threatened attack. Aye, indeed, thinking of those three brickbats, I and my chimney have had narrow escapes.

It is now some seven years since I have stirred from my home. My city friends all wonder why I don't come to see them, as in former times. They think I am getting sour and unsocial. Some say that I have become a sort of mossy old misanthrope, while all the time the fact is, I am simply standing guard over my mossy old chimney; for it is resolved between me and my chimney, that I and my chimney will never surrender.

FINAL PROJECT

Correct and rewrite all essays and place them in your Final Portfolio.

SUGGESTED
Weekly *Implementation*

DAY 1	DAY 2	DAY 3	DAY 4	DAY 5
Prayer journal.	**Prayer journal.**	**Prayer journal.**	**Prayer journal.**	**Prayer journal.**
Review the required reading(s) *before* the assigned lesson begins.	Review reading(s) from next lesson.	Write rough drafts of all assigned essays.	Rewrite corrected copies of essays due tomorrow.	Essays are due.
Teacher may want to discuss assigned reading(s) with students.	Outline essays due at the end of the week.	The teacher and/or a peer evaluator may correct rough drafts.		Take Lesson 12 test.
Teacher and students will decide on required essays for this lesson, choosing two or three essays.	Per teacher instructions, students may answer orally in a group setting some of the essays that are not assigned as formal essays.			Reading ahead: Review "Oh Captain! My Captain!" Walt Whitman; Negro Spirituals; "The Gettysburg Address," Abraham Lincoln; and "Surrender Speech," Chief Joseph.
The rest of the essays can be outlined, answered with shorter answers, or skipped.				Guide: Is Whitman a Romantic? What were the purposes of the Negro Spirituals?
Review all readings for Lesson 12.				

The American Civil War

BACKGROUND

The southerner Mary Chestnut wrote, as the Civil War was beginning to unfold, "We [the North and the South] are divorced because we have hated each other so!" This hatred led to a bloody and horrible civil war.

For years the question, "What caused The Civil war?" has puzzled historians. They suggest many reasons, but what is the main cause? Slavery was the chief irritant but did not cause the conflict. For example, both Rachel and Samuel Cormany, Civil War contemporaries, supported their government's efforts to quell the southern rebellion, but neither of them was irritated by slavery. Rachel blamed the war on the "hotheadness of the South, and the invisibleness of the North." They were not in favor of freeing the slaves. They represented most of the North. In fact, there were many things that contributed to the Civil War—some more than others. Certainly slavery was *a* cause but not *the* cause.

The Civil War was caused because Southern and Northern Americans chose not to live together. Again, the operative word is *chose*. They chose to fight a war. The North and the South were always two nations, and by 1860 it was difficult, but not impossible, to live together in the same house. They had solved their problems before—in 1820 and 1850 for instance. However, in 1860, the political system failed.

The Civil war was neither the fault of the South nor the North—rather it was the fault of both. The combination of an expanding economy, a flood of immigrants, the second Great Awakening, Manifest Destiny, and the failure of the American political system brought the young republic to the brink of Civil War. Ultimately, though, the failure of nerve manifested by American political leaders thrust the nation into the bloodiest war in American history.

Reflected in the literature of this nation, no war quite captured the minds and hearts of Americans as this war did.

You will analyze: "Oh Captain! My Captain!" Walt Whitman; Negro Spirituals; "The Gettysburg Address," Abraham Lincoln; and "Surrender Speech," Chief Joseph.

Reading Ahead: *Narrative of the Life of Frederick Douglass*, Frederick Douglass.

Guide Question: How was Douglass' life typical or atypical of most African-American slave lives?

Walt Whitman

BACKGROUND

© Arttoday.com

Whitman was one of the first American poets to abandon most of the Romanticism of earlier poetry and to create a distinctly American idiom to address those he celebrated as the "American masses." Walt Whitman, and later Carl Sandburg, spoke for a nation. Whitman and Emily Dickinson were the first modern American poets.

O Captain! My Captain!
Walt Whitman

O CAPTAIN! my Captain! our fearful trip is done;
The ship has weather'd every rack, the prize we
    sought is won;
The port is near, the bells I hear, the people all exult-
    ing,
While follow eyes the steady keel, the vessel grim and
    daring:

But O heart! heart! heart!
O the bleeding drops of red,
Where on the deck my Captain lies,
Fallen cold and dead.

O Captain! my Captain! rise up and hear the bells;
Rise up—for you the flag is flung—for you the bugle
　　　trills;
For you bouquets and ribbon'd wreaths—for you the
　　　shores a-crowding;
For you they call, the swaying mass, their eager faces
　　　turning;
Here Captain! dear father!
This arm beneath your head;
It is some dream that on the deck,
You've fallen cold and dead.

My Captain does not answer, his lips are pale and still;
My father does not feel my arm, he has no pulse nor
　　　will;
The ship is anchor'd safe and sound, its voyage closed
　　　and done;
From fearful trip, the victor ship, comes in with object
　　　won;
Exult, O shores, and ring, O bells!
But I, with mournful tread,
Walk the deck my Captain lies,
Fallen cold and dead.
http://www.petama.ch/PROJ-07-A.htm

Negro Spirituals

BACKGROUND

Spirituals were the sacred hymns of the African-American slave community. They usually taught a lesson and told a story, both from the Old Testament.

The most grievous historical metaphor for the African-American community is chattel slavery. It is the quintessential image of the apparent triumph of white racism in American civilization. This unhappy time captures the African-American heart as strongly as the Egyptian bondage motif captures the Old Testament community. Slavery presented African-Americans with a disconcerting contradiction: legally they were defined as property; but at the same time, they were called upon to act in sentient, articulate, and human ways.

Within the context of chattel slavery, the African-American community created patterns of resistance.

Spirituals were a form of slave resistance. The dominant white community did not allow the African-American community to express overtly their frustration. Therefore, the African-American slave community used the spiritual hymn and the folktale to teach survival skills, to express hostility toward their masters, and to impart wisdom to the young. In the folktale "The Tar Baby Tricks Brer Rabbit," Brer Rabbit slyly convinced his arch enemies—Fox and Bear—to throw him into the brier patch rather than into the well. Of course that was exactly what Bear and Fox did and exactly what Brer Rabbit wanted them to do since Brer Rabbit escaped through the brier patch! The African-American slave community resisted slavery in every possible way. From the beginning the African Community saw itself in an adversarial role to the white community and sought to escape into its own culture as a way to defend itself against white domination.

The ultimate goal of many African peoples was preservation and promotion of community—not retribution and revenge. This community spirit of beneficence, forbearance, practical wisdom, improvisation, forgiveness, and justice was nurtured, preserved, and celebrated in the African-American community—but only at great personal sacrifice. Therefore, African-American resistance was a uniquely American phenomenon, resulting from three hundred years of historical oppression.

Negro Spirituals:
Go Down Moses

When Israel was in Egypt's land
Let my people go
Oppressed so hard they could not stand
Let my people go

Go down Moses
Way down in Egypt land
Tell old Pharaoh
Let my people go

Thus spoke the Lord, bold Moses said
Let my people go

If not I'll smite your first born dead
Let my people go

No more in bondage shall they toil
Let my people go

Let them come out with Egypt's spoil
Let my people go.
http://xroads.virginia.edu/~HYPER/TWH/TWH_index.htm

Deep River

Deep river, my home is over Jordan
Deep river,
Lord, I want to cross over into campground
Lord, I want to cross over into campground
Lord, I want to cross over into campground
Lord, I want to cross over into campground

Oh, chillun
Oh, don't you want to go, to that gospel feast
That promised land, that land where all is peace?
Walk into heaven, and take a seat
And cast my crown at Jesus feet

Lord, I want to cross over into campground
Lord, I want to cross over into campground
Lord, I want to cross over into campground
Lord, I want to cross over into campground
http://xroads.virginia.edu/~HYPER/TWH/TWH_index.htm

Roll Jordan, Roll

Roll Jordan, roll
Roll Jordan, roll
I wanter go to heav'n when I die
To hear ol' Jordan roll
O brethren
Roll Jordan, roll
Roll Jordan, roll
I wanter go to heav'n when I die
To hear ol' Jordan roll

Oh, brothers you oughter been dere
Yes my Lord
A-sittin' in the Kingdom
To hear ol' Jordan roll

Sing it over
Oh, sinner you oughter been dere
Yes my Lord
A-sittin' in the Kingdom
To hear ol' Jordan roll
http://xroads.virginia.edu/~HYPER/TWH/TWH_index.htm,Roll

Swing Low, Sweet Chariot

Swing low, sweet chariot,
Coming for to carry me home
Swing low, sweet chariot,
Coming for to carry me home

I looked over Jordan, and what did I see
Coming for to carry me home?
A band of angels coming after me
Coming for to carry me home

If you get there before I do
Coming for to carry me home
Tell all my friends I coming too
Coming for to carry me home

I'm sometimes up, I'm sometimes down
Coming for to carry me home
But still my soul feels heavenly bound
Coming for to carry me home
http://xroads.virginia.edu/~HYPER/TWH/TWH_index.htm

Abraham Lincoln

BACKGROUND

Sometimes great literature takes months, even years to create. Apparently, Lincoln wrote this most famous of small speeches while traveling on a train from Washington, D. C., to Gettysburg, PA. It was presented on November 19, 1863, to dedicate a cemetery interning Union war dead who feel at the Battle of Gettysburg, July 1-3, 1863.

Gettysburg Address

Fourscore and seven years ago our fathers brought forth on this continent a new nation, conceived in liberty and dedicated to the proposition that all men are created equal. Now we are engaged in a great civil war, testing whether that nation or any nation so conceived and so dedicated can long endure. We are met on a great battlefield of that war. We have come to dedicate a portion of that field as a final resting-place for those who here gave their lives that that nation might live. It is altogether fitting and proper that we should do this. But in a larger sense, we cannot dedicate, we cannot consecrate, we cannot hallow this ground. The brave men, living and dead who struggled here have consecrated it far above our poor power to add or detract.

© Arttoday.com

The world will little note nor long remember what we say here, but it can never forget what they did here. It is for us the living rather to be dedicated here to the unfinished work which they who fought here have thus far so nobly advanced. It is rather for us to be here dedicated to the great task remaining before us—that from these honored dead we take increased devotion to that cause for which they gave the last full measure of devotion—that we here highly resolve that these dead shall not have died in vain, that this nation under God shall have a new birth of freedom, and that government of the people, by the people, for the people shall not perish from the earth.

http://www.law.ou.edu/hist/getty.html

Chief Joseph of the Nez Perce

BACKGROUND

Chief Joseph (1840?-1904), was chief of the Nez Perce and one of the leaders of Native American resistance to white assimilation and domination in the western United States. Following his father's example, Chief Joseph continued a policy of noncompliance to an 1863 treaty that confined the

Nez Perce to a government reservation. In 1877 hostilities broke out. The Nez Perce were ordered to leave the Oregon territory and relocate to a reservation in Idaho. Joseph reluctantly agreed to the demand, but when a few of his men killed a group of whites, he decided to lead several hundred people on a march to find refuge in Canada. He defeated United States Army units that tried to stop him on the Big Hole River in Montana but was stopped about 48 miles from the border where he presented the following speech:

I will Fight No More Forever
1877

I will fight no more forever.
I am tired of fighting.
Our chiefs are killed.
Looking Glass is dead.
Toohulhulsote is dead.
The old men are all dead.
It is the young men who say no and yes.
He who led the young men is dead.
It is cold and we have no blankets.
The little children are freezing to death.
My people, some of them,
Have run away to the hills
And have no blankets, no food.
No one knows where they are
Perhaps they are freezing to death.
I want to have time to look for my children
And see how many of them I can find.
Maybe I shall find them among the dead.
Hear me, my chiefs, I am tired.
My heart is sad and sick.
From where the sun now stands
I will fight no more forever.

http://www.4literature.net/Chief_Joseph/

CRITICAL THINKING

A. In "Oh Captain! My Captain!" what metaphor does Whitman use to communicate his grief at the death of Abraham Lincoln?

B. In what sense is this poetry modern? In what sense is this poetry Romantic?

BIBLICAL APPLICATION

In what ways were Negro spirituals a form of resistance to chattel slavery?

ENRICHMENT

Other than Chief Joseph, the most famous Native war chief was Geronimo. Geronimo (1829-1909) was chief of an Apache tribe in present-day Arizona. In 1876 the United States government attempted to move the Apaches from their ancestral home to New Mexico. Geronimo then began a ten year war against white settlements. Utimately, Geronomo was captured and converted to Christianity before he died. The following is from Geronimo's autobiography:

About ten years later some more white men came. These were all warriors. They made their camp on the Gila River south of Hot Springs. At first they were friendly and we did not dislike them, but they were not as good as those who came first.

After about a year some trouble arose between them and the Indians, and I took the war path as a warrior, not as a chief. I had not been wronged, but some of my people bad been, and I fought with my tribe; for the soldiers and not the Indians were at fault.

Not long after this some of the officers of the United States troops invited our leaders to hold a conference at Apache Pass (Fort Bowie). Just before noon the Indians were shown into a tent and told that they would be given something to eat. When in the tent they were attacked by soldiers. Our chief, Mangus-Colorado, and several other warriors, by cutting through the tent, escaped; but most of the warriors were killed or captured. Among the Bedonkohe Apaches killed at this time were Sanza, Kladetahe, Niyokahe, and Gopi. After this treachery the Indians went back to the mountains and left the fort entirely alone. I do not think that the agent had anything to do with planning this, for he had always treated us well. I believe it was entirely planned by the soldiers.

From the very first the soldiers sent out to our western country, and the officers in charge of them, did not hesitate to wrong the Indians. They never explained to the Government when an Indian was wronged, but always reported the misdeeds of the Indians. Much that was done by mean white men was reported at Washington as the deeds of my people.

The Indians always tried to live peaceably with the white soldiers and settlers. One day during the time that the soldiers were stationed at Apache Pass I made a treaty with the post. This was done by shaking hands and promising to be brothers. Cochise and Mangus-Colorado did likewise. I do not know the name of the officer in command, but this was the first regiment that ever came to Apache Pass. This treaty was made about a year before we were attacked in a tent, as above related. In a few days after the attack at Apache Pass we organized in the mountains and returned to fight the soldiers. There were two tribes—the Bedonkohe and the Chokonen Apaches, both commanded by Cochise. After a few days' skirmishing we attacked a freight train that was coming in with supplies for the Fort. We killed some of the men and captured the others. These prisoners our chief offered to trade for the Indians whom the soldiers had captured at the massacre in the tent. This the officers refused, so we killed our prisoners, disbanded, and went into hiding in the mountains. Of those who took part in this affair I am the only one now living.

In a few days troops were sent out to search for us, but as we were disbanded, it was, of course, impossible for them to locate any hostile camp. During the time they were searching for us many of our warriors (who were thought by the soldiers to be peaceable Indians) talked to the officers and men, advising them where they might find the camp they sought, and while they searched we watched them from our hiding places and laughed at their failures.

After this trouble all of the Indians agreed not to be friendly with the white men any more. There was no general engagement, but a long struggle followed. Sometimes we attacked the white men, sometimes they attacked us. First a few Indians would be killed and then a few soldiers. I think the killing was about equal on each side. The number killed in these troubles did not amount to much, but this treachery on the part of the soldiers had angered the Indians and revived memories of other wrongs, so that we never again trusted the United States troops.

http://odur.let.rug.nl/~usa/B/geronimo/

What does Geronimo say is the primary reason whites and Native Americans did not get along?

FINAL PROJECT

Correct and rewrite all essays and place them in your
Final Portfolio.

SUGGESTED
Weekly *Implementation*

DAY 1	DAY 2	DAY 3	DAY 4	DAY 5
Prayer journal. Review the required reading(s) *before* the assigned lesson begins. Teacher may want to discuss assigned reading(s) with students. Teacher and students will decide on required essays for this lesson, choosing two or three essays. The rest of the essays can be outlined, answered with shorter answers, or skipped. Review all readings for Lesson 13.	**Prayer journal.** Review reading(s) from next lesson. Student should outline essays due at the end of the week. Per teacher instructions, students may answer orally in a group setting some of the essays that are not assigned as formal essays.	**Prayer journal.** Write rough drafts of all assigned essays. The teacher and/or a peer evaluator may correct rough drafts.	**Prayer journal.** Rewrite corrected copies of essays due tomorrow.	**Prayer journal.** Essays are due. Take Lesson 13 test. Reading ahead: Review Reading Ahead: *Narrative of the Life of Frederick Douglass*, Frederick Douglass. Guide: How was Douglass' life typical or atypical of most African-American slave lives?

DIVISION, WAR, AND RECONCILIATION *1855-1865* *(Part 2)*

Narrative of the Life of Frederick Douglass

Frederick Douglass

BACKGROUND

Frederick Douglass was born into slavery sometime in 1817 or 1818. Like many slaves, he was unsure of his exact date of birth. Douglass was separated from his mother, Harriet Bailey, soon after his birth. His father was most likely their white master, Captain Anthony. Captain Anthony was the clerk of a rich man named Colonel Lloyd. Lloyd owned hundreds of slaves. Life on any of Lloyd's plantations, like that on many Southern plantations, was brutal. In 1845, just seven years after his escape from slavery, the young Frederick Douglass published the powerful account of his life in bondage.

CRITICAL THINKING

A. Douglass writes in a very eloquent style, which contributes to the effectiveness of his work. Many people who thought African-Americans were inferior in intelligence were shown to be mistaken with the writings of Frederick Douglass. Discuss the form that Douglass employs in his masterpiece.

> **You will analyze:** *Narrative of the Life of Frederick Douglass*, Frederick Douglass.
>
> **Reading Ahead:** *The Adventures of Huckleberry Finn*, by Mark Twain.
>
> **Guide Question:** Is Twain writing a humorous farce or is he writing a very serious, even cynical, novel?

B. What does Douglass learn that is the key to freedom?

BIBLICAL APPLICATION

Discuss Douglass's faith journey.

ENRICHMENT

Compare Phillis Wheatley and Frederick Douglass.

FINAL PROJECT

Correct and rewrite all essays and place them in your Final Portfolio.

SUGGESTED
Weekly *Implementation*

DAY 1	DAY 2	DAY 3	DAY 4	DAY 5
Prayer journal.	Prayer journal.	Prayer journal.	Prayer journal.	Prayer journal.
Review the required reading(s) *before* the assigned lesson begins.	Review reading(s) from next lesson.	Write rough drafts of all assigned essays.	Rewrite corrected copies of essays due tomorrow.	Essays are due.
Teacher may want to discuss assigned reading(s) with students.	Outline essays due at the end of the week.	The teacher and/or a peer evaluator may correct rough drafts.		Take Lesson 14 test.

Reading ahead: Review: *The Adventures of Huckleberry Finn*, by Mark Twain. |
Teacher and students will decide on required essay for this lesson, choosing two or three essays.	Per teacher instructions, students may answer orally in a group setting some of the essays that are not assigned as formal essays.			Guide: Is Twain writing a humorous farce or is he writing a very serious, even cynical, novel?
The rest of the essays can be outlined, answered with shorter answers, or skipped.				
Review all readings for Lesson 14.				

REALISM, NATURALISM, AND THE FRONTIER, *1865-1915* (Part 1)

The Adventures of Huckleberry Finn

Mark Twain (1884)

© Arttoday.com

In the final paragraph of *The Adventures of Huckleberry Finn*, Huck says, "...so there ain't nothing more to write about, and I am rotten glad of it, because if I'd 'a' knowed what a trouble it was to make a book I wouldn't 'a' tackled it, and ain't a' going to no more." As you'll see when you've read the novel, the mock-sentiment is very much in character; but you can also read it as an expression of Mark Twain's relief at finishing the most difficult book he ever wrote. The book had taken him more than seven years to complete! At one point he was so frustrated with it that he considered burning what he'd written. Instead, he put it aside and worked on three other books that were published before *Huck Finn*. The modern American novelist Ernest Hemingway said: ". . . all modern American literature comes from one book by Mark Twain called Huckleberry Finn." This is an exaggeration, to be sure, but in this novel we have all the elements of the American ethos: a journey, race relations, inter-generational rivalry, and mutability. On one level *Huckleberry Finn* is a hilarious adventure of a free spirited young American doing what we all want to do: live in the woods and have no responsibilities. On another level, however, Twain is exploring the more despondent side of humanity. At the end of his life Twain had to endure many unhappy tragedies. His wife died in 1904. In 1909 his youngest daughter died, leaving Twain a sick and unhappy man. As you read *Huckleberry Finn*, see if you can identify both Mark Twains.

ABOUT THE AUTHOR

Samuel Langhorne Clemens—Mark Twain—(1835-1910), was born in Florida, Missouri, but grew up on the Mississippi River in Hannibal, Missouri. He happily lived as a river pilot on the Mississippi River until the Civil War ended river traffic. In 1861 Twain moved west. It was in the West that he wrote "The Celebrated Jumping Frog of Calavaras County." Throughout his life Twain enjoyed entertaining Americans with his whimsical writings, but below the surface, Twain was a complicated, and, many felt, a bitter man. At the end of his life, Mark Twain said, *"Everything human is pathetic. The secret source of humor itself is not joy but sorrow. There is no humor in heaven."*
http://www.brainyquote.com/quotes/quotes/

Other Notable Works
The Adventures of Tom Sawyer (1876)
Life on the Mississippi (1883)
A Connecticut Yankee in King Arthur's Court (1889)

SUGGESTED VOCABULARY WORDS

Use these words in essays that you write this week.

V	temperance	
IX	reticule	
XVII	wince	pensive
XX	degraded	histrionic
XXV	obsequies	
XXIX	ingenious	

A literary movement called realism began with the writings of Mark Twain. Realism is defined as the faithful representation in literature of the actual events of life. Realism grew out of a protest against romanticism—a literary movement that sentimentalized nature.

I conceive that the right way to write a story for boys is to write so that it will not only interest boys but strongly interest any man who has been a boy. That immensely enlarges the audience (Mark Twain).

BIBLICAL APPLICATION

Compare Huckleberry Finn to the young Samuel of the Old Testament (1 Sam.1-3).

CRITICAL THINKING

A. As *Huck Finn* progresses we learn to love Jim. Loyal to a fault, trusting, and hardworking, the reader is drawn to this pillar of fecundity. Describe in detail the way that Twain develops this character.

B. Huck is not a static character. As the novel progresses, he matures. What additional knowledge about the problems of life has Huck acquired by the time he gets to the Phelps' farm? In an essay, explain how Huck has changed by this point.

C. Ironically, Jim and Huck are trying to escape from slavery by floating down the Mississippi River. Why is this escape ironic?

Principles Of Realism	1. Insistence upon the experienced commonplace. 2. Character more important than plot. 3. Attack upon Romanticism and Romantic writers. 4. Morality is fluid not static. Situation ethics is the rule of the day. 5. Concept of realism as a realization of democracy.
Identifying Characteristics Of Realistic Writing	1. The purpose of writing is to instruct and to entertain. Realists were pragmatic, relativistic, democratic, and experimental. 2. The subject matter of Realism is drawn from the common, the average, the non-extreme, the representative, the probable. 3. The morality of Realism is intrinsic and relativistic. 4. Emphasis is placed upon scenic presentation, de-emphasizing authorial comment and evaluation. Realistic novels rarely use the omniscient point of view.
Realistic Characterization	Realists believe that humans control their destinies; characters act on their environment rather than simply reacting to it. Character is superior to circumstance.
The Use Of Symbolism And Imagery	Realists generally reject the kind of symbolism suggested by Emerson when he said, "Every natural fact is a symbol of some spiritual fact." Their use of symbolism is controlled and limited; they depend more on the use of images.
Writing Techniques	1. Settings thoroughly familiar to the writer. 2. Plots emphasizing the norm of daily experience. 3. Ordinary characters, studied in depth. 4. Complete authorial objectivity. 5. A world truly reported.

D. Mark Twain used several literary devices. Look up the meaning of each of the following literary terms and find at least one example for the book.

1. satire
2. symbolism
3. allegory
4. foreshadowing

E. Twain uses first person point of view to tell his story. What advantages and disadvantages does this present Twain?

ENRICHMENT

A. Can you imagine Huck joining the transcendentalist Henry David Thoreau for a year on the edge of Walden Pond? Why or why not?

B. Define Realism. Give examples of Realism in *Huckleberry Finn*.

C. Realism, which is an ideological cousin to Naturalism, attacks the two most important tenants of Christianity. The basic ontological (i.e., science of beginnings) axiom is the living God. It is theoretically as legitimate for a Christian theist to view God as the cause of the universe as for a realist to view nature as a chaos that happened to arise. Next, the basic epistemological (i.e., science of knowledge) axiom is divine revelation. To the realist, there is no divine revelation. The realist's base of operation lies in rationalism and experience. The Christian theist's base of operation lies in God's divine revelation. Find contemporary examples where Christian theism is clashing with realism.

FINAL PROJECT

Correct and rewrite all essays and place them in your Final Portfolio.

SUGGESTED
Weekly *Implementation*

DAY 1	DAY 2	DAY 3	DAY 4	DAY 5
Prayer journal. Review the required reading(s) before the assigned lesson begins. Teacher may want to discuss assigned reading(s) with students. Teacher and students will decide on required essays for this lesson, choosing two or three essays. The rest of the essays can be outlined, answered with shorter answers, or skipped. Review all readings for Lesson 15	**Prayer journal.** Review reading(s) from next lesson. Outline essays due at the end of the week. Per teacher instructions, students may answer orally in a group setting some of the essays that are not assigned as formal essays.	**Prayer journal.** Write rough drafts of all assigned essays. The teacher and/or a peer evaluator may correct rough drafts.	**Prayer journal.** Rewrite corrected copies of essays due tomorrow.	**Prayer journal.** Essays are due. Take Lesson 15 test. Reading ahead: Review *The Red Badge of Courage*, by Stephen Crane. Guide: Who is the "god" the reader encounters in this seminal, naturalistic novel?

REALISM, NATURALISM, AND THE FRONTIER *1865-1915*
(Part 2)

The Adventures of Huckleberry Finn (Continued)
Mark Twain

You will analyze: *The Adventures of Huckleberry Finn*, Mark Twain.

Read Ahead: *Red Badge of Courage*, Stephen Crane.

Guide Question: Who is the "god" the reader encounters in this seminal, naturalistic novel?

CRITICAL THINKING

A. Some critics find the end of the novel to be very disappointing. They feel that after Huck arrives at the Phelps' house, the plot deteriorates rapidly. On the other hand, many critics find the end of the book to be entirely consistent with the tone of the book. What do you think? Defend your answer with specific details from the book.

B. Twain's handling of Christianity wavers between outright scorn and mockery (Chapter I) to veiled superstition. Describe Twain's attitudes toward Christianity in *Huckleberry Finn*. Defend your answer with specific passages from the book.

C. Give at least one example of Twain's cynicism.

D. Every journey must have a goal. What is the goal of Huck's journey?

ENRICHMENT: THE HISTORICAL SETTING

A. Though only twenty-five percent of the colonial population owned slaves, and most of those lived below the Mason-Dixon Line, slavery factored heavily in the economy of all the British North American colonies, and not just in the plantation economy of the South. As one historian explained, "While many southerners found slavery morally repugnant, there was a clear business rationale: in the long run, it was cheaper to acquire Africans than to hire laborers. The North also profited immensely from the international trade in Africans.

Its booming industries—shipbuilding, sail making, iron foundries, sawmills, and rum distilleries—were an integral part of the trading triangle between Europe, Africa, and North America."

As a business enterprise, slavery did well in isolated pockets up North, especially in the farming regions of New York and New Jersey, Delaware, and Rhode Island. During the pre-Revolution days, sixty-one percent of all American slaves—nearly 145,000—lived in Virginia and Maryland, working the tobacco fields in small to medium-sized gangs. This distribution changed as southern planters moved into Mississippi, Alabama, and Tennessee. In any event, most slave owners owned no more than two or three slaves. The rule of thumb was that if you were a slave, you probably lived on a large plantation. If you were a white planter, you owned fewer than 10 slaves.

By the very important year of 1750, both free and enslaved black people, despite the hardships of their lives, manifested a deepening attachment to America. By then, the majority of blacks had been born in America rather than in Africa.

There were a few free blacks. By 1810 the free black population had swelled to 186,446, but slavery too, continued to flourish and spread westward with

> Everything human is pathetic. The secret source of Humor itself is not joy but sorrow. There is no humor in heaven. . . Man is the only animal that blushes. Or needs to.
>
> (Mark Twain)

© Arttoday.com

the growing new nation. As one historian explained, "During its first 50 years, the United States transformed itself from a small republic into an expansive democracy for white Americans. The nation tripled its population, doubled in size, and extended slavery to parts of the Western frontier. For black Americans, this same period was a contradictory mix of community-building for free blacks and entrenched enslavement for those not yet emancipated. Slavery grew stronger, as the invention of the cotton gin and a booming Southern economy fueled the push westward. In cities like Philadelphia, free blacks sought equal participation in American society by building churches and schools, forming beneficial societies, and petitioning their state legislature. In the aftermath of the Haitian Revolution (1791-1804), several slave uprisings, including Gabriel's Rebellion (1800), Denmark Vesey's Plot (1822), and Nat Turner's Revolt (1831), were poignant reminders of the human desire for freedom—regardless of the bloody consequences.

What about the Church and slavery?

In the decades after the American Revolution, Northern states gradually began to abolish slavery. As a result, sharper differences emerged between the experiences of enslaved peoples in the South and North. Northern African Americans were now relatively free. By 1810 the slave trade to the United States had come to an end, and the slave population began to increase

naturally, giving rise to an increasingly large native-born population of African Americans. With fewer migrants who had experienced Africa personally, these transformations allowed the myriad cultures and language groups of enslaved Africans to blend together, making way for the preservation and transmission of religious practices that were increasingly "African-American." This transition coincided with the period of intense religious revivalism known as "awakenings." In the Southern states beginning in the 1770s, increasing numbers of slaves converted to evangelical religions such as the Methodist and Baptist faiths. Many clergy within these denominations actively promoted the idea that all Christians were equal in the sight of God, a message that provided hope and sustenance to the slaves. They also encouraged worship in ways that many Africans found to be similar, or at least adaptable, to African worship patterns, with enthusiastic singing, clapping, dancing, and even spirit-possession. Still, many white owners and clergy preached a message of strict obedience to white orthodoxy. They feared that religion, like education, would become an opportunity for rebellion. It is clear that many blacks saw these white churches, in which ministers promoted obedience to one's master as the highest religious ideal, as a mockery of the "true" Christian message of equality and liberation as they knew it. In the slave quarters, however, African Americans organized their own religious activities. These religious gatherings were a mixture of Evangelical Christianity and African phenomenology.

Although there was some hope immediately after the Revolution that the ideals of independence and equality would extend to African-Americans, this hope died with the invention of the cotton gin in 1793. With the gin (short for engine), raw cotton could be quickly cleaned. Suddenly, cotton became a hugely profitable crop. It was the growth industry of antebellum America, which transformed southern economy and changed the dynamics of slavery. The first federal census of 1790 counted 697,897 slaves; by 1810, there were 1.2 million slaves, a 70 percent increase. Within 10 years after the cotton gin was put into use, the value of the total United States crop leaped from $150,000 to more than $8 million (*Africans in America*, www.pbs.org). The success of this plantation crop made it much more difficult for slaves to purchase their freedom or obtain it through the good will of their masters. Cotton became the foundation for the developing textile industry in New England, spurring the industrial revolution which transformed America in the 19th century. Cotton was truly king!

A. Write a five-page <u>research paper</u> on chattel slavery in the United States as it evolved from 1619 to the American Civil War (1861). (For students who are unfamiliar with the writing of research papers, please refer to a thorough writing handbook: *Warriner's; Hodges Harbrace College*, etc.)

B. Huck's decision to run away with Jim—a slave—is an unlawful act. Huck, though, decides to commit a civil disobedient act. When, if ever, is civil disobedience appropriate? In your answer, reference writings from Thoreau.

C. Compare the tone of the following short story with the tone in *Huck Finn*.

The Celebrated Jumping Frog of Calaveras County

Mark Twain

http://www.classicallibrary.org/twain/celebrated/
01-celebrated.htm

In compliance with the request of a friend of mine, who wrote me from the East, I called on good-natured, garrulous old Simon Wheeler, and inquired after my friend's friend, Leonidas W. Smiley, as requested to do, and I hereunto append the result. I have a lurking suspicion that *Leonidas W.* Smiley is a myth; that my friend never knew such a personage; and that he only conjectured that, if I asked old Wheeler about him, it would remind him of his infamous *Jim* Smiley, and he would go to work and bore me nearly to death with some infernal reminiscence of him as long and tedious as it should be useless to me. If that was the design, it certainly succeeded.

I found Simon Wheeler dozing comfortably by the barroom stove of the old, dilapidated tavern in the ancient mining camp of Angel's, and I noticed that he was fat and bald-headed, and had an expression of winning gentleness and simplicity upon his tranquil countenance. He roused up and gave me good-day. I told him a friend of mine had commissioned me to make some inquiries about a cherished companion of his boyhood named *Leonidas W.* Smiley—*Rev. Leonidas W.* Smiley, young minister of the Gospel, who he had heard was at one time a resident of Angel's Camp. I added that, if Mr. Wheeler could tell me anything about this Rev. Leonidas W. Smiley, I would feel under many obligations to him.

Simon Wheeler backed me into a corner and blockaded me there with his chair, and then sat me down and reeled off the monotonous narrative which follows this paragraph. He never smiled, he never frowned, he never changed his voice from the gentle-flowing key to which he tuned the initial sentence, he never betrayed the slightest suspicion of enthusiasm; but all through the interminable narrative there ran a vein of impressive earnestness and sincerity, which showed me plainly that, so far from his imagining that there was anything ridiculous or funny about his story, he regarded it as a really important matter, and admired its two heroes as men of transcendent genius in *finesse*. I let him go on in his own way, and never interrupted him once.

"Rev. Leonidas W. H'm, Reverend Le—well, there was a feller here once by the name of *Jim* Smiley, in the winter of '49—or maybe it was the spring of '50—I don't recollect exactly, somehow, though what makes me think it was one or the other is because I remember the big flume wasn't finished when he first came to the camp; but anyway, he was the curiousest man about always betting on anything that turned up you ever see, if he could get anybody to bet on the other side; and if he couldn't, he'd change sides. Any way that suited the other man would suit *him*—any way just so's he got a bet, *he* was satisfied. But still he was lucky, uncommon lucky; he most always come out winner. He was always ready and laying for a chance; there couldn't be no solit'ry thing mentioned but that feller'd offer to bet on it, and take any side you please, as I was just telling you. If there was a horse race, you'd find him flush, or you'd find him busted at the end of it; if there was a dogfight, he'd bet on it; if there was a cat-fight, he'd bet on it; if there was a chicken-fight, he'd bet on it; why, if there was two birds setting on a fence, he would bet you which one would fly first; or if there was a camp meeting, he would be there reg'lar, to bet on Parson Walker, which he judged to be the best exhorter about here, and so he was, too, and a good man. If he even seen a straddlebug start to go anywheres, he would bet you how long it would take him to get wherever he was going to, and if you took him up, he would foller that straddlebug to Mexico but what he would find out where he was bound for and how long he was on the road. Lots of the boys here has seen that Smiley, and can tell you about him. Why, it never made no difference to *him*—he would bet on *anything*—the dangdest feller. Parson Walker's wife laid very sick once, for a good while, and it seemed as if they warn't going to save her; but one morning he come in, and Smiley asked how she was, and he said she was considerable better—thank the Lord for his inf'nit mercy—and coming on so smart that, with the blessing of Prov'dence, she'd get well yet; and Smiley, before he thought, says, 'Well, I'll risk two-and-a-half that she don't, anyway.'

Thish-yer Smiley had a mare—the boys called her the fifteen-minute nag, but that was only in fun, you know, because, of course, she was faster than that—and he used to win money on that horse, for all she was so slow and always had the asthma, or the distemper, or the consumption, or something of that kind. They used to give her two or three hundred yards start, and then pass her under way; but always at the fag end of the race she'd get excited and desperate-like, and come cavorting and straddling up, and scattering her legs around limber, sometimes in the air, and sometimes out to one side amongst the fences, and kicking up m-o-r-e dust, and raising m-o-r-e racket with her coughing and sneezing and blowing her nose—and always fetch up at the stand just about a neck ahead, as near as you could cipher it down.

And he had a little small bull pup, that to look at him you'd think he wan't worth a cent, but to set around and look ornery, and lay for a chance to steal something. But as soon as money was up on him, he was a different dog; his underjaw'd begin to stick out like the fo-castle of a steamboat, and his teeth would uncover, and shine savage like the furnaces. And a dog might tackle him, and bullyrag him, and bite him, and throw him over his shoulder two or three times, and Andrew Jackson—which was the name of the pup— Andrew Jackson would never let on but what *he* was satisfied, and hadn't expected nothing else—and the bets being doubled and doubled on the other side all the time, till the money was all up; and then all of a sudden he would grab that other dog jest by the j'int of his hind leg and freeze to it—not chaw, you understand, but only jest grip and hang on till they throwed up the sponge, if it was a year. Smiley always come out winner on that pup, till he harnessed a dog once that didn't have no hind legs, because they'd been sawed off by a circular saw, and when the thing had gone along far enough, and the money was all up, and he come to make a snatch for his pet holt, he saw in a minute how he'd been imposed on, and how the other dog had him in the door, so to speak, and he 'peared surprised, and then he looked sorter discouraged-like, and didn't try no more to win the fight, and so he got shucked out bad. He give Smiley a look, as much as to say his heart was broke, and it was *his* fault for putting up a dog that had-n't no hind legs for him to take holt of, which was his main dependence in a fight, and then he limped off a piece and laid down and died. It was a good pup, was that Andrew Jackson, and would have made a name for hisself if he'd lived, for the stuff was in him, and he had genius—I know it, because he hadn't had no opportu-

nities to speak of, and it don't stand to reason that a dog could make such a fight as he could under them circumstances, if he hadn't no talent. It always makes me feel sorry when I think of that last fight of his'n, and the way it turned out.

Well, thish-yer Smiley had rat-tarriers, and chicken cocks, and tomcats, and all them kind of things, till you couldn't rest, and you couldn't fetch nothing for him to bet on but he'd match you. He ketched a frog one day, and took him home, and said he cal'klated to edercate him; and so he never done nothing for three months but set in his back yard and learn that frog to jump. And you bet you he *did* learn him too. He'd give him a little punch behind, and the next minute you'd see that frog whirling in the air like a doughnut—see him turn one summerset, or may be a couple, if he got a good start, and come down flatfooted and all right, like a cat. He got him up so in the matter of catching flies, and kept him in practice so constant, that he'd nail a fly every time as far as he could see him. Smiley said all a frog wanted was education, and he could do most any-thing—and I believe him. Why, I've seen him set Dan'l Webster down here on this floor—Dan'l Webster was the name of the frog—and sing out, "Flies, Dan'l, flies!" and quicker'n you could wink, he'd spring straight up, and snake a fly off'n the counter there, and flop down on the floor again as solid as a gob of mud, and fall to scratching the side of his head with his hind foot as indifferent as if he hadn't no idea he'd been doin' any more'n any frog might do. You never see a frog so mod-est and straightfor'ard as he was, for all he was so gifted. And when it came to fair and square jumping on a dead level, he could get over more ground at one straddle than any animal of his breed you ever see. Jumping on a dead level was his strong suit, you under-stand; and when it come to that, Smiley would ante up money on him as long as he had a red. Smiley was mon-strous proud of his frog, and well he might be, for fellers that had traveled and been everywheres, all said he laid over any frog that ever *they* see.

Well, Smiley kept the beast in a little lattice box, and he used to fetch him downtown sometimes and lay for a bet. One day a feller—a stranger in the camp, he was—come across him with his box, and says:

"What might it be that you've got in the box?"

And Smiley says, sorter indifferent like, "It might be a parrot, or it might be a canary, maybe, but it ain't—it's only just a frog."

And the feller took it, and looked at it careful, and turned it round this way and that, and says, "H'm—so 'tis. Well, what's *he* good for?"

"Well," Smiley says, easy and careless, "he's good enough for *one* thing, I should judge—he can outjump ary frog in Calaveras county."

The feller took the box again, and took another long, particular look, and give it back to Smiley, and says, very deliberate, "Well, I don't see no p'ints about that frog that's any better'n any other frog."

"Maybe you don't," Smiley says. "Maybe you understand frogs, and maybe you don't understand 'em; maybe you've had experience, and maybe you ain't only a amature, as it were. Anyways, I've got *my* opinion, and I'll risk forty dollars that he can outjump any frog in Calaveras county."

And the feller studied a minute, and then says, kinder sad like, "Well, I'm only a stranger here, and I ain't got no frog; but if I had a frog, I'd bet you."

And then Smiley says, "That's all right—that's all right—if you'll hold my box a minute, I'll go and get you a frog." And so the feller took the box, and put up his forty dollars along with Smiley's and set down to wait.

So he set there a good while thinking and thinking to hisself, and then he got the frog out and prized his mouth open and took a teaspoon and filled him full of quail shot—filled him pretty near up to his chin—and set him on the floor. Smiley he went to the swamp and slopped around in the mud for a long time, and finally he ketched a frog, and fetched him in, and give him to this feller, and says:

"Now, if you're ready, set him alongside of Dan'l, with his fore-paws just even with Dan'l and I'll give the word." Then he says, "one—two—three—jump!" and him and the feller touched up the frogs from behind, and the new frog hopped off, but Dan'l give a heave, and hysted up his shoulders—so—like a French-man, but it wan't no use—he couldn't budge; he was planted as solid as an anvil, and he couldn't no more stir than if he was anchored out. Smiley was a good deal surprised, and he was disgusted too, but he didn't have no idea what the matter was, of course.

The feller took the money and started away; and when he was going out at the door, he sorter jerked his thumb over his shoulders—this way—at Dan'l, and says again, very deliberate, "Well, *I* don't see no p'ints about that frog that's any better'n any other frog."

Smiley he stood scratching his head and looking down at Dan'l a long time, and at last he says, "I do

wonder what in the nation that frog throw'd off for—I wonder if there ain't something the matter with him—he 'pears to look might baggy, somehow." And he ketched Dan'l by the nap of the neck, and lifted him up and says, "Why, blame my cats, if he don't weigh five pound!" and turned him upside down, and he belched out a double handful of shot. And then he see how it was, and he was the maddest man—he set the frog down and took out after that feller, but he never ketched him. And—

(Here Simon Wheeler heard his name called from the front yard, and got up to see what was wanted.) And turning to me as he moved away, he said: "Just set where you are, stranger, and rest easy—I an't going to be gone a second."

But, by your leave, I did not think that a continuation of the history of the enterprising vagabond *Jim* Smiley would be likely to afford me much information concerning the *Rev. Leonidas W.* Smiley, and so I started away.

At the door I met the sociable Wheeler returning, and he buttonholed me and recommenced:

Well, thish-yer Smiley had a yaller one-eyed cow that didn't have no tail, only jest a short stump like a bannanner, and—"

However, lacking both time and inclination, I did not wait to hear about the afflicted cow, but took my leave.

D. *Huckleberry Finn* is one of the earliest novels in which the issue of motivation and self are paramount. In his book *The Saturated Self: Dilemmas of Identity in Contemporary Life*, Kenneth J. Gergen argues that self motivation appeared by the end of the 20th century as a sort of selfishness that was very destructive to Christianity. As Huckleberry regularly relativized his situation on the banks of the Mississippi, many modern Americans conducted their lives in the same way. Agree or disagree with this statement and offer evidence to support your answer.

FINAL PROJECT

Correct and rewrite all essays and place them in your Final Portfolio.

SUGGESTED
Weekly *Implementation*

DAY 1	DAY 2	DAY 3	DAY 4	DAY 5
Prayer journal. Review the required reading(s) before the assigned lesson begins. Teacher may want to discuss assigned reading(s) with students. Teacher and students will decide on required essays for this lesson, choosing two or three essays. The rest of the essays can be outlined, answered with shorter answers, or skipped. Review all readings for Lesson 16	**Prayer journal.** Review reading(s) from next lesson. Outline essays due at the end of the week. Per teacher instructions, students may answer orally in a group setting some of the essays that are not assigned as formal essays.	**Prayer journal.** Write rough drafts of all assigned essays. The teacher and/or a peer evaluator may correct rough drafts.	**Prayer journal.** Rewrite corrected copies of essays due tomorrow.	**Prayer journal.** Essays are due. Take Lesson 16 test. Reading ahead: Review *Red Badge of Courage*, Stephen Crane. Guide: Who is the "god" the reader encounters in this seminal, naturalistic novel?

REALISM, NATURALISM, AND THE FRONTIER, *1865-1915* (Part 3)

The Red Badge of Courage
Stephen Crane (1895)

BACKGROUND

This impressive novel is one of the few unchallenged classics of modern American literature. Stephen Crane's immense talent is everywhere evident in his great work. This is not to say, though, that Crane's vision is correct regarding Christian Worldview. No, Crane's novel is full of Naturalism—a germinating and menacing worldview still spreading across America. The Naturalistic stories and novels of Stephen Crane truly mark the maturation of modernity. Major revealing features of *modernity* are an unrestrained, individual freedom—the goal of which is to liberate one from all restrictions, constraints, traditions, and all social patterning—all of which are *ipso facto* presumed to be dehumanizing. Modernity has contempt for viewpoints beyond its own. Ironically, in its nihilistic pursuit of tolerance it becomes intolerant! Modernity is reductionist Naturalism. *What does the word "reductionist" mean?* Crane's works are wholly modern in both philosophy and technique. While remnants of Romanticism may be found in the poems of Dickinson and Whitman, and some in Melville, none remain in Crane. At one point Henry faces death and "he had been to touch the great death, and found that, after all, it was but the great death. He was a man." The man that Crane and his contemporaries create is not the man created in the image of God, the man who is precious and vital; rather, he is a man in a mob, a man who has no

You will analyze: *Red Badge of Courage*, Stephen Crane.

Reading Ahead: Students should review "Outcasts of Poker Flat," Bret Harte; "The Story of an Hour," Kate Chopin; "Luke Havergal" and "Credo" Edwin Arlington Robinson; "Lucinda Matlock," Edgar Lee Masters. (Lesson 19)

Guide: What new styles and themes emerge in these late 19th century works?

future. Crane offers his reader no salvation, no hope. Crane only validates the *now, the sensory touch, the empirical*.

Since the fall of the Berlin Wall, by the way, many historians have argued that we are in a *post-modern* era. Now, many Americans are suspicious of science and any authority. This viewpoint has as a central credo: "Anything goes if I believe it sincerely." Stephen Crane brought us well along on this slippery trail.

The following statements, then, summarize how history has unfolded in the last six centuries:

In the scheme of things *The Red Badge of Courage* and Naturalism ushered in a new philosophical era. It was one of the genuinely new cultural revolutions in American history. It was not to be the last.

Naturalism: If God does exist, He is pretty wimpish. Only the laws of nature have any force. God is either uninterested or downright mean.

ABOUT THE AUTHOR

Stephen Crane's life was full of tragedy. Born into a pastor's family, his beloved father died when Stephen was eight years old. Crane himself was twenty-eight when he died of tuberculosis. Never popular in his lifetime, Crane lived in virtual poverty. However, in his two plus decades Crane wrote some of the best American literature of all time.

Other Notable Works

Maggie: A Girl of the Streets (1893)

SUGGESTED VOCABULARY WORDS

I hilarious
III impregnable
III impetus
     perambulating
VI imprecations
     querulous
IX trepidation
X perfunctory
XIX petulantly
     deprecating
XXI temerity
XXIV imperious
     expletive
     stentorian

BACKGROUND

The U.S. Civil War (1861-1865) between the industrial North and the agricultural South was a turning point in American history. The innocent optimism of the young nation gave way, after the war, to a period of exhaustion. Reconstruction grew out of this fatigue—it was as if the American political system was not going to try to

If Nature is so pernicious, if only the strongest survive, if there is no order to life, then one is free to do whatever satisfies one's momentary sensory needs.

In his book *The Cross of Christ* (1986), John R. W. Stott argues that naturalism ignores the central problem of the human condition: sin. Sin cannot be dismissed as merely a circumstantial event determined by Nature. No, man is responsible for his bad choices. As the theologian and Christian psychologist Karl Menninger laments, sins that were once crimes are now behaviors determined by the environment. Thus, criminals receive "treatment" not "punishment."

solve its problems. Before the war, Idealists and Romantics championed human rights, especially the abolition of slavery; after the war, Americans increasingly idealized progress and the self-made man. Ralph Waldo Emerson and Henry David Thoreau remained as icons of inevitable American progress. However, many philosophical changes were in the air. This was the era of the millionaire manufacturer and the speculator, robber barons and trust busters, when Darwinian evolution and the "survival of the fittest" seemed to sanction the sometimes unethical methods of the successful business tycoon. Naturalism grew naturally out of the fertile ground of social Darwinism. This so-called "Gilded Age," a term coined by Mark Twain, was an age of thoughtless excess.

Business boomed after the war. The new intercontinental rail system, inaugurated in 1869, and the transcontinental telegraph, which began operating in 1861, gave industry access to materials, markets, and communications. The constant influx of immigrants provided a seemingly endless supply of inexpensive labor as well. More than 23 million foreigners—German, Scandinavian, and Irish in the early years, and increasingly Central and Southern Europeans thereafter—flowed into the United States between 1860 and 1910. American business interests imported Asian contract laborers on the West Coast. This created tensions that remain in America even today. In 1860, most Americans lived on farms or in small villages, but by 1919 half the population was concentrated in about twelve cities. Problems of urbanization and industrialization appeared. From 1860 to 1914, the United States changed from a small, young, agricultural country to a huge, modern, industrial nation.

America, however, was full of problems. The differences among people groups were immense and growing larger. It was to this world that men like Stephen Crane wrote. He attacked social problems. American literature openly discussed significant social problems. Previously, American fiction was entertaining and didactic but not evaluative. Characteristic American novels of the period, Stephen Crane's *Maggie: A Girl of the Streets*; Jack London's *Martin Eden*; and later Theodore Dreiser's *An American Tragedy*, depict the damage of economic forces and alienation of the vulnerable individual. Survivors, like Twain's *Huck Finn*; Humphrey Vanderveyden's (in London) *The Sea-Wolf*; Hemingway's Frederick Henry in *A Farewell to Arms*; and Dreiser's *Sister Carrie*, endure through inner strength and above all, individuality. No longer is there a hint in American literature that there is a loving, caring God. The world that Anne Bradstreet knew is dead.

CRITICAL THINKING

A. When he wrote *The Red Badge of Courage*, Crane had never shot a gun in anger or seen a battle. Can you tell?

B. Define maturity. How was Henry more mature at the end of the novel than he was at the beginning?

C. Compare and contrast Stephen Crane's view of death with Jack London's view of death in the following short story. They are both Naturalist writers.

To Build a Fire

Jack London

http://www.classicreader.com/read.php/sid.6/bookid.698/

Day had broken cold and grey, exceedingly cold and grey, when the man turned aside from the main Yukon trail and climbed the high earth-bank, where a dim and little-travelled trail led eastward through the fat spruce timberland. It was a steep bank, and he paused for breath at the top, excusing the act to himself by looking at his watch. It was nine o'clock. There was no sun nor hint of sun, though there was not a cloud in the sky. It was a clear day, and yet there seemed an intangible pall over the face of things, a subtle gloom that made the day dark, and that was due to the absence of sun. This fact did not worry the man. He was used to the lack of sun. It had been days since he had seen the sun, and he knew that a few more days must pass before that cheerful orb, due south, would just peep above the sky-line and dip immediately from view.

The man flung a look back along the way he had

come. The Yukon lay a mile wide and hidden under three feet of ice. On top of this ice were as many feet of snow. It was all pure white, rolling in gentle undulations where the ice-jams of the freeze-up had formed. North and south, as far as his eye could see, it was unbroken white, save for a dark hair-line that curved and twisted from around the spruce-covered island to the south, and that curved and twisted away into the north, where it disappeared behind another spruce-covered island. This dark hair-line was the trail—the main trail—that led south five hundred miles to the Chilcoot Pass, Dyea, and salt water; and that led north seventy miles to Dawson, and still on to the north a thousand miles to Nulato, and finally to St. Michael on Bering Sea, a thousand miles and half a thousand more.

But all this—the mysterious, far-reaching hairline trail, the absence of sun from the sky, the tremendous cold, and the strangeness and weirdness of it all—made no impression on the man. It was not because he was long used to it. He was a new-comer in the land, a chechaquo, and this was his first winter. The trouble with him was that he was without imagination. He was quick and alert in the things of life, but only in the things, and not in the significances. Fifty degrees below zero meant eighty odd degrees of frost. Such fact impressed him as being cold and uncomfortable, and that was all. It did not lead him to meditate upon his frailty as a creature of temperature, and upon man's frailty in general, able only to live within certain narrow limits of heat and cold; and from there on it did not lead him to the conjectural field of immortality and man's place in the universe. Fifty degrees below zero stood for a bite of frost that hurt and that must be guarded against by the use of mittens, ear-flaps, warm moccasins, and thick socks. Fifty degrees below zero was to him just precisely fifty degrees below zero. That there should be anything more to it than that was a thought that never entered his head.

As he turned to go on, he spat speculatively. There was a sharp, explosive crackle that startled him. He spat again. And again, in the air, before it could fall to the snow, the spittle crackled. He knew that at fifty below spittle crackled on the snow, but this spittle had crackled in the air. Undoubtedly it was colder than fifty below—how much colder he did not know. But the temperature did not matter. He was bound for the old claim on the left fork of Henderson Creek, where the boys were already. They had come over across the divide from the Indian Creek country, while he had come the roundabout way to take a look at the possibilities of getting out logs in the spring from the islands in the

Yukon. He would be in to camp by six o'clock; a bit after dark, it was true, but the boys would be there, a fire would be going, and a hot supper would be ready. As for lunch, he pressed his hand against the protruding bundle under his jacket. It was also under his shirt, wrapped up in a handkerchief and lying against the naked skin. It was the only way to keep the biscuits from freezing. He smiled agreeably to himself as he thought of those biscuits, each cut open and sopped in bacon grease, and each enclosing a generous slice of fried bacon.

He plunged in among the big spruce trees. The trail was faint. A foot of snow had fallen since the last sled had passed over, and he was glad he was without a sled, travelling light. In fact, he carried nothing but the lunch wrapped in the handkerchief. He was surprised, however, at the cold. It certainly was cold, he concluded, as he rubbed his numbed nose and cheek-bones with his mittened hand. He was a warm-whiskered man, but the hair on his face did not protect the high cheek-bones and the eager nose that thrust itself aggressively into the frosty air.

At the man's heels trotted a dog, a big native husky, the proper wolf-dog, grey-coated and without any visible or temperamental difference from its brother, the wild wolf. The animal was depressed by the tremendous cold. It knew that it was no time for travelling. Its instinct told it a truer tale than was told to the man by the man's judgment. In reality, it was not merely colder than fifty below zero; it was colder than sixty below, than seventy below. It was seventy-five below zero. Since the freezing-point is thirty-two above zero, it meant that one hundred and seven degrees of frost obtained. The dog did not know anything about thermometers. Possibly in its brain there was no sharp consciousness of a condition of very cold such as was in the man's brain. But the brute had its instinct. It experienced a vague but menacing apprehension that subdued it and made it slink along at the man's heels, and that made it question eagerly every unwonted movement of the man as if expecting him to go into camp or to seek shelter somewhere and build a fire. The dog had learned fire, and it wanted fire, or else to burrow under the snow and cuddle its warmth away from the air.

The frozen moisture of its breathing had settled on its fur in a fine powder of frost, and especially were its jowls, muzzle, and eyelashes whitened by its crystalled breath. The man's red beard and moustache were likewise frosted, but more solidly, the deposit taking the form of ice and increasing with every warm, moist breath he exhaled. Also, the man was chewing tobacco, and the muzzle of ice held his lips so rigidly that he was unable to clear his chin when he expelled the juice. The result was that a crystal beard of the colour and solidity of amber was increasing its length on his chin. If he fell down it would shatter itself, like glass, into brittle fragments. But he did not mind the appendage. It was the penalty all tobacco-chewers paid in that country, and he had been out before in two cold snaps. They had not been so cold as this, he knew, but by the spirit thermometer at Sixty Mile he knew they had been registered at fifty below and at fifty-five.

He held on through the level stretch of woods for several miles, crossed a wide flat of nigger-heads, and dropped down a bank to the frozen bed of a small stream. This was Henderson Creek, and he knew he was ten miles from the forks. He looked at his watch. It was ten o'clock. He was making four miles an hour, and he calculated that he would arrive at the forks at half-past twelve. He decided to celebrate that event by eating his lunch there.

The dog dropped in again at his heels, with a tail drooping discouragement, as the man swung along the creek-bed. The furrow of the old sled-trail was plainly visible, but a dozen inches of snow covered the marks of the last runners. In a month no man had come up or down that silent creek. The man held steadily on. He was not much given to thinking, and just then particularly he had nothing to think about save that he would eat lunch at the forks and that at six o'clock he would be in camp with the boys. There was nobody to talk to and, had there been, speech would have been impossible because of the ice-muzzle on his mouth. So he continued monotonously to chew tobacco and to increase the length of his amber beard.

Once in a while the thought reiterated itself that it was very cold and that he had never experienced such cold. As he walked along he rubbed his cheek-bones and nose with the back of his mittened hand. He did this automatically, now and again changing hands. But rub as he would, the instant he stopped his cheek-bones went numb, and the following instant the end of his nose went numb. He was sure to frost his cheeks; he knew that, and experienced a pang of regret that he had not devised a nose-strap of the sort Bud wore in cold snaps. Such a strap passed across the cheeks, as well, and saved them. But it didn't matter much, after all. What were frosted cheeks? A bit painful, that was all; they were never serious.

Empty as the man's mind was of thoughts, he was keenly observant, and he noticed the changes in the creek, the curves and bends and timber-jams, and always he sharply noted where he placed his feet. Once, coming around a bend, he shied abruptly, like a startled horse, curved away from the place where he had been walking, and retreated several paces back along the trail. The creek he knew was frozen clear to the bottom—no creek could contain water in that arctic winter—but he knew also that there were springs that bubbled out from the hillsides and ran along under the snow and on top the ice of the creek. He knew that the coldest snaps never froze these springs, and he knew likewise their danger. They were traps. They hid pools of water under the snow that might be three inches deep, or three feet. Sometimes a skin of ice half an inch thick covered them, and in turn was covered by the snow. Sometimes there were alternate layers of water and ice-skin, so that when one broke through he kept on breaking through for a while, sometimes wetting himself to the waist.

That was why he had shied in such panic. He had felt the give under his feet and heard the crackle of a snow-hidden ice-skin. And to get his feet wet in such a temperature meant trouble and danger. At the very least it meant delay, for he would be forced to stop and build a fire, and under its protection to bare his feet while he dried his socks and moccasins. He stood and studied the creek-bed and its banks, and decided that the flow of water came from the right. He reflected awhile, rubbing his nose and cheeks, then skirted to the left, stepping gingerly and testing the footing for each step. Once clear of the danger, he took a fresh chew of tobacco and swung along at his four-mile gait.

In the course of the next two hours he came upon several similar traps. Usually the snow above the hidden pools had a sunken, candied appearance that advertised the danger. Once again, however, he had a close call; and once, suspecting danger, he compelled the dog to go on in front. The dog did not want to go. It hung back until the man shoved it forward, and then it went quickly across the white, unbroken surface. Suddenly it broke through, floundered to one side, and got away to firmer footing. It had wet its forefeet and legs, and almost immediately the water that clung to it turned to ice. It made quick efforts to lick the ice off its legs, then dropped down in the snow and began to bite out the ice that had formed between the toes. This was a matter of instinct. To permit the ice to remain would mean sore feet. It did not know this. It merely obeyed the mysterious prompting that arose from the deep crypts of its being. But the man knew, having achieved a judgment on the subject, and he removed the mitten from his right hand and helped tear out the ice-parti-

cles. He did not expose his fingers more than a minute, and was astonished at the swift numbness that smote them. It certainly was cold. He pulled on the mitten hastily, and beat the hand savagely across his chest.

At twelve o'clock the day was at its brightest. Yet the sun was too far south on its winter journey to clear the horizon. The bulge of the earth intervened between it and Henderson Creek, where the man walked under a clear sky at noon and cast no shadow. At half-past twelve, to the minute, he arrived at the forks of the creek. He was pleased at the speed he had made. If he kept it up, he would certainly be with the boys by six. He unbuttoned his jacket and shirt and drew forth his lunch. The action consumed no more than a quarter of a minute, yet in that brief moment the numbness laid hold of the exposed fingers. He did not put the mitten on, but, instead, struck the fingers a dozen sharp smashes against his leg. Then he sat down on a snow-covered log to eat. The sting that followed upon the striking of his fingers against his leg ceased so quickly that he was startled, he had had no chance to take a bite of biscuit. He struck the fingers repeatedly and returned them to the mitten, baring the other hand for the purpose of eating. He tried to take a mouthful, but the ice-muzzle prevented. He had forgotten to build a fire and thaw out. He chuckled at his foolishness, and as he chuckled he noted the numbness creeping into the exposed fingers. Also, he noted that the stinging which had first come to his toes when he sat down was already passing away. He wondered whether the toes were warm or numbed. He moved them inside the moccasins and decided that they were numbed.

He pulled the mitten on hurriedly and stood up. He was a bit frightened. He stamped up and down until the stinging returned into the feet. It certainly was cold, was his thought. That man from Sulphur Creek had spoken the truth when telling how cold it sometimes got in the country. And he had laughed at him at the time! That showed one must not be too sure of things. There was no mistake about it, it was cold. He strode up and down, stamping his feet and threshing his arms, until reassured by the returning warmth. Then he got out matches and proceeded to make a fire. From the undergrowth, where high water of the previous spring had lodged a supply of seasoned twigs, he got his firewood. Working carefully from a small beginning, he soon had a roaring fire, over which he thawed the ice from his face and in the protection of which he ate his biscuits. For the moment the cold of space was outwitted. The dog took satisfaction in the fire, stretching out close enough for warmth and far enough away to escape being singed.

When the man had finished, he filled his pipe and took his comfortable time over a smoke. Then he pulled on his mittens, settled the ear-flaps of his cap firmly about his ears, and took the creek trail up the left fork. The dog was disappointed and yearned back toward the fire. This man did not know cold. Possibly all the generations of his ancestry had been ignorant of cold, of real cold, of cold one hundred and seven degrees below freezing-point. But the dog knew; all its ancestry knew, and it had inherited the knowledge. And it knew that it was not good to walk abroad in such fearful cold. It was the time to lie snug in a hole in the snow and wait for a curtain of cloud to be drawn across the face of outer space whence this cold came. On the other hand, there was keen intimacy between the dog and the man. The one was the toil-slave of the other, and the only caresses it had ever received were the caresses of the whip-lash and of harsh and menacing throat-sounds that threatened the whip-lash. So the dog made no effort to communicate its apprehension to the man. It was not concerned in the welfare of the man; it was for its own sake that it yearned back toward the fire. But the man whistled, and spoke to it with the sound of whip-lashes, and the dog swung in at the man's heels and followed after.

The man took a chew of tobacco and proceeded to start a new amber beard. Also, his moist breath quickly powdered with white his moustache, eyebrows, and lashes. There did not seem to be so many springs on the left fork of the Henderson, and for half an hour the man saw no signs of any. And then it happened. At a place where there were no signs, where the soft, unbroken snow seemed to advertise solidity beneath, the man broke through. It was not deep. He wetted himself half-way to the knees before he floundered out to the firm crust.

He was angry, and cursed his luck aloud. He had hoped to get into camp with the boys at six o'clock, and this would delay him an hour, for he would have to build a fire and dry out his foot-gear. This was imperative at that low temperature—he knew that much; and he turned aside to the bank, which he climbed. On top, tangled in the underbrush about the trunks of several small spruce trees, was a high-water deposit of dry firewood—sticks and twigs principally, but also larger portions of seasoned branches and fine, dry, last-year's grasses. He threw down several large pieces on top of the snow. This served for a foundation and prevented the young flame from drowning itself in the snow it otherwise would melt. The flame he got by touching a match to a small shred of birch-bark that he took from his pocket. This burned even more readily than paper. Placing it on the foundation, he fed the young flame with wisps of dry grass and with the tiniest dry twigs.

He worked slowly and carefully, keenly aware of his danger. Gradually, as the flame grew stronger, he increased the size of the twigs with which he fed it. He squatted in the snow, pulling the twigs out from their entanglement in the brush and feeding directly to the flame. He knew there must be no failure. When it is seventy-five below zero, a man must not fail in his first attempt to build a fire—that is, if his feet are wet. If his feet are dry, and he fails, he can run along the trail for half a mile and restore his circulation. But the circulation of wet and freezing feet cannot be restored by running when it is seventy-five below. No matter how fast he runs, the wet feet will freeze the harder.

All this the man knew. The old-timer on Sulphur Creek had told him about it the previous fall, and now he was appreciating the advice. Already all sensation had gone out of his feet. To build the fire he had been forced to remove his mittens, and the fingers had quickly gone numb. His pace of four miles an hour had kept his heart pumping blood to the surface of his body and to all the extremities. But the instant he stopped, the action of the pump eased down. The cold of space smote the unprotected tip of the planet, and he, being on that unprotected tip, received the full force of the blow. The blood of his body recoiled before it. The blood was alive, like the dog, and like the dog it wanted to hide away and cover itself up from the fearful cold. So long as he walked four miles an hour, he pumped that blood, willy-nilly, to the surface; but now it ebbed away and sank down into the recesses of his body. The extremities were the first to feel its absence. His wet feet froze the faster, and his exposed fingers numbed the faster, though they had not yet begun to freeze. Nose and cheeks were already freezing, while the skin of all his body chilled as it lost its blood.

But he was safe. Toes and nose and cheeks would be only touched by the frost, for the fire was beginning to burn with strength. He was feeding it with twigs the size of his finger. In another minute he would be able to feed it with branches the size of his wrist, and then he could remove his wet foot-gear, and, while it dried, he could keep his naked feet warm by the fire, rubbing them at first, of course, with snow. The fire was a success. He was safe. He remembered the advice of the old-timer on Sulphur Creek, and smiled. The old-timer had been very serious in laying down the law that no man must travel alone in the Klondike after fifty below. Well, here he was; he had had the accident; he was alone; and he had saved himself. Those old-timers were rather womanish, some of them, he thought. All a man had to do was to keep his head, and he was all right. Any man who was a man could travel alone. But it was surprising, the rapidity with which his cheeks and nose were freezing. And he had not thought his fingers could go lifeless in so short a time. Lifeless they were, for he could scarcely make them move together to grip a twig, and they seemed remote from his body and from him. When he touched a twig, he had to look and see whether or not he had hold of it. The wires were pretty well down between him and his finger-ends.

All of which counted for little. There was the fire, snapping and crackling and promising life with every dancing flame. He started to untie his moccasins. They were coated with ice; the thick German socks were like sheaths of iron half-way to the knees; and the mocassin strings were like rods of steel all twisted and knotted as by some conflagration. For a moment he tugged with his numbed fingers, then, realizing the folly of it, he drew his sheath-knife.

But before he could cut the strings, it happened. It was his own fault or, rather, his mistake. He should not have built the fire under the spruce tree. He should have built it in the open. But it had been easier to pull the twigs from the brush and drop them directly on the fire. Now the tree under which he had done this carried a weight of snow on its boughs. No wind had blown for weeks, and each bough was fully freighted. Each time he had pulled a twig he had communicated a slight agitation to the tree—an imperceptible agitation, so far as he was concerned, but an agitation sufficient to bring about the disaster. High up in the tree one bough capsized its load of snow. This fell on the boughs beneath, capsizing them. This process continued, spreading out and involving the whole tree. It grew like an avalanche, and it descended without warning upon the man and the fire, and the fire was blotted out! Where it had burned was a mantle of fresh and disordered snow.

The man was shocked. It was as though he had just heard his own sentence of death. For a moment he sat and stared at the spot where the fire had been. Then he grew very calm. Perhaps the old-timer on Sulphur Creek was right. If he had only had a trail-mate he would have been in no danger now. The trail-mate could have built the fire. Well, it was up to him to build the fire over again, and this second time there must be no failure. Even if he succeeded, he would most likely lose some toes. His feet must be badly frozen by now, and there would be some time before the second fire was ready.

Such were his thoughts, but he did not sit and think them. He was busy all the time they were passing through his mind, he made a new foundation for a fire, this time in the open; where no treacherous tree could blot it out. Next, he gathered dry grasses and tiny twigs from the high-water flotsam. He could not bring his fingers together to pull them out, but he was able to gather them by the handful. In this way he got many rotten twigs and bits of green moss that were undesirable, but it was the best he could do. He worked methodically, even collecting an armful of the larger branches to be used later when the fire gathered strength. And all the while the dog sat and watched him, a certain yearning wistfulness in its eyes, for it looked upon him as the fire-provider, and the fire was slow in coming.

When all was ready, the man reached in his pocket for a second piece of birch-bark. He knew the bark was there, and, though he could not feel it with his fingers, he could hear its crisp rustling as he fumbled for it. Try as he would, he could not clutch hold of it. And all the time, in his consciousness, was the knowledge that each instant his feet were freezing. This thought tended to put him in a panic, but he fought against it and kept calm. He pulled on his mittens with his teeth, and threshed his arms back and forth, beating his hands with all his might against his sides. He did this sitting down, and he stood up to do it; and all the while the dog sat in the snow, its wolf-brush of a tail curled around warmly over its forefeet, its sharp wolf-ears pricked forward intently as it watched the man. And the man as he beat and threshed with his arms and hands, felt a great surge of envy as he regarded the creature that was warm and secure in its natural covering.

After a time he was aware of the first far-away signals of sensation in his beaten fingers. The faint tingling grew stronger till it evolved into a stinging ache that was excruciating, but which the man hailed with satisfaction. He stripped the mitten from his right hand and fetched forth the birch-bark. The exposed fingers were quickly going numb again. Next he brought out his bunch of sulphur matches. But the tremendous cold had already driven the life out of his fingers. In his effort to separate one match from the others, the whole bunch fell in the snow. He tried to pick it out of the snow, but failed. The dead fingers could neither touch nor clutch. He was very careful. He drove the thought of his freezing feet; and nose, and cheeks, out of his mind, devoting his whole soul to the matches. He watched, using the sense of vision in place of that of touch, and when he saw his fingers on each side the bunch, he closed them—that is, he willed to close them, for the wires were drawn, and the fingers did not obey. He pulled the mitten on the right hand, and beat it fiercely against his knee. Then, with both mittened hands, he scooped the bunch of matches, along with much snow, into his lap. Yet he was no better off.

After some manipulation he managed to get the bunch between the heels of his mittened hands. In this fashion he carried it to his mouth. The ice crackled and snapped when by a violent effort he opened his mouth. He drew the lower jaw in, curled the upper lip out of the way, and scraped the bunch with his upper teeth in order to separate a match. He succeeded in getting one, which he dropped on his lap. He was no better off. He could not pick it up. Then he devised a way. He picked it up in his teeth and scratched it on his leg. Twenty times he scratched before he succeeded in lighting it. As it flamed he held it with his teeth to the birch-bark. But the burning brimstone went up his nostrils and into his lungs, causing him to cough spasmodically. The match fell into the snow and went out.

The old-timer on Sulphur Creek was right, he thought in the moment of controlled despair that ensued: after fifty below, a man should travel with a partner. He beat his hands, but failed in exciting any sensation. Suddenly he bared both hands, removing the mittens with his teeth. He caught the whole bunch between the heels of his hands. His arm-muscles not being frozen enabled him to press the hand-heels tightly against the matches. Then he scratched the bunch along his leg. It flared into flame, seventy sulphur matches at once! There was no wind to blow them out. He kept his head to one side to escape the strangling fumes, and held the blazing bunch to the birch-bark. As he so held it, he became aware of sensation in his hand. His flesh was burning. He could smell it. Deep down below the surface he could feel it. The sensation developed into pain that grew acute. And still he endured it, holding the flame of the matches clumsily to the bark that would not light readily because his own burning hands were in the way, absorbing most of the flame.

At last, when he could endure no more, he jerked his hands apart. The blazing matches fell sizzling into the snow, but the birch-bark was alight. He began laying dry grasses and the tiniest twigs on the flame. He could not pick and choose, for he had to lift the fuel between the heels of his hands. Small pieces of rotten wood and green moss clung to the twigs, and he bit them off as well as he could with his teeth. He cherished the flame carefully and awkwardly. It meant life, and it must not perish. The withdrawal of blood from the sur-

face of his body now made him begin to shiver, and he grew more awkward. A large piece of green moss fell squarely on the little fire. He tried to poke it out with his fingers, but his shivering frame made him poke too far, and he disrupted the nucleus of the little fire, the burning grasses and tiny twigs separating and scattering. He tried to poke them together again, but in spite of the tenseness of the effort, his shivering got away with him, and the twigs were hopelessly scattered. Each twig gushed a puff of smoke and went out. The fire-provider had failed. As he looked apathetically about him, his eyes chanced on the dog, sitting across the ruins of the fire from him, in the snow, making restless, hunching movements, slightly lifting one forefoot and then the other, shifting its weight back and forth on them with wistful eagerness.

The sight of the dog put a wild idea into his head. He remembered the tale of the man, caught in a blizzard, who killed a steer and crawled inside the carcass, and so was saved. He would kill the dog and bury his hands in the warm body until the numbness went out of them. Then he could build another fire. He spoke to the dog, calling it to him; but in his voice was a strange note of fear that frightened the animal, who had never known the man to speak in such way before. Something was the matter, and its suspicious nature sensed danger—it knew not what danger but somewhere, somehow, in its brain arose an apprehension of the man. It flattened its ears down at the sound of the man's voice, and its restless, hunching movements and the liftings and shiftings of its forefeet became more pronounced but it would not come to the man. He got on his hands and knees and crawled toward the dog. This unusual posture again excited suspicion, and the animal sidled mincingly away.

The man sat up in the snow for a moment and struggled for calmness. Then he pulled on his mittens, by means of his teeth, and got upon his feet. He glanced down at first in order to assure himself that he was really standing up, for the absence of sensation in his feet left him unrelated to the earth. His erect position in itself started to drive the webs of suspicion from the dog's mind; and when he spoke peremptorily, with the sound of whip-lashes in his voice, the dog rendered its customary allegiance and came to him. As it came within reaching distance, the man lost his control. His arms flashed out to the dog, and he experienced genuine surprise when he discovered that his hands could not clutch, that there was neither bend nor feeling in the fingers. He had forgotten for the moment that they were frozen and that they were freezing more and more. All this happened quickly, and before the animal could get away, he encircled its body with his arms. He sat down in the snow, and in this fashion held the dog, while it snarled and whined and struggled.

But it was all he could do, hold its body encircled in his arms and sit there. He realized that he could not kill the dog. There was no way to do it. With his helpless hands he could neither draw nor hold his sheath-knife nor throttle the animal. He released it, and it plunged wildly away, with tail between its legs, and still snarling. It halted forty feet away and surveyed him curiously, with ears sharply pricked forward. The man looked down at his hands in order to locate them, and found them hanging on the ends of his arms. It struck him as curious that one should have to use his eyes in order to find out where his hands were. He began threshing his arms back and forth, beating the mittened hands against his sides. He did this for five minutes, violently, and his heart pumped enough blood up to the surface to put a stop to his shivering. But no sensation was aroused in the hands. He had an impression that they hung like weights on the ends of his arms, but when he tried to run the impression down, he could not find it.

A certain fear of death, dull and oppressive, came to him. This fear quickly became poignant as he realized that it was no longer a mere matter of freezing his fingers and toes, or of losing his hands and feet, but that it was a matter of life and death with the chances against him. This threw him into a panic, and he turned and ran up the creek-bed along the old, dim trail. The dog joined in behind and kept up with him. He ran blindly, without intention, in fear such as he had never known in his life. Slowly, as he ploughed and floundered through the snow, he began to see things again—the banks of the creek, the old timber-jams, the leafless aspens, and the sky. The running made him feel better. He did not shiver. Maybe, if he ran on, his feet would thaw out; and, anyway, if he ran far enough, he would reach camp and the boys. Without doubt he would lose some fingers and toes and some of his face; but the boys would take care of him, and save the rest of him when he got there. And at the same time there was another thought in his mind that said he would never get to the camp and the boys; that it was too many miles away, that the freezing had too great a start on him, and that he would soon be stiff and dead. This thought he kept in the background and refused to consider. Sometimes it pushed itself forward and demanded to be heard, but he thrust it back and strove to think of other things.

It struck him as curious that he could run at all on feet so frozen that he could not feel them when they struck the earth and took the weight of his body. He seemed to himself to skim along above the surface and to have no connection with the earth. Somewhere he had once seen a winged Mercury, and he wondered if Mercury felt as he felt when skimming over the earth.

His theory of running until he reached camp and the boys had one flaw in it: he lacked the endurance. Several times he stumbled, and finally he tottered, crumpled up, and fell. When he tried to rise, he failed. He must sit and rest, he decided, and next time he would merely walk and keep on going. As he sat and regained his breath, he noted that he was feeling quite warm and comfortable. He was not shivering, and it even seemed that a warm glow had come to his chest and trunk. And yet, when he touched his nose or cheeks, there was no sensation. Running would not thaw them out. Nor would it thaw out his hands and feet. Then the thought came to him that the frozen portions of his body must be extending. He tried to keep this thought down, to forget it, to think of something else; he was aware of the panicky feeling that it caused, and he was afraid of the panic. But the thought asserted itself, and persisted, until it produced a vision of his body totally frozen. This was too much, and he made another wild run along the trail. Once he slowed down to a walk, but the thought of the freezing extending itself made him run again.

And all the time the dog ran with him, at his heels. When he fell down a second time, it curled its tail over its forefeet and sat in front of him facing him curiously eager and intent. The warmth and security of the animal angered him, and he cursed it till it flattened down its ears appeasingly. This time the shivering came more quickly upon the man. He was losing in his battle with the frost. It was creeping into his body from all sides. The thought of it drove him on, but he ran no more than a hundred feet, when he staggered and pitched headlong. It was his last panic. When he had recovered his breath and control, he sat up and entertained in his mind the conception of meeting death with dignity. However, the conception did not come to him in such terms. His idea of it was that he had been making a fool of himself, running around like a chicken with its head cut off—such was the simile that occurred to him. Well, he was bound to freeze anyway, and he might as well take it decently. With this new-found peace of mind came the first glimmerings of drowsiness. A good idea, he thought, to sleep off to death. It was like taking an anaesthetic. Freezing was not so bad as people thought. There were lots worse ways to die.

He pictured the boys finding his body next day. Suddenly he found himself with them, coming along the trail and looking for himself. And, still with them, he came around a turn in the trail and found himself lying in the snow. He did not belong with himself any more, for even then he was out of himself, standing with the boys and looking at himself in the snow. It certainly was cold, was his thought. When he got back to the States he could tell the folks what real cold was. He drifted on from this to a vision of the old-timer on Sulphur Creek. He could see him quite clearly, warm and comfortable, and smoking a pipe.

"You were right, old hoss; you were right," the man mumbled to the old-timer of Sulphur Creek.

Then the man drowsed off into what seemed to him the most comfortable and satisfying sleep he had ever known. The dog sat facing him and waiting. The brief day drew to a close in a long, slow twilight. There were no signs of a fire to be made, and, besides, never in the dog's experience had it known a man to sit like that in the snow and make no fire. As the twilight drew on, its eager yearning for the fire mastered it, and with a great lifting and shifting of forefeet, it whined softly, then flattened its ears down in anticipation of being chidden by the man. But the man remained silent. Later, the dog whined loudly. And still later it crept close to the man and caught the scent of death. This made the animal bristle and back away. A little longer it delayed, howling under the stars that leaped and danced and shone brightly in the cold sky. Then it turned and trotted up the trail in the direction of the camp it knew, where were the other food-providers and fire-providers.

BIBLICAL APPLICATION

A man said to the universe: "Sir, I exist!" "However," replied the universe, "The fact has not created in me a sense of obligation." (In Humanity, http://quotes.prolix, mi/Authors/).

He never created a Hester Prynne who gave her life to absolute truth or a Huck Finn who had affectionate tolerance toward differing opinions. Crane's world was cynical and very dangerous. His world was full of opportunistic "demons" who sought to do him in. He was "A man adrift on a slim spar/A horizon smaller than the rim of a bottle/Tented waves rearing lashy dark points/The near whine of froth in circles./God is cold" (from the poem "Adrift on a Spar," http://www.americanpoems.com/F) In a short story entitled "The Open

> Tone: the author's attitude toward his subject as expressed in a literary work. Tone is conveyed through the author's choice of words, his inclusion of certain details, and his description of characters and events.

Boat" Crane hauntingly described the frustration of being in an open boat near enough to see the shore but unable to reach the shore and safety (http://www.gonzaga.edu/faculty/campbell/crane/):

> If I am going to be drowned—if I am going to be drowned—if I am going to be drowned, why, in the name of the seven mad gods who rule the sea, was I allowed to come thus far and contemplate sand and trees? Was I brought here merely to have my nose dragged away as I was about to nibble the sacred cheese of life?

The moribundity expressed by Crane becomes a recurring theme in American literature. Gone is the God of the Puritans and even the God whom Hester Prynne so faithfully served. The great-great-grandchildren of Anne Bradstreet doubted God really loved them at all. "Fate" was the true power that determined their future.

Find examples of this hopelessness in modern movies, television programs, and music. Why, as Christian believers, should we reject this pessimism?

ENRICHMENT

A contemporary and very popular proponent of Naturalism is B. F. Skinner. In his book *Beyond Freedom and Dignity,* Skinner argues that the problems we face today are caused by outside forces (e.g., Nature) and can be solved by also changing these outside forces. Changing hearts is irrelevant. Agree or disagree.

FINAL PORTFOLIO

Correct and re-write required essays and place in your Portfolio.

SUGGESTED
Weekly *Implementation*

DAY 1	DAY 2	DAY 3	DAY 4	DAY 5
Prayer journal. Review the required reading(s) before the assigned lesson begins. Teacher may want to discuss assigned reading(s) with students. Teacher and students will decide on required essays for this lesson, choosing two or three essays. The rest of the essays can be outlined, answered with shorter answers, or skipped. Review all readings for Lesson 17	**Prayer journal.** Review reading(s) from next lesson. Outline essays due at the end of the week. Per teacher instructions, students may answer orally in a group setting some of the essays that are not assigned as formal essays.	**Prayer journal.** Write rough drafts of all assigned essays. The teacher and/or a peer evaluator may correct rough drafts.	**Prayer journal.** Rewrite corrected copies of essays due tomorrow.	**Prayer journal.** Essays are due. Take Lesson 17 test. Reading Ahead: Review "Outcasts of Poker Flat," Bret Harte; "The Story of an Hour," Kate Chopin; "Luke Havergal" and "Credo," Edwin Arlington Robinson; "Lucinda Matlock," Edgar Lee Masters. (Lesson 19) Guide: What new styles and themes emerge in these late 19th century works?

LESSON 18

REALISM, NATURALISM, AND THE FRONTIER, *1865-1915*
(Part 4)

Red Badge of Courage

(*continued*)

Stephen Crane

BACKGROUND

In his book *Sister Carrie* the Naturalist writer Theodore Dreiser wrote:

Oh, Carrie. Oh, Carrie. Oh, blind striving of the human heart . . . In your rocking-chair, by your window dreaming, shall you long, alone. In your rocking-chair, by your window, shall you dream such happiness as you may never feel.

http://wyllie.lib.virginia.edu:8086/perl/toccer-new?id=DreSist.sgm&images=images/modeng&data=/texts/english/modeng/parsed&tag=public&part=47&di

CRITICAL THINKING

A. The plot of *Red Badge of Courage*, to some critics, has major flaws. For instance, after running farther and faster than anyone else, Henry Fleming proves to be one of the bravest soldiers in the regiment. Some critics feel that this is unbelievable. Do you agree? If you feel that the transformation is believable, explain why you do with reasons from the book

B. Analyze Crane's tone and writing style.

C. Pretend that Henry was court marshaled for desertion. Should he be convicted? Why or why not?

D. To Crane, nature has lost all contact with humanity. "It was surprising that Nature had gone tranquilly on with her golden process in the midst of so much devilment." Contrast this view with some of the earlier Romantic writers (e.g., Hawthorne).

BIBLICAL APPLICATION

Naturalism stresses the discoverable, deterministic laws

You will analyze: *Red Badge of Courage*, Stephen Crane.

Reading Ahead: "Outcasts of Poker Flat," Bret Harte; "The Story of an Hour," Kate Chopin; "Luke Havergal" and "Credo," Edwin Arlington Robinson; "Lucinda Matlock," Edgar Lee Masters.

Guide Question: What new styles and themes emerge in these late 19th century works?

of nature. If God exists in the naturalistic word, He is, like nature, cold and indifferent. As the fleeing Henry trips over his dead friend, he notices that a squirrel is playing innocently around his dead friend's body. The birds sing beautiful songs impervious to the death occurring all around them. The contrast of the carnage of human warfare and the malevolent beauty of nature is at the heart of Naturalism. Naturalism posits that nature is both ubiquitous and impersonal. What Scripture verses can you find that contradict this view? Write an essay that argues your perspective.

ENRICHMENT

A. How was Crane affected by Social Darwinism? Social Darwinism was a social theory popular at the end of the nineteenth century. It argued that a social structure and a human organism both survive according to natural laws; i.e., survival of the fittest.

B. In *Principles of Psychology* (1855) Herbert Spencer, a British philosopher, took Darwin's theory into the social realm. He influenced a generation of sociologists and authors like Stephen Crane. He wrote

The Red Badge of Courage has a very simple but well-written plot. A good plot has a purpose; it grows naturally out of events, and it is related to the main idea in the story.

that all organic matter originated in a unified state and that individual characteristics gradually developed through evolution. The evolutionary progression from simple to more complex and diverse states was an important theme in most of Spencer's later works. In summary, Spencer argued that the strongest individuals and social systems survive. The weakest do not. This was an example of a scientific theory being transposed on human society and experience. The same thing happened with Einstein's theory of relativity. "Who would imagine that this simple law (constancy of the velocity of light) has plunged the conscientiously thoughtful physicist into the greatest intellectual difficulties?" Einstein wrote. (www.bartleby.com) He was horrified that social scientists took his theory about the quantum nature of light, a description of molecular motion, and the special theory of relativity and created a social theory called Relativism. Relativism argued that persons should make decisions based upon the "relative worth" of that decision based on circumstances. In other words, people were free to do what was relatively beneficial to their situation regardless of the consequences to others. Why do social scientists indulge themselves in such contrived chicanery and what are its ramifications?

C. Read the following short story by Crane entitled "Blue Hotel" (1898) and write an essay highlighting its Naturalistic themes.

Blue Hotel

The Palace Hotel at Fort Romper was painted a light blue, a shade that is on the legs of a kind of heron, causing the bird to declare its position against any background. The Palace Hotel, then, was always screaming and howling in a way that made the dazzling winter landscape of Nebraska seem only a gray swampish hush. It stood alone on the prairie, and when the snow was falling the town two hundred yards away was not visible. But when the traveler alighted at the railway station he was obliged to pass the Palace Hotel before he could come upon the company of low clapboard houses which composed Fort Romper, and it was not to be thought that any traveler could pass the Palace Hotel without looking at it. Pat Scully, the proprietor, had proved himself a master of strategy when he chose his paints. It is true that on clear days, when the great trans-continental expresses, long lines of swaying Pullmans, swept through Fort Romper, passengers were overcome at the sight, and the cult that knows the brown-reds and the subdivisions of the dark greens of the East expressed shame, pity, horror, in a laugh. But to the citizens of this prairie town, and to the people who would naturally stop there, Pat Scully had performed a feat. With this opulence and splendor, these creeds, classes, egotisms, that streamed through Romper on the rails day after day, they had no color in common.

As if the displayed delights of such a blue hotel were not sufficiently enticing, it was Scully's habit to go every morning and evening to meet the leisurely trains that stopped at Romper and work his seductions upon any man that he might see wavering, gripsack in hand.

One morning, when a snow-crusted engine dragged its long string of freight cars and its one passenger coach to the station, Scully performed the marvel of catching three men. One was a shaky and quick-eyed Swede, with a great shining cheap valise; one was a tall bronzed cowboy, who was on his way to a ranch near the Dakota line; one was a little silent man from the East, who didn't look it, and didn't announce it. Scully practically made them prisoners. He was so nimble and merry and kindly that each probably felt it would be the height of brutality to try to escape. They trudged off over the creaking board sidewalks in the wake of the eager little Irishman.

He wore a heavy fur cap squeezed tightly down on his head. It caused his two red ears to stick out stiffly, as if they were made of tin. At last, Scully, elaborately, with boisterous hospitality, conducted them through the portals of the blue hotel. The room which they entered was small. It seemed to be merely a proper temple for an enormous stove, which, in the center, was humming with godlike violence. At various points on its surface the iron had become luminous and glowed yellow from the heat. Beside the stove Scully's son Johnnie was playing High-Five with an old farmer who had whiskers both gray and sandy. They were quarreling. Frequently the old farmer turned his face toward a box of sawdust-colored brown from tobacco juice that was behind the stove, and spat with an air of great impatience and irritation. With a loud flourish of words Scully destroyed the game of cards, and bustled his son upstairs with part of the baggage of the new guests. He himself conducted them to three basins of the coldest water in the world. The cowboy and the Easterner burnished themselves fiery red with this water, until it seemed to be some kind of a metal polish. The Swede, however, merely dipped his fingers gingerly and with trepidation. It was notable that throughout this series of small ceremonies the three travelers were made to feel that Scully was very benevolent. He was conferring great favors upon them. He handed the towel from one to the other with an air of philanthropic impulse.

Afterward they went to the first room, and, sitting about the stove, listened to Scully's officious clamor at his daughters, who were preparing the midday meal. They reflected in the silence of experienced men who tread carefully amid new people. Nevertheless, the old farmer, stationary, invincible in his chair near the warmest part of the stove, turned his face from the sawdust box frequently and addressed a glowing commonplace to the strangers. Usually he was answered in short but adequate sentences by either the cowboy or the Easterner. The Swede said nothing. He seemed to be occupied in making furtive estimates of each man in the room. One might have thought that he had the sense of silly suspicion which comes to guilt. He resembled a badly frightened man.

Later, at dinner, he spoke a little, addressing his conversation entirely to Scully. He volunteered that he had come from New York, where for ten years he had worked as a tailor. These facts seem to strike Scull as fascinating, and afterward he volunteered that he had lived at Romper for fourteen years. The Swede asked about the crops and the price of labor. He seemed barely to listen to Scully's extended replies. His eyes continued to rove from man to man.

Finally, with a laugh and a wink, he said that some of these Western Communities were very dangerous; and after his statement he straightened his legs under the table, tilted his head, and laughed again, loudly. It was plain that the demonstration had no meaning to the others. They looked at him wondering and in silence.

As the men trooped heavily back into the front room, the two little windows presented views of a turmoiling sea of snow. The huge arms of the wind were making attempts—mighty, circular, futile to embrace the flakes as they sped. A gate-post like a still man with a blanched face stood aghast amid this profligate fury. In a hearty voice Scully announced the presence of a blizzard. The guests of the blue hotel, lighting their pipes, assented with grunts of lazy masculine contentment. No island of the sea could be exempt in the degree of this little room with its humming stove. Johnnie, son of Scully, in a tone which defined his opinion of his ability as a card-player, challenged the old farmer of both gray and sandy whiskers to a game of High-Five. The farmer agreed with a contemptuous and bitter scoff. They sat close to the stove, and squared their knees under a wide board. The cowboy and the Easterner watched the game with interest. The Swede remained near the window, aloof, but with a countenance that showed signs of an inexplicable excitement.

The play of Johnnie and the gray-beard was suddenly ended by another quarrel. The old man arose while casting a look of heated scorn at his adversary. He slowly buttoned his coat, and then stalked with fabulous dignity from the room. In the discreet silence of all other men the Swede laughed. His laughter rang somehow childishly. Men by this time had begun to look at him askance, as if they wished to inquire what ailed him.

A new game was formed jocosely. The cowboy volunteered to become the partner of Johnnie, and them all then turned to ask the Swede to throw in his lot with the little Easterner. He asked some questions about the game, and learning that it wore many names, and that he had played it when it was under an alias, he accepted the invitation. He strode toward the men nervously, as if he expected to be assaulted. Finally, seated, he gazed from face to face and laughed shrilly. This laugh was so strange that the Easterner looked up quickly, the cowboy sat intent and with his mouth open, and Johnnie paused, holding the cards with still fingers. Afterward there was a short silence. Then Johnnie said: "Well, let's get at it. Come on now!" They pulled their chairs forward until their knees were bunched under the board. They began to play, and their interest in the game caused the others to forget the manner of the Swede.

The cowboy was a board-whacker. Each time that he held superior cards he whanged them, one by one, with exceeding force, down upon the improvised table, and took the tricks with a glowing air of prowess and pride that sent thrills of indignation into the hearts of his opponents. A game with a board-whacker in it is sure to become intense. The countenances of the Easterner and the Swede were miserable whenever the cowboy thundered down his aces and kings, while Johnnie, his eyes gleaming with joy, chuckled and chuckled. Because of the absorbing play none considered the strange ways of the Swede. They paid strict heed to the game. Finally, during a lull caused by a new deal, the Swede suddenly addressed Johnnie: "I suppose there have been a good many men killed in this room." The jaws of the others dropped and they looked at him. "What in hell are you talking about?" said Johnnie. The Swede laughed again his blatant laugh, full of a kind of false courage and defiance. "Oh, you know what I mean all right," he answered.

"I'm a liar if I do!" Johnnie protested. The card was halted, and the men stared at the Swede. Johnnie evidently felt that as the son of the proprietor he should make a direct inquiry. "Now, what might you be drivin' at, mister?" he asked. The Swede winked at him. It was a wink full of cunning. His fingers shook on the edge of the board. "Oh, maybe you think I have been to nowheres. Maybe you think I'm a tenderfoot?"

"I don't know nothin' about you," answered Johnnie, "and I don't give a damn where you've been. All I got to say is that I don't know what you're driving at. There hain't never been nobody killed in this room."

The cowboy, who had been steadily gazing at the Swede, then spoke. "What's wrong with you, mister?"

Apparently it seemed to the Swede that he was formidably menaced. He shivered and turned white near the corners of his mouth. He sent an appealing glance in the direction of the little Easterner. During these moments he did not forget to wear his air of advanced pot-valor.

"They say they don't know what I mean," he remarked mockingly to the Easterner.

The latter answered after prolonged and cautious reflection. "I don't understand you," he said, impassively.

The Swede made a movement then which announced that he thought he had encountered treachery from the only quarter where he had expected sympathy if not help. "Oh, I see you are all against me. I see-" The cowboy was in a state of deep stupefaction. "Say," he cried, as he tumbled the deck violently down upon the board. "Say, what are you gittin' at, hey?"

The Swede sprang up with the celerity of a man escaping from a snake on the floor. "I don't want to fight!" he shouted. "I don't want to fight!"

The cowboy stretched his long legs indolently and deliberately. His hands were in his pockets. He spat into the sawdust box. "Well, who the hell thought you did?" he inquired.

The Swede backed rapidly toward a corner of the room. His hands were out protectingly in front of his chest, but he was making an obvious struggle to control his fright. "Gentlemen," he quavered, "I suppose I am going to be killed before I can leave this house! I suppose I am going to be killed before I can leave this house." In his eyes was the dying swan look. Through the windows could be seen the snow turning blue in the shadow of dusk. The wind tore at the house and some loose thing beat regularly against the clapboard like a spirit tapping.

A door opened, and Scully himself entered. He paused in surprise as he noted the tragic attitude of the Swede. Then he said: "What's the matter here?"

The Swede answered him swiftly and eagerly: "These men are going to kill me."

"Kill you!" ejaculated Scully. "Kill you! What are you talkin'?"

The Swede made the gesture of a martyr.

Scully wheeled sternly upon his son. "What is this, Johnnie?"

The lad had grown sullen. "Damned if I know," he answered. "I can't make no sense to it." He began to shuffle the cards, fluttering them together with an angry snap. "He says a good many men have been killed in this room, or something like that. And he says he's goin' to be killed here too. I don't know what ails him. He's crazy, I shouldn't wonder."

Scully then looked for explanation to the cowboy, but the cowboy simply shrugged his shoulders.

"Kill you?" said Scully again to the Swede. "Kill you? Man, you're off your nut."

"Oh, I know," burst out the Swede. "I know what will happen. Yes, I'm crazy—yes. Yes, of course, I'm crazy—yes. But I know one thing—" There was a sort of sweat of misery and terror upon his face. "I know I won't get out of here alive."

The cowboy drew a deep breath, as if his mind was passing into the last stages of dissolution. "Well, I'm dog-goned," he whispered to himself.

Scully wheeled suddenly and faced his son. "You've been troublin' this man!"

Johnnie's voice was loud with its burden of grievance. "Why, good Gawd, I ain't done nothin' to 'im."

The Swede broke in. "Gentlemen, do not disturb yourselves. I will leave this house. I will go 'way because—" He accused them dramatically with his glance. "Because I do not want to be killed."

Scully was furious with his son. "Will you tell me what is the matter, you young divil? What's the matter, anyhow? Speak out!"

"Blame it," cried Johnnie in despair, "don't I tell you I don't know. He—he says we want to kill him, and that's all I know. I can't tell what ails him."

The Swede continued to repeat: "Never mind, Mr. Scully, never mind. I will leave this house. I will go away, because I do not wish to be killed. Yes, of course, I am crazy—yes. But I know one thing! I will go away. I will leave this house. Never mind, Mr. Scully, never mind. I will go away."

"You will not go 'way," said Scully. "You will not go 'way until I hear the reason of this business. If anybody has troubled you I will take care of him. This is my house. You are under my roof, and I will not allow any peaceable man to be troubled here." He cast a terrible eye upon Johnnie, the cowboy, and the Easterner.

"Never mind, Mr. Scully; never mind. I will go 'way. I do not wish to be killed." The Swede moved toward the door, which opened upon the stairs. It was evidently his intention to go at once for his baggage.

"No, no," shouted Scully peremptorily; but the whitefaced man slid by him and disappeared. "Now," said Scully severely, "what does this mane?"

Johnnie and the cowboy cried together: "Why, we didn't do nothin' to 'im!"

Scully's eyes were cold. "No," he said, "you didn't?"

Johnnie swore a deep oath. "Why, this is the wildest loon I ever see. We didn't do nothin' at all. We were jest sittin' here playin' cards and he—" The father suddenly spoke to the Easterner. "Mr. Blanc," he asked, "what has these boys been doin'?"

The Easterner reflected again. "I didn't see anything wrong at all," he said at last slowly.

Scully began to howl. "But what does it mane?" He stared ferociously at his son. "I have a mind to lather you for this, me boy."

Johnnie was frantic. "Well, what have I done?" he bawled at his father.

"I think you are tongue-tied," said Scully finally to his son, the cowboy and the Easterner, and at the end of this scornful sentence he left the room.

Upstairs the Swede was swiftly fastening the straps of his great valise. Once his back happened to be half-turned toward the door, and hearing a noise there, he wheeled and sprang up, uttering a loud cry. Scully's wrinkled visage showed grimly in the light of the small lamp he carried. This yellow effulgence, streaming upward, colored only his prominent features, and left his eyes, for instance, in mysterious shadow. He resembled a murderer.

"Man, man!" he exclaimed, "have you gone daffy?"

"Oh, no! Oh, no!" rejoined the other. "There are people in this world who know pretty nearly as much as you do—understand?" For a moment they stood gazing at each other. Upon the Swede's deathly pale cheeks were two spots brightly crimson and sharply edged, as if they had been carefully painted. Scully placed the light on the table and sat himself on the edge of the bed. He spoke ruminatively. "By cracky, I never heard of such a thing in my life. It's a complete muddle. I can't for the soul of me think how you ever got this idea into your head." Presently he lifted his eyes and asked: "And did you sure think they were going to kill you?" The Swede scanned the old man as if he wished to see into

his mind. "I did," he said at last. He obviously suspected that this answer might precipitate an outbreak. As he pulled on a strap his whole arm shook, the elbow wavering like a bit of paper.

Scully banged his hand impressively on the footboard of the bed. "Why, man, we're goin' to have a line of ilictric street-cars in this town next spring."

"'A line of electric street-cars,'" repeated the Swede stupidly.

"And," said Scully, "there's a new railroad goin' to be built down from Broken Arm to here. Not to mention the four churches and the smashin' big brick schoolhouse. Then there's the big factory, too. Why, in two years Romper'll be a met-tro-pol-is."

Having finished the preparation of his baggage, the Swede straightened himself. "Mr. Scully," he said with sudden hardihood, "how much do I owe you?"

"You don't owe me anythin'," said the old man angrily. "Yes, I do," retorted the Swede. He took seventy-five cents from his pocket and tendered it to Scully; but the latter snapped his fingers in disdainful refusal. However, it happened that they both stood gazing in a strange fashion at three silver pieces in the Swede's open palm.

"I'll not take your money," said Scully at last. "Not after what's been goin' on here." Then a plan seemed to strike him. "Here," he cried, picking up his lamp and moving toward the door. "Here! Come with me a minute."

"No," said the Swede in overwhelming alarm.

"Yes," urged the old man. "Come on! I want you to come and see a picter—just across the hall—in my room."

The Swede must have concluded that his hour was come. His jaw dropped and his teeth showed like a dead man's. He ultimately followed Scully across the corridor, but he had the step of one hung in chains.

Scully flashed the light high on the wall of his own chamber. There was revealed a ridiculous photograph of a little girl. She was leaning against a balustrade of gorgeous decoration, and the formidable bang to her hair was prominent. The figure was as graceful as an upright sled-stake, and, withal, it was of the hue of lead. "There," said Scully tenderly. "That's the picter of my little girl that died. Her name was Carrie. She had the purtiest hair you ever saw! I was that fond of her, she—" Turning then he saw that the Swede was not contemplating the picture at all, but, instead, was keeping keen watch on the gloom in the rear.

"Look, man!" shouted Scully heartily. "That's the picter of my little gal that died. Her name was Carrie.

And then here's the picter of my oldest boy, Michael. He's a lawyer in Lincoln an' doin' well. I gave that boy a grand eddycation, and I'm glad for it now. He's a fine boy. Look at 'im now. Ain't he bold as blazes, him there in Lincoln, an honored an' respicted gintleman. An honored an' respicted gintleman," concluded Scully with a flourish. And so saying, he smote the Swede jovially on the back.

The Swede faintly smiled.

"Now," said the old man, "there's only one more thing." He dropped suddenly to the floor and thrust his head beneath the bed. The Swede could hear his muffled voice. "I'd keep it under me piller if it wasn't for that boy Johnnie. Then there's the old woman—Where is it now? I never put it twice in the same place. Ah, now come out with you!"

Presently he backed clumsily from under the bed, dragging with him an old coat rolled into a bundle. "I've fetched him" he muttered. Kneeling on the floor he unrolled the coat and extracted from its heart a large yellow-brown whisky bottle.

His first maneuver was to hold the bottle up to the light. Reassured, apparently, that nobody had been tampering with it, he thrust it with a generous movement toward the Swede.

The weak-kneed Swede was about to eagerly clutch this element of strength, but he suddenly jerked his hand away and cast a look of horror upon Scully.

"Drink," said the old man affectionately. He had arisen to his feet, and now stood facing the Swede.

There was a silence. Then again Scully said: "Drink!"

The Swede laughed wildly. He grabbed the bottle, put it to his mouth, and as his lips curled absurdly around the opening and his throat worked, he kept his glance burning with hatred upon the old man's face.

IV

After the departure of Scully the three men, with the card-board still upon their knees, preserved for a long time an astounded silence. Then Johnnie said: "That's the dod-dangest Swede I ever see."

"He ain't no Swede," said the cowboy scornfully.

"Well, what is he then?" cried Johnnie. "What is he then?"

"It's my opinion," replied the cowboy deliberately, "he's some kind of a Dutchman." It was a venerable custom of the country to entitle as Swedes all light-haired men who spoke with a heavy tongue. In consequence the idea of the cowboy was not without its daring. "Yes, sir," he repeated. "It's my opinion this feller is some kind of a Dutchman."

"Well, he says he's a Swede, anyhow," muttered Johnnie sulkily. He turned to the Easterner: "What do you think, Mr. Blanc?"

"Oh, I don't know," replied the Easterner.

"Well, what do you think makes him act that way?" asked the cowboy.

"Why, he's frightened!" The Easterner knocked his pipe against a rim of the stove. "He's clear frightened out of his boots."

"What at?" cried Johnnie and cowboy together.

The Easterner reflected over his answer.

"What at?" cried the others again.

"Oh, I don't know, but it seems to me this man has been reading dime-novels, and he thinks he's right out in the middle of it—the shootin' and stabbin' and all."

"But," said the cowboy, deeply scandalized, "this ain't Wyoming, ner none of them places. This is Nebrasker."

"Yes," added Johnnie, "an' why don't he wait till he gits out West?"

The traveled Easterner laughed. "It isn't different there even—not in these days. But he thinks he's right in the middle of hell."

Johnnie and the cowboy mused long.

"It's awful funny," remarked Johnnie at last.

"Yes," said the cowboy. "This is a queer game. I hope we don't git snowed in, because then we'd have to stand this here man bein' around with us all the time. That wouldn't be no good."

"I wish pop would throw him out," said Johnnie.

Presently they heard a loud stamping on the stairs, accompanied by ringing jokes in the voice of old Scully, and laughter, evidently from the Swede. The men around the stove stared vacantly at each other. "Gosh," said the cowboy. The door flew open, and old Scully, flushed and anecdotal, came into the room. He was jabbering at the Swede, who followed him, laughing bravely. It was the entry of two roysterers from a banquet hall.

"Come now," said Scully sharply to the three seated men, "move up and give us a chance at the stove." The cowboy and the Easterner obediently sidled their chairs to make room for the newcomers. Johnnie, however, simply arranged himself in a more indolent attitude, and then remained motionless.

"Come! Git over, there," said Scully.

"Plenty of room on the other side of the stove," said Johnnie.

"Do you think we want to sit in the draught?" roared the father.

But the Swede here interposed with a grandeur of

confidence. "No, no. Let the boy sit where he likes," he cried in a bullying voice to the father.

"All right! All right!" said Scully deferentially. The cowboy and the Easterner exchanged glances of wonder.

The five chairs were formed in a crescent about one side of the stove. The Swede began to talk; he talked arrogantly, profanely, angrily. Johnnie, the cowboy and the Easterner maintained a morose silence, while old Scully appeared to be receptive and eager, breaking in constantly with sympathetic ejaculations.

Finally the Swede announced that he was thirsty. He moved in his chair, and said that he would go for a drink of water.

"I'll git it for you," cried Scully at once.

"No," said the Swede contemptuously. "I'll get it for myself." He arose and stalked with the air of an owner off into the executive parts of the hotel.

As soon as the Swede was out of hearing Scully sprang to his feet and whispered intensely to the others. "Upstairs he thought I was tryin' to poison 'im."

"Say," said Johnnie, "this makes me sick. Why don't you throw 'im out in the snow?"

"Why, he's all right now," declared Scully. "It was only that he was from the East and he thought this was a tough place. That's all. He's all right now."

The cowboy looked with admiration upon the Easterner. "You were straight," he said, "You were on to that there Dutchman."

"Well," said Johnnie to his father, "he may be all right now, but I don't see it. Other time he was scared, and now he's too fresh."

Scully's speech was always a combination of Irish brogue and idiom, Western twang and idiom, and scraps of curiously formal diction taken from the story-books and newspapers. He now hurled a strange mass of language at the head of his son. "What do I keep? What do I keep? What do I keep?" he demanded in a voice of thunder. He slapped his knee impressively, to indicate that he himself was going to make reply, and that all should heed. "I keep a hotel," he shouted. "A hotel, do you mind? A guest under my roof has sacred privileges. He is to be intimidated by none. Not one word shall he hear that would prijudice him in favor of goin' away. I'll not have it. There's no place in this here town where they can say they iver took in a guest of mine because he was afraid to stay here." He wheeled suddenly upon the cowboy and the Easterner. "Am I right?"

"Yes, Mr. Scully," said the cowboy, "I think you're right."

"Yes, Mr. Scully," said the Easterner, "I think you're right."

V

At six-o'clock supper, the Swede fizzed like a firewheel. He sometimes seemed on the point of bursting into riotous song, and in all his madness he was encouraged by old Scully. The Easterner was incased in reserve; the cowboy sat in wide-mouthed amazement, forgetting to eat, while Johnnie wrathily demolished great plates of food. The daughters of the house when they were obliged to replenish the biscuits approached as warily as Indians, and, having succeeded in their purposes, fled with ill-concealed trepidation. The Swede domineered the whole feast, and he gave it the appearance of a cruel bacchanal. He seemed to have grown suddenly taller; he gazed, brutally disdainful, into every face. His voice rang through the room. Once when he jabbed out harpoon-fashion with his fork to pinion a biscuit the weapon nearly impaled the hand of the Easterner which had been stretched quietly out for the same biscuit. After supper, as the men filed toward the other room, the Swede smote Scully ruthlessly on the shoulder. "Well, old boy, that was a good square meal." Johnnie looked hopefully at his father; he knew that shoulder was tender from an old fall; and indeed it appeared for a moment as if Scully was going to flame out over the matter, but in the end he smiled a sickly smile and remained silent. The others understood from his manner that he was admitting his responsibility for the Swede's new viewpoint.

Johnnie, however, addressed his parent in an aside. "Why don't you license somebody to kick you downstairs?" Scully scowled darkly by way of reply.

When they were gathered about the stove, the Swede insisted on another game of High-Five. Scully gently deprecated the plan at first, but the Swede turned a wolfish glare upon him. The old man subsided, and the Swede canvassed the others. In his tone there was always a great threat. The cowboy and the Easterner both remarked indifferently that they would play. Scully said that he would presently have to go to meet the 6.58 train, and so the Swede turned menacingly upon Johnnie. For a moment their glances crossed like blades, and then Johnnie smiled and said: "Yes, I'll play."

They formed a square with the little board on their knees. The Easterner and the Swede were again partners. As the play went on, it was noticeable that the cowboy was not board-whacking as usual. Meanwhile, Scully, near the lamp, had put on his spectacles and, with an appearance curiously like an old priest, was reading a newspaper. In time he went out to meet the 6.58 train, and, despite his precautions, a gust of polar wind whirled into the room as he opened the door.

Besides scattering the cards, it chilled the players to the marrow. The Swede cursed frightfully. When Scully returned, his entrance disturbed a cozy and friendly scene. The Swede again cursed. But presently they were once more intent, their heads bent forward and their hands moving swiftly. The Swede had adopted the fashion of board-whacking.

Scully took up his paper and for a long time remained immersed in matters which were extraordinarily remote from him. The lamp burned badly, and once he stopped to adjust the wick. The newspaper as he turned from page to page rustled with a slow and comfortable sound. Then suddenly he heard three terrible words: "You are cheatin'!"

Such scenes often prove that there can be little of dramatic import in environment. Any room can present a tragic front; any room can be comic. This little den was now hideous as a torture-chamber. The new faces of the men themselves had changed it upon the instant. The Swede held a huge fist in front of Johnnie's face, while the latter looked steadily over it into the blazing orbs of his accuser. The Easterner had grown pallid; the cowboy's jaw had dropped in that expression of bovine amazement which was one of his important mannerisms. After the three words, the first sound in the room was made by Scully's paper as it floated forgotten to his feet. His spectacles had also fallen from his nose, but by a clutch he had saved them in air. His hand, grasping the spectacles, now remained poised awkwardly and near his shoulder. He stared at the card-players.

Probably the silence was while a second elapsed. Then, if the floor had been suddenly twitched out from under the men they could not have moved quicker. The five had projected themselves headlong toward a common point. It happened that Johnnie in rising to hurl himself upon the Swede had stumbled slightly because of his curiously instinctive care for the cards and the board. The loss of the moment allowed time for the arrival of Scully, and also allowed the cowboy time to give the Swede a great push which sent him staggering back. The men found tongue together, and hoarse shouts or rage, appeal or fear burst from every throat. The cowboy pushed and jostled feverishly at the Swede, and the Easterner and Scully clung wildly to Johnnie; but, through the smoky air, above the swaying bodies of the peace-compellers, the eyes of the two warriors ever sought each other in glances of challenge that were at once hot and steely.

Of course the board had been overturned, and now the whole company of cards was scattered over the floor, where the boots of the men trampled the fat and

painted kings and queens as they gazed with their silly eyes at the war that was waging above them.

Scully's voice was dominating the yells. "Stop now! Stop, I say! Stop, now—"

Johnnie, as he struggled to burst through the rank formed by Scully and the Easterner, was crying: "Well, he says I cheated! He says I cheated! I won't allow no man to say I cheated! If he says I cheated, he's a—!"

The cowboy was telling the Swede: "Quit, now! Quit, d'ye hear—"

The screams of the Swede never ceased. "He did cheat! I saw him! I saw him—"

As for the Easterner, he was importuning in a voice that was not heeded. "Wait a moment, can't you? Oh, wait a moment. What's the good of a fight over a game of cards? Wait a moment—"

In this tumult no complete sentences were clear. "Cheat"—"Quit"—"He says"—These fragments pierced the uproar and rang out sharply. It was remarkable that whereas Scully undoubtedly made the most noise, he was the least heard of any of the riotous band.

Then suddenly there was a great cessation. It was as if each man had paused for breath, and although the room was still lighted with the anger of men, it could be seen that there was no danger of immediate conflict, and at once Johnnie, shouldering his ways forward, almost succeeded in confronting the Swede. "What did you say I cheated for? What did you say I cheated for? I don't cheat and I won't let no man say I do!"

The Swede said: "I saw you! I saw you!"

"Well," cried Johnnie, "I'll fight any man what says I cheat!"

"No, you won't," said the cowboy. "Not here."

"Ah, be still, can't you?" said Scully, coming between them.

The quiet was sufficient to allow the Easterner's voice to be heard.

He was repeating: "Oh, wait a moment, can't you? What's the good of a fight over a game of cards? Wait a moment."

Johnnie, his red face appearing above his father's shoulder, hailed the Swede again. "Did you say I cheated?"

The Swede showed his teeth. "Yes."

"Then," said Johnnie, "we must fight."

"Yes, fight," roared the Swede. He was like a demoniac. "Yes, fight! I'll show you what kind of a man I am! I'll show you who you want to fight! Maybe you think I can't fight! Maybe you think I can't! I'll show you, you skin, you card-sharp! Yes, you cheated! You cheated! You cheated!"

"Well, let's git at it, then, mister," said Johnnie coolly.

The cowboy's brow was beaded with sweat from his efforts in intercepting all sorts of raids. He turned in despair to Scully. "What are you goin' to do now?"

A change had come over the Celtic visage of the old man. He now seemed all eagerness; his eyes glowed.

"We'll let them fight," he answered stalwartly. "I can't put up with it any longer. I've stood this damned Swede till I'm sick. We'll let them fight."

VI

The men prepared to go out of doors. The Easterner was so nervous that he had great difficulty in getting his arms into the sleeves of his new leather-coat. As the cowboy drew his fur-cap down over his ears his hands trembled. In fact, Johnnie and old Scully were the only ones who displayed no agitation. These preliminaries were conducted without words.

Scully threw open the door. "Well, come on," he said. Instantly a terrific wind caused the flame of the lamp to struggle at its wick, while a puff of black smoke sprang from the chimney-top. The stove was in mid-current of the blast, and its voice swelled to equal the roar of the storm. Some of the scarred and bedabbled cards were caught up from the floor and dashed helplessly against the further wall. The men lowered their heads and plunged into the tempest as into a sea.

No snow was falling, but great whirls and clouds of flakes, swept up from the ground by the frantic winds, were streaming southward with the speed of bullets. The covered land was blue with the sheen of an unearthly satin, and there was no other hue save where at the low black railway station—which seemed incredibly distant—one light gleamed like a tiny jewel. As the men floundered into a thigh-deep drift, it was known that the Swede was bawling out something. Scully went to him, put a hand on his shoulder and projected an ear.

"What's that you say?" he shouted.

"I say," bawled the Swede again, "I won't stand much show against this gang. I know you'll all pitch on me."

Scully smote him reproachfully on the arm. "Tut, man," he yelled. The wind tore the words from Scully's lips and scattered them far a-lee.

"You are all a gang of—" boomed the Swede, but the storm also seized the remainder of this sentence.

Immediately turning their backs upon the wind, the men had swung around a corner to the sheltered side of the hotel. It was the function of the little house to preserve here, amid this great devastation of snow, an irregular V-shape of heavily-incrusted grass, which crackled beneath the feet. One could imagine the great drifts piled against the windward side. When the party reached the comparative peace of this spot it was found that the Swede was still bellowing.

"Oh, I know what kind of a thing this is! I know you'll all pitch on me. I can't lick you all!"

Scully turned upon him panther-fashion. "You'll not have to whip all of us. You'll have to whip my son Johnnie. An' the man what troubles you durin' that time will have me to dale with."

The arrangements were swiftly made. The two men faced each other, obedient to the harsh commands of Scully, whose face, in the subtly luminous gloom, could be seen set in the austere impersonal lines that are pictured on the countenances of the Roman veterans. The Easterner's teeth were chattering, and he was hopping up and down like a mechanical toy. The cowboy stood rock-like.

The contestants had not stripped off any clothing. Each was in his ordinary attire. Their fists were up, and they eyed each other in a calm that had the elements of leonine cruelty in it.

During this pause, the Easterner's mind, like a film, took lasting impressions of three men—the iron-nerved master of the ceremony; the Swede, pale, motionless, terrible; and Johnnie, serene yet ferocious, brutish yet heroic. The entire prelude had in it a tragedy greater than the tragedy of action, and this aspect was accentuated by the long mellow cry of the blizzard, as it sped the tumbling and wailing flakes into the black abyss of the south.

"Now!" said Scully.

The two combatants leaped forward and crashed together like bullocks. There was heard the cushioned sound of blows, and of a curse squeezing out from between the tight teeth of one.

As for the spectators, the Easterner's pent-up breath exploded from him with a pop of relief, absolute relief from the tension of the preliminaries. The cowboy bounded into the air with a yowl. Scully was immovable as from supreme amazement and fear at the fury of the fight which he himself had permitted and arranged.

For a time the encounter in the darkness was such a perplexity of flying arms that it presented no more detail than would a swiftly-revolving wheel. Occasionally a face, as if illumined by a flash of light, would shine out, ghastly and marked with pink spots. A moment later, the men might have been known as shadows, if it were not for the involuntary utterance of oaths that came from them in whispers.

Suddenly a holocaust of warlike desire caught the

cowboy, and he bolted forward with the speed of a broncho. "Go it, Johnnie; go it! Kill him! Kill him!"

Scully confronted him. "Kape back," he said; and by his glance the cowboy could tell that this man was Johnnie's father.

To the Easterner there was a monotony of unchangeable fighting that was an abomination. This confused mingling was eternal to his sense, which was concentrated in a longing for the end, the priceless end. Once the fighters lurched near him, and as he scrambled hastily backward, he heard them breathe like men on the rack.

"Kill him, Johnnie! Kill him! Kill him! Kill him!" The cowboy's face was contorted like one of those agony masks in museums.

"Keep still," said Scully icily.

Then there was a sudden loud grunt, incomplete, cut short, and Johnnie's body swung away from the Swede and fell with sickening heaviness to the grass. The cowboy was barely in time to prevent the mad Swede from flinging himself upon his prone adversary. "No, you don't," said the cowboy, interposing an arm. "Wait a second."

Scully was at his son's side. "Johnnie! Johnnie, me boy?" His voice had a quality of melancholy tenderness. "Johnnie? Can you go on with it?" He looked anxiously down into the bloody pulpy face of his son.

There was a moment of silence, and then Johnnie answered in his ordinary voice: "Yes, I—it –yes."

Assisted by his father he struggled to his feet. "Wait a bit now till you git your wind," said the old man.

A few paces away the cowboy was lecturing the Swede. "No, you don't! Wait a second!"

The Easterner was plucking at Scully's sleeve. "Oh, this is enough," he pleaded. "This is enough! Let it go as it stands. This is enough!"

"Bill," said Scully, "git out of the road." The cowboy stepped aside. "Now." The combatants were actuated by a new caution as they advanced toward collision. They glared at each other, and then the Swede aimed a lightning blow that carried with it his entire weight. Johnnie was evidently half-stupid from weakness, but he miraculously dodged, and his fist sent the over-balanced Swede sprawling.

The cowboy, Scully and the Easterner burst into a cheer that was like a chorus of triumphant soldiery, but before its conclusion the Swede had scuffled agilely to his feet and come in berserk abandon at his foe. There was another perplexity of flying arms, and Johnnie's body again swung away and fell, even as a bundle might fall from a roof. The Swede instantly staggered to

a little wind-waved tree and leaned upon it, breathing like an engine, while his savage and flame-lit eyes roamed from face to face as the men bent over Johnnie. There was a splendor of isolation in his situation at this time which the Easterner felt once when, lifting his eyes from the man on the ground, he beheld that mysterious and lonely figure, waiting. "Are you any good yet, Johnnie?" asked Scully in a broken voice.

The son gasped and opened his eyes languidly. After a moment he answered: "No—I ain't—any good—any—more." Then, from shame and bodily ill, he began to weep, the tears furrowing down through the bloodstains on his face. "He was too—too—too heavy for me."

Scully straightened and addressed the waiting figure. "Stranger," he said, evenly, "it's all up with our side." Then his voice changed into that vibrant huskiness which is commonly the tone of the most simple and deadly announcements. "Johnnie is whipped."

Without replying, the victor moved off on the route to the front door of the hotel.

The cowboy was formulating new and unspellable blasphemies. The Easterner was startled to find that they were out in a wind that seemed to come direct from the shadowed arctic floes. He heard again the wail of the snow as it was flung to its grave in the south. He knew now that all this time the cold had been sinking into him deeper and deeper, and he wondered that he had not perished. He felt indifferent to the condition of the vanquished man.

"Johnnie, can you walk?" asked Scully.

"Did I hurt—hurt him any?" asked the son.

"Can you walk, boy? Can you walk?"

Johnnie's voice was suddenly strong. There was a robust impatience

in it. "I asked you whether I hurt him any!"

"Yes, yes, Johnnie," answered the cowboy consolingly; "he's hurt a good deal."

They raised him from the ground, and as soon as he was on his feet he went tottering off, rebuffing all attempts at assistance. When the party rounded the corner they were fairly blinded by the pelting of the snow. It burned their faces like fire. The cowboy carried Johnnie through the drift to the door. As they entered some cards again rose from the floor and beat against the wall.

The Easterner rushed to the stove. He was so profoundly chilled that he almost dared to embrace the glowing iron. The Swede was not in the room. Johnnie sank into a chair, and folding his arms on his knees, buried his face in them. Scully, warming one foot and then the other at the rim of the stove, muttered to himself with Celtic mournfulness. The cowboy had removed his fur-cap, and with a dazed and rueful air he was now running one hand through his tousled locks. From overhead they could hear the creaking of boards, as the Swede tramped here and there in his room.

The sad quiet was broken by the sudden flinging open of a door that led toward the kitchen. It was instantly followed by an inrush of women. They precipitated themselves upon Johnnie amid a chorus of lamentation. Before they carried their prey off to the kitchen, there to be bathed and harangued with a mixture of sympathy and abuse which is a feat of their sex, the mother straightened herself and fixed old Scully with an eye of stern reproach. "Shame be upon you, Patrick Scully!" she cried, "Your own son, too. Shame be upon you!"

"There, now! Be quiet, now!" said the old man weakly.

"Shame be upon you, Patrick Scully!" The girls rallying to this slogan, sniffed disdainfully in the direction of those trembling accomplices, the cowboy and the Easterner. Presently they bore Johnnie away, and left the three men to dismal reflection.

VII

"I'd like to fight this here Dutchman myself," said the cowboy, breaking a long silence.

Scully wagged his head sadly. "No, that wouldn't do. It wouldn't be right. It wouldn't be right."

"Well, why wouldn't it?" argued the cowboy. "I don't see no harm in it."

"No," answered Scully with mournful heroism. "It wouldn't be right. It was Johnnie's fight, and now we mustn't whip the man just because he whipped Johnnie."

"Yes, that's true enough," said the cowboy; "but—he better not get fresh with me, because I couldn't stand no more of it."

"You'll not say a word to him," commanded Scully, and even then they heard the tread of the Swede on the stairs. His entrance was made theatric. He swept the door back with a bang and swaggered to the middle of the room. No one looked at him. "Well," he cried, insolently, at Scully, "I s'pose you'll tell me now how much I owe you?"

The old man remained stolid. "You don't owe me nothin'."

"Huh!" said the Swede, "huh! Don't owe 'im nothin'."

The cowboy addressed the Swede. "Stranger, I don't see how you come to be so gay around here."

Old Scully was instantly alert. "Stop!" he shouted, holding his hand forth, fingers upward. "Bill, you shut up!"

The cowboy spat carelessly into the sawdust box. "I didn't say a word, did I?" he asked.

"Mr. Scully," called the Swede, "how much do I owe you?" It was seen that he was attired for departure, and that he had his valise in his hand.

"You don't owe me nothin'," repeated Scully in his same imperturbable way.

"Huh!" said the Swede. "I guess you're right. I guess if it was any way at all, you'd owe me somethin'. That's what I guess." He turned to the cowboy, "'Kill him! Kill him! Kill him!'" he mimicked, and then guffawed victoriously. "'Kill him!'" He was convulsed with ironical humor.

But he might have been jeering the dead. The three men were immovable and silent, staring with glassy eyes at the stove.

The Swede opened the door and passed into the storm, giving one derisive glance backward at the still group.

As soon as the door was closed, Scully and the cowboy leaped to their feet and began to curse. They trampled to and fro, waving their arms and smashing into the air with their fists. "Oh, but that was a hard minute! Him there leerin' and scoffin'! One bang at his nose was worth forty dollars to me that minute! How did you stand it, Bill?"

"How did I stand it?" cried the cowboy in a quivering voice. "How did I stand it? Oh!"

The old man burst into sudden brogue. "I'd loike to take that Swade," he wailed, "and hould 'im down on a shtone flure and bate 'im to a jelly wid a shtick!"

The cowboy groaned in sympathy. "I'd like to git him by the neck and ha-ammer him"—he brought his hand down on a chair with a noise like a pistol-shot—"hammer that there Dutchman until he couldn't tell himself from a dead coyote!"

"I'd bate 'im until he—"

"I'd show him some things—"

And then together they raised a yearning fanatic cry. "Oh-o-oh! if we only could—"

"Yes!"

"Yes!"

"And then I'd—"

"O-o-oh!"

VIII

The Swede, tightly gripping his valise, tacked across the face of the storm as if he carried sails. He was following a line of little naked gasping trees, which he knew must mark the way of the road. His face, fresh from the pounding of Johnnie's fists, felt more pleasure than pain in the wind and the driving snow. A number of square shapes loomed upon him finally, and he knew them as the houses of the main body of the town. He found a street and made travel along it, leaning heavily upon the wind whenever, at a corner, a terrific blast caught him.

He might have been in a deserted village. We picture the world as thick with conquering and elate humanity, but here, with the bugles of the tempest pealing, it was hard to imagine a peopled earth. One viewed the existence of man then as a marvel, and conceded a glamour of wonder to these lice which were caused to cling to a whirling, fire-smote, ice-locked, disease-stricken, space-lost bulb. The conceit of man was explained by this storm to be the very engine of life. One was a coxcomb not to die in it. However, the Swede found a saloon.

In front of it an indomitable red light was burning, and the snowflakes were made blood-color as they flew through the circumscribed territory of the lamp's shining. The Swede pushed open the door of the saloon and entered. A sanded expanse was before him, and at the end of it four men sat about a table drinking. Down one side of the room extended a radiant bar, and its guardian was leaning upon his elbows listening to the talk of the men at the table. The Swede dropped his valise upon the floor, and, smiling fraternally upon the barkeeper, said: "Gimme some whisky, will you?" The man placed a bottle, a whisky-glass, and glass of ice-thick water upon the bar. The Swede poured himself an abnormal portion of whisky and drank it in three gulps. "Pretty bad night," remarked the bartender indifferently. He was making the pretension of blindness, which is usually a distinction of his class; but it could have been seen that he was furtively studying the half-erased blood-stains on the face of the Swede. "Bad night," he said again.

"Oh, it's good enough for me," replied the Swede, hardily, as he poured himself some more whisky. The barkeeper took his coin and maneuvered it through its reception by the highly-nickeled cash-machine. A bell rang; a card labeled "20 cts." had appeared.

"No," continued the Swede, "this isn't too bad weather. It's good enough for me."

"So?" murmured the barkeeper languidly.

The copious drams made the Swede's eyes swim, and he breathed a trifle heavier. "Yes, I like this weather. I like it. It suits me." It was apparently his design to impart a deep significance to these words.

"So?" murmured the bartender again. He turned to gaze dreamily at the scroll-like birds and bird-like scrolls which had been drawn with soap upon the mirrors back of the bar.

"Well, I guess I'll take another drink," said the Swede presently. "Have something?"

"No, thanks; I'm not drinkin'," answered the bartender. Afterward he asked: "How did you hurt your face?"

The Swede immediately began to boast loudly. "Why, in a fight. I thumped the soul out of a man down here at Scully's hotel."

The interest of the four men at the table was at last aroused.

"Who was it?" said one.

"Johnnie Scully," blustered the Swede. "Son of the man what runs it. He will be pretty near dead for some weeks, I can tell you. I made a nice thing of him, I did. He couldn't get up. They carried him in the house. Have a drink?"

Instantly the men in some subtle way incased themselves in reserve. "No, thanks," said one. The group was of curious formation. Two were prominent local business men; one was the district-attorney; and one was a professional gambler of the kind known as "square." But a scrutiny of the group would not have enabled an observer to pick the gambler from the men of more reputable pursuits. He was, in fact, a man so delicate in manner, when among people of fair class, and so judicious in his choice of victims, that in the strictly masculine part of the town's life he had come to be explicitly trusted and admired. People called him a thorough-bred. The fear and contempt with which his craft was regarded was undoubtedly the reason that his quiet dignity shone conspicuous above the quiet dignity of men who might be merely hatters, billiard-markers or grocery clerks. Beyond an occasional unwary traveler, who came by rail, this gambler was supposed to prey solely upon reckless and senile farmers, who, when flush with good crops, drove into town in all the pride and confidence of an absolutely invulnerable stupidity. Hearing at times in circuitous fashion of the despoilment of such a farmer, the important men of Romper invariably laughed in contempt of the victim, and if they thought of the wolf at all, it was with a kind of pride at the knowledge that he would never dare think of attacking their wisdom and courage. Besides, it was popular that this gambler had a real wife, and two real children in a neat cottage in a suburb, where he led an exemplary home life, and when any one even suggested a discrepancy in his character, the crowd immediately vociferated descriptions of this virtuous family circle. Then men who led exemplary home lives, and men who did not lead exemplary home lives, all subsided in a bunch, remarking that there was nothing more to be said.

However, when a restriction was placed upon him—as, for instance, when a strong clique of members of the new Pollywog Club refused to permit him, even as a spectator, to appear in the rooms of the organization—the candor and gentleness with which he accepted the judgment disarmed many of his foes and made his friends more desperately partisan. He invariably distinguished between himself and a respectable Romper man so quickly and frankly that his manner actually appeared to be a continual broadcast compliment.

And one must not forget to declare the fundamental fact of his entire position in Romper. It is irrefutable that in all affairs outside of his business, in all matters that occur eternally and commonly between man and man, this thieving card-player was so generous, so just, so moral, that, in a contest, he could have put to flight the consciences of nine-tenths of the citizens of Romper.

And so it happened that he was seated in this saloon with the two prominent local merchants and the district-attorney.

The Swede continued to drink raw whisky, meanwhile babbling at the barkeeper and trying to induce him to indulge in potations. "Come on. Have a drink. Come on. What—no? Well, have a little one then. By gawd, I've whipped a man to-night, and I want to celebrate. I whipped him good, too. Gentlemen," the Swede cried to the men at the table, "have a drink?"

"Ssh!" said the barkeeper.

The group at the table, although furtively attentive, had been pretending to be deep in talk, but now a man lifted his eyes toward the Swede and said shortly: "Thanks. We don't want any more." At this reply the Swede ruffled out his chest like a rooster. "Well," he exploded, "it seems I can't get anybody to drink with me in this town. Seems so, don't it? Well!"

"Ssh!" said the barkeeper.

"Say," snarled the Swede, "don't you try to shut me up. I won't have it. I'm a gentleman, and I want people to drink with me. And I want 'em to drink with me now. Now—do you understand?" He rapped the bar with his knuckles.

Years of experience had calloused the bartender. He merely grew sulky. "I hear you," he answered.

"Well," cried the Swede, "listen hard then. See those men over there? Well, they're going to drink with me, and don't you forget it. Now you watch."

"Hi!" yelled the barkeeper, "this won't do!"

"Why won't it?" demanded the Swede. He stalked over to the table, and by chance laid his hand upon the shoulder of the gambler. "How about this?" he asked, wrathfully. "I asked you to drink with me."

The gambler simply twisted his head and spoke over his shoulder. "My friend, I don't know you."

"Oh, hell!" answered the Swede, "come and have a drink."

"Now, my boy," advised the gambler kindly, "take your hand off my shoulder and go 'way and mind your own business." He was a little slim man, and it seemed strange to hear him use this tone of heroic patronage to the burly Swede. The other men at the table said nothing.

"What? You won't drink with me, you little dude! I'll make you then! I'll make you!" The Swede had grasped the gambler frenziedly at the throat, and was dragging him from his chair. The other men sprang up. The barkeeper dashed around the corner of his bar. There was a great tumult, and then was seen a long blade in the hand of the gambler. It shot forward, and a human body, this citadel of virtue, wisdom, power, was pierced as easily as if it had been a melon. The Swede fell with a cry of supreme astonishment. The prominent merchants and the district-attorney must have at once tumbled out of the place backward. The bartender found himself hanging limply to the arm of a chair and gazing into the eyes of a murderer.

"Henry," said the latter, as he wiped his knife on one of the towels that hung beneath the bar-rail, "you tell 'em where to find me. I'll be home, waiting for 'em." Then he vanished. A moment afterward the barkeeper was in the street dinning through the storm for help, and, moreover, companionship.

The corpse of the Swede, alone in the saloon, had its eyes fixed upon a dreadful legend that dwelt a-top of the cash-machine. "This registers the amount of your purchase."

IX

Months later, the cowboy was frying pork over the stove of a little ranch near the Dakota line, when there was a quick thud of hoofs outside, and, presently, the Easterner entered with the letters and the papers. "Well," said the Easterner at once, "the chap that killed the Swede has got three years. Wasn't much, was it?"

"He has? Three years?" The cowboy poised his pan of pork, while he ruminated upon the news. "Three years. That ain't much."

"No. It was a light sentence," replied the Easterner as he unbuckled his spurs. "Seems there was a good deal of sympathy for him in Romper."

"If the bartender had been any good," observed the cowboy thoughtfully, "he would have gone in and cracked that there Dutchman on the head with a bottle in the beginnin' of it and stopped all this here murderin'."

"Yes, a thousand things might have happened," said the Easterner tartly.

The cowboy returned his pan of pork to the fire, but his philosophy continued. "It's funny, ain't it? If he hadn't said Johnnie was cheatin' he'd be alive this minute. He was an awful fool. Game played for fun, too. Not for money. I believe he was crazy."

"I feel sorry for that gambler," said the Easterner.

"Oh, so do I," said the cowboy. "He don't deserve none of it for killin' who he did."

"The Swede might not have been killed if everything had been square."

"Might not have been killed?" exclaimed the cowboy. "Everythin' square? Why, when he said that Johnnie was cheatin' and acted like such a jackass? And then in the saloon he fairly walked up to git hurt?" With these arguments the cowboy browbeat the Easterner and reduced him to rage.

"You're a fool!" cried the Easterner viciously. "You're a bigger jackass than the Swede by a million majority. Now let me tell you one thing. Let me tell you something. Listen! Johnnie was cheating!"

"'Johnnie,'" said the cowboy blankly. There was a minute of silence, and then he said robustly: "Why, no. The game was only for fun."

"Fun or not," said the Easterner, "Johnnie was cheating. I saw him. I know it. I saw him. And I refused to stand up and be a man. I let the Swede fight it out alone. And you—you were simply puffing around the place and wanting to fight. And then old Scully himself! We are all in it! This poor gambler isn't even a noun. He is kind of an adverb. Every sin is the result of a collaboration. We, five of us, have collaborated in the murder of this Swede. Usually there are from a dozen to forty women really involved in every murder, but in this case it seems to be only five men—you, I, Johnnie, old Scully, and that fool of an unfortunate gambler came merely as a culmination, the apex of a human movement, and gets all the punishment."

The cowboy, injured and rebellious, cried out

blindly into this fog of mysterious theory. "Well, I didn't do anythin', did I?"

http://www.gonzaga.edu/faculty/campbell/crane/

D. Naturalism is essentially a literary expression of determinism. Associated with bleak, realistic depictions of lower-class life, determinism denies Christianity as a motivating force in the world and instead perceives the universe as a machine. It is hard to imagine that a born again Christian could be a naturalist. Eighteenth century Enlightenment thinkers also imagined the world as a machine, but as a perfect one, invented by God and tending toward progress and human betterment. Naturalists imagined society, instead, as a blind machine, godless and out of control.

The 19th-century American historian and social thinker Henry Adams constructed an elaborate theory of history involving the idea of the dynamo, or machine force, and entropy, or decay of force. Instead of progress, Adams saw inevitable decline in human society. This pessimism was reinforced by the rise of Social Darwinism (the survival of the fittest). God is dead in American literature. God in American literature died when Nathaniel Hawthorne set aside his pen after writing *The Scarlet Letter*.

Speaking of the loss of God most succinctly Stephen Crane said:

A man said to the universe: "Sir, I exist!"

"However," replied the universe,

"The fact has not created in me a sense of obligation."

Like romanticism, Naturalism first appeared in Europe. Naturalism flourished as Americans became urbanized and aware of the importance of large, impersonal economic and social forces.

FINAL PROJECT

Correct and rewrite all essays and place them in your Final Portfolio.

SUGGESTED
Weekly *Implementation*

DAY 1	DAY 2	DAY 3	DAY 4	DAY 5
Prayer journal. Review the required reading(s) *before* the assigned lesson begins. Teacher may want to discuss assigned reading(s) with students. Teacher and students will decide on required essays for this lesson, choosing two or three essays. The rest of the essays can be outlined, answered with shorter answers, or skipped. Review all readings for Lesson 18	**Prayer journal.** Review reading(s) from next lesson. Outline essays due at the end of the week. Per teacher instructions, students may answer orally in a group setting some of the essays that are not assigned as formal essays.	**Prayer journal.** Write rough drafts of all assigned essays. The teacher and/or a peer evaluator may correct rough drafts.	**Prayer journal.** Rewrite corrected copies of essays due tomorrow.	**Prayer journal.** Essays are due. Take Lesson 18 test. Reading Ahead: Students should review "Outcasts of Poker Flat," Bret Harte; "The Story of an Hour," Kate Chopin; "Luke Havergal" and "Credo," Edwin Arlington Robinson; "Lucinda Matlock," Edgar Lee Masters. Guide: What new styles and themes emerge in these late 19th century works?

REALISM, NATURALISM, AND THE FRONTIER *1865-1915* (Part 5)

Bret Harte

BACKGROUND

Bret Harte, (1836-1902), American writer, is best known for his short stories set in the American West. In 1868 Harte became editor of the *Overland Monthly*, which published many of his best-known stories, including "The Outcasts of Poker Flat" (1869). Despite the fact that these stories shocked many readers, these works have come to be regarded as classics of American regional literature and were noted for their descriptions of the mining camps and towns of California in the middle 19th century.

The Outcasts of Poker Flat

Bret Harte

http://www.angeltowns.com/members/shortstories/hartepoker.html

As Mr. John Oakhurst, gambler, stepped into the main street of Poker Flat on the morning of the twenty-third of November, 1850, he was conscious of a change in its moral atmosphere since the preceding night. Two or three men, conversing earnestly together, ceased as he approached, and exchanged significant glances. There was a Sabbath lull in the air which, in a settlement unused to Sabbath influences, looked ominous.

Mr. Oakhurst's calm, handsome face betrayed small concern in these indications. Whether he was conscious of any predisposing cause was another question. "I reckon they're after somebody," he reflected; "likely it's me." He returned to his pocket the handkerchief with which he had been whipping away the red dust of

You will analyze: "Outcasts of Poker Flat," Bret Harte; "The Story of an Hour," Kate Chopin; "Luke Havergal" and "Credo," Edwin Arlington Robinson; "Lucinda Matlock," Edgar Lee Masters.

Reading Ahead: *Ethan Frome*, Edith Wharton.

Guide Question: In what way is *Ethan Frome* a

Poker Flat from his neat boots, and quietly discharged his mind of any further conjecture.

In point of fact, Poker Flat was "after somebody." It had lately suffered the loss of several thousand dollars, two valuable horses, and a prominent citizen. It was experiencing a spasm of virtuous reaction, quite as lawless and ungovernable as any of the acts that had provoked it. A secret committee had determined to rid the town of all improper persons. This was done permanently in regard of two men who were then hanging from the boughs of a sycamore in the gulch, and temporarily in the banishment of certain other objectionable characters. I regret to say that some of these were ladies. It is but due to the sex, however, to state that their impropriety was professional, and it was only in such easily established standards of evil that Poker Flat ventured to sit in judgment.

Mr. Oakhurst was right in supposing that he was included in this category. A few of the committee had urged hanging him as a possible example, and a sure method of reimbursing themselves from his pockets of the sums he had won from them. "It's agin justice," said Jim Wheeler, "to let this yer young man from Roaring Camp—an entire stranger—carry away our money." But a crude sentiment of equity residing in the breasts of those who had been fortunate enough to win from Mr. Oakhurst overruled this narrower local prejudice.

Mr. Oakhurst received his sentence with philosophic calmness, none the less coolly that he was aware of the hesitation of his judges. He was too much of a gambler not to accept Fate. With him life was at best an uncertain game, and he recognized the usual percentage in favor of the dealer.

A body of armed men accompanied the deported wickedness of Poker Flat to the outskirts of the settlement. Besides Mr. Oakhurst, who was known to be a coolly desperate man, and for whose intimidation the armed escort was intended, the expatriated party consisted of a young woman familiarly known as the "Duchess"; another, who had won the title of "Mother Shipton"; and "Uncle Billy," a suspected sluice-robber and confirmed drunkard. The cavalcade provoked no comments from the spectators, nor was any word uttered by the escort. Only, when the gulch which marked the uttermost limit of Poker Flat was reached, the leader spoke briefly and to the point. The exiles were forbidden to return at the peril of their lives.

As the escort disappeared, their pent-up feelings found vent in a few hysterical tears from the Duchess, some bad language from Mother Shipton, and a Parthian volley of expletives from Uncle Billy. The philosophic Oakhurst alone remained silent. He listened calmly to Mother Shipton's desire to cut somebody's heart out, to the repeated statements of the Duchess that she would die in the road, and to the alarming oaths that seemed to be bumped out of Uncle Billy as he rode forward. With the easy good humor characteristic of his class, he insisted upon exchanging his own riding horse, "Five Spot," for the sorry mule which the Duchess rode. But even this act did not draw the party into any closer sympathy. The young woman readjusted her somewhat draggled plumes with a feeble, faded coquetry; Mother Shipton eyed the possessor of "Five Spot" with malevolence, and Uncle Billy included the whole party in one sweeping anathema.

The road to Sandy Bar—a camp that, not having as yet experienced the regenerating influences of Poker Flat, consequently seemed to offer some invitation to the emigrants—lay over a steep mountain range. It was distant a day's severe travel. In that advanced season, the party soon passed out of the moist, temperate regions of the foothills into the dry, cold, bracing air of the Sierras. The trail was narrow and difficult. At noon the Duchess, rolling out of her saddle upon the ground, declared her intention of going no farther, and the party halted.

The spot was singularly wild and impressive. A wooded amphitheater, surrounded on three sides by precipitous cliffs of naked granite, sloped gently toward the crest of another precipice that overlooked the valley. It was, undoubtedly, the most suitable spot for a camp, had camping been advisable. But Mr. Oakhurst knew that scarcely half the journey to Sandy Bar was accomplished, and the party were not equipped or provisioned for delay. This fact he pointed out to his companions curtly, with a philosophic commentary on the folly of "throwing up their hand before the game was played out." But they were furnished with liquor, which in this emergency stood them in place of food, fuel, rest, and prescience. In spite of his remonstrances, it was not long before they were more or less under its influence. Uncle Billy passed rapidly from a bellicose state into one of stupor, the Duchess became maudlin, and Mother Shipton snored. Mr. Oakhurst alone remained erect, leaning against a rock, calmly surveying them.

Mr. Oakhurst did not drink. It interfered with a profession which required coolness, impassiveness, and presence of mind, and, in his own language, he "couldn't afford it." As he gazed at his recumbent fellow exiles, the loneliness begotten of his pariah trade, his habits of life, his very vices, for the first time seriously oppressed him. He bestirred himself in dusting his black clothes, washing his hands and face, and other acts characteristic of his studiously neat habits, and for a moment forgot his annoyance. The thought of deserting his weaker and more pitiable companions never perhaps occurred to him. Yet he could not help feeling the want of that excitement which, singularly enough, was most conducive to that calm equanimity for which he was notorious. He looked at the gloomy walls that rose a thousand feet sheer above the circling pines around him; at the sky, ominously clouded; at the valley below, already deepening into shadow. And, doing so, suddenly he heard his own name called.

A horseman slowly ascended the trail. In the fresh, open face of the newcomer Mr. Oakhurst recognized Tom Simson, otherwise known as the "Innocent" of Sandy Bar. He had met him some months before over a "little game," and had, with perfect equanimity, won the entire fortune—amounting to some forty dollars—of that guileless youth. After the game was finished, Mr. Oakhurst drew the youthful speculator behind the door and thus addressed him: "Tommy, you're a good little man, but you can't gamble worth a cent. Don't try it over again." He then handed him his money back, pushed him gently from the room, and so made a devoted slave of Tom Simson.

There was a remembrance of this in his boyish and enthusiastic greeting of Mr. Oakhurst. He had started, he said, to go to Poker Flat to seek his fortune. "Alone?" No, not exactly alone; in fact (a giggle), he had run away with Piney Woods. Didn't Mr. Oakhurst remember Piney? She that used to wait on the table at the Temperance House? They had been engaged a long time, but old Jake Woods had objected, and so they had run away, and were going to Poker Flat to be married, and here they were. And they were tired out, and how lucky it was they had found a place to camp and company. All this the Innocent delivered rapidly, while Piney, a stout, comely damsel of fifteen, emerged from behind the pine tree, where she had been blushing unseen, and rode to the side of her lover.

Mr. Oakhurst seldom troubled himself with sentiment, still less with propriety; but he had a vague idea that the situation was not fortunate. He retained, however, his presence of mind sufficiently to kick Uncle Billy, who was about to say something, and Uncle Billy was sober enough to recognize in Mr. Oakhurst's kick a superior power that would not bear trifling. He then endeavored to dissuade Tom Simson from delaying further, but in vain. He even pointed out the fact that there was no provision, nor means of making a camp. But, unluckily, the Innocent met this objection by assuring the party that he was provided with an extra mule loaded with provisions and by the discovery of a rude attempt at a log house near the trail. "Piney can stay with Mrs. Oakhurst," said the Innocent, pointing to the Duchess, "and I can shift for myself."

Nothing but Mr. Oakhurst's admonishing foot saved Uncle Billy from bursting into a roar of laughter. As it was, he felt compelled to retire up the canyon until he could recover his gravity. There he confided the joke to the tall pine trees, with many slaps of his leg, contortions of his face, and the usual profanity. But when he returned to the party, he found them seated by a fire—for the air had grown strangely chill and the sky overcast—in apparently amicable conversation. Piney was actually talking in an impulsive, girlish fashion to the Duchess, who was listening with an interest and animation she had not shown for many days. The Innocent was holding forth, apparently with equal effect, to Mr. Oakhurst and Mother Shipton, who was actually relaxing into amiability. "Is this yer a —picnic?" said Uncle Billy with inward scorn as he surveyed the sylvan group, the glancing firelight, and the tethered animals in the foreground. Suddenly an idea mingled with the alcoholic fumes that disturbed his brain. It was apparently of a jocular nature, for he felt impelled to slap his leg again and cram his fist into his mouth.

As the shadows crept slowly up the mountain, a slight breeze rocked the tops of the pine trees, and moaned through their long and gloomy aisles. The ruined cabin, patched and covered with pine boughs, was set apart for the ladies. As the lovers parted, they unaffectedly exchanged a kiss, so honest and sincere

that it might have been heard above the swaying pines. The frail Duchess and the malevolent Mother Shipton were probably too stunned to remark upon this last evidence of simplicity, and so turned without a word to the hut. The fire was replenished, the men lay down before the door, and in a few minutes were asleep.

Mr. Oakhurst was a light sleeper. Toward morning he awoke benumbed and cold. As he stirred the dying fire, the wind, which was now blowing strongly, brought to his cheek that which caused the blood to leave it—snow!

He started to his feet with the intention of awakening the sleepers, for there was no time to lose. But turning to where Uncle Billy had been lying, he found him gone. A suspicion leaped to his brain and a curse to his lips. He ran to the spot where the mules had been tethered; they were no longer there. The tracks were already rapidly disappearing in the snow.

The momentary excitement brought Mr. Oakhurst back to the fire with his usual calm. He did not waken the sleepers. The Innocent slumbered peacefully, with a smile on his good-humored, freckled face; the virgin Piney slept beside her frailer sisters as sweetly as though attended by celestial guardians; and Mr. Oakhurst, drawing his blanket over his shoulders, stroked his mustaches and waited for the dawn. It came slowly in a whirling mist of snowflakes that dazzled and confused the eye. What could be seen of the landscape appeared magically changed. He looked over the valley, and summed up the present and future in two words— "snowed in!"

A careful inventory of the provisions, which, fortunately for the party, had been stored within the hut and so escaped the felonious fingers of Uncle Billy, disclosed the fact that with care and prudence they might last ten days longer. "That is," said Mr. Oakhurst, sotto voce to the Innocent, "if you're willing to board us. If you ain't—and perhaps you'd better not—you can wait till Uncle Billy gets back with provisions." For some occult reason, Mr. Oakhurst could not bring himself to disclose Uncle Billy's rascality, and so offered the hypothesis that he had wandered from the camp and had accidentally stampeded the animals. He dropped a warning to the Duchess and Mother Shipton, who of course knew the facts of their associate's defection. "They'll find out the truth about us all when they find out anything," he added, significantly, "and there's no good frightening them now."

Simson not only put all his worldly store at the disposal of Mr. Oakhurst, but seemed to enjoy the prospect of their enforced seclusion. "We'll have a good camp for a week, and then the snow'll melt, and we'll all go back together." The cheerful gaiety of the young man, and Mr. Oakhurst's calm, infected the others. The Innocent with the aid of pine boughs extemporized a thatch for the roofless cabin, and the Duchess directed Piney in the rearrangement of the interior with a taste and tact that opened the blue eyes of that provincial maiden to their fullest extent. "I reckon now you're used to fine things at Poker Flat," said Piney. The Duchess turned away sharply to conceal something that reddened her cheeks through its professional tint, and Mother Shipton requested Piney not to "chatter." But when Mr. Oakhurst returned from a weary search for the trail, he heard the sound of happy laughter echoed from the rocks. He stopped in some alarm, and his thoughts first naturally reverted to the whisky, which he had prudently cached. "And yet it don't somehow sound like whisky," said the gambler. It was not until he caught sight of the blazing fire through the still-blinding storm and the group around it that he settled to the conviction that it was "square fun."

Whether Mr. Oakhurst had cached his cards with the whisky as something debarred the free access of the community, I cannot say. It was certain that, in Mother Shipton's words, he "didn't say cards once" during that evening. Haply the time was beguiled by an accordion, produced somewhat ostentatiously by Tom Simson from his pack. Notwithstanding some difficulties attending the manipulation of this instrument, Piney Woods managed to pluck several reluctant melodies from its keys, to an accompaniment by the Innocent on a pair of bone castanets. But the crowning festivity of the evening was reached in a rude camp-meeting hymn, which the lovers, joining hands, sang with great earnestness and vociferation. I fear that a certain defiant tone and Covenanter's swing to its chorus, rather than any devotional quality, caused it speedily to infect the others, who at last joined in the refrain:

"I'm proud to live in the service of the Lord,
And I'm bound to die in His army."

The pines rocked, the storm eddied and whirled above the miserable group, and the flames of their altar leaped heavenward as if in token of the vow.

At midnight the storm abated, the rolling clouds parted, and the stars glittered keenly above the sleeping camp. Mr. Oakhurst, whose professional habits had enabled him to live on the smallest possible amount of sleep, in dividing the watch with Tom Simson somehow managed to take upon himself the greater part of that duty. He excused himself to the Innocent by saying that he had "often been a week without sleep." "Doing what?" asked Tom. "Poker!" replied Oakhurst, sententiously; "when a man gets a streak of luck he don't get tired. The luck gives in first. Luck," continued the gambler, reflectively, "is a mighty queer thing. All you know about it for certain is that it's bound to change. And it's finding out when it's going to change that makes you. We've had a streak of bad luck since we left Poker Flat—you come along, and slap you get into it, too. If you can hold your cards right along you're all right. For," added the gambler, with cheerful irrelevance,

"I'm proud to live in the service of the Lord,
And I'm bound to die in His army."

The third day came, and the sun, looking through the white-curtained valley, saw the outcasts divide their slowly decreasing store of provisions for the morning meal. It was one of the peculiarities of that mountain climate that its rays diffused a kindly warmth over the wintry landscape, as if in regretful commiseration of the past. But it revealed drift on drift of snow piled high around the hut—a hopeless, uncharted, trackless sea of white lying below the rocky shores to which the castaways still clung. Through the marvelously clear air the smoke of the pastoral village of Poker Flat rose miles away. Mother Shipton saw it, and from a remote pinnacle of her rocky fastness hurled in that direction a final malediction. It was her last vituperative attempt, and perhaps for that reason was invested with a certain degree of sublimity. It did her good, she privately informed the Duchess. "Just you go out there and cuss, and see." She then set herself to the task of amusing "the child," as she and the Duchess were pleased to call Piney. Piney was no chicken, but it was a soothing and original theory of the pair thus to account for the fact that she didn't swear and wasn't improper.

When night crept up again through the gorges, the reedy notes of the accordion rose and fell in fitful spasms and long-drawn gasps by the flickering campfire. But music failed to fill entirely the aching void left by insufficient food, and a new diversion was proposed by Piney—storytelling. Neither Mr. Oakhurst nor his female companions caring to relate their personal experiences, this plan would have failed too but for the Innocent. Some months before he had chanced upon a stray copy of Mr. Pope's ingenious translation of the *Iliad*. He now proposed to narrate the principal incidents of that poem—having thoroughly mastered the argument and fairly forgotten the words—in the current vernacular of Sandy Bar. And so for the rest of that night the Homeric demigods again walked the earth. Trojan bully and wily Greek wrestled in the winds, and the great pines in the canyon seemed to bow to the wrath of the son of Peleus. Mr. Oakhurst listened with quiet satisfaction. Most especially was he interested in the fate of "Ash-heels," as the Innocent persisted in denominating the "swift-footed Achilles."

So with small food and much of Homer and the accordion, a week passed over the heads of the outcasts. The sun again forsook them, and again from leaden skies the snowflakes were sifted over the land. Day by day closer around them drew the snowy circle, until at last they looked from their prison over drifted walls of dazzling white that towered twenty feet above their heads. It became more and more difficult to replenish their fires, even from the fallen trees beside them, now half-hidden in the drifts. And yet no one complained. The lovers turned from the dreary prospect and looked into each other's eyes, and were happy. Mr. Oakhurst settled himself coolly to the losing game before him. The Duchess, more cheerful than she had been, assumed the care of Piney. Only Mother Shipton—once the strongest of the party—seemed to sicken and fade. At midnight on the tenth day she called Oakhurst to her side. "I'm going," she said, in a voice of querulous weakness, "but don't say anything about it. Don't waken the kids. Take the bundle from under my head and open it." Mr. Oakhurst did so. It contained Mother Shipton's rations for the last week, untouched. "Give 'em to the child," she said, pointing to the sleeping Piney. "You've starved yourself," said the gambler. "That's what they call it," said the woman, querulously, as she lay down again and, turning her face to the wall, passed quietly away.

The accordion and the bones were put aside that day, and Homer was forgotten. When the body of Mother Shipton had been committed to the snow, Mr. Oakhurst took the Innocent aside, and showed him a pair of snowshoes, which he had fashioned from the old pack saddle. "There's one chance in a hundred to save her yet," he said, pointing to Piney; "but it's there," he added, pointing toward Poker Flat. "If you can reach there in two days she's safe." "And you?" asked Tom Simson. "I'll stay here," was the curt reply.

The lovers parted with a long embrace. "You are not going, too?" said the Duchess as she saw Mr. Oakhurst apparently waiting to accompany him. "As far as the canyon," he replied. He turned suddenly, and kissed the Duchess, leaving her pallid face aflame and her trembling limbs rigid with amazement.

Night came, but not Mr. Oakhurst. It brought the storm again and the whirling snow. Then the Duchess, feeding the fire, found that someone had quietly piled beside the hut enough fuel to last a few days longer. The tears rose to her eyes, but she hid them from Piney.

The women slept but little. In the morning, looking into each other's faces, they read their fate. Neither spoke; but Piney, accepting the position of the stronger, drew near and placed her arm around the Duchess's waist. They kept this attitude for the rest of the day. That night the storm reached its greatest fury, and, rending asunder the protecting pines, invaded the very hut.

Toward morning they found themselves unable to feed the fire, which gradually died away. As the embers slowly blackened, the Duchess crept closer to Piney, and broke the silence of many hours: "Piney, can you pray?" "No, dear," said Piney, simply. The Duchess, without knowing exactly why, felt relieved, and, putting her head upon Piney's shoulder, spoke no more. And so reclining, the younger and purer pillowing the head of her soiled sister upon her virgin breast, they fell asleep.

The wind lulled as if it feared to waken them. Feathery drifts of snow, shaken from the long pine boughs, flew like white-winged birds, and settled about them as they slept. The moon through the rifted clouds looked down upon what had been the camp. But all human stain, all trace of earthly travail, was hidden beneath the spotless mantle mercifully flung from above.

They slept all that day and the next, nor did they waken when voices and footsteps broke the silence of the camp. And when pitying fingers brushed the snow from their wan faces, you could scarcely have told from the equal peace that dwelt upon them which was she that had sinned. Even the law of Poker Flat recognized this, and turned away, leaving them still locked in each other's arms.

But at the head of the gulch, on one of the largest pine trees, they found the deuce of clubs pinned to the bark with a bowie knife. It bore the following, written in pencil, in a firm hand:

BENEATH THIS TREE
LIES THE BODY
OF
JOHN OAKHURST,
WHO STRUCK A STREAK OF BAD LUCK
ON THE 23D OF NOVEMBER, 1850,
AND
HANDED IN HIS CHECKS
ON THE 7TH DECEMBER, 1850.

And pulseless and cold, with a Derringer by his side and a bullet in his heart, though still calm as in life, beneath the snow lay he who was at once the strongest and yet the weakest of the outcasts of Poker Flat.
http://www.geocities.com/short_stories

Kate Chopin

BACKGROUND

Kate Chopin (1850-1904) was known for her depictions of culture in New Orleans, Louisiana, and of the struggles of 19th century women. For more than a decade following her first published story in 1889, Chopin was one of the first American writers to depict the manners, customs, speech, and surroundings of a people group. Two collections of her short fiction were published in the 1890s: *Bayou Folk* (1894) and *A Night in Acadie* (1897). Her later stories such as "The Story of an Hour," emphasized women's need for self-reliance.

The Story of an Hour
Kate Chopin

http://classiclit.about.com/library/bl-etexts/kchopin/bl-kchop-story.htm

Knowing that Mrs. Mallard was afflicted with a heart trouble, great care was taken to break to her as gently as possible the news of her husband's death.

It was her sister Josephine who told her, in broken sentences; veiled hints that revealed in half concealing. Her husband's friend Richards was there, too, near her. It was he who had been in the newspaper office when intelligence of the railroad disaster was received, with Brently Mallard's name leading the list of "killed." He had only taken the time to assure himself of its truth by a second telegram, and had hastened to forestall any less careful, less tender friend in bearing the sad message.

She did not hear the story as many women have heard the same, with a paralyzed inability to accept its significance. She wept at once, with sudden, wild abandonment, in her sister's arms. When the storm of grief had spent itself she went away to her room alone. She would have no one follow her.

There stood, facing the open window, a comfort-able, roomy armchair. Into this she sank, pressed down by a physical exhaustion that haunted her body and seemed to reach into her soul.

She could see in the open square before her house the tops of trees that were all aquiver with the new spring life. The delicious breath of rain was in the air. In the street below a peddler was crying his wares. The notes of a distant song which some one was singing reached her faintly, and countless sparrows were twittering in the eaves.

There were patches of blue sky showing here and there through the clouds that had met and piled one above the other in the west facing her window.

She sat with her head thrown back upon the cushion of the chair, quite motionless, except when a sob came up into her throat and shook her, as a child who has cried itself to sleep continues to sob in its dreams.

She was young, with a fair, calm face, whose lines bespoke repression and even a certain strength. But now there was a dull stare in her eyes, whose gaze was fixed away off yonder on one of those patches of blue sky. It was not a glance of reflection, but rather indicated a suspension of intelligent thought.

There was something coming to her and she was waiting for it, fearfully. What was it? She did not know; it was too subtle and elusive to name. But she felt it, creeping out of the sky, reaching toward her through the sounds, the scents, the color that filled the air.

Now her bosom rose and fell tumultuously. She was beginning to recognize this thing that was approaching to possess her, and she was striving to beat it back with her will—as powerless as her two white slender hands would have been.

When she abandoned herself a little whispered word escaped her slightly parted lips. She said it over and over under her breath: "free, free, free!" The vacant stare and the look of terror that had followed it went from her eyes. They stayed keen and bright. Her pulses beat fast, and the coursing blood warmed and relaxed every inch of her body.

She did not stop to ask if it were or were not a monstrous joy that held her. A clear and exalted perception enabled her to dismiss the suggestion as trivial.

She knew that she would weep again when she saw the kind, tender hands folded in death; the face that had never looked save with love upon her, fixed and gray and dead. But she saw beyond that bitter moment a long procession of years to come that would belong to her absolutely. And she opened and spread her arms out to them in welcome.

There would be no one to live for during those coming years; she would live for herself. There would be no powerful will bending hers in that blind persistence with which men and women believe they have a right to impose a private will upon a fellow-creature. A kind intention or a cruel intention made the act seem no less a crime as she looked upon it in that brief moment of illumination.

And yet she had loved him—sometimes. Often she had not. What did it matter! What could love, the unsolved mystery, count for in face of this possession of self-assertion which she suddenly recognized as the strongest impulse of her being!

"Free! Body and soul free!" she kept whispering.

Josephine was kneeling before the closed door with her lips to the keyhole, imploring for admission. "Louise, open the door! I beg, open the door—you will make yourself ill. What are you doing Louise? For heaven's sake open the door."

"Go away. I am not making myself ill." No; she was drinking in a very elixir of life through that open window.

Her fancy was running riot along those days ahead of her. Spring days, and summer days, and all sorts of days that would be her own. She breathed a quick prayer that life might be long. It was only yesterday she had thought with a shudder that life might be long.

She arose at length and opened the door to her sister's importunities. There was a feverish triumph in her eyes, and she carried herself unwittingly like a goddess of Victory. She clasped her sister's waist, and together they descended the stairs. Richards stood waiting for them at the bottom.

Some one was opening the front door with a latchkey. It was Brently Mallard who entered, a little travel-stained, composedly carrying his grip-sack and umbrella. He had been far from the scene of accident, and did not even know there had been one. He stood amazed at Josephine's piercing cry; at Richards' quick motion to screen him from the view of his wife.

But Richards was too late.

When the doctors came they said she had died of heart disease—of joy that kills.

http://www.geocities.com/

Edwin Arlington Robinson

Edwin Arlington Robinson (1869-1935) was no doubt one of the finest poets America ever produced. His life was full of tragedy, which affected his writings. During the early 1890s the family's fortunes began to decline,

triggering a series of tragedies that influenced Robinson's life and poetry. In 1892 his father died, and the panic of 1893 bankrupted the family. Robinson's brother Dean became addicted to morphine and returned home in failing health. Robinson was forced to leave Harvard because of the family's financial difficulties and his mother's failing health. She died in 1896 of "black diphtheria," and the brothers had to lay out their mother, dig the grave, and bury her. Robinson persevered and became the first major American poet of the twentieth century, unique in that he devoted his life to poetry and paid the price in poverty and obscurity.

Luke Havergal
Edwin Arlington Robinson
http://www.theotherpages.org/poems/robin01.html

Go to the western gate, Luke Havergal,
There where the vines cling crimson on the wall,
And in the twilight wait for what will come.
The wind will moan, the leaves will whisper some
Whisper of her, and strike you as they fall;
But go, and if you trust her she will call.
Go to the western gate, Luke Havergal
Luke Havergal
No, there is not a dawn in eastern skies
To rift the fiery night that's in your eyes;
But there, where western glooms are gathering,
The dark will end the dark, if anything:
God slays Himself with every leaf that flies,
And hell is more than half of paradise.
No, there is not a dawn in eastern skies
In eastern skies.
Out of a grave I come to tell you this,
Out of a grave I come to quench the kiss
That flames upon your forehead with a glow
That blinds you to the way that you must go.
Yes, there is yet one way to where she is,
Bitter, but one that faith can never miss.
Out of a grave I come to tell you this
To tell you this.
There is the western gate, Luke Havergal,
There are the crimson leaves upon the wall. Go,

for the winds are tearing them away,
Nor think to riddle the dead words they say,
Nor any more to feel them as they fall;
But go! and if you trust her she will call.
There is the western gate, Luke Havergal
Luke Havergal.

Credo

http://www.theotherpages.org/poems/robin01.html

I cannot find my way: there is no star
In all the shrouded heavens anywhere;
And there is not a whisper in the air
Of any living voice but one so far
That I can hear it only as a bar
Of lost, imperial music, played when fair
And angel fingers wove, and unaware,
Dead leaves to garlands where no roses are.
No, there is not a glimmer, nor a call,
For one that welcomes, welcomes when he fears,
The black and awful chaos of the night;
For through it all, above, beyond it all,
I know the far-sent message of the years,
I feel the coming glory of the Light!

Edgar Lee Masters

BACKGROUND

Edgar Lee Masters (1869-1950) wrote *A Book of Verses* (1898) and several plays before gaining fame with *Spoon River Anthology* (1915), a collection of poems in free verse about the secret lives of the inhabitants of Spoon River, a small Midwestern fictional town. Masters presents the poems as the voices of the occupants of the town's graveyard, talking honestly about their lives. In "Lucinda Matlock," Edgar Lee Masters demonstrates the literary devices of Realism (which is also a worldview). This style normally includes the devices of irony, simplicity, morals and values, and symbols.

Lucinda Matlock

http://www.theotherpages.org/poems/masters01.html#2

I went to the dances at Chandlerville,
And played snap-out at Winchester.
One time we changed partners,
Driving home in the moonlight of middle June,
And then I found Davis.
We were married and lived together for seventy years,
Enjoying, working, raising the twelve children,
Eight of whom we lost
Ere I had reached the age of sixty.
I spun, I wove, I kept the house, I nursed the sick,
I made the garden, and for holiday
Rambled over the fields where sang the larks,
And by Spoon River gathering many a shell,
And many a flower and medicinal weed—
Shouting to the wooded hills, singing to the green
    valleys.
At ninety-six I had lived enough, that is all,
And passed to a sweet repose.
What is this I hear of sorrow and weariness,
Anger, discontent and drooping hopes?
Degenerate sons and daughters,
Life is too strong for you—
It takes life to love Life.

CRITICAL THINKING

A. How does Bret Harte create humor in his short story "Outcasts of Poker Flat?"

B. What was the joy that killed Mrs. Mallard?

C. What does Robinson mean by these lines "God slays Himself with every leaf that flies,/ And hell is more than half of paradise?"

D. What does Lucinda Matlock mean when she says, "It takes life to love Life?"

ENRICHMENT

Compare Mrs. Mallard to Lucinda Matlock.

FINAL PROJECT

Correct and rewrite all essays and place them in your Final Portfolio.

SUGGESTED
Weekly *Implementation*

DAY 1	DAY 2	DAY 3	DAY 4	DAY 5
Prayer journal.	**Prayer journal.**	**Prayer journal.**	**Prayer journal.**	**Prayer journal.**
Review the required reading(s) *before* the assigned lesson begins.	Review reading(s) from next lesson.	Write rough drafts of all assigned essays.	Rewrite corrected copies of essays due tomorrow.	Essays are due.
Teacher may want to discuss assigned reading(s) with students.	Outline essays due at the end of the week.	The teacher and/or a peer evaluator may correct rough drafts.		Take the Lesson 19 test.
Teacher and students will decide on required essays for this lesson choosing two or three essays.	Per teacher instructions, students may answer orally in a group setting some of the essays that are not assigned as formal essays.			Reading Ahead: Review *Ethan Frome*, Edith Wharton.
The rest of the essays can be outlined, answered with shorter answers, or skipped.				Guide: In what way is *Ethan Frome* a Naturalistic novel?
Review all readings for Lesson 19				

THE MODERN AGE, 1915-1946: LATE ROMANTICISM/ NATURALISM *(Part 1)*

Ethan Frome

Edith Wharton (1911)

BACKGROUND

It's hard to imagine a less likely author for *Ethan Frome* than Edith Wharton, for this story of a poverty-stricken, lonely New England farmer was written by a wealthy, middle-aged member of New York City's high society. Edith Wharton probably never spent a day of her life outside of high society, New York City society. Even so, she draws a realistic picture of the dark, cramped, cheerless rooms of the Frome farm and the emptiness of their hearts.

Ethan Frome is an exceptionally well-written novel. With barely more than 150 pages Edith Wharton takes us into the human heart. We do not much like what we see. Her novels are psychological novels: a study of human motivation and ethos. Wharton is a masterful storyteller. Her story is a story of life itself: the story of a man and two women captured by the exigencies of life, two people who make a decision one day that permanently changes the lives of an entire community. Wharton uses the dialect and scenery of a late nineteenth century New England rural community to take the reader into her own heart.

The following is Edith Wharton's explanation of why she wrote *Ethan Frome*:

I had known something of New England village life long before I made my home in the same county as my imaginary Starkfield; though, during the years spent there, certain of its aspects became much more familiar to me.

Even before that final initiation, however, I had had an uneasy sense that the New England of fiction bore little—except a vague botanical and dialectical—resemblance to the harsh and beautiful land as I had seen it. Even the abundant enumeration of sweet-fern, asters and mountain-laurel, and the conscientious reproduction of the vernacular, left me with the feeling that the outcropping granite had in both cases been overlooked. I give the impression merely as a personal one; it accounts for *Ethan Frome*, and may, to some readers, in a measure justify it.

So much for the origin of the story; there is nothing else of interest to say of it, except as concerns its construction.

The problem before me, as I saw in the first flash, was this: I had to deal with a subject of which the dramatic climax, or rather the anti-climax, occurs a generation later than the first acts of the tragedy. This enforced lapse of time would seem to anyone persuaded—as I have always been—that every subject (in the novelist's sense of the term) implicitly contains its own form and dimensions, to mark Ethan Frome as the subject for a novel. But I never thought this for a moment, for I had felt, at the same time, that the theme of my tale was not one on which many variations could be played. It must be treated as starkly and summarily as life had always presented itself to my protagonists; any attempt to elaborate and complicate their sentiments would necessarily have falsified the whole. They were, in truth, these figures, my granite outcroppings; but half-emerged from the soil, and scarcely more articulate.

This incompatibility between subject and plan would perhaps have seemed to suggest that my "situation" was after all one to be rejected. Every novelist has been visited by the insinuating wraiths of false "good situations," siren-subjects luring his cockle-shell to the rocks; their voice is oftenest heard, and their mirage-sea beheld, as he traverses the waterless desert which awaits him half-way through whatever work is actually in hand. I knew well enough what song those sirens sang, and had often tied myself to my dull job until they were out of hearing—perhaps carrying a lost master-piece in their rainbow veils. But I had no such fear of them in the case of Ethan Frome. It was the first sub-ject I had ever approached with full confidence in its value, for my own purpose, and a relative faith in my power to render at least a part of what I saw in it. Every novelist, again, who "intends upon" his art, has lit upon such subjects, and been fascinated by the difficulty of presenting them in the fullest relief, yet without an added ornament, or a trick of drapery or lighting. This was my task, if I were to tell the story of Ethan Frome; and my scheme of construction—which met with the immediate and unqualified disapproval of the few friends to whom I tentatively outlined it—I still think justified in the given case. It appears to me, indeed, that, while an air of artificiality is lent to a tale of com-plex and sophisticated people which the novelist causes to be guessed at and interpreted by any mere looker-on, there need be no such drawback if the looker-on is sophisticated, and the people he interprets are simple. If he is capable of seeing all around them, no violence is done to probability in allowing him to exercise this fac-ulty; it is natural enough that he should act as the sym-pathizing intermediary between his rudimentary characters and the more complicated minds to whom he is trying to present them. But this is all self-evident, and needs explaining only to those who have never thought of fiction as an art of composition.

The real merit of my construction seems to me to lie in a minor detail. I had to find means to bring my tragedy, in a way at once natural and picture-making, to the knowledge of its narrator. I might have sat him down before a village gossip who would have poured out the whole affair to him in a breath, but in doing this I should have been false to two essential elements of my picture: first, the deep-rooted reticence and inarticu-lateness of the people I was trying to draw, and sec-ondly the effect of "roundness" (in the plastic sense) produced by letting their case be seen through eyes as different as those of Harmon Gow and Mrs. Ned Hale. Each of my chroniclers contributes to the narrative just so much as he or she is capable of understanding of what, to them, is a complicated and mysterious case;

and only the narrator of the tale has scope enough to see it all, to resolve it back into simplicity, and to put it in its rightful place among his larger categories.

I make no claim for originality in following a method of which "La Grande Breteche" and "The Ring and the Book" had set me the magnificent example; my one merit is, perhaps, to have guessed that the proceed-ing there employed was also applicable to my small tale.

I have written this brief analysis—the first I have ever published of any of my books—because, as an author's introduction to his work, I can imagine nothing of any value to his readers except a statement as to why he decided to attempt the work in question, and why he selected one form rather than another for its embodiment. These primary aims, the only ones that can be explicitly stated, must, by the artist, be almost instinctively felt and acted upon before there can pass into his creation that imponderable something more which causes life to circu-late in it, and preserves it for a little from decay.

ABOUT THE AUTHOR

Edith Wharton (1832-1937), whose real name was Newbold Jones, was a member of a wealthy New York family. Deeply influenced by Naturalism and realism, Wharton still tried to place a sense of moral values in her novels. She is one of the few significant twentieth century American writers who did so.

OTHER NOTABLE WORKS

The Age of Innocence
Tales of Men and Ghosts

VOCABULARY WORDS

Prologue	taciturnity
	exanimate
Chapter I	sardonically
	oblique
Chapter III	scintillating
	querulous
Chapter V	languidly
Chapter VI	ominous

CRITICAL THINKING

A. The man telling the story is never real. Why?

Theme: a belief about life expressed in a prose/poetry/ dramatic piece. A theme is usually subtly presented in the literary piece. A theme should not be confused with a moral. A moral is a lesson for actual life. A theme is a comment on life.

B. Time and time again the reader is invited to interpret the story through Ethan's eyes. We watch Mattie dance, for instance, through Ethan's eyes before we meet her. This technique is called *stream of consciousness*. What effect does this technique have on the story?

C. The life span of a story—or the number of years that it will be read—is determined to a large degree by its deeper meaning, or *theme*. Apart from the characters, apart from the plot a book must have a powerful theme or it will die. *The Odyssey*, by Homer, for instance, is such a story. The theme of journey is eternal and always interesting. The theme of someone returning to someone he loves is equally interesting. What is the theme of *Ethan Frome*?

D. This tragic book is marked by *irony*. *Irony* is defined as a contradiction between what is said and what is expected. Mattie ironically becomes the opposite of what she was as a youth. How do Zeena and Ethan change by the end of the novel? What other instances of irony do you find in Mrs. Hale's conversation?

E. Find examples of *imagery* in this book.

F. How does the narrator draw the reader into this story?

G. How is interest increased by the conversation between Mattie and Denis Eady?

BIBLICAL APPLICATION

A. Why do you think Ethan did or did not have a right to leave Zeena? What does the Bible say?

B. Wharton herself was struggling in a difficult marriage. Do you think this helped her make this novel more credible? How much do you think the personal lives of authors affect their writing style?

C. At the end of the novel we observe three people captured by unforgiveness. They are, in effect, in a "living hell." What does the Bible say about unforgiveness? How can you forgive someone who has grievously wronged you? In fact, *Ethan Frome* has a similar theme to the existential play *No Exit*, by the French writer Jean Paul Sartre. Read this short play and compare it to *Ethan Frome* in an essay.

ENRICHMENT

© Arttoday.com

A. Research the problems of the American city at the end of the nineteenth century. Contrast the views of Wharton with Dwight L. Moody an urban evangelist who transformed Chicago. This book presages the pessimism that grew after the First World War. In what ways is this novel a pessimistic view of life? In what ways does Wharton retain some moral vision?

B. One individual who had a profound effect on America when Edith Wharton was alive was Charles Darwin (1809-1882). In 1859 Charles Darwin published *On The Origin of Species by Means of Natural Selection*, or the *Preservation of Favoured Races in the Struggle for Life*. In 1858 Darwin had co-authored (with Alfred Russel Wallace) the theory of natural selection, which says that superior biological variations tend to be preserved. In the struggle for existence, the fit are not those who survive but those who reproduce. Natural selection also leads to diversification as different organisms adapt to particular ecological circumstances. Darwin said all biological similarities and differences are caused by descent with modification. He concluded that all organisms are descended from only one ancestor. Evolution is the name for this biological process that goes back to one common ancestor 3-1/2 billion years ago. Charles Darwin, then, was the father of the theory of evolution:

http://www.classicreader.com/booktoc.php/sid.2/bookid.107/

We have reason to believe, as stated in the first chapter, that a change in the conditions of life, by specially acting on the reproductive system, causes or increases variability; and in the foregoing case the conditions of life are supposed to have undergone a change, and this would manifestly be favourable to natural selection, by giving a better chance of profitable variations occurring; and unless profitable variations do occur, natural selection can do nothing. Not that, as I believe, any extreme amount of variability is necessary; as man can certainly produce great results by adding up in any given direction mere individual differences, so could Nature, but far more easily, from having incomparably longer time at her disposal. Nor do I believe that any great physical change, as of climate, or any unusual degree of isolation to check immigration, is actually necessary to produce new and unoccupied places for natural selection to fill up by modifying and improving some of the varying inhabitants. For as all the inhabitants of each country are struggling together with nicely balanced forces, extremely slight modifications in the structure or habits of one inhabitant would often give it an advantage over others; and still further modifications of the same kind would often still further increase the advantage.—*The Origin of Species*

Define natural selection and explain why this scientific theory is anti-Christian?

C. Producing interest in the plot is called creating *suspense*. How does Wharton create suspense?

D. Wharton knew much too well the frustration of a failed marriage—such as Ethan and Zeena's. Teddy Wharton was thirteen years older than his wife and a totally unsuitable mate for her. She bored him, and he scoffed at her literary and intellectual pursuits. When Teddy's health began to fail, the marriage became still more strained. He crabbed and complained much of the time. In fits of temper he verbally abused his wife. Twice he suffered nervous breakdowns. Edith Wharton told the story of her marriage in various writings, including her literary autobiography, *A Backward Glance* (1934). If Wharton's version is accurate, though, she wins our sympathy as the wronged partner in the marriage, just as most readers sympathize with Ethan Frome for being stuck with Zeena, his sickly, ill-tempered wife. However, Ethan's is also a one-sided story. We can only guess what Zeena thinks about him by reading between the lines. It seems certain, however, that Ethan Frome is a product of Edith Wharton's long and serious contemplation of the mutual obligations of marriage partners. Ethan chose to die rather than stay with his spouse. That wasn't a satisfactory solution for Wharton, though. In 1913, two years after *Ethan Frome* was published, she filed for divorce. Pretend that you are Ethan Frome's and/or Edith Wharton's pastor. What would be your advice to them? What would you say to Frome after he tried to commit suicide?

FINAL PORTFOLIO

Correct and re-write required essays and place in your Portfolio.

SUGGESTED
Weekly *Implementation*

DAY 1	DAY 2	DAY 3	DAY 4	DAY 5
Prayer journal. Review the required reading(s) before the assigned lesson begins. Teacher may want to discuss assigned reading(s) with students. Teacher and students will decide on required essays for this lesson, choosing two or three essays. The rest of the essays can be outlined, answered with shorter answers, or skipped. Review all readings for Lesson 20	**Prayer journal.** Review reading(s) from next lesson. Outline essays due at the end of the week. Per teacher instructions, students may answer orally in a group setting some of the essays that are not assigned as formal essays.	**Prayer journal.** Write rough drafts of all assigned essays. The teacher and/or a peer evaluator may correct rough drafts.	**Prayer journal.** Rewrite corrected copies of essays due tomorrow.	**Prayer journal.** Essays are due. Take Lesson 20 test. Reading ahead: 20th century poetry (provided in text) Guide: What worldviews in this old genre surface in this new century?

THE MODERN AGE, 1915-1946: LATE ROMANTICISM/ NATURALISM *(Part 2)*

20th Century Poetry

BACKGROUND

Twentieth century poetry grew out of the century in which it was produced. In particular most of the poets represented in this lesson grew up in the turbulent 1920s.

During the 1920s, the United States experienced unparalleled prosperity. The benefits of the 19th century Industrial Revolution were becoming obvious. After World War I, a postwar boom began and continued unabated until the 1929 stock market collapse. The 1920s marked the climax of the "second industrial revolution."

During the last half of the 19th century, American industry had primarily manufactured goods intended for other producers. By 1920 industry was focusing on such goods and consumables as silk stockings, washing machines, and cars (Nash, et al., *The American People*). Powering this great revolution was electricity. The technology surrounding electricity advanced as radically as space technology in the middle decades of the 20th century. Electricity had as profound an effect on American culture as any technology in modern times.

Where electricity could not take Americans, the gasoline-powered engine did. Americans had a love affair with the auto from the beginning. There were 8000 motor vehicles in 1900 and nearly a million in 1912. By 1929 Americans were purchasing 4.5 million cars, and by the end of the year 27 million were registered. The automobile caused American cities to expand beyond their natural barriers. Great distances could be covered by automobiles in a relatively short amount of time. A novelty for Americans was that they could live in the suburbs and work in the cities. The census of 1920 indicated that for the first time, more Americans lived in and near cities than in the country. These advances, however, created problems.

Such modern technologies as radio and movies promoted a national secular culture. This new culture emphasized consumption and pleasure, not discipline and sacrifice. Religious and moral values came under

> **You will analyze:** 20th century poetry.
>
> **Reading Ahead:** *A Farewell to Arms*, Ernest Hemingway.
>
> **Guide Question:** How is the protagonist Frederick Henry in *A Farewell to Arms* similar to Henry Fleming in *A Red Badge of Courage*? Stylistically, how is *A Farewell to Arms* similar to *The Adventures of Huckleberry Finn?*

attack. The most famous example of this attack was the famous Scopes trial in 1925. John Scopes, a young biology teacher, broke a Tennessee law and taught evolution in his classes. He was arrested, and a famous trial was held in Dayton, Tennessee. While Scopes was convicted, Fundamentalist Christianity was ridiculed. For the first time Americans were publicly invited to mock their faith. It would not be the last time.

In 1900 Americans were regularly connected to close friends and family. The only connection to the outside world was through an occasional, old newspaper and low-circulation magazine. In spite of military victories all over the globe, Americans simply did not have a global perspective.

In a sense, World War I changed all that. It was hard to keep a farm boy home after he had seen Paris. At the same time, technological innovations also brought radical changes. By 1940, network radio linked millions of listeners together. Mass transportation, the telephone, and the automobile made it possible for people to communicate while living great distances apart (Fenton, *A New American History*). The Sears & Roebuck catalogue and other mail order catalogues created a common fashion culture. Regardless of socio-economic

> The home school movement and Christian private school movement in the middle of the 20th century was partly in response to the excesses originating in the 1920s.

status and literally for the first time, Americans could wear the same type of underwear and hats. National magazines were read by millions of readers, who saw the same photographs and read the same stories. In darkened movie houses patrons cried through the same scenes, in the same movies (Fenton). For the first time, Americans had a national cultural identity as well as a national political identity.

In the middle of the 1920s, two young sociologists, Robert and Helen Lynd, made a city the object of their study and suggested certain sociological commonalities. They found some astounding statistics, values, and attitudes. For the first time in American history, Americans no longer wished to have 6 or 8 children. On the contrary, Americans sought to have 2 or 3 children. Quality of life issues were suddenly more important than child-bearing. The shift was from the Victorian image of child-bearing to the modern image of child-rearing (Fenton). The former dominance of the home in the child's life was threatened. Young people spent less time in the home than their parents who grew up in the 1890s. The growth of suburbs and residential cities offered less yard space. Most importantly, however, was the growth of public education.

The lure of the kindergarten to 4 and 5 year olds was irresistible. The invention of the high school was even more influential. Athletics, dramatics, and societies all conspired to take time away from the American family. Young people began driving automobiles. They participated in "dates" which replaced older notions of "courtship." As a result, the rate of unwed pregnancies skyrocketed. As the Lynds put it:

> The more sophisticated social life of today has brought with it another "problem" much discussed by parents. This problem is the apparently increasing relaxation of some of the traditional prohibitions upon the approaches of boys and girls to each other's persons. Here again new inventions of the last 35 years have played a part. In 1890 a "well-brought-up" boy and girl were commonly forbidden to sit together in the dark. But motion pictures and the automobile have lifted this taboo, and, once lifted, it is easy for the practice to become widely extended. Buggy-riding in 1890 allowed only a narrow range of mobility. Three to eight were generally accepted hours for riding, and being out after 8:30 without a chaperone was forbidden. In an auto, however, a party may go to a city halfway across the state in an after-noon or evening. And un-chaperoned automobile parties as late as midnight, while subject to criticism, are not exceptional.

http://www.bsu.edu/libraries/

However, not all cultural advances were bad. Young people and parents, for the first time in some cases, openly discussed private and personal issues. A more democratic form of relationship arose. Death from disease decreased. Everyone had more leisure time, which produced a vast market for American poetry — in fact, never before had Americans read that much poetry.

Ezra Pound

(1885-1972)

© Arttoday.com

Ezra Pound was one of the most influential American poets of the 20th century. From 1908 to 1920, he lived in London, where he associated with many writers, including William Butler Yeats, for whom he worked as a secretary, and T.S. Eliot, whose *Waste Land* he drastically edited and improved. He eventually moved to Italy, where he became caught up in Italian Fascism: Pound was a racist and fascist.

Pound's interests and reading were universal. His life-work was *The Cantos*, which he wrote and published until his death. They contain brilliant passages, but their allusions to works of literature and art from many eras and cultures make them difficult. Pound's poetry is best known for its clear, visual images, fresh rhythms, and muscular, intelligent, unusual lines, such as, in Canto LXXXI, "The ant's a centaur in his dragon world," or in poems inspired by Japanese haiku, such as "In a Station of the Metro" (1916):

20th century poetry clearly moved from Naturalism and Realism into Existentialism and Absurdism

The apparition of these faces in the crowd;
Petals on a wet, black bough.

Pound's subject matter was modern and realistic. He was involved in the early stages of surrealism.

T.S. Eliot

(1888-1965)

© Arttoday.com

T. S. Eliot was both an American and a British writer of unprecedented stature. He was considered the best. He lived on two continents, but he belonged only to God. One of the most respected poets of his day, his iconoclastic poetry had revolutionary impact. He also wrote influential essays and dramas, and championed the importance of literary and social traditions for the modern poet.

The famous beginning of Eliot's "Prufrock" invites the reader into tawdry alleys:

Prufrock

Let us go then, you and I,
When the evening is spread out against the sky
Like a patient etherized upon a table;
Let us go, through certain half-deserted streets,
The muttering retreats
Of restless nights in one-night cheap hotels
And sawdust restaurants with oyster-shells:
Streets that follow like a tedious argument
Of insidious intent
To lead you to an overwhelming question...

Works by Ezra Pound can be found at 20th Century Poetry http://www.lit.kobe_u.ac.jp/~hishika/pound.htm

T.S. Eliot met the Lord late in life and wrote some of the most inspiring prose and poetry in the English language.

Oh, do not ask, "What is it?"
Let us go and make our visit.
www.classicreader.com/read.php/sid.1bookid.8/sec.13/

Similar imagery pervades *The Waste Land* (1922), which echoes Dante's Inferno to evoke London's thronged streets around the time of World War I:

Unreal City,
Under the brown fog of a winter dawn,
A crowd flowed over London Bridge, so many I had not thought death had undone so many... (I, 60-63)
http://www.bartleby.com/201/1.html

The Waste Land's vision is ultimately apocalyptic (i.e., end times) and worldwide:

Cracks and reforms and bursts in the violet air
Falling towers Jerusalem, Athens, Alexandria, Vienna
London Unreal (V, 373-377)
http://www.bartleby.com/201/1.html

Eliot's vision of the world is decidedly hopeless and Naturalistic—that is until he commits his life to Christ. At the end of his life, Eliot had a profound experience with Christ that profoundly changed his views of the past and future. In fact, one of the most Christian Theistic pieces of literature in the English language is Eliot's *Murder in the Cathedral*, written at the end of his life.

Hippopotamus

http://www.bartleby.com/201/1.html

The broad-backed hippopotamus
Rests on his belly in the mud;
Although he seems so firm to us
He is merely flesh and blood.

Flesh-and-blood is weak and frail,
Susceptible to nervous shock;
While the True Church can never fail
For it is based upon a rock.

The hippo's feeble steps may err
In compassing material ends,
While the True Church need never stir
To gather in its dividends.

The 'potamus can never reach
The mango on the mango-tree;
But fruits of pomegranate and peach
Refresh the Church from over sea.

At mating time the hippo's voice
Betrays inliexions hoarse and odd,
But every week we hear rejoice
The Church, at being one with God.

The hippopotamus's day
Is passed in sleep; at night he hunts;
God works in a mysterious way—
The Church can sleep and feed at once.

I saw the 'potamus take wing
Ascending from the damp savannas,
And quiring angels round him sing
The praise of God, in loud hosannas.

Blood of the Lamb shall wash him clean
And him shall heavenly arms enfold,
Among the saints he shall be seen
Performing on a harp of gold.

He shall be washed as white as snow,
By all the martyr'd virgins kiss,
While the True Church remains below
Wrapt in the old miasmal mist.

Robert Frost
(1874-1963)

© Arttoday.com

Robert Lee Frost was born in California but was raised on a farm in New England until the age of 10. The New England countryside became Frost's favorite setting. A charismatic public reader, he was renowned for his tours. He read an original work at the inauguration of President John F. Kennedy in 1961 that helped spark a national interest in poetry. His popularity is easy to explain: He wrote of traditional farm life, appealing to nostalgia for the old ways. His themes were universal and immutable—apple picking, stone walls, fences, country roads. His subjects were ordinary people. He was one of the few modern poets who used rhyme. This endeared him to American readers.

Frost's work is often deceptively simple. Many poems suggest a deeper meaning. For example, a quiet snowy evening by an almost hypnotic rhyme scheme may suggest the not entirely unwelcome approach of death. Beneath the falling snow and gentle raindrops are pain and unhappiness. Some critics blame Frost's perspectives on the early years of his marriage when he tried to make a living on an inhospitable New England farm. From "Stopping by Woods on a Snowy Evening" (1923):

The woods are lovely, dark and deep,
But I have promises to keep,
And miles to go before I sleep,
And miles to go before I sleep.
www.classicreader.com

> When you read Robert Frost, see if you can find evidence of Naturalism.

Wallace Stevens
(1879-1955)

© Arttoday.com

Stevens's poetry argues for the belief that the order of art corresponds with an order in nature. His vocabulary is rich: He writes with generous imagery.

Some of Stevens's poems draw upon popular culture, while others poke fun at sophisticated society or soar into an intellectual heaven. He is known for his exuberant

> For more information on Stevens, including his poems, access this web-site http://www.english.upenn.edu/~afilreis /Stevens/home.html

> It is alleged that Stevens was converted at the end of his life. Father Arthur Hanley visited Wallace in the hospital and reported afterwards that Wallace had been baptized and said "I will see you in heaven." Wallace died soon after.

word play: "Soon, with a noise like tambourines / Came her attendant Byzantines."

Stevens's work is full of surprising insights. Sometimes he plays tricks on the reader, as in "Disillusionment of Ten O'clock" (1931):

The houses are haunted
By white night-gowns.
None are green,
Or purple with green rings,
Or green with yellow rings,
Or yellow with blue rings. . .
http://www.theotherpages.org/poems/stevens1.html

This poem seems to complain about unimaginative lives (plain white nightgowns) but actually brings up bright images in the reader's mind. Stevens' poetry is not easy but is well worth the effort.

William Carlos Williams
(1883-1963)

William Carlos Williams was a practicing pediatrician throughout his life; he delivered more than 2,000 babies and wrote poems on his prescription pads. His sympathy for ordinary working people, children, and everyday events in modern urban settings make his poetry attractive and accessible. "The Red Wheelbarrow" (1923), like a Dutch still life, finds interest and beauty in everyday objects.

> The student may find Williams' poems at this site http://www.library.utoronto.ca/utel/rp/authors/wcw.html

e. e. cummings
(1894-1962)

A painter, e. e. cummings was the first American poet to recognize that poetry had become primarily a visual, not an oral, art; his poems used much unusual spacing and indentation, as well as dropping all use of capital letters.

Like Williams, Cummings also used colloquial language, sharp imagery, and words from popular culture. Also like Williams, he took creative liberties with layout. His poem "in Just" (1920) invites the reader to fill in the missing ideas.

> e. e. cummings is a nontraditional poet.

> Poems by e. e. cummings can be found at this web-site: http://www.poets.org/poets/

Hart Crane
(1899-1932)

Hart Crane was a disturbed young poet who committed suicide at age 33 by leaping into the sea. He left striking poems, including an epic, *The Bridge* (1930), which was inspired by the Brooklyn Bridge, in which he ambitiously attempted to review the American cultural experience and recast it in affirmative terms. His exuberant style works best in such short poems as "Voyages" (1923, 1926) and "At Melville's Tomb" (1926); the ending is a suitable epitaph for Crane: *This fabulous shadow only the sea keeps.*

> Hart Crane's poetry can be found at http://www.poets.org/poems/

Edna St. Vincent Millay

(1892-1950)

Millay won a Pulitzer Prize for poetry (for the *Harp Weaver and Other Poems*). While her verse was notorious for archetypal images and unoriginal metaphors, it was enjoyed for its easy and lively manner, and she is noted for her mastery of the sonnet form. Her poetry was full of emotion. It seemed to belong to another age. Her poetry was more like Elizabeth Barrett Browning's poetry than some of her contemporaries.

God's World

http://www.bartleby.com/131/4.html

O world, I cannot hold thee close enough!
Thy winds, thy wide grey skies!
Thy mists, that roll and rise!
Thy woods, this autumn day, that ache and sag
And all but cry with colour! That gaunt crag
To crush! To lift the lean of that black bluff!
World, World, I cannot get thee close enough!
Long have I known a glory in it all,
But never knew I this;
Here such a passion is
As stretcheth me apart,—Lord, I do fear
Thou'st made the world too beautiful this year;
My soul is all but out of me,—let fall
No burning leaf; prithee, let no bird calls.

Renascence

http://www.bartleby.com/131/1.html

All I could see from where I stood
Was three long mountains and a wood;
I turned and looked the other way,
And saw three islands in a bay.
So with my eyes I traced the line

Of the horizon, thin and fine,
Straight around till I was come
Back to where I'd started from;
And all I saw from where I stood
Was three long mountains and a wood.

Over these things I could not see:
These were the things that bounded me;
And I could touch them with my hand,
Almost, I thought, from where I stand.
And all at once things seemed so small

My breath came short, and scarce at all.
But, sure, the sky is big, I said;
Miles and miles above my head;
So here upon my back I'll lie
And look my fill into the sky.

And so I looked, and, after all,
The sky was not so very tall.
The sky, I said, must somewhere stop,
And—sure enough!—I see the top!
The sky, I thought, is not so grand;

I 'most could touch it with my hand!
And reaching up my hand to try,
I screamed to feel it touch the sky.
I screamed, and—lo!—Infinity
Came down and settled over me;

Forced back my scream into my chest,
Bent back my arm upon my breast,
And, pressing of the Undefined
The definition on my mind,
Held up before my eyes a glass

Through which my shrinking sight did pass
Until it seemed I must behold
Immensity made manifold;
Whispered to me a word whose sound
Deafened the air for worlds around,

And brought unmuffled to my ears
The gossiping of friendly spheres,
The creaking of the tented sky,
The ticking of Eternity.
I saw and heard and knew at last

The How and Why of all things, past,
And present, and forevermore.
The Universe, cleft to the core,
Lay open to my probing sense
That, sick'ning, I would fain pluck thence

But could not,—nay! But needs must suck
At the great wound, and could not pluck
My lips away till I had drawn

All venom out.—Ah, fearful pawn!
For my omniscience paid I toll

In infinite remorse of soul.
All sin was of my sinning, all
Atoning mine, and mine the gall
Of all regret. Mine was the weight
Of every brooded wrong, the hate

That stood behind each envious thrust,
Mine every greed, mine every lust.
And all the while for every grief,
Each suffering, I craved relief
With individual desire,—

Craved all in vain! And felt fierce fire
About a thousand people crawl;
Perished with each,—then mourned for all!
A man was starving in Capri;
He moved his eyes and looked at me;

I felt his gaze, I heard his moan,
And knew his hunger as my own.
I saw at sea a great fog bank
Between two ships that struck and sank;
A thousand screams the heavens smote;

And every scream tore through my throat.
No hurt I did not feel, no death
That was not mine; mine each last breath
That, crying, met an answering cry
From the compassion that was I.

All suffering mine, and mine its rod;
Mine, pity like the pity of God.
Ah, awful weight! Infinity
Pressed down upon the finite Me!
My anguished spirit, like a bird,

Beating against my lips I heard;
Yet lay the weight so close about
There was no room for it without.
And so beneath the weight lay I
And suffered death, but could not die.

Long had I lain thus, craving death,
When quietly the earth beneath
Gave way, and inch by inch, so great
At last had grown the crushing weight,
Into the earth I sank till I

Full six feet under ground did lie,
And sank no more,—there is no weight
Can follow here, however great.
From off my breast I felt it roll,
And as it went my tortured soul

Burst forth and fled in such a gust
That all about me swirled the dust.
Deep in the earth I rested now;
Cool is its hand upon the brow
And soft its breast beneath the head

Of one who is so gladly dead.
And all at once, and over all
The pitying rain began to fall;
I lay and heard each pattering hoof
Upon my lowly, thatchèd roof,
And seemed to love the sound far more
Than ever I had done before.
For rain it hath a friendly sound
To one who's six feet under ground;
And scarce the friendly voice or face:

A grave is such a quiet place.

The rain, I said, is kind to come
And speak to me in my new home.
I would I were alive again
To kiss the fingers of the rain,

To drink into my eyes the shine
Of every slanting silver line,
To catch the freshened, fragrant breeze
From drenched and dripping apple-trees.
For soon the shower will be done,

And then the broad face of the sun
Will laugh above the rain-soaked earth
Until the world with answering mirth
Shakes joyously, and each round drop
Rolls, twinkling, from its grass-blade top.

How can I bear it; buried here,
While overhead the sky grows clear
And blue again after the storm?
O, multi-colored, multiform,
Beloved beauty over me,

That I shall never, never see
Again! Spring-silver, autumn-gold,
That I shall never more behold!

Sleeping your myriad magics through,
Close-sepulchred away from you!
O God, I cried, give me new birth,
And put me back upon the earth!
Upset each cloud's gigantic gourd
And let the heavy rain, down-poured
In one big torrent, set me free,

Washing my grave away from me!

I ceased; and through the breathless hush
That answered me, the far-off rush
Of herald wings came whispering
Like music down the vibrant string

Of my ascending prayer, and—crash!
Before the wild wind's whistling lash
The startled storm-clouds reared on high
And plunged in terror down the sky,
And the big rain in one black wave

Fell from the sky and struck my grave.
I know not how such things can be;
I only know there came to me
A fragrance such as never clings
To aught save happy living things;

A sound as of some joyous elf
Singing sweet songs to please himself,
And, through and over everything,
A sense of glad awakening.
The grass, a-tiptoe at my ear,

Whispering to me I could hear;
I felt the rain's cool finger-tips
Brushed tenderly across my lips,
Laid gently on my sealèèd sight,
And all at once the heavy night

Fell from my eyes and I could see,—
A drenched and dripping apple-tree,
A last long line of silver rain,
A sky grown clear and blue again.
And as I looked a quickening gust

Of wind blew up to me and thrust
Into my face a miracle
Of orchard-breath, and with the smell,—
I know not how such things can be!—
I breathed my soul back into me.

Ah! Up then from the ground sprang I
And hailed the earth with such a cry
As is not heard save from a man
Who has been dead, and lives again.
About the trees my arms I wound

Like one gone mad I hugged the ground;
I raised my quivering arms on high;
I laughed and laughed into the sky,
Till at my throat a strangling sob
Caught fiercely, and a great heart-throb

Sent instant tears into my eyes;
O God, I cried, no dark disguise
Can e'er hereafter hide from me
Thy radiant identity!
Thou canst not move across the grass
But my quick eyes will see Thee pass,
Nor speak, however silently,
But my hushed voice will answer Thee.
I know the path that tells Thy way
Through the cool eve of every day;

God, I can push the grass apart
And lay my finger on Thy heart!

The world stands out on either side
No wider than the heart is wide;
Above the world is stretched the sky,—

No higher than the soul is high.
The heart can push the sea and land
Farther away on either hand;
The soul can split the sky in two,
And let the face of God shine through.

But East and West will pinch the heart
That can not keep them pushed apart;
And he whose soul is flat—the sky
Will cave in on him by and by.
www.barleby.com

Marianne Moore

(1887-1972)

Marianne Moore once wrote that poems were "imaginary gardens with real toads in them." Her poems are conversational, yet elaborate and subtle in their syllabic versification, drawing upon extremely precise description and historical and scientific fact. A "poet's poet,"

© Arttoday.com

she influenced such later poets as her young friend Elizabeth Bishop. In his 1925 essay "Marianne Moore," William Carlos Williams wrote about Moore's style: Moore guides the reader into minute details ". . . in looking at some apparently small object, one feels the swirl of great events."

Langston Hughes

(1902-1967)

© Arttoday.com

One of many talented poets of the Harlem Renaissance of the 1920s, in the company of James Weldon Johnson and others, was Langston Hughes. He embraced African American jazz rhythms and was one of the first black writers to attempt to make a profitable career out of his writing. Hughes incorporated blues, spirituals, colloquial speech, and folkways in his poetry. Hughes was part of the Great Migration. For many blacks, the years after the Civil War were very much like the years before the Civil War. While they were legally free, economically and socially they were still in bondage. "Jim Crow" laws made sure of this. The demon of racism manifested itself in unjust laws promulgated by white governments to maintain its hegemony over its black population.

CRITICAL THINKING

A. Ezra Pound was a notorious racist and supporter of the Nazi party in Germany. Do you see evidence of his racism in his poems? Should we avoid reading his poetry because he is a racist?

B. Agree or disagree with each critic below:

At his best, of course, Frost does not philosophize.

The anecdote is absorbed into symbol. The method of indirection operates fully: the senses of realistic detail, the air of casual comment, are employed to build up and intensify a serious effect. (Cleanth Brooks, *Modern Poetry*, p. 113)

Despite his great virtues, you cannot read a great deal of Frost without this effect of the *deja vu*. Sententiousness and a relative absence of formal daring are his main defects. Even in his finest work, the conventionality of rhythm and rhyme contributes a certain tedium, temporarily relegated to a dim corner of the reader's consciousness. (M.L. Rosenthal, *The Modern Poets*, pp. 112-113)

C. Read "Home Burial" and "Death of a Hired Hand" by Robert Frost—another New England writer— and compare the themes of these poems with *Ethan Frome*, Edith Wharton. Identify elements of naturalism and realism in these literary works. How does nature function in these two writer's prose/poetry? How does each author use irony? Why is irony a particularly effective literary device for naturalistic writers to use?

D. Read as many of Langston Hughes' poems as you can. Do you find examples of anger in his poetry? Explain.

E. Compare and contrast "Cassandra," "Richard Cory," and "Mr. Flood's Party" by Edwin Arlington Robinson.

F. Some scholars argue that Edna St. Vincent Millay is a second-rate poet. What do you think about this criticism?

G. In Robert Frost's poem *Fire and Ice*, what is the speaker's tone of voice in the first two lines? Is it surprising? How does his tone suit or contrast with the content of what he is saying? What gives the poetry its power?

ENRICHMENT

You are retained by a major publisher to put together an anthology of the best American poetry of the 20th century. What 5 American poets and poems would you include and why?

FINAL PROJECT

Correct and rewrite all essays and place them in your Final Portfolio.

SUGGESTED
Weekly *Implementation*

DAY 1	DAY 2	DAY 3	DAY 4	DAY 5
Prayer journal. Review the required reading(s) *before* the assigned lesson begins. Teacher may want to discuss assigned reading(s) with students. Teacher and students will decide on required essays for this lesson, choosing two or three essays. The rest of the essays can be outlined, answered with shorter answers, or skipped. Review all readings for Lesson 21	Prayer journal. Review reading(s) from next lesson. Outline essays due at the end of the week. Per teacher instructions, students may answer orally in a group setting some of the essays that are not assigned as formal essays.	Prayer journal. Write rough drafts of all assigned essays. The teacher and/or a peer evaluator may correct rough drafts.	Prayer journal. Rewrite corrected copies of essays due tomorrow.	Prayer journal. Essays are due. Take Lesson 21 test. Reading ahead: review *A Farewell to Arms*, Ernest Hemingway. Guide: How is the protagonist Frederick Henry in *A Farewell to Arms* similar to Henry Fleming in *A Red Badge of Courage?* Stylistically, how is *A Farewell to Arms* similar to *The Adventures of Huckleberry Finn?*

THE MODERN AGE, 1915-1946: LATE ROMANTICISM/ NATURALISM *(Part 3)*

A Farewell to Arms

Ernest Hemingway (1929)

BACKGROUND

A Farewell to Arms is a powerful story. Wrought with naturalism, the vision of Ernest Hemingway is a bleak one. The following quote is from the end of *A Farewell to Arms:*

> "Once in camp I put a log on top of the fire and it was full of ants. As it commenced to burn, the ants swarmed out and went first toward the centre where the fire was; then turned back and ran toward the end. When there were enough on the end they fell off into the fire. Some got out, their bodies burnt and flattened, and went off not knowing where they were going. But most of them went toward the fire and then back toward the end and swarmed on the cool end and finally fell off into the fire. I remember thinking at the time that it was the end of the world. . . That was what you did. You died. You did not now what it was about. You never had time to learn. They threw you in and told you the rules and the first time they caught you off base they killed you . . . You could count on that. Stay around and they would kill you."

Americans have journeyed a long way from the Christian theism of Jonathan Edwards. Unfortunately, the naturalism of Ernest Hemingway is quite close to the contemporary American vision.

The Hemingway story is the post-World War I story. The period between the two world wars was the United States' traumatic "coming of age," despite the fact that U.S. direct involvement was relatively brief (1917-1918) and its casualties many fewer than those of its European allies and foes. Entering World War I, the war to "end all wars," the horror of trench warfare dis-

You will analyze: *A Farewell to Arms*, by Ernest Hemingway.

Reading Ahead: Review *Their Eyes Were Watching God*, Zora Neale Hurston.

Guide Question: How does Janie develop as a character?

illusioned a generation. The American author John Dos Passos expressed America's postwar disillusionment in the novel *Three Soldiers* (1921), when he noted that civilization was a "vast edifice of sham, and the war, instead of its crumbling, was its fullest and most ultimate expression." Shocked and permanently changed, Americans returned to their homeland but could never regain their innocence. The carnage of World War I had permanently changed the American heart.

Many returning farm-boy soldiers moved into the city. Millions of southern African Americans moved into Northern urban centers. For the first time, many Americans enrolled in higher education—in the 1920s college enrollment doubled. For the first time colleges had more applicants than places available. Americans experienced a cultural revolution when the radio and

electric lights were added to their homes. Like the businessman protagonist of Sinclair Lewis's novel *Babbitt* (1922), the average American approved of new conveniences because they were modern and because most were American inventions and American-made. Most people went to the movies once a week. Prohibition—a nationwide ban on the production, transport, and sale of alcohol instituted through the 18th Amendment to the U.S. Constitution—began in 1919,

© Arttoday.com

introducing underground "speakeasies" and nightclubs, featuring jazz music, cocktails, and daring modes of dress and dance. Dancing, movie going, automobile touring, and radio were national crazes. American women, in particular, felt liberated. Many had left farms and villages for home-front duty in American cities during World War I and had become resolutely modern. They cut their hair short ("bobbed"), wore short "flapper" dresses, and gloried in the right to vote assured by the 19th Amendment to the Constitution, passed in 1920. They boldly spoke their mind and took public roles in society. My own grandmother, Helen Stobaugh, did something unthinkable earlier in the century: She divorced her first husband! She was a 1920 flapper!

A new, liberated world was dawning in America. Youths, too, were rebelling, angry and disillusioned with the savage war, the older generation they held responsible, and difficult postwar economic conditions that, ironically, allowed Americans with dollars—like writers F. Scott Fitzgerald, Ernest Hemingway, Gertrude Stein, and Ezra Pound—to live overseas on very little money. Intellectual currents, particularly Freudian psychology and to a lesser extent Marxism (like the earlier Darwinian theory of evolution), implied a "godless" worldview and contributed to the breakdown of traditional values. Totalitarianism was growing in Italy and Germany and was openly embraced by intellectuals like Ezra Pound. Americans abroad absorbed these views and brought them back to the United States, firing the imagination of young writers and artists. William Faulkner, for example,

employed Freudian elements in all his works, as did virtually all serious American fiction writers after World War I. Faulkner was an existentialist—someone who put a lot of emphasis on experience. For the first time Americans were having "an identity crisis." Despite outward unparalleled material prosperity, young Americans of the 1920s were the first of many on "the lost generations"—so named by essayist Gertrude Stein. As Bob Dylan expressed the soul of the later generation, Hemingway's *The Sun Also Rises* (1926) and Fitzgerald's *This Side of Paradise* (1920) decried the extravagance and disillusionment of their lost generation. In T.S. Eliot's long poem *The Waste Land* (1922), Western civilization was symbolized by a bleak desert in desperate need of rain (spiritual renewal). The following is a portion of T. S. Eliot's poem "The Love Song of J. Alfred Prufrock."

F. Scott Fitzgerald and his wife Zelda

The Love Song of J. Alfred Prufrock

http://www.classicreader.com/read.php/sid.1/bookid.8/sec.13/

Let us go then, you and I,
When the evening is spread out against the sky
Like a patient etherized upon a table;
Let us go, through certain half-deserted streets,
The muttering retreats
Of restless nights in one-night cheap hotels
And sawdust restaurants with oyster-shells:
Streets that follow like a tedious argument
Of insidious intent
To lead you to an overwhelming question....
Oh, do not ask, "What is it?"
Let us go and make our visit.

In the room the women come and go
Talking of Michelangelo.

The yellow fog that rubs its back upon the window-
   panes,
The yellow smoke that rubs its muzzle on the window-
   panes

Licked its tongue into the corners of the evening,
Lingered upon the pools that stand in drains,
Let fall upon its back the soot that falls from
   chimneys,
Slipped by the terrace, made a sudden leap,
And seeing that it was a soft October night,
Curled once about the house, and fell asleep.

And indeed there will be time
For the yellow smoke that slides along the street,
Rubbing its back upon the window panes;
There will be time, there will be time
To prepare a face to meet the faces that you meet
There will be time to murder and create,
And time for all the works and days of hands
That lift and drop a question on your plate;
Time for you and time for me,
And time yet for a hundred indecisions,
And for a hundred visions and revisions,
Before the taking of a toast and tea.

The prosperity of the 1920s was a distant memory in 1929 when the stock market crashed. The ensuing world depression of the 1930s affected most of the United States. Workers lost their jobs, and factories shut down; businesses and banks failed; farmers could not pay their debts and lost their farms. Midwestern droughts turned the "breadbasket" of America into a dust bowl. Many farmers left the Midwest for California in search of jobs, as vividly described in John Steinbeck's *The Grapes of Wrath* (1939). At the peak of the Depression, one-third of all Americans were out of work. Soup kitchens, shanty towns, and armies of hobos became part of national life. Hard times had hit America and deeply affected American literature and culture.

Hemingway saying good-bye to his family as he goes to Italy to fight in World War I.

ABOUT THE AUTHOR

Born in Oak Park, IL, in 1899, Ernest Hemingway served in World War I as an ambulance driver with the Italian army. The story in this book is approximately autobiographical. After the war, Hemingway joined other expatriates in Paris. He served as a war correspondent during the Spanish Civil War and World War II. Hemingway was a disturbed man, and in 1961 committed suicide.

OTHER NOTABLE WORKS

The Sun Also Rises (1926)
The Old Man and the Sea (1952)

SUGGESTED VOCABULARY WORDS

Chapter VII feigned
Chapter XV felicitations

CRITICAL THINKING

A. Who is the narrator of *A Farewell to Arms*? What effect does this form of narration have on the story?

B. Hemingway writes in a journalistic *style*. Give examples of this style and contrast it to the style that we read in *The Scarlet Letter*.

C. Hemingway's vision was deeply impacted by Social Darwinism and to a lesser degree by the philosopher Frederick Nietzsche. In his book *The Meaning of Evolution*, George Gaylord Simpson writes: "Man is the result of a purposeless and materialistic process that did not have him in mind. He was not planned . . . discovery that the universe . . . lacked any purpose or plan has the inevitable corollary that the workings of the universe cannot provide any automatic, universal, eternal, or absolute criteria of Right and wrong." Find evidence of this worldview in this book.

D. Critics have suggested that Hemingway calls his character Henry because he wants to compare him with Henry Fleming in *The Red Badge of Courage*. Compare and contrast these two literary characters.

E. Many find Hemingway's vision of truth to be quite disturbing—in fact rather hopeless. What about you? Evidence your views from the text.

Narrator: The person who tells a story. The author can use several point of view techniques: first person (I . . .), third person (observer only—we do not see inside any character's mind), limited omniscient (we see into the mind of only one character), or omniscient (we see inside the mind of all characters).

F. Hemingway uses several characters—e.g., Rinaldi and Ferguson—to develop his main characters. These characters are called *foils*. Tell how Hemingway uses these foils.

G. The British historian Paul Johnson and other historians argue that the decline and ultimately the collapse of the religious impulse would leave a huge vacuum. They suggest that the way this vacuum is filled is the story of the modern world. Agree or disagree with this theory and evidence your answer by referencing *A Farewell to Arms*.

BIBLICAL APPLICATION

Catherine and Henry sin—openly and without apology. What does the Bible say about fornication? Is there any justification for their actions?

ENRICHMENT

A. Write a report on World War I.

B. Research Hemingway's life. How autobiographical was this book?

C. In his book *Modern Art and the Death of Culture*, H. R. Rookmaaker—who was deeply influenced by Francis Shaeffer—argues that art has experienced four stages:

1. **Pre-enlightenment (Middle Ages to 18th Century).** Reflects a belief in an ordered universe, transcendent values, and absolute morality.

2. **Enlightenment Art (18th Century).** Reflects Naturalism. Art ceases to reflect transcendent convictions. The seeds of modern art are planted.

3. **Impressionism (19th century).** Reflects the sense experience between painter and object. Feelings are important.

4. **Absurdism (early 20th century).** Reflects an admission that there is no meaning.

Based on what you have studied this year, in what ways does Western literature mirror the same stages?

D. Compare and contrast the beginning of Stephen Crane's *A Red Badge of Courage* and the beginning of *A Farewell to Arms*.

The cold passed reluctantly from the earth, and the retiring fogs revealed an army stretched out on the hills, resting. As the landscape changed from brown to green, the army awakened, and began to tremble with eagerness at the noise of rumors. It cast its eyes upon the roads, which were growing from long troughs of liquid mud to proper thoroughfares. A river, amber-tinted in the shadow of its banks, purled at the army's feet; and at night, when the stream had become of a sorrowful blackness, one could see across it the red, eyelike gleam of hostile camp-fires set in the low brows of distant hills.

Once a certain tall soldier developed virtues and went resolutely to wash a shirt. He came flying back from a brook waving his garment bannerlike. He was swelled with a tale he had heard from a reliable friend, who had heard it from a truthful cavalryman, who had heard it from his trustworthy brother, one of the orderlies at division headquarters. He adopted the important air of a herald in red and gold.

"We're goin' t' move t'morrah—sure," he said pompously to a group in the company street. "We're goin' 'way up the river, cut across, an' come around in behint 'em."

To his attentive audience he drew a loud and elaborate plan of a very brilliant campaign. When he had finished, the blue-clothed men scattered into small arguing groups between the rows of squat brown huts. A Negro teamster who had been dancing upon a cracker box with the hilarious encouragement of twoscore soldiers was deserted. He sat mournfully down. Smoke drifted lazily from a multitude of quaint chimneys.

"It's a lie! that's all it is—a thunderin' lie!" said another private loudly. His smooth face was flushed, and his hands were thrust sulkily into his trouser's pockets. He took the matter as an affront to him. "I don't believe the derned old army's ever going to move. We're set. I've got ready to move eight times in the last two weeks, and we ain't moved yet."

The tall soldier felt called upon to defend the truth of a rumor he himself had introduced. He and the loud one came near to fighting over it.

A corporal began to swear before the assemblage. He had just put a costly board floor in his house, he said. During the early spring he had refrained from adding extensively to the comfort of his environment because he had felt that the army might start on the march at any moment. Of late, however, he had been impressed that they were in a sort of eternal camp.

Many of the men engaged in a spirited debate. One outlined in a peculiarly lucid manner all the plans of the commanding general. He was opposed by men who advocated that there were other plans of campaign. They clamored at each other, numbers making futile bids for the popular attention. Meanwhile, the soldier who had fetched the rumor bustled about with much importance. He was continually assailed by questions.

"What's up, Jim?"

"Th' army's goin' t' move."

"Ah, what yeh talkin' about? How yeh know it is?"

"Well, yeh kin b'lieve me er not, jest as yeh like. I don't care a hang." There was much food for thought in the manner in which he replied. He came near to convincing them by disdaining to produce proofs. They grew much excited over it.

There was a youthful private who listened with eager ears to the words of the tall soldier and to the varied comments of his comrades. After receiving a fill of discussions concerning marches and attacks, he went to his hut and crawled through an intricate hole that served it as a door. He wished to be alone with some new thoughts that had lately come to him. He lay down on a wide bunk that stretched across the end of the room. In the other end, cracker boxes were made to serve as furniture. They were grouped about the fireplace. A picture from an illustrated weekly was upon the log walls, and three rifles were paralleled on pegs. Equipments hung on handy projections, and some tin dishes lay upon a small pile of firewood. A folded tent was serving as a roof. The sunlight, without, beating upon it, made it glow a light yellow shade. A small window shot an oblique square of whiter light upon the cluttered floor. The smoke from the fire at times neglected the clay chimney and wreathed into the room, and this flimsy chimney of clay and sticks made endless threats to set ablaze the whole establishment.

The youth was in a little trance of astonishment. So they were at last going to fight. On the morrow, perhaps, there would be a battle, and he would be in it. For a time he was obliged to labor to make himself believe. He could not accept with assurance an omen that he was about to mingle in one of those great affairs of the earth.

He had, of course, dreamed of battles all his life — of vague and bloody conflicts that had thrilled him with their sweep and fire. In visions he had seen himself in many struggles. He had imagined peoples secure in the shadow of his eagle-eyed prowess. But awake he had regarded battles as crimson blotches on the pages of the past. He had put them as things of the bygone with his thought-images of heavy crowns and high castles. There was a portion of the world's history which he had regarded as the time of wars, but it, he thought, had been long gone over the horizon and had disappeared forever.

From his home his youthful eyes had looked upon the war in his own country with distrust. It must be some sort of a play affair. He had long despaired of witnessing a Greeklike struggle. Such would be no more, he had said. Men were better, or more timid. Secular and religious education had effaced the throat-grappling instinct, or else firm finance held in check the passions.

http://wyllie.lib.virginia.edu:8086/perl/toccer-new?id=CraRedb.sgm&images=images/modeng&data=texts/english/modeng/parsed&tag=public&part=1&di

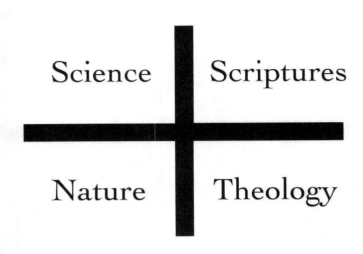

G. In her book *On Looking into the Abyss*, Gertrude Himmelfarb argues that in the field of literature the great works are no longer read—or if they are, there are essentially no rules for interpreting them; in philosophy, truth and reality are considered non-existent. In historical studies the historian comes to any conclusions he chooses. Some philosophers call this view *nihilism*. In what way does Himmelfarb capture the world of Catherine and Henry?

H. Hemingway argued that no new novel had been written since Twain wrote *Huckleberry Finn*. In what ways are *A Farewell* and *Huckleberry Finn* similar? Explore the realism used in both novels.

I. In his book *Not the Way it is Supposed to Be: A Breviary of Sin*, Cornelius Plantinga argues we need a healthy reminder of our sin and guilt. Not only do we need a healthy reminder of how sin affects us personally, we must remember that the truth of traditional Christianity saws against the grain of much in contemporary culture and therefore needs constant sharpening. In light of the sinful life that Catherine and Henry lived, and the results of that sin, what application does Plantinga's view have on this hapless couple?

FINAL PORTFOLIO

Correct and re-write required essays and place in your Portfolio.

E. Write an alternative ending to this book.

F. Hemingway was a Hegelian. The philosopher Hegel believed strongly in the dialectic. He starts with a thesis (a position put forward for argument). Opposed to this is a contradictory statement or antithesis. Out of their opposition comes a synthesis which embraces both. But since the truth lies only in the whole system, this first synthesis is not yet the truth of the matter, but becomes a new thesis, with its corresponding antithesis and synthesis. And so on. Truth, then, is not absolute and is always open to interpretation. Truth lies in the "search" in the "system." Find examples of Hegelian thought in Hemingway's writings.

SUGGESTED
Weekly *Implementation*

DAY 1	DAY 2	DAY 3	DAY 4	DAY 5
Prayer journal.	**Prayer journal.**	**Prayer journal.**	**Prayer journal.**	**Prayer journal.**
Review the required reading(s) *before* the assigned lesson begins.	Review reading(s) from next lesson.	Write rough drafts of all assigned essays.	Rewrite corrected copies of essays due tomorrow.	Essays are due.
Teacher may want to discuss assigned reading(s) with students.	Outline essays due at the end of the week.	The teacher and/or a peer evaluator may correct rough drafts.		Take Lesson 22 test.
Teacher and students will decide on required essays for this lesson, choosing two or three essays.	Per teacher instructions, students may answer orally in a group setting some of the essays that are not assigned as formal essays.			Reading ahead: Review *Their Eyes Were Watching God*, Zora Neale Hurston.
The rest of the essays can be outlined, answered with shorter answers, or skipped.				Guide: How does Janie develop as a character?
Review all readings for Lesson 22.				

THE MODERN AGE, 1915-1946: LATE ROMANTICISM/ NATURALISM (Part 4)

Their Eyes Were Watching God

Zora Neale Hurston (1937)

Students will analyze: *Their Eyes Were Watching God*, Zora Neale Hurston.

Reading Ahead: *The Unvanquished*, William Faulkner.

Guide Question: Is Bayard a Romantic? Naturalist? Realist?

BACKGROUND

Zora Neale Hurston was born around 1900 in Alabama but moved when she was still very young to Eatonville, Florida. For the rest of her life she explored the mystery of being born in and then living for the majority of her life in this small town. She died January 28, 1960.

Hurston was an American folk writer, whose works influenced a generation of African-American authors; she wrote an anthropological study of her racial heritage at a time when African-American culture was not a popular field of study.

Hurston was a member of the Harlem Renaissance, an African American cultural movement of the late 1920s and early 1930s in the Harlem section of New York City. For the first time, African-American literature attracted significant attention. African-American artists shared a strong sense of racial pride. Major prose writers in the movement were W. E. B. Du Bois and Langston Hughes. Thurston profoundly influenced the Harlem Renaissance writers of the 1930s and was influenced by them. She also greatly inspired later African-American authors such as Toni Morrison. However, this theistic writer wrote with spirit and joy absent from so many writers like Ralph Ellison and Tony Morrison.

Hurston was educated at Howard University, at Barnard College, and at Columbia University. Like Ashley Bryan, Zora Hurston collected African-American folklore. *Mules and Men* (1935), one of her best known folklore collections, was based on her field research in the American South. *Tell My Horse* (1938) described folk customs in Haiti and Jamaica. Her best known novel is *Their Eyes Were Watching God* (1937), in which she tracked a Southern black woman's search, over 25 years and 3 marriages, for her true identity and a community in which she could develop that identity.

OTHER WORLDS

Mules and Men (1935)

CRITICAL THINKING

A. Discuss the form that Hurston employs to tell her story. What are advantages and disadvantages of using this form?

B. Hurston was a highly educated African-American woman, yet she wrote in an African-American dialect. Why?

C. Discuss Hurston's narrative technique.

D. What are two themes in this book? How does Hurston develop them?

BIBLICAL APPLICATION

Draw parallels between Janie's life and Hannah's life.

ENRICHMENT

A. Zora Neale Hurston's protagonist and her family had very little to do with the white community. In fact Hurston says very little about interactions between the races (the main source of prejudice is exhibited by another African-American, Mrs. Turner). How have other American authors handled race-mixing in American culture?

B. William Faulkner, another southern author, describes race relations in this way:

> There are two of them . . . Uncle Buck and Uncle Buddy . . . They lived in a two-room log house with about a dozen dogs, and they kept the niggers in the manor house. It don't have any windows now and a child with a hairpin could unlock any lock in it, but every night when the niggers come up from the fields Uncle Buck or Uncle Buddy would drive them into the house and lock the door with a key almost as big as a horse pistol; probably they would still be locking the front door long after the last nigger has escaped out the back. And folks said that Uncle Buck and Uncle Buddy knew this and that the niggers knew that they knew it . . . ("The Country Shall not Perish," in Collected Stories, New York: Random House, 1971, 114-115.

Faulkner saw race relations in what historians call "paternalism." What is paternalism and what is disturbing about this view of race relations?

FINAL PROJECT

Correct and rewrite all essays and place them in your Final Portfolio.

SUGGESTED
Weekly *Implementation*

DAY 1	DAY 2	DAY 3	DAY 4	DAY 5
Prayer journal. Review the required reading(s) *before* the assigned lesson begins. Teacher may want to discuss assigned reading(s) with students. Teacher and students will decide on required essays for this lesson, choosing two or three essays. The rest of the essays can be outlined, answered with shorter answers, or skipped. Review all readings for Lesson 23.	**Prayer journal.** Review reading(s) from next lesson. Outline essays due at the end of the week. Per teacher instructions, students may answer orally in a group setting some of the essays that are not assigned as formal essays.	**Prayer journal.** Write rough drafts of all assigned essays. The teacher and/or a peer evaluator may correct rough drafts.	**Prayer journal.** Rewrite corrected copies of essays due tomorrow.	**Prayer journal.** Essays are due. Take Lesson 23 test. Reading Ahead: Review *The Unvanquished*, William Faulkner. Guide: Is Bayard a Romantic? Naturalist? Realist?

THE MODERN AGE, 1915-1946: LATE ROMANTICISM/ NATURALISM *(Part 5)*

The Unvanquished

William Faulkner (1934)

BACKGROUND

The Unvanquished is not the best book written by William Faulkner— arguably the best novelist in all of world history— but it is one of his best and one of his most readable. The story occurs during the Civil War and begins the Sartoris legends.

ABOUT THE AUTHOR

Faulkner (1897-1962) came from an old Mississippi family alive with Southern tradition. He created a fictional location, Yoknapatawpha County, which captured the essence of Southern life. Faulkner was a prolific writer and has left our nation with a rich corpus of literature.

OTHER NOTABLE WORKS

The Sound and the Fury (1929)
Light in August (1932)

VOCABULARY WORDS

Chapter	Word
I, 2	impunity *(immunity)*
	dispensation *(allocation)*
II, 2	cajoling *(coaxing)*
	annihilation *(destruction)*
	inviolate *(hallowed)*

You will analyze: *The Unvanquished* and "The Tall Men," William Faulkner.

Reading Ahead: *The Pearl,* John Steinbeck.

Guide Question: What themes does Steinbeck develop in this short novel?

Setting: the time, place, and general environment in which a piece of fiction occurs.

CRITICAL THINKING

A. Why is the setting so important to this story?

B. What is the point of view? Why does it make this book more effective?

C. Faulkner's prose is so powerful that it seems like poetry, a technique accomplished by his puissant imagery. Search for examples of this imagery in the text.

> Imagery: concrete words or details that appeal to the senses.

D. On the other hand, there is a great deal of colloquial language in this story. How important is the informal language? How important is the use of a Southern dialect? How do you feel about Faulkner's frequent use of the word *nigger*?

E. Who is the main character? Granny? Bayard? Colonel Sartoris? Defend your answer.

F. The chapter "An Odor of Verbena" has been criticized as being an entirely different story, or a story within a story. Some critics wonder if it really belongs. What do you think? Why?

BIBLICAL APPLICATION

Faulkner discusses in great detail the whole issue of "family sin." In one novel, *Absalom, Absalom*, he blames the destruction of an entire family upon the sins of a father. The Snopes—an unprincipled, materialistic family—are the natural result of the South (see *The Hamlet*, *The Town*, and *The Mansion*). Like rats in an empty house, they move in and take over as the moneyed, educated aristocracy self-destructs. In this book, Bayard and the Sartoris family are in a steady but definite decline. Compare the results of David and Bathsheba's relationship with what Faulkner's characters experience.

ENRICHMENT

The writing of history is the selection of information and the synthesis of this information into a narrative that will stand the critical eye of time. However, history is never static. One never creates the definitive theory of an historical event. Some historians invite each generation to re-examine its own story and to reinterpret past events in light of present circumstances.

The creation of this story is more difficult than it seems. From the beginning the historian is forced to decide what sort of human motivations matter most: Economic? Political? Religious?

For instance, what causes the American Revolution? The historian Bernard Bailyn argues that ideology or the history of thought causes the American Revolution. Historian Oscar Handlin argues the Revolution is caused by social upheaval (i.e., the dislocation of groups and classes of people). Sydney Ahlstrom argues that religion is an important cause of the American Revolution. The historian will look at several theories of history and primary source material and then decide for himself what really happened, sometimes resulting in what is called "revisionist" history.

The Tall Men

CRITICAL THINKING

A. Compare and contrast the worldview of the state draft investigator and the marshal.

B. Why is Faulkner's title for this story appropriate?

C. Describe Faulkner's narrative technique. How does it enhance his story?

D. Even though very little real action occurs in this story, the plot develops very well. How does Faulkner accomplish this development?

E. Compare and contrast in style and substance this short story with *Unvanquished*.

ENRICHMENT

A. To Faulkner, and to most southerners, land, people, and history were vital. In that context, what does Faulkner mean in the following quote? "And I knew them too. I had seen them too, who had never been further . . . than I could return by night to sleep. It was these places . . . the places that men and women have lived in and loved whether they had anything to paint pictures of them or not, all the little places quiet enough to be lived in and loved and the names of them before they were quiet enough, and the names of the deeds that made them quiet enough and the names of the men and the women who did the deeds, who lasted and endured and fought the battles and lost them and fought again because they didn't even know they had been whipped, and tamed the wilderness and overpassed the mountains and deserts and died and still went on as the shape of the United States grew and went on. I knew them too: the men and women still powerful seventy-five years and twice that and twice that again afterward, still powerful and still dangerous and still coming, North and South and East and West, until the name of what they did and what they died for became just one single word, louder than any thunder. It was America, and it covered all the western earth." (William Faulkner, "The Country Shall not Perish," in *Collected Stories*, New York: Random House, 1971, 114-115.)

B. Most of us think that writing history is pretty simple: we merely find out what happened and write down the facts, but it isn't that simple. The reason the Civil War occurred is open to great debate. To some, the war resulted from a conspiracy of slave owners committed to an immoral institution; others depicted an aggressive North determined to destroy the South—slavery was not the cause of the war. Later slavery expansion was seen as the cause;

still others argued for states' rights. What do you think? Research the causes of the Civil War as depicted through literature as well as through historical accounts.

C. William Faulkner was deeply influenced by the American short story writer Sherwood Anderson. In a one to two page essay, discuss similarities between the following short story and "The Tall Men."

The New Englander

Sherwood Anderson

http://www.angeltowns.com/

Elsie Leander and her girlhood was spent on her father's farm in Vermont. For several generations the Leanders had all lived on the same farm and had all married thin women, and so she was thin. The farm lay in the shadow of a mountain and the soil was not very rich. From the beginning and for several generations there had been a great many sons and few daughters in the family. The sons had gone west or to New York City and the daughters had stayed at home and thought such thoughts as come to New England women who see the sons of their father's neighbour slipping, away, one by one, into the West.

Her father's house was a small white frame affair, and when you went out at the back door, past a small barn and a chicken house, you got into a path that ran up the side of a hill and into an orchard. The trees were all old and gnarled. At the back of the orchard the hill dropped away and bare rocks showed.

Inside the fence a large grey rock stuck high up out of the ground. As Elsie sat with her back to the rock, with a mangled hillside at her feet, she could see several large mountains, apparently but a short distance away, and between herself and the mountains lay many tiny fields surrounded by neatly built stone walls. Everywhere rocks appeared. Large ones, too heavy to be moved, stuck out of the ground in the center of the fields. The fields were like cups filled with a green liquid that turned grey in the fall and white in the winter. The mountains, far off but apparently near at hand, were like giants ready at any moment to reach out their hands and take the cups one by one and drink off the green liquid. The large rocks in the fields were like the thumbs of the giants.

Elsie had three brothers, born ahead of her, but they had all gone away. Two of them had gone to live with her uncle in the West and her elder brother had gone to New York City where he had married and prospered. All through his youth and manhood her father had worked hard and had lived a hard life, but his son in New York City had begun to send money home, and after that things went better. He still worked every day about the barn or in the fields but he did not worry about the future. Elsie's mother did house work in the mornings and in the afternoons sat in a rocking chair in her tiny living room and thought of her sons while she crocheted table covers and tidies for the backs of chairs. She was a silent woman, very thin and with very thin bony hands. She did not ease herself into a rocking chair but sat down and got up suddenly, and when she crocheted her back was as straight as the back of a drill sergeant.

The mother rarely spoke to the daughter. Sometimes in the afternoons as the younger woman went up the hillside to her place by the rock at the back of the orchard, her father came out of the barn and stopped her. He put a hand on her shoulder and asked where she was going. "To the rock," she said and her father laughed. His laughter was like the creaking of a rusty barn door hinge and the hand he had laid on her shoulder was thin like her own hands and like her mother's hands. The father went into the barn shaking his head. "She's like her mother. She is herself like a rock," he thought. At the head of the path that led from the house to the orchard there was a great cluster of bayberry bushes. The New England farmer came out of his barn to watch his daughter go along the path, but she had disappeared behind the bushes. He looked away past his house to the fields and to the mountains in the distance. He also saw the green cup-like fields and the grim mountains. There was an almost imperceptible tightening of the muscles of his half worn-out old body. For a long time he stood in silence and then, knowing from long experience the danger of having thoughts, he went back into the barn and busied himself with the mending of an agricultural tool that had been mended many times before.

The son of the Leanders who went to live in New York City was the father of one son, a thin sensitive boy who looked like Elsie. The son died when he was twenty-three years old and some years later the father died and left his money to the old people on the New England farm. The two Leanders who had gone west had lived there with their father's brother, a farmer, until they grew into manhood. Then Will, the younger, got a job on a railroad. He was killed one winter morning. It was a cold snowy day and when the freight train he was in charge of as conductor left the city of Des Moines, he started to run over the tops of the cars. His feet slipped and he shot down into space. That was the end of him.

Of the new generation there was only Elsie and her brother Tom, whom she had never seen, left alive. Her father and mother talked of going west to Tom for two years before they came to a decision. Then it took another year to dispose of the farm and make preparations. During the whole time Elsie did not think much about the change about to take place in her life.

The trip west on the railroad train jolted Elsie out of herself. In spite of her detached attitude toward life she became excited. Her mother sat up very straight and stiff in the seat in the sleeping car and her father walked up and down in the aisle. After a night when the younger of the two women did not sleep but lay awake with red burning cheeks and with her thin fingers incessantly picking at the bed-clothes in her berth while the train went through towns and cities, crawled up the sides of hills and fell down into forest-clad valleys, she got up and dressed to sit all day looking at a new kind of land. The train ran for a day and through another sleepless night in a flat land where every field was as large as a farm in her own country. Towns appeared and disappeared in a continual procession. The whole land was so unlike anything she had ever known that she began to feel unlike herself. In the valley where she had been born and where she had lived all her days everything had an air of finality. Nothing could be changed. The tiny fields were chained to the earth. They were fixed in their places and surrounded by aged stone walls. The fields like the mountains that looked down at them were as unchangeable as the passing days. She had a feeling they had always been so, would always be so.

Elsie sat like her mother upright in the car seat and with a back like the back of a drill sergeant. The train ran swiftly along through Ohio and Indiana. Her thin hands like her mother's hands were crossed and locked. One passing casually through the car might have thought both women prisoners handcuffed and bound to their seats. Night came on and she again got into her berth. Again she lay awake and her thin cheeks became flushed, but she thought new thoughts. Her hands were no longer gripped together and she did not pick at the bed clothes. Twice during the night she stretched herself and yawned, a thing she had never in her life done before. The train stopped at a town on the prairies, and as there was something the matter with one of the

wheels of the car in which she lay the trainsmen came with flaming torches to tinker it. There was a great pounding and shouting. When the train went on its way she wanted to get out of her berth and run up and down in the aisle of the car. The fancy had come to her that the men tinkering with the car wheel were new men out of the new land who had broken with strong hammers the doors of her prison away. They had destroyed forever the programme she had made for her life.

Elsie was filled with joy at the thought that the train was still going on into the West. She wanted to go on for ever in a straight line into the unknown. She fancied herself no longer on a train and imagined she had become a winged thing flying through space. Her long years of sitting alone by the rock on the New England farm had got her into the habit of expressing her thoughts aloud. Her thin voice broke the silence that lay over the sleeping car and her father and mother, both also lying awake, sat up in their berth to listen.

Tom Leander, the only living male representative of the new generation of Leanders, was a loosely built man of forty inclined to corpulency. At twenty he had married the daughter of a neighboring farmer, and when his wife inherited some money she and Tom moved into the town of Apple Junction in Iowa where Tom opened a grocery. The venture prospered as did Tom's matrimonial venture. When his brother died in New York City and his father, mother, and sister decided to come west Tom was already the father of a daughter and four sons.

On the prairies north of town and in the midst of a vast level stretch of corn fields, there was a partly completed brick house that had belonged to a rich farmer named Russell, who had begun to build the house intending to make it the most magnificent place in the county, but when it was almost completed he had found himself without money and heavily in debt. The farm, consisting of several hundred acres of corn land, had been split into three farms and sold. No one had wanted the huge unfinished brick house. For years it had stood vacant, its windows staring out over the fields that had been planted almost up to the door.

In buying the Russell house Tom was moved by two motives. He had a notion that in New England the Leanders had been rather magnificent people. His memory of his father's place in the Vermont valley was shadowy, but in speaking of it to his wife he became very definite. "We had good blood in us, we Leanders," he said, straightening his shoulders. "We lived in a big house. We were important people."

Wanting his father and mother to feel at home in the new place, Tom had also another motive. He was not a very energetic man and, although he had done well enough as keeper of a grocery, his success was largely due to the boundless energy of his wife. She did not pay much attention to her household and her children, like little animals, had to take care of themselves, but in any matter concerning the store her word was law.

To have his father the owner of the Russell Place Tom felt would establish him as a man of consequence in the eyes of his neighbor. "I can tell you what, they're used to a big house," he said to his wife. "I tell you what, my people are used to living in style."

The exaltation that had come over Elsie on the train wore away in the presence of grey empty Iowa fields, but something of the effect of it remained with her for months. In the big brick house life went on much as it had in the tiny New England house where she had always lived. The Leanders installed themselves in three or four rooms on the ground floor. After a few weeks the furniture that had been shipped by freight arrived and was hauled out from town in one of Tom's grocery wagons. There were three or four acres of ground covered with great piles of boards the unsuccessful farmer had intended to use in the building of stables. Tom sent men to haul the boards away and Elsie's father prepared to plant a garden. They had come west in April and as soon as they were installed in the house ploughing and planting began in the fields near by. The habit of a lifetime returned to the daughter of the house. In the new place there was no gnarled orchard surrounded by a half-ruined stone fence. All of the fences in all of the fields that stretched away out of sight to the north, south, east, and west were made of wire and looked like spider webs against the blackness of the ground when it had been freshly ploughed.

There was, however, the house itself. It was like an island rising out of the sea. In an odd way the house, although it was less than ten years old, was very old. Its unnecessary bigness represented an old impulse in men. Elsie felt that. At the east side there was a door leading to a stairway that ran into the upper part of the house that was kept locked. Two or three stone steps led up to it. Elsie could sit on the top step with her back against the door and gaze into the distance without being disturbed. Almost at her feet began the fields that seemed to go on and on for ever. The fields were like the waters of a sea. Men came to plough and plant. Giant horses moved in a procession across the prairies. A young man who drove six horses came directly toward her. She was fascinated. The breasts of the horses as they came for-

ward with bowed heads seemed like the breasts of giants. The soft spring air that lay over the fields was also like a sea. The horses were giants walking on the floor of a sea. With their breasts they pushed the waters of the sea before them. They were pushing the waters out of the basin of the sea. The young man who drove them was also a giant.

Elsie pressed her body against the closed door at the top of the steps. In the garden back of the house she could hear her father at work. He was raking dry masses of weeds off the ground preparatory to spading the ground for a family garden. He had always worked in a tiny confined place and would do the same thing here. In this vast open place he would work with small tools, doing little things with infinite care, raising little vegetables. In the house her mother would crochet little tidies. She herself would be small. She would press her body against the door of the house, try to get herself out of sight. Only the feeling that sometimes took possession of her, and that did not form itself into a thought, would be large.

The six horses turned at the fence and the outside horse got entangled in the traces. The driver swore vigorously. Then he turned and stared at the pale New Englander and with another oath pulled the heads of the horses about and drove away into the distance. The field in which he was ploughing contained two hundred acres. Elsie did not wait for him to return but went into the house and sat with folded arms in a room. The house she thought was a ship floating in a sea on the floor of which giants went up and down.

May came and then June. In the great fields work was always going on and Elsie became somewhat used to the sight of the young man in the field that came down to the steps. Sometimes when he drove his horses down to the wire fence he smiled and nodded. In the month of August, when it is very hot, the corn in Iowa fields grows until the corn stalks resemble young trees. The corn fields become forests. The time for the cultivating of the corn has passed and weeds grow thick between the corn rows. The men with their giant horses have gone away. Over the immense fields silence broods.

When the time of the laying-by of the crop came that first summer after Elsie's arrival in the West her mind, partially awakened by the strangeness of the railroad trip, awakened again. She did not feel like a staid thin woman with a back like the back of a drill sergeant, but like something new and as strange as the new land into which she had come to live. For a time she did not know what was the matter. In the field the corn had grown so high that she could not see into the distance. The corn was like a wall and the little bare spot of land on which her father's house stood was like a house built behind the walls of a prison. For a time she was depressed, thinking that she had come west into a wide open country, only to find herself locked up more closely than ever.

An impulse came to her. She arose and going down three or four steps seated herself almost on a level with the ground.

Immediately she got a sense of release. She could not see over the corn but she could see under it. The corn had long wide leaves that met over the rows. The rows became long tunnels running away into infinity. Out of the black ground grew weeds that made a soft carpet of green. From above light sifted down. The corn rows were mysteriously beautiful. They were warm passageways running out into life. She got up from the steps, and walking timidly to the wire fence that separated her from the field, put her hand between the wires and took hold of one of the corn stalks. For some reason after she had touched the strong young stalk and had held it for a moment firmly in her hand she grew afraid. Running quickly back to the step she sat down and covered her face with her hands. Her body trembled. She tried to imagine herself crawling through the fence and wandering along one of the passageways. The thought of trying the experiment fascinated but at the same time terrified. She got quickly up and went into the house.

One Saturday night in August Elsie found herself unable to sleep. Thoughts, more definite than any she had ever known before, came into her mind. It was a quiet hot night and her bed stood near a window. Her room was the only one the Leanders occupied on the second floor of the house. At midnight a little breeze came up from the south and when she sat up in bed the floor of corn tassels lying below her line of sight looked in the moonlight like the face of a sea just stirred by a gentle breeze.

A murmuring began in the corn and murmuring thoughts and memories awoke in her mind. The long wide succulent leaves had begun to dry in the intense heat of the August days and as the wind stirred the corn they rubbed against each other. A call, far away, as of a thousand voices arose. She imagined the voices were like the voices of children. They were not like her brother Tom's children, noisy boisterous little animals, but something quite different, tiny little things with large eyes and thin sensitive hands. One after another they crept into her arms. She became so excited over

the fancy that she sat up in bed and taking a pillow into her arms held it against her breast. The figure of her cousin, the pale sensitive young Leander who had lived with his father in New York City and who had died at the age of twenty-three, came sharply into her mind. It was as though the young man had come suddenly into the room. She dropped the pillow and sat waiting, intense, expectant.

Young Harry Leander had come to visit his cousin on the New England farm during the late summer of the year before he died. He had stayed there for a month and almost every afternoon had gone with Elsie to sit by the rock at the back of the orchard. One afternoon when they had both been for a long time silent he began to talk. "I want to go live in the West," he said. "I want to go live in the West. I want to grow strong and be a man," he repeated. Tears came into his eyes.

They got up to return to the house, Elsie walking in silence beside the young man. The moment marked a high spot in her life. A strange trembling eagerness for something she had not realized in her experience of life had taken possession of her. They went in silence through the orchard but when they came to the bayberry bush her cousin stopped in the path and turned to face her. "I want you to kiss me," he said eagerly, stepping toward her.

A fluttering uncertainty had taken possession of Elsie and had been transmitted to her cousin. After he had made the sudden and unexpected demand and had stepped so close to her that his breath could be felt on her cheek, his own cheeks became scarlet and his hand that had taken her hand trembled. "Well, I wish I were strong. I only wish I were strong," he said hesitatingly and turning walked away along the path toward the house. And in the strange new house, set like an island in its sea of corn, Harry Leander's voice seemed to arise again above the fancied voices of the children that had been coming out of the fields. Elsie got out of bed and walked up and down in the dim light coming through the window. Her body trembled violently. "I want you to kiss me," the voice said again and to quiet it and to quiet also the answering voice in herself she went to kneel by the bed and taking the pillow again into her arms pressed it against her face.

Tom Leander came with his wife and family to visit his father and mother on Sundays. The family appeared at about ten o'clock in the morning. When the wagon turned out of the road that ran past the Russell Place Tom shouted. There was a field between the house and the road and the wagon could not be seen as it came along the narrow way through the corn. After Tom had shouted, his daughter Elizabeth, a tall girl of sixteen, jumped out of the wagon. All five children came tearing toward the house through the corn. A series of wild shouts arose on the still morning air.

The grocery man had brought food from the store. When the horse had been unhitched and put into a shed he and his wife began to carry packages into the house. The four Leander boys, accompanied by their sister, disappeared into the near-by fields. Three dogs that had trotted out from town under the wagon accompanied the children. Two or three children and occasionally a young man from a neighboring farm had come to join in the fun. Elsie's sister-in-law dismissed them all with a wave of her hand. With a wave of her hand she also brushed Elsie aside. Fires were lighted and the house reeked with the smell of cooking. Elsie went to sit on the step at the side of the house. The corn fields that had been so quiet rang with shouts and with the barking of dogs.

Tom Leander's oldest child, Elizabeth, was like her mother, full of energy. She was thin and tall like the women of her father's house but very strong and alive. In secret she wanted to be a lady but when she tried her brothers, led by her father and mother, made fun of her. "Don't put on airs," they said. When she got into the country with no one but her brothers and two or three neighboring farm boys she herself became a boy. With the boys she went tearing through the fields, following the dogs in pursuit of rabbits. Sometimes a young man came with the children from a near-by farm. Then she did not know what to do with herself. She wanted to walk demurely along the rows through the corn but was afraid her brothers would laugh and in desperation outdid the boys in roughness and noisiness. She screamed and shouted and running wildly tore her dress on the wire fences as she scrambled over in pursuit of the dogs. When a rabbit was caught and killed she rushed in and tore it out of the grasp of the dogs. The blood of the little dying animal dripped on her clothes. She swung it over her head and shouted.

The farm hand who had worked all summer in the field within sight of Elsie became enamored of the young woman from town. When the grocery man's family appeared on Sunday mornings he also appeared but did not come to the house. When the boys and dogs came tearing through the fields he joined them. He was also self-conscious and did not want the boys to know the purpose of his coming and when he and Elizabeth found themselves alone together he became embarrassed. For a moment they walked together in silence. In a wide circle about them, in the forest of the corn,

ran the boys and dogs. The young man had something he wanted to say, but when he tried to find words his tongue became thick and his lips felt hot and dry. "Well," he began, "let's you and me—me"

Words failed him and Elizabeth turned and ran after her brothers and for the rest of the day he could not manage to get her out of their sight. When he went to join them she became the noisiest member of the party. A frenzy of activity took possession of her. With hair hanging down her back, with clothes torn, and with cheeks and hands scratched and bleeding she led her brothers in the endless wild pursuit of the rabbits.

The Sunday in August that followed Elsie Leander's sleepless night was hot and cloudy. In the morning she was half ill and as soon as the visitors from town arrived she crept away to sit on the step at the side of the house. The children ran away into the fields. An almost overpowering desire to run with them, shouting and playing along the corn rows took possession of her. She arose and went to the back of the house. Her father was at work in the garden, pulling weeds from between rows of vegetables. Inside the house she could hear her sister-in-law moving about. On the front porch her brother Tom was asleep with his mother beside him. Elsie went back on the step and then arose and went to where the corn came down to the fence. She climbed awkwardly over and went a little way along one of the rows. Putting out her hand she touched the firm hard stalks and then, becoming afraid, dropped to her knees on the carpet of weeds that covered the ground. For a long time she stayed thus listening to the voices of the children in the distance.

An hour slipped away. Presently it was time for dinner and her sister-in-law came to the back door and shouted. There was an answering whoop from the distance and the children came running through the fields. They climbed over the fence and ran shouting across her father's garden. Elsie also arose. She was about to attempt to climb back over the fence unobserved when she heard a rustling in the corn. Young Elizabeth Leander appeared. Beside her walked the ploughman who but a few months earlier had planted the corn in the field where Elsie now stood. She could see the two people coming slowly along the rows. An understanding had been established between them. The man reached through between the corn stalks and touched the hand of the girl who laughed awkwardly and running to the fence climbed quickly over. In her hand she held the limp body of a rabbit the dogs had killed.

The farm hand went away and when Elizabeth had gone into the house Elsie climbed over the fence. Her niece stood just within the kitchen door holding the dead rabbit by one leg. The other leg had been torn away by the dogs. At sight of the New England woman, who seemed to look at her with hard unsympathetic eyes, she was ashamed and went quickly into the house. She threw the rabbit upon a table in the parlor and then ran out of the room. Its blood ran out on the delicate flowers of a white crocheted table cover that had been made by Elsie's mother.

The Sunday dinner with all the living Leanders gathered about the table was gone through in a heavy lumbering silence. When the dinner was over and Tom and his wife had washed the dishes they went to sit with the older people on the front porch. Presently they were both asleep. Elsie returned to the step at the side of the house but when the desire to go again into the cornfields came sweeping over her she got up and went indoors.

The woman of thirty-five tip-toed about the big house like a frightened child. The dead rabbit that lay on the table in the parlor had become cold and stiff. Its blood had dried on the white table cover. She went upstairs but did not go to her own room. A spirit of adventure had hold of her. In the upper part of the house there were many rooms and in some of them no glass had been put into the windows. The windows had been boarded up and narrow streaks of light crept in through the cracks between the boards.

Elsie tip-toed up the flight of stairs past the room in which she slept and opening doors went into other rooms. Dust lay thick on the floors. In the silence she could hear her brother snoring as he slept in the chair on the front porch. From what seemed a far away place there came the shrill cries of the children. The cries became soft. They were like the cries of unborn children that had called to her out of the fields on the night before. Into her mind came the intense silent figure of her mother sitting on the porch beside her son and waiting for the day to wear itself out into night. The thought brought a lump into her throat. She wanted something and did not know what it was. Her own mood frightened her. In a windowless room at the back of the house one of the boards over a window had been broken and a bird had flown in and become imprisoned.

The presence of the woman frightened the bird. It flew wildly about. Its beating wings stirred up dust that danced in the air. Elsie stood perfectly still, also frightened, not by the presence of the bird but by the presence of life. Like the bird she was a prisoner. The thought gripped her. She wanted to go outdoors where her niece Elizabeth walked with the young ploughman through the corn, but was like the bird in the room—a prisoner. She moved restlessly about. The bird flew back and forth across the room. It alighted on the window sill near the place where the board was broken away. She stared into the frightened eyes of the bird that in turn stared into her eyes. Then the bird flew away, out through the window, and Elsie turned and ran nervously downstairs and out into the yard. She climbed over the wire fence and ran with stooped shoulders along one of the tunnels.

Elsie ran into the vastness of the cornfields filled with but one desire. She wanted to get out of her life and into some new and sweeter life she felt must be hidden away somewhere in the fields. After she had run a long way she came to a wire fence and crawled over. Her hair became unloosed and fell down over her shoulders. Her cheeks became flushed and for the moment she looked like a young girl. When she climbed over the fence she tore a great hole in the front of her dress. For a moment her tiny breasts were exposed and then her hand clutched and held nervously the sides of the tear. In the distance she could hear the voices of the boys and the barking of the dogs. A summer storm had been threatening for days and now black clouds had begun to spread themselves over the sky. As she ran nervously forward, stopping to listen and then running on again, the dry corn blades brushed against her shoulders and a fine shower of yellow dust from the corn tassels fell on her hair. A continued crackling noise accompanied her progress. The dust made a golden crown about her head. From the sky overhead a low rumbling sound, like the growling of giant dogs, came to her ears.

The thought that having at last ventured into the corn she would never escape became fixed in the mind of the running woman. Sharp pains shot through her body. Presently she was compelled to stop and sit on the ground. For a long time she sat with her closed eyes. Her dress became soiled. Little insects that live in the ground under the corn came out of their holes and crawled over her legs.

Following some obscure impulse the tired woman threw herself on her back and lay still with closed eyes. Her fright passed. It was warm and close in the room-like tunnels. The pain in her side went away. She opened her eyes and between the wide green corn blades could see patches of a black threatening sky. She did not want to be alarmed and so closed her eyes again. Her thin hand no longer gripped the tear in her dress and her tiny breasts were exposed. They expanded and contracted in little spasmodic jerks. She threw her hands back over her head and lay still.

It seemed to Elsie that hours passed as she lay thus, quiet and passive under the corn. Deep within her there was a feeling that something was about to happen, something that would lift her out of herself, that would tear her away from her past and the past of her people. Her thoughts were not definite. She lay still and waited as she had waited for days and months by the rock at the back of the orchard on the Vermont farm when she was a girl. A deep grumbling noise went on in the sky overhead but the sky and everything she had ever known seemed very far away, no part of herself.

After a long silence, when it seemed to her that she was lost from herself as in a dream, Elsie heard a man's voice calling. "Aho, aho, aho," shouted the voice and after another period of silence there arose answering voices and then the sound of bodies crashing through the corn and the excited chatter of children. A dog came running along the row where she lay and stood beside her. His cold nose touched her face and she sat up. The dog ran away. The Leander boys passed. She could see their bare legs flashing in and out across one of the tunnels. Her brother had become alarmed by the rapid approach of the thunder storm and wanted to get his family to town. His voice kept calling from the house and the voices of the children answered from the fields.

Elsie sat on the ground with her hands pressed together. An odd feeling of disappointment had possession of her. She arose and walked slowly along in the general direction taken by the children. She came to a fence and crawled over, tearing her dress in a new place. One of her stockings had become unloosed and had slipped down over her shoe top. The long sharp weeds had scratched her leg so that it was criss-crossed with red lines, but she was not conscious of any pain.

The distraught woman followed the children until she came within sight of her father's house and then stopped and again sat on the ground. There was another loud crash of thunder and Tom Leander's voice called again, this time half angrily. The name of the girl Elizabeth was shouted in loud masculine tones that rolled and echoed like the thunder along the aisles under the corn.

And then Elizabeth came into sight accompanied by the young ploughman. They stopped near Elsie and the man took the girl into his arms. At the sound of their approach Elsie had thrown herself face downward on the ground and had twisted herself into a position where she could see without being seen. When their lips met her tense hands grasped one of the corn stalks.

Her lips pressed themselves into the dust. When they had gone on their way she raised her head. A dusty powder covered her lips.

What seemed another long period of silence fell over the fields. A strong wind began to blow and the corn rocked back and forth. The murmuring voices of unborn children, her imagination had created in the whispering fields, became a vast shout. The wind blew harder and harder. The corn stalks were twisted and bent. Elizabeth went thoughtfully out of the field and climbing the fence confronted her father. "Where you been? What you been a doing?" he asked. "Don't you know we got to get out of here?"

When Elizabeth went toward the house Elsie followed, creeping on her hands and knees like a little animal, and when she had come within sight of the fence surrounding the house she sat on the ground and put her hands over her face. Something within herself was being twisted and whirled about as the tops of the corn stalks were now being twisted and whirled by the wind. She sat so that she did not look toward the house and when she opened her eyes she could again see along the long mysterious aisles.

Her brother, with his wife and children, went away. By turning her head Elsie could see them driving at a trot out of the yard back of her father's house. With the going of the younger woman the farm house in the midst of the cornfield rocked by the winds seemed the most desolate place in the world.

Her mother came out at the back door of the house. She ran to the steps where she knew her daughter was in the habit of sitting and then in alarm began to call. It did not occur to Elsie to answer. The voice of the older woman did not seem to have anything to do with herself. It was a thin voice and was quickly lost in the wind and in the crashing sound that arose out of the fields. With her head turned toward the house Elsie stared at her mother who ran wildly around the house and then went indoors. The back door of the house went shut with a bang.

The storm that had been threatening broke with a roar. Broad sheets of water swept over the cornfields. Sheets of water swept over the woman's body. The storm that had for years been gathering in her also broke. Sobs arose out of her throat. She abandoned herself to a storm of grief that was only partially grief. Tears ran out of her eyes and made little furrows through the dust on her face. In the lulls that occasionally came in the storm she raised her head and heard, through the tangled mass of wet hair that covered her ears and above the sound of millions of rain-drops that alighted on the earthen floor inside the house of the corn, the thin voices of her mother and father calling to her out of the Leander house.

> Only God can change history.

COMMENTARY:

The past, or at least the *interpretation* of the past, is constantly changing according to new scholarship discoveries. Therefore, as new sources are discovered, and old ones reexamined, the historian understands that *theories* of history may change. "Every true history is contemporary history," historians Gerald Grob and George Billias write. Students are asked to make the *theories* of historical events personal and contemporary.

While historians know that they can never be completely neutral about history, scholarly historical inquiry demands that they implement the following principles:

Historians must evaluate the veracity of sources. There must be a hierarchy of historical sources.

Historians must be committed to telling both sides of the historical story. They may choose to lobby for one view over the other, but historians must fairly present all theories.

Historians must avoid stereotypes and archetypes. They must overcome personal prejudices and dispassionately view history in ruthlessly objective terms.

Historians must be committed to the truth no matter where their scholarship leads them. At times historians will discover unflattering information about their nation/state. They must not hesitate to accept and then to tell the truth.

Finally, historians understand that real, abiding, and eternal history ultimately is made only by people who obey God at all costs.

After everything is said and done, historians are only *studying* the past. They cannot really *change* the past. Theories about the past come and go and change with each generation. However, the past is past. It is over. Historians debate about history, but they can never change history—they can re-write history, but they cannot change it.

God alone can change history of the future. When a person is reborn, his present, future, and, yes, even his past is changed. History is literarily rewritten. He is a new creation. That bad choice, that sin, that catastrophe is placed under the blood of the Lamb through the grace of Jesus and everything starts fresh and new: a new history for a new person.

Let me illustrate. My great-great-great grandfather was a slave owner in Eastern Tennessee 139 years ago; his passion was to kill Yankees. From that inheritance, like most white southerners who grew up in the 1960s, I grew up to mistrust, even to hate African-Americans. Like so many people captured by their history and culture, my present and future came from my past. However, when I was a senior in high school, Jesus Christ became my Lord and Savior. My attitudes changed. It took time and work and purposeful re-newing of my mind, but prejudices gradually disappeared. Ultimately, I married my New Jersey wife, and we have three African-American adopted children—whose ancestors, by the way, may have been owned by my great-great-great uncle! My children's children — African-American children—will be my grandchildren. Imagine! Quite literally, my legacy has been rewritten. It has been changed irrevocably by my decision to invite Jesus Christ to be Savior of my life. In a real sense, family prejudice and death existing for generations ended in this generation. The destructive, historical cycle that was part of my history has ended. No one can accomplish that but the Lord Jesus. *History is being rewritten!* My prayer is that if you do not know this God who can change history—even your history—that these historical literary units may encourage you to listen to Jesus Christ who wants to come into your heart as Savior.

FINAL PROJECT

Correct and rewrite all essays and place them in your Final Portfolio.

SUGGESTED
Weekly *Implementation*

DAY 1	DAY 2	DAY 3	DAY 4	DAY 5
Prayer journal. Review the required reading(s) *before* the assigned lesson begins. Teacher may want to discuss assigned reading(s) with students. Teacher and students will decide on required essays for this lesson, choosing two or three essays. The rest of the essays can be outlined, answered with shorter answers, or skipped. Review all readings for Lesson 24.	**Prayer journal.** Review reading(s) from next lesson. Outline essays due at the end of the week. Per teacher instructions, students may answer orally in a group setting some of the essays that are not assigned as formal essays.	**Prayer journal.** Write rough drafts of all assigned essays. The teacher and/or a peer evaluator may correct rough drafts.	**Prayer journal.** Rewrite corrected copies of essays due tomorrow.	**Prayer journal.** Essays are due. Take Lesson 24 test. Reading Ahead: Review *The Pearl*, John Steinbeck. Guide: What themes does Steinbeck develop in this short novel?

THE MODERN AGE, 1915-1946: LATE ROMANTICISM/ NATURALISM *(Part 6)*

The Pearl

John Steinbeck (1947)

BACKGROUND

President Herbert Hoover had been in office only 7 months when the stock market crashed. This great crash ended the Roaring 20s and was followed by the Great Depression. The American dream seemed to have gone sour. Most Americans blamed themselves for the Depression. Americans believed that if they worked hard enough they would prosper, but that was no longer possible for millions of Americans. The Great Depression destroyed America's confidence in the future. This hopelessness is reflected in all of John Steinbeck's fiction.

There had been recessions and depressions in American history but nothing close to what Americans experienced in the 1930s. At one point, almost one-half of Americans were unemployed, and there was no welfare "safety net." People had no food stamps or welfare checks. They had to rely upon friends, family members, and the Church, and it wasn't enough.

In spite of President Hoover's innovative efforts, the Great Depression only worsened. When Franklin D. Roosevelt became president in 1932, Americans were ready for a change.

The Great Depression lasted from about 1929 to the beginning of America's involvement in World War II (1941). Roosevelt attacked the Great Depression forcefully and with innovative tactics. His politics of intervention can be divided into two phases. He promised a "new deal" for the American people. The first was from 1933-1935 and focused mainly on helping the poor and unemployed. With Congressional support, Roosevelt authorized massive spending to employ millions of people through such projects as the Civilian Conservation Corps and the Tennessee Valley Authority. While Roosevelt did not implement socialism, he did superimpose a welfare state on a capitalistic society with controversial results. Steinbeck and other intellectuals were strong proponents of socialism.

> **You will analyze:** *The Pearl*, John Steinbeck.
>
> **Reading Ahead:** *The Emperor Jones*, Eugene O'Neill.
>
> **Guide Question:** Is the Emperor Jones a victim of his circumstances or the perpetrator of his own destruction?

Socialism advocated that the means of production were owned and controlled by the state. There was no private ownership of property. Socialists sought to champion the rights of the poor and the disenfranchised—much like the protagonist in *The Pearl*. This radical social theory gained thousands of proponents in the 1930s.

The so-called second new deal occurred from 1935-1937. During this period, Roosevelt emphasized social reform and social justice. To accomplish his goals, he established the Works Progress Administration (WPA) that helped many poor people and built massive projects (like the Blue Ridge Parkway). Next, he enacted the Social Security Act that provided a safety net and retirement income for workers.

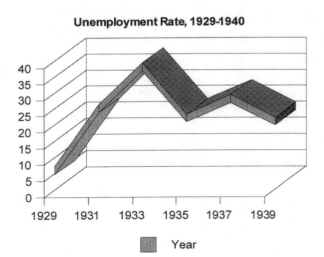

Unemployment Rate, 1929-1940

Finally, during 1937-1938, Roosevelt implemented a third new deal the purpose of which was to help homeless farmers and agricultural workers.

The New Deal failed to stop the Great Depression. Only World War II could end the Depression. However, the New Deal convinced most Americans that their government had a moral and legal right to intervene in public and private affairs if the general good of the public demanded it. America, for better or for worse, was never to be the same. While the economic picture improved, the spiritual damage was done. Many Americans, including John Steinbeck, remained bitter the rest of their lives. Steinbeck turned his bitterness toward God and exhibited a particularly harsh form of Naturalism in his writings.

ABOUT THE AUTHOR

John Steinbeck, American writer and Nobel *laureate*, wrote about his life in fictional books. He described in his work the struggle of people who were marginalized in American society. Steinbeck never wrote an autobiography, but all of his writing contains pieces of his life story. The settings of most of the books are the areas near Monterey, California, where Steinbeck was born and lived most of his life. Kino, a poor Mexican pearl fisherman, finds a very valuable pearl. However, instead of bringing great rewards, the pearl brings tragedy and misfortune to Kino and his family. Finally, in disgust and grief poor Kino returns the pearl to the ocean.

OTHER NOTABLE WORKS

1935 *Tortilla Flat*
1937 *Of Mice and Men*
1939 *The Grapes of Wrath*
1945 *Cannery Row*
1952 *East of Eden*
1961 *The Winter of our Discontent*
1962 *Travels with Charley*

VOCABULARY WORDS

Chapter	Word
Epilogue	Parable
I	detachment
	frantically
III	fiercely
	prophecy
VI	lumbered

CRITICAL THINKING

A. How does Steinbeck use foreshadowing in his book?

B. How does Steinbeck use ants to make some points?

C. How does Steinbeck present the priest in *The Pearl*?

D. List several themes in *The Pearl*.

BIBLICAL APPLICATION

A. What does this book tell you about the way the naturalist Steinbeck sees God?

B. Respond to the Priest's sermon which stated "Each man and woman is like a soldier sent by God to guard some part of the castle of the Universe."

ENRICHMENT

Even though Juana knows that the pearl will cause disaster, she returns it to her husband after it was lost. Why would she do this?

FINAL PROJECT

Correct and rewrite all essays and place them in your Final Portfolio.

SUGGESTED
Weekly *Implementation*

DAY 1	DAY 2	DAY 3	DAY 4	DAY 5
Prayer journal.	Prayer journal.	Prayer journal.	Prayer journal.	Prayer journal.
Review the required reading(s) *before* the assigned lesson begins.	Review reading(s) from next lesson.	Write rough drafts of all assigned essays.	Rewrite corrected copies of essays due tomorrow.	Essays are due.
Teacher may want to discuss assigned reading(s) with students.	Outline essays due at the end of the week.	The teacher and/or a peer evaluator may correct rough drafts.		Take Lesson 25 test.
Teacher and students will decide on required essays for this lesson, choosing two or three essays.	Per teacher instructions, students may answer orally in a group setting some of the essays that are not assigned as formal essays.			Reading Ahead: Review *The Emperor Jones*, Eugene O'Neill.
The rest of the essays can be outlined, answered with shorter answers, or skipped.				Guide: Is the Emperor Jones a victim of his circumstances or the perpetrator of his own destruction?
Review all readings for Lesson 25.				

LESSON 26

THE MODERN AGE, 1946-1960: REALISM/ NATURALISM
(Part 1)

The Emperor Jones

Eugene O'Neill

BACKGROUND

You will analyze: *The Emperor Jones*, Eugene O'Neill.

Reading Ahead: *Little Foxes*, Lillian Hellman.

Guide Question: In what ways are the characters dysfunctional?

© Arttoday.com

American playwright Eugene Gladstone O'Neill revolutionized American drama. His plays made American drama a major player on the stage of Western theater. He moved American theater from flippant comedies to earthy naturalistic plays. There is perhaps no more tragic figure in American literary history than the brilliant Eugene O'Neill. His drug-addicted mother tried to commit suicide but failed, he tried and failed, and his son tried and succeeded. He struggled with depression all his life. He openly renounced his faith in God. In short, he was the quintessential modern man. All his plays concern protagonists as Naturalistic beings who lost their old harmony with nature, the harmony which they used to have as an animal and have not yet acquired in a spiritual way. Thus, not being able to find harmony either on earth or in heaven, they are in the middle, trying to make peace with themselves and their world. As Harvard Professor Harvey Cox explained, "Once, Americans had dreams and no technology to accomplish those dreams. Now, Americans have plenty of technology but no dreams left to fulfill." (Unpublished Lecture, Harvard University, 1976).

CRITICAL THINKING

A. Discuss in detail how O'Neill builds suspense in this play.

B. There are several layers of conflict in this play. Comment on the several kinds of conflict that arise.

C. Find several instances of Naturalism in this play.

D. What is the setting and how does it affect the outcome of this play?

E. Who is Smithers and what is his purpose in this play?

ENRICHMENT

One scholar observed that O'Neill makes an "effort to interpret life in consonance with the findings of science, especially Freudian psychology, and at the same time a longing to find cosmic release in a mystical universe." Discuss this observation with your educator.

BIBLICAL APPLICATION

A. The Emperor Jones was haunted by unforgiveness that had been visited on him by others. Tragically, he was destroyed by that unforgiveness. Twenty years after World War II, a psychologist conducted a study of survivors of the Nazi concentration camps and their guards. To his horror, he discovered that the survivors had a higher divorce rate, suicide rate, and even higher rate of death by cancer than the concentration camp guards. In spite of the fact that the guards were guilty of heinous crimes, and the former inmates were innocent victims, it was the innocent victims who fared much poorer. Propose a reason for why this was so.

B. The following is a story of this author's call into the ministry. Do you have someone who deeply affected your life and encouraged you in your faith? Describe him/her.

Brother Palmer Garner

He was an ordinary pastor, Brother Garner, the sort of pastor you would expect a church board to send to my south Arkansas town in 1965.

South Arkansas was unprepared to face the present, much less the future. The Civil War hung like a heavy shroud on this declining railroad town. Less than 100 years before, Yankee soldiers had unceremoniously marched through our swamps to Vicksburg. To our eternal shame, no significant resistance was offered, except a brief unsuccessful skirmish at Boggy Bayou.

A pastor distinguished only by his mediocrity, Palmer Garner seemed committed to irrelevance. Despite the fact that desegregation was fracturing our fragile community and some of our neighbors and relatives were warring with the Army Reserve units at Central High School in Little Rock, Arkansas, Garner was warning us of "immoral thoughts." Most of us had not had an "immoral thought" since Elvis Presley played in the old VA gym.

The only redeeming feature of Brother Garner's sermons was that they were mercifully short. They allowed us to get to Lawson Cafe's hickory-smoked pork ribs before the Southern Baptists!

We never liked Garner's sensitivity. It seemed so effeminate—un-Christian, really. He seemed to be an incorrigible sentimentalist, and while Southern ethos was full of tradition and veiled sentimentalism, we fiercely hid our true feelings.

For instance, when Mr. Bubba Sinclair tried to kill himself, no one expressed surprise or shock. Such an act was expected of an unstable person whose alcoholism had brought dishonor on his family and town. The only thing that bothered us was that he failed. Such a vulnerable act demanded resolution, and we per-versely expected Bubba to act like a man and finish the job. Although we never said anything to him, he knew what was expected, and he finally did it.

Garner was, however, a greater threat to our fragile equilibrium. Dwight Washington, a high school scholar and track star, had a conversion experience at one of our revival services. He foolishly thought that since Jesus loved him, we would too. So, he tried to attend our Sunday morning worship service. But he was politely asked to leave during the assurance of pardon—because "nigras" should go to their own churches.

Garner saw everything and was obviously displeased. Not that he castigated us. We could handle that. We enjoyed pastors who scolded us for our sins. We tolerated, even enjoyed his paternalistic diatribes. No, Garner did the intolerable: he wept. Right in the middle of morning worship, right where great preachers like Muzon Mann had labored, where our children were baptized, Garner wept! Right in the middle of morning worship, as if it was part of the liturgy, he started crying! Not loud, uncontrollable sobs, but quiet, deep crying. Like a man who was overwhelmed by the exigencies of life.

Old Man Henley, senile and almost deaf, remembering the last time he cried—when his wife died—started crying too. And then the children. How we hated Palmer Garner! If we ever doubted, Garner was obviously an outsider to our community . . .

Brother Garner did not last the year. He was moved to an obscure church in North Arkansas, and I heard he died in ignominiousness.

I never forgot that day. It changed my life. As I grew older, the embarrassment of watching my pastor cry was replaced first by admiration and then awe. What a courageous man! I owe so much to Palmer Garner. He taught me how to cry and what to cry for. He showed me that the really important changes required time, courage, and tears. (James P. Stobaugh)

FINAL PROJECT

Correct and rewrite all essays and place them in your Final Portfolio.

SUGGESTED
Weekly *Implementation*

DAY 1	DAY 2	DAY 3	DAY 4	DAY 5
Prayer journal. Review the required reading(s) *before* the assigned lesson begins. Teacher may want to discuss assigned reading(s) with students. Teacher and students will decide on required essays for this lesson, choosing two or three essays. The rest of the essays can be outlined, answered with shorter answers, or skipped. Review all readings for Lesson 26.	**Prayer journal.** Review reading(s) from next lesson. Outline essays due at the end of the week. Per teacher instructions, students may answer orally in a group setting some of the essays that are not assigned as formal essays.	**Prayer journal.** Write rough drafts of all assigned essays. The teacher and/or a peer evaluator may correct rough drafts.	**Prayer journal.** Rewrite corrected copies of essays due tomorrow.	**Prayer journal.** Essays are due. Take Lesson 26 test. Reading Ahead: Review *The Little Foxes*, Lillian Hellman. Guide: In what ways are the characters dysfunctional?

LESSON 27

THE MODERN AGE, 1946-1960: REALISM/NATURALISM (Part 2)

The Little Foxes
Lillian Hellman (1939)

BACKGROUND

"Cynicism is an unpleasant way to tell the truth," Hellman says in her play *The Little Foxes*, and this more-or-less sums up her life. Lillian Hellman (1905-1984) became a writer at a time when there was no television, much less any internet, and when writers were celebrities. She more than held her own in this department. To Fitzgerald, Hemingway, Faulkner, and Hammett, Lillian Hellman was an *avant guard* radical. She maintained a lavish and controversial lifestyle that offended many Americans.

Born in New Orleans, Louisiana, Hellman had many avaricious and colorful relatives, who later appeared in her plays. Since her family moved back and forth from New York City, she was absorbed into the New York artistic scene. Later, she moved to Hollywood where she spent the remainder of her life

> **You will analyze:** *The Little Foxes*, by Lillian Hellman.
> **Read Ahead:** *The Glass Menagerie*, Tennessee Williams.
> **Guide Question:** What is the worldview of the narrator and why does Williams use him to tell the story?

writing for MGM. She never forgot her southern roots, and they reappeared in all her literary works.

The Little Foxes is perhaps Hellman's most famous achievement. In the chicanery of the Hubbard family we have one of the best pictures of the rise of Southern industrialism in the post-Civil War period.

CRITICAL THINKING

A. Describe in great detail the relationship of Horace and his wife Regina. This relationship is a key element of the play.

B. Why did you enjoy (not enjoy) this play? Evaluate the play according to how well Hellman presented a credible plot, setting, characterization, conflict, and resolution.

C. Find several instances of realism in this play.

D. Faulkner, Hellman, Williams, Welty, Ransom, O'Connor and other great writers came from the South. Why do you think so much great literature has come out of the South in this century?

(See Lesson 32: Introduction to the Southern Renaissance.)

BIBLICAL APPLICATION

Compare Regina Giddens to Jezebel.

ENRICHMENT

React to the following assessment of contemporary culture: Our culture deifies self-reflection and existential possibilities. Unless Christians stand to say, "Why?" we will lose the sense of irony. There will be no individual essence to which we remain true or committed. As the boundaries of definition give way, so does the assumption of self-identity. "Who am I?" is a teeming world of provisional possibilities. A question other generations dared not ask. A question that is asked all the time now. Who will answer that question for this generation . . . (Kenneth J. Gergen, *The Saturated Self: Dilemmas of Identity in Contemporary Life*)

SUGGESTED
Weekly *Implementation*

DAY 1	DAY 2	DAY 3	DAY 4	DAY 5
Prayer journal.	**Prayer journal.**	**Prayer journal.**	**Prayer journal.**	**Prayer journal.**
Review the required reading(s) *before* the assigned lesson begins.	Review reading(s) from next lesson.	Write rough drafts of all assigned essays.	Rewrite corrected copies of essays due tomorrow.	Essays are due.
Teacher may want to discuss assigned reading(s) with students.	Student should outline essays due at the end of the week.	The teacher and/or a peer evaluator may correct rough drafts.		Take Lesson 27 test.
Teacher and students will decide on required essays for this lesson, choosing two or three essays. The rest of the essays can be outlined, answered with shorter answers, or skipped.	Per teacher instructions, students may answer orally in a group setting some of the essays that are not assigned as formal essays.			Reading Ahead: Review *The Glass Menagerie*, Tennessee Williams.

Guide: What is the worldview of the narrator and why does Williams use him to tell the story? |
| Review all readings for Lesson 27. | | | | |

THE MODERN AGE, 1946-1960: REALISM/ NATURALISM
(Part 3)

The Glass Menagerie
Tennessee Williams (1944)

BACKGROUND

In his book *Mist* the great religious Spanish writer Unamuno creates a character, Augusto Perez, who, through omniscient narration, turns to his maker (e.g., Unamuno) and cries: "Am I to die as a creature of fiction?" Such is the cry of the characters in *The Glass Menagerie*. The Christian author and Harvard Professor Robert Coles laments that "we have the right to think of ourselves, so rich in today's America, as in jeopardy *sub specie aeternitatis*, no matter the size and diversification of his [sic] stock portfolio." It seems, at times that we are lost. "The sense of being lost, displaced, and homeless is pervasive in contemporary culture," Walter Brueggemann writes. "The yearning to belong somewhere, to have a home, to be in a safe place, is a deep and moving pursuit." This world does not provide what the characters in these plays need. Harvard Divinity School's Dr. Forrest Church, now pastor in a Unitarian Church in New York City, writes, "In our faith God is not a given; God is a question . . . God is defined by us. Our views are shaped and changed by our experiences. We create a faith in which we can live and struggle to live up to it . . . compared to lov[ing] a distant God [who] has no allure." From a Christian perspective, Forrest captures the devastating essence of our modern dilemma.

Tennessee Williams, among others, ushered in the post-Christian age, which had its roots in the 1920s but really rose to the forefront in the 1990s. The post-Christian age is dominated by anxiety, irrationality, and helplessness. In such a world, consciousness is adrift, unable to anchor itself to any universal ground of justice, truth or reason. Consciousness itself is thus "decentered": no longer agent of action in the world, but a function through which impersonal forces pass and intersect. (Patricia Waugh in Gene Edward Veith, Jr., *Postmodern Times: A Christian Guide to Contemporary Thought and Culture*)

You will analyze: *The Glass Menagerie*, by Tennessee Williams.

Reading Ahead: Review *The Crucible*, Arthur Miller (Lesson 30).

Guide Question: Should John Proctor pretend that he is a witch in order to save his life?

Enter now the post-Christian era of tentativeness, of glass-fragile-figures—that glass menagerie which is so much a part of modern America . . .

Of all Broadway plays, the remarkable *The Glass Menagerie*, has some of the most powerful insights into the human heart. It was Tennessee Williams' first successful play; it won the New York Critics' Circle Award as the best play of the 1944-45 Broadway season. Less than three years later, *A Streetcar Named Desire* opened, and it, too, captured the Critics' Circle Award, also winning the Pulitzer Prize.

CRITICAL THINKING

A. Describe in detail the characters in this play.

B. What is the conflict?

C. Why does Williams title his play "The Glass Menagerie"?

D. Describe the dreams of Laura, Amanda, Tom, and Jim. Do any of them fully attain their dreams?

BIBLICAL APPLICATION

Compare and contrast the way that Amanda handles disappointment with the way that the biblical character Joseph handles disappointment.

FINAL PORTFOLIO

Correct and rewrite all essays and place them in your Final Portfolio.

SUGGESTED
Weekly *Implementation*

DAY 1	DAY 2	DAY 3	DAY 4	DAY 5
Prayer journal.	**Prayer journal.**	**Prayer journal.**	**Prayer journal.**	**Prayer journal.**
Review the required reading(s) *before* the assigned lesson begins. Teacher may want to discuss assigned reading(s) with students. Teacher and students will decide on required essays for this lesson, choosing two or three essays. The rest of the essays can be outlined, answered with shorter answers, or skipped. Review all readings for Lesson 28.	Review reading(s) from next lesson. Outline essays due at the end of the week. Per teacher instructions, students may answer orally in a group setting some of the essays that are not assigned as formal essays.	Write rough drafts of all assigned essays. The teacher and/or a peer evaluator may correct rough drafts.	Rewrite corrected copies of essays due tomorrow.	Essays are due. Take Lesson 28 test. Reading Ahead: Review *The Crucible*, Arthur Miller (Lesson 30). Guide: Should John Proctor pretend that he is a witch in order to save his life?

LESSON 29

THE MODERN AGE, 1946-1960: REALISM/ NATURALISM
(Part 4)

CRITICAL THINKING

A. Is Amanda Wingfield more like Regina Giddens or Horace Giddens? Why?

B. *Chariots of Fire*, a famous and popular movie, by most accounts, has a Christian message and most pastors recommended it to their congregations during its heyday. However, this movie includes actors who obviously are not Christians, and it is owned by Hollywood studios who care nothing about Judeo-Christian values. Should Christians support movies that help non-Christian people prosper? What about Mel Gibson's *The Passion of the Christ*?

C. Pretend that Anne Bradstreet, Ralph Waldo Emerson, Nathaniel Hawthorne, Stephen Crane, Ernest Hemingway, and Tennessee Williams have a conversation about the following topics: God, the Bible, Salvation, Nature, Fate. Complete the following chart with phrases they might use in their conversations:

> **You will analyze:** *The Glass Menagerie,* Tennessee Williams.
>
> **Reading Ahead:** *The Crucible*, Arthur Miller.
>
> **Guide Question:** Should John Proctor pretend he is a witch in order to save his life?

D. Amanda believes in several common myths about success and hard work. She thinks that if she had only married one of those rich gentlemen callers, she would be successful. She admires the imaginary groups in her magazines. Likewise, she believes in the American dream—if one works hard enough, he will prosper. Ironically, the "gentleman caller" Jim O'Connor agrees with Amanda. He also has big plans. Only Laura and Tom seem to face reality squarely.

The personal failure of all the characters in the play in some ways parallels the larger failure of Depression era America. The Depression turned millions of American dreams into nightmares.

	Anne Bradstreet	Ralph Waldo Emerson	Nathaniel Hawthorne	Stephen Crane	Ernest Hemingway	Tennessee Williams
GOD						
BIBLE						
SALVATION						
NATURE						
FATE						

The New Deal failed to stop the Great Depression. Only World War II which brought full employment could end the Depression. Unfortunately, however, there was no solution to the dilemma facing Jim, Laura, Tom and Amanda, at least not in this world.

What is the American dream at the beginning of the 21st century? Is it attainable?

ENRICHMENT

Read another Tennessee Williams' play and compare it to this one.

FINAL PORTFOLIO

Correct and rewrite all essays and place them in your Final Portfolio.

SUGGESTED
Weekly *Implementation*

DAY 1	DAY 2	DAY 3	DAY 4	DAY 5
Prayer journal. Review the required reading(s) *before* the assigned lesson begins. Teacher may want to discuss assigned reading(s) with students. Teacher and students will decide on required essays for this lesson, choosing two or three essays. The rest of the essays can be outlined, answered with shorter answers, or skipped. Review all readings for Lesson 29.	**Prayer journal.** Review reading(s) from next lesson. Outline essays due at the end of the week. Per teacher instructions, students may answer orally in a group setting some of the essays that are not assigned as formal essays.	**Prayer journal.** Write rough drafts of all assigned essays. The teacher and/or a peer evaluator may correct rough drafts.	**Prayer journal.** Rewrite corrected copies of essays due tomorrow.	**Prayer journal.** Essays are due. Take Lesson 29 test. Reading Ahead: *The Crucible*, Arthur Miller. Guide: Should John Proctor pretend he is a witch in order to save his life?

THE MODERN AGE, 1946-1960: REALISM/ NATURALISM
(Part 5)

The Crucible

Arthur Miller

BACKGROUND

Arthur Miller (1915-) is one of the finest American playwrights of the last century. Miller's play *The Crucible* (1953), although concerned with the Salem witchcraft trials, was actually aimed at the then widespread congressional investigation of subversive activities in the United States. The drama won the 1953 Tony Award. Arthur Miller championed the worldview Realism in literature and drama.

CRITICAL THINKING

A. Is John Proctor a realistic character? Does he seem more a product of the 1950s than a character living in the 17th century?

B. How could a 17th century court justify executing people accused of witches?

C. What is Elizabeth Proctor's role?

You will analyze: *The Crucible*, Arthur Miller.

Reading Ahead: *A Separate Peace*, John Knowles.

Guide Question: Did Gene hurt Finny on purpose?

ENRICHMENT

Arthur Miller wrote *The Crucible* as a criticism of the excesses of the 1950 McCarthy Hearings. These were a series of congressional hearings to reveal Communist spies and sympathizers in the United States government. No doubt there were excesses and some innocent people had their reputations ruined. On the other hand, there really was some illegal, very harmful espionage occurring in high places in the United States government. In light of September 11, 2001, how can the government protect its people without resorting to excesses?

FINAL PORTFOLIO

Correct and re-write required essays and place in your Final Portfolio.

SUGGESTED

Weekly *Implementation*

DAY 1	DAY 2	DAY 3	DAY 4	DAY 5
Prayer journal.	**Prayer journal.**	**Prayer journal.**	**Prayer journal.**	**Prayer journal.**
Review the required reading(s) *before* the assigned lesson begins.	Review reading(s) from next lesson.	Write rough drafts of all assigned essays.	Rewrite corrected copies of essays due tomorrow.	Essays are due.
Teacher may want to discuss assigned reading(s) with students.	Outline essays due at the end of the week.	The teacher and/or a peer evaluator may correct rough drafts.		Take Lesson 30 test.
Teacher and students will decide on required essays for this lesson, choosing two or three essays.	Per teacher instructions, students may answer orally in a group setting some of the essays that are not assigned as formal essays.			Reading Ahead: Review *A Separate Peace*, John Knowles.
The rest of the essays can be outlined, answered with shorter answers, or skipped.				Guide: Did Gene purposely hurt Finny?
Review all readings for Lesson 30.				

LESSON 31
CONTEMPORARY WRITERS, 1960-PRESENT *(Part 1)*

Post-World War II Literature

The period after World War II ushered in a period of confusion and, then, optimism. There was no profound disillusionment that followed World War I. However, by the 1960s this self-assured buoyancy had deteriorated into selfish individualism and unchecked egalitarianism. This narcissism spawned a literary and artistic movement called Absurdism. The central premise of Absurdism is that there was no meaning, no structure to life. Absurdism argued that we live in veiled chaos unencumbered by any scientific or sociological law or system. Champions of this movement were/are John Barth and Kurt Vonnegut, Jr. A similar artistic/literary movement in Europe was the Existentialism of Jean Paul Sartre and Albert Camus.

The Separate Peace was set during World War II, but it was a product of the 1950s. During the 1950s, Americans experienced unprecedented prosperity. This prosperity invited most Americans to a new form of conservatism that posited the view point that "if it works, don't fix it." Therefore, conformity and uniformity were watchmen on the walls of early 1950 American culture. The camaraderie and community engendered in World War II invited Americans to embrace the security of group conformity. Most Americans craved the security of a simpler world of the 1930s rather than the uncomfortable, risky, unknown world that was to come.

> While a cold war raged overseas, a culture war broke out at home.

Post-war Americans preferred to maintain old, traditional values, not to invent new ones. This included job choices and home life. Though men and women had been forced into new employment patterns during World War II, once the war was over, traditional roles were reaffirmed. As soon as the War ended, women basically went home to be housewives. Again, returning soldiers expected to be the breadwinners; women, even when they worked, assumed their proper place was at

> **You will analyze:** *A Separate Peace*, John Knowles.
>
> **Reading Ahead:** "Everything That Rises Must Converge," Flannery O'Connor; "A Worn Path," Eudora Welty; "The Jilting of Granny Weatherall," Katherine Anne Porter.
>
> **Guide Question:** What themes emerge in Southern literature?

home. Now they could return home. Sociologist David Riesman observed the importance of peer-group expectations in his influential book, *The Lonely Crowd*. He called this new society "other-directed," and maintained that such societies led to stability as well as conformity. Television contributed to the homogenizing trend by providing young and old with a shared experience reflecting accepted social patterns. Radio and then television created an American culture that competed with local culture. This new culture invited conformity.

However, not all Americans conformed to such cultural norms. A number of writers and other artists rebelled against conventional values. Stressing spontaneity and spirituality, they asserted intuition over reason, Existentialism and Mysticism over denominational faith. This new worldview was reminiscent of the Transcendental movement of the previous century. These new cultural rebels went out of their way to challenge the patterns of respectability and shock the rest of the culture.

Their literary work displayed their penchant for non-conformity. Jack Kerouac typed his best-selling novel *On the Road* on a 75-meter roll of paper. Lacking accepted punctuation and paragraph structure, the book glorified the possibilities of the free life. Poet Allen Ginsberg gained similar notoriety for his poetry. John Lennon and *The Beatles* broke new ground. The movie *The Blob* established new patterns when Steve McQueen and his teenage friends, unable to rely on adult superiors, took matters into their own hands, broke the law, and ultimately figured out themselves how to kill this monster. The viewer knew without any doubt that youth unencumbered by adult supervision was the hope for America's future.

This was only the beginning. More iconoclastic, artistic movements quickly followed. Elvis Presley, who seems fairly tame to later generations, in fact revolutionized non-conformity music. Born in Tupelo, Mississippi, Elvis Presley popularized African American soul music and took it a step further. In effect he created a new music genre: rock and roll. Presley shocked Americans with his long hair, seductive lyrics, and undulating hips.

Other artists followed. Painter Jackson Pollock discarded easels and laid out gigantic canvases on the floor and then applied paint, sand and other materials in wild splashes of color. Akin to Dadaism and Surrealism, this new abstract, called "modern art" invited the participant to new levels of subjectivity, individualism, and narcissism. Meaning now resided in the viewer, not in the artists. Americans could now find meaning in their own experience rather than in socially accepted norms and rituals. These artists and authors, whatever their medium, provided fertile ground for the more radical social revolutions of the 1960s.

What makes *A Separate Peace* so important is that within its pages a moral vision, albeit a fractured one, returns to American literature. Perhaps literature is headed back in the direction of the Puritans!

A Separate Peace

John Knowles

ABOUT THE AUTHOR

John Knowles was only 33 years old when *A Separate Peace* was published in England in 1959 and then in the United States in 1960. The book was an immediate and stunning success, receiving the William Faulkner Foundation Award and the Rosenthal Award of the National Institute of Arts and Letters. However, John Knowles had begun writing seriously a decade before the success of *A Separate Peace* enabled him to abandon full-time employment. He was assistant editor for the Yale Alumni Magazine where he had attended college; he worked as a reporter and drama critic for the Hartford Courant; and then he wrote his first novel, *Descent into Proselito*, while living in Italy and France.

That novel was never published; his friend and teacher, the playwright Thornton Wilder, felt it was not good enough. Knowles was born in Fairmont, West Virginia, on September 16, 1926, the third of four children. During World War II at age fifteen, he went away to boarding school, the Phillips Exeter Academy in New Hampshire. The pressures of this environment at such a dire and impressionable time in his life laid the foundation for *A Separate Peace*—and even before that novel, for a short story called "Phineas," which takes us through the events of the first half of the novel. What makes this novel so unique is that it celebrates many old fashioned values: honesty, hard work, and integrity.

CRITICAL THINKING

A. Gene feels challenged and stifled by the Devon School. He enjoys the community but finds it debilitating too. In the same way, many of John Knowles' major characters fight to achieve an understanding with where they are, testing themselves constantly against their current situations. Give examples of these internal conflicts from the text.

B. Gene is the narrator of the story. He tells us what is going on; we see everything through his eyes. How reliable a narrator is Gene? Would Finny (until his death) be a better narrator? Why not have a teacher or a parent relate the story? Would it matter?

C. Did Gene cause Finny to fall from the tree?

D. How important is the setting?

E. Give one or two themes of this novel.

ENRICHMENT

Predict what themes, characters, and plots will emerge in 20 years.

FINAL PORTFOLIO

Correct and re-write required essays and place in your Final Portfolio.

SUGGESTED
Weekly *Implementation*

DAY 1	DAY 2	DAY 3	DAY 4	DAY 5
Prayer journal.	**Prayer journal.**	**Prayer journal.**	**Prayer journal.**	**Prayer journal.**
Review the required reading(s) *before* the assigned lesson begins.	Review reading(s) from next lesson.	Write rough drafts of all assigned essays.	Rewrite corrected copies of essays due tomorrow.	Essays are due.
Teacher may want to discuss assigned reading(s) with students.	Outline essays due at the end of the week.	The teacher and/or a peer evaluator may correct rough drafts.		Take Lesson 31 test.
Teacher and students will decide on required essays for this lesson, choosing two or three essays.	Per teacher instructions, students may answer orally in a group setting some of the essays that are not assigned as formal essays.			Reading Ahead: Review "Everything That Rises Must Converge," Flannery O'Connor; "A Worn Path," Eudora Welty; "The Jilting of Granny Weatherall," Katherine Anne Porter.
The rest of the essays can be outlined, answered with shorter answers, or skipped.				Guide: What themes emerge in Southern literature?
Review all readings for Lesson 31.				

CONTEMPORARY WRITERS, 1960-PRESENT: THE SOUTHERN RENAISSANCE *(Part 2)*

Southern Renaissance

BACKGROUND

In the early and middle part of the 20th century there was a renaissance of Southern literature that was unprecedented since the New England Renaissance that occurred a century before. Southern literature, deeply affected, ironically, by the Ohio writer Sherwood Anderson, emphasized the unique. More than that though, Southern prose literature was just plain good story-telling.

The roots of the Southern Renaissance began at Vanderbilt University in the 1920s with a group called "the fugitive poets," including poets John Crowe Ransom ("The Equilibrist") and Allen Tate ("Ode to a Confederate Dead"). To some extent Robert Penn Warren was associated with this movement, as was Cleanth Brooks, a literary critic. They were linked with the "agrarian" movement in larger southern culture.

Characteristics of the Agrarian Movement in the Southern Renaissance include reaction against northern modernism which they saw as dehumanizing, against abstraction, and against the clock-punching mentality that was seen as coming at the expense of the value of human life. The Agrarian Movement was interested in the whole person—not in people as machines and producers. Associates of the movement valued religious sensibilities, especially Catholic, and celebrated and protected the south's agrarian past. The south traditionally valued a sense of place and traditions related to the Bible, excellent criteria for good literature growth. It is not surprising that the south produced such exceptional authors, poets, and playwrights with this strain of culture.

Poetry from the Agrarian Movement had classical traits because the poets worked from the ancient Greek concepts of democracy and balance. The Agrarian Movement was inherently conservative in that the north was viewed as progressive and all about change and advancement; the south was about valuing past and what already existed. Southern Renaissance literature

> **You will analyze:** "Everything That Rises Must Converge," Flannery O'Connor; "A Worn Path," Eudora Welty; "The Jilting of Granny Weatherall," Katherine Anne Porter.
>
> **Reading Ahead:** *Cold Sassy Tree*, Olive Ann Burns.
>
> **Guide Question:** How does the protagonist mature both physically and spiritually?

is against using utility as the measuring stick for worth. The book *I'll take My Stand: The South and the Agrarian Tradition* compiles twelve southern authors and critics who discuss and define these traits and views.

William Faulkner and other Southern authors grew out of these roots. Faulkner was pure literary genius,

but his success was not necessarily related to the Agrarian Movement—he would have been a genius regardless of when he was born. Other writers after Faulkner have all had to reckon with his influence. Even though Flannery O'Connor was influenced by him and other Agrarians, she was a writer in her own right.

Southern literature, in general, rejected much of the progressive modernism that permeated American art and literature. Faulkner's stream of consciousness (e.g. *The Sound and the Fury*) and O'Connor's neo-theism stood in stark contrast to the surrealistic world that invaded post World War I Europe and America.

One seminal figure was Gertrude Stein (1874-1946). Stein did for literature what Picasso was doing for art. One is tempted to ignore Stein, but her contribution to literature was so strong that she profoundly influenced Ernest Hemingway and F. Scott Fitzgerald.

In any event, an ominous movement was emerging: art and literature were divorced from both reality and morality. The platonic notion that knowledge was good was sorely tested.

This notion was exacerbated by the rise of new technologies. Technological innovation was synonymous with "good." It was not until the horrors of the World War II concentration camps—perhaps the greatest technological achievement of the 20th century—did people question the notion of unlimited technological progress.

Photography was important to the modern artist. Metaphor was out. The real, in-your-face art was in. Even Surrealism, that was itself strange, invited sensory expressions that were often earthy.

Flannery O'Connor burst on the scene with a refreshing exception to the hopelessness that permeated American literature in the 20th century. She considered that dealing with reality with accurate reproduction of what influenced a character was paramount.

Everything That Rises Must Converge
Flannery O'Connor

Flannery O'Connor (1925-1964) was born in Savannah, Georgia on March 25, 1925, and died of lupus in Milledgeville, Georgia on August 3, 1964. In these 39 years, she contributed a brief, powerful canon (2 novels, 32 short stories, plus reviews and commentaries). O'Connor is considered one of the most important voices in American literature. Her short novels and short stories are some of the best in American literature. A born-again Christian, O'Connor, to a certain measure, reintroduced Christian theism into American literature at a time when naturalism, realism, and existentialism dominated the literary landscape. "Everything That Rises Must Converge" was written a year before O'Connor's death and reflects the racial tensions endemic to 1960 America.

CRITICAL THINKING

A. In what ways are Julian and his mother similar? Different? How does O'Connor communicate these differences to the reader?

B. Why is it ironic that both Julian and his mother focus their dreams on the same things?

C. What does the title mean?

> New Criticism at Vanderbilt University, Nashville, Tennessee, pushed the reader beyond objectivity to a form of subjectivity that invited him to an "insight." As a result, old paradigms and archetypes were questioned and new literary insights emerged.

D. Henry James, William Faulkner, and many other American writers experimented with fictional points of view (some are still doing so). James often restricted the information in the novel to what a single character would have known. In his novel *The Sound and the Fury* Faulkner breaks up the narrative into four sections, each giving the viewpoint of a different character (including a mentally retarded boy). *As I Lay Dying* employs a similar approach. In "Everything That Rises Must Converge" Flannery O'Connor also employs a fairly sophisticated point of view. What is it?

E. What kills Julian's mother: her shock at seeing an African-American wearing the same dress as she is wearing or the way Julian is treating her?

BIBLICAL APPLICATION

A. Julian is sure that he is captured by unforgiveness for the rest of his life. Write another ending to this story. It is five years later. Julian comes to your church. You engage him in conversation and discover that he is unhappy because he cannot forgive himself. What will you say to him? Use the Bible to support your statements.

B. In my small 1950s church there was a very kind, godly man who faithfully attended church every Sunday morning and even taught Sunday school. In fact, he was an officer on our administrative board. All the children called him Uncle George. The problem was he was the Grand Wizard of the state Ku Klux Klan. Should he have been allowed to hold important offices in the church? Should he have been allowed to attend church at all? Was he saved?

ENRICHMENT

Race affects where we live, the jobs we hold, the person we marry. No matter where we are, or who we are, in one way or another, our lives are affected by racial issues. To suggest in 1997 that racial difficulties are no longer a reality in American culture is to ignore reality. Americans inherit a history—good and bad—of racial interaction that profoundly affects individual and corporate worldviews. Race as a category in politics, social welfare policy, and religion became significant for the first time in open discussions in the 1960's and 1970's. These discussions continue today. Whether in a conversation on the edge of an indigo field outside Columbia, South Carolina, in 1730 or in inner-city Philadelphia in 1997, racial discussions inevitably generated controversy. Racial anger is a reaction to the perceived failure of these discussions and their inability to bring expected results. In her own way Flannery O'Connor captures some of this struggle in the lives her two protagonists in "Everything That Rises Must Converge."

Do you struggle with race issues? How do they affect you?

BACKGROUND

Eudora Welty (1909-2001) was born in Jackson, Mississippi and lived her whole life there. Her descriptions of human character and personality are legendary.

A Worn Path
Eudora Welty

CRITICAL THINKING

A. Discuss how Welty uses the journey motif to advance the action in "A Worn Path."

B. What is the purpose of Welty's introducing the hunter and clinic?

ENRICHMENT

What universal truth is revealed in "A Worn Path"?

The Jilting of Granny Weatherall
Katherine Anne Porter

BACKGROUND

Katherine Anne Porter (1890-1980) was a descendent of Daniel Boone, legendary pioneer and explorer. Born in Indian Creek, Texas, Katherine Anne Porter she grew up in Texas and Louisiana. Her mother died when Katherine was two, and she was reared by her paternal grandmother. Porter was educated in convent schools. At the age of sixteen she ran away and married the first of her three husbands. A few years later she left the first husband to work as an actress. Porter contracted tuberculosis and during her recovery she decided to become a writer. Subsequently she earned her living as a journalist in Chicago, Illinois, and in Denver, Colorado.

CRITICAL THINKING

A. What are the qualities that Granny owned which helped her live successfully?

B. How does Porter use steam of consciousness and dialogue to advance the action of her story?

FINAL PROJECT

Correct and rewrite all essays and place them in your Final Portfolio.

SUGGESTED
Weekly *Implementation*

DAY 1	DAY 2	DAY 3	DAY 4	DAY 5
Prayer journal. Review the required reading(s) *before* the assigned lesson begins. Teacher may want to discuss assigned reading(s) with students. Teacher and students will decide on required essays for this lesson, choosing two or three essays. The rest of the essays can be outlined, answered with shorter answers, or skipped. Review all readings for Lesson 32.	**Prayer journal.** Review reading(s) from next lesson. Outline essays due at the end of the week. Per teacher instructions, students may answer orally in a group setting some of the essays that are not assigned as formal essays.	**Prayer journal.** Write rough drafts of all assigned essays. The teacher and/or a peer evaluator may correct rough drafts.	**Prayer journal.** Rewrite corrected copies of essays due tomorrow.	**Prayer journal.** Essays are due. Take Lesson 32 test. Reading Ahead: Review *Cold Sassy Tree*, Olive Ann Burns. Guide: How does the protagonist mature both physically and spiritually?

CONTEMPORARY WRITERS, 1960-PRESENT *(Part 3)*

Cold Sassy Tree

Olive Ann Burns

BACKGROUND

Olive Ann Burns (1924-1990) once described her writing in this way, "It has been said that growing up in the South and becoming a writer is like spending your life riding in a wagon, seated in a chair that is always facing backwards. I don't face life looking backwards, but I have written about past times and past people."

CRITICAL THINKING

A. What is the central conflict in this novel?

B. The narrator in this novel is a young boy. How reliable is he?

C. In what ways has the narrator matured? What objects does Burns use to show maturity or lack of maturity?

D. Are the female characters in *Cold Sassy Tree* real or archetypal?

You will analyze: *Cold Sassy Tree*, Olive Ann Burns.

Reading Ahead: *The Chosen*, Chiam Potok.

Guide Question: Did Danny make the right choice?

BIBLICAL APPLICATION

Discuss Will's faith journey.

FINAL PORTFOLIO

Correct and re-write required essays for this lesson and place in your Portfolio.

SUGGESTED
Weekly *Implementation*

DAY 1	DAY 2	DAY 3	DAY 4	DAY 5
Prayer journal. Review the required reading(s) *before* the assigned lesson begins. Teacher may want to discuss assigned reading(s) with students. Teacher and students will decide on required essays for this lesson, choosing two or three essays. The rest of the essays can be outlined, answered with shorter answers, or skipped. Review all readings for Lesson 33.	Prayer journal. Review reading(s) from next lesson. Outline essays due at the end of the week. Per teacher instructions, students may answer orally in a group setting some of the essays that are not assigned as formal essays.	**Prayer journal.** Write rough drafts of all assigned essays. The teacher and/or a peer evaluator may correct rough drafts.	**Prayer journal.** Rewrite corrected copies of essays due tomorrow.	**Prayer journal.** Essays are due. Take Lesson 33 test. Reading Ahead: Review *The Chosen*, Chiam Potok. Question: Did Danny make the right choice?

LESSON 34

CONTEMPORARY WRITERS, 1960-PRESENT *(Part 4)*

The Chosen

Chiam Potok

BACKGROUND

The Chosen is basically the story of two cultures colliding. On one level it is the story of Orthodox Judaism vs. Hasidic Judaism. On the other hand, it embraces life at many different levels. It also celebrates such human virtues as respect and loyalty.

Chiam Potok (1929-) born Herman Harold Potok, was the son of Polish immigrants and was reared in an Orthodox Jewish home, important because his background deeply affected his writings. Potok began his career as an author and novelist with the publication of *The Chosen* (1967), which stands as the first book from a major publisher to portray Orthodox Judaism in the United States. Potok followed *The Chosen* with a sequel two years later called *The Promise*. Potok returned to the subject of Hasidism for a third time with *My Name is Asher Lev* (1972), the story of a young artist and his conflict with the traditions of his family and community. Potok followed this novel with a sequel, as well, publishing *The Gift of Asher Lev* (1990). Potok continued to examine the conflict between secular and religious interests in his other novels as well, including *In the Beginning* (1975), *The Book of Lights* (1981), and *Davita's Harp* (1985). His most recent works include *I am the Clay* (1992), The *Tree of Here* (1993), *The Sky of Now* (1995), and *The Gates of November* (1996).

You will analyze: *The Chosen*, Chiam Potok.

Prepare Final Portfolio for American Literature.

CRITICAL THINKING

A. Should Danny have become a psychotherapist even though it violated his father's wishes?

B. Do you like the ending of the book? Why?

C. Potok is a master story-teller. In some ways *what he does not write* is as important as *what he does write*. Explain.

D. What roles to women have in this novel?

E. Why does Potok tell the story from Reuven's perspective rather than Danny's?

FINAL PORTFOLIO

Correct and re-write required essays and place in your Final Portfolio. Check your Portfolio for final presentation to a peer group.

SUGGESTED
Weekly *Implementation*

DAY 1	DAY 2	DAY 3	DAY 4	DAY 5
Prayer journal.	**Prayer journal.**	**Prayer journal.**	**Prayer journal.**	**Prayer journal.**
Review the required reading(s) *before* the assigned lesson begins.	Review reading(s) from next lesson.	Write rough drafts of all assigned essays.	Rewrite corrected copies of essays due tomorrow.	Essays are due.
Teacher may want to discuss assigned reading(s) with students.	Outline essays due at the end of the week.	The teacher and/or a peer evaluator may correct rough drafts.		Students should take Lesson 34 test.
Teacher and students will decide on required essays for this lesson, choosing two or three essays.	Per teacher instructions, students may answer orally in a group setting some of the essays that are not assigned as formal essays.			**Prepare Final Portfolio in American Literature** for presentation to peer, family, or co-op group.
The rest of the essays can be outlined, answered with shorter answers, or skipped.				
Review all readings for Lesson 34.				

LESSON 35

AMERICAN LITERATURE PORTFOLIO: SUBMIT THIS WEEK.

This Final Portfolio is composed of what you have accomplished this year through *American Literature: Encouraging Thoughtful Christians to be World Changers.*

Consider this project a portfolio of your academic progress for this academic year. You should arrange to have an exhibition for peers, parents, and other academicians. You should keep your American Literature Portfolio as a record of your development as a writer, as a critical thinker, and as an American Literature scholar. It could also serve as a Biblical Application Journal if you have opted to complete the biblical application questions.

The **American Literature Portfolio** should contain the following in an attractive binder, clearly labeled with title, academic year, and your name:

AMERICAN LITERATURE PORTFOLIO

Table of Contents

Corrected Literary Essays

Literary Checkups

Writing Journals

Pictures (or paraphernalia, or travel journals) from field trips

Supplemental Material (or other pertinent information)

Vocabulary cards (in a separate pocket-type folder)

AMERICAN LITERATURE

ENCOURAGING THOUGHTFUL CHRISTIANS
TO BE WORLD CHANGERS

APPENDICES

APPENDIX A

Writing Tips

How do students produce concise, well-written essays?

GENERAL STATEMENTS

- Essays should be written in the context of the other social sciences. This means that essays should be written on all topics: science topics, history topics, social science topics, etc.
- Some essays should be rewritten, depending on the assignment and the purpose of the writing; definitely those essays which are to be presented to various readers or a public audience should be rewritten for their best presentation. Parents and other educators should discuss with their students which and how many essays will be rewritten. Generally speaking, I suggest that students rewrite at least one essay per week.
- Students should write something every day and read something every day. Students will be prompted to read assigned whole books before they are due. It is imperative that students read ahead as they write present essays or they will not be able to read all the material. Remember this too: students tend to write what they read. Poor material—material that is too juvenile—will be echoed in the vocabulary and syntax of student essays.
- Students should begin writing assignments immediately after they are assigned. A suggested implementation schedule is provided. Generally speaking, students will write about one hour per day to accomplish the writing component of this course.
- Students should revise their papers as soon as they are evaluated. Follow the implementation schedule at the end of each course.

Every essay includes a *prewriting phase, an outlining phase, a writing phase, a revision phase,* and for the purposes of this course, *a publishing phase.*

PRE-WRITING THINKING CHALLENGE

ISSUE
State problem/issue in five sentences.

State problem/issue in two sentences.

State problem/issue in one sentence.

NAME THREE OR MORE SUBTOPICS OF THE PROBLEM.

NAME THREE OR MORE SUBTOPICS OF THE SUBTOPICS.

WHAT INFORMATION MUST BE KNOWN TO SOLVE THE PROBLEM OR TO ANSWER THE QUESTION?

STATE THE ANSWER TO THE QUESTION/
PROBLEM
—In five sentences.

—In two sentences.

—In one sentence.

STATED IN TERMS OF OUTCOMES, WHAT
EVIDENCES DO I SEE THAT CONFIRM THAT I
HAVE MADE THE RIGHT DECISION?

ONCE THE PROBLEM/QUESTION IS
ANSWERED/SOLVED, WHAT ONE OR TWO
NEW PROBLEMS/ANSWERS MAY ARISE?

ABBREVIATED PRE-WRITING THINKING CHALLENGE

What is the issue?
State problem/issue in five sentences.
State problem/issue in two sentences.
State problem/issue in one sentence.
Name three or more subtopics of problem.
Name three or more subtopics of the subtopics.
What information must be known to solve the problem
or to answer the question?
State the answer to the question/problem
—in five sentences —in two sentences —in one sentence.
Stated in terms of outcomes, what evidences do I see
that confirm that I have made the right decision?

Once the problem or question is answered or solved,
what are one or two new problems or answers that
could arise?

PRE-WRITING PHASE

Often called the brainstorming phase, the pre-writing
phase is the time you decide on exactly what your topic
is. What questions must you answer? You should articulate a thesis (a one sentence statement of purpose for

why you are writing about this topic. The thesis typically has two to four specific points contained within
it). You should decide what sort of essay this is—for
instance, a definition, an exposition, a persuasive argument—and then design a strategy. For example, a
clearly persuasive essay will demand that you state the
issue and give your opinion in the opening paragraph.

Next, after a thesis statement, you will write an outline. *No matter what length the essay may be, 20 pages or one
paragraph, you should create an outline.*

Outline
Thesis: In his poem *The Raven*, Edgar Allan Poe
uses literary devices to describe such weighty topics as
death and *unrequited love*, which draw the reader to an
insightful and many times emotional moment. (Note
that this thesis informs the reader that the author will
be exploring *death* and *unrequited love*.)

I.   Introduction (Opens to the reader the explo-
     ration of the writing and tells the reader what
     to expect.)
II. Body (This particular essay will include two
     main points developed in two main para-
     graphs, one paragraph about death and one
     paragraph about emotions. The second para-
     graph will be introduced by means of a transi-
     tion word or phrase or sentence.)
     A. Imagining Death
     B. Feeling Emotions
III. Conclusions (A paragraph which draws con-
     clusions or solves the problem mentioned in
     the thesis statement.)

One of the best ways to organize your thoughts is
to spend time in concentrated thinking, what some call
brainstorming. Thinking through what you want to
write is a way to narrow your topic.

Sample Outline:
Persuasive Paper with Three Major Points (Arguments)

I. Introduction: <u>Thesis statement</u> includes a listing or a summary of the three supportive arguments and introduces the paper.

II. Body
A. Argument 1
   Evidence
   (transition words or phrases or sentences to the next topic)
B. Argument 2
   Evidence
   (transition words or phrases or sentences to the next topic)
C. Argument 3
   Evidence
   (transition words or phrases or sentences to the conclusion)

III. Conclusion: Restatement of arguments and evidence used throughout the paper (do not use the words *in conclusion*—just conclude).

NOTE: For greater detail and explanation of outlining, refer to a composition handbook. Careful attention should be paid to parallel structure with words or phrases, to correct form with headings and subheadings, to punctuation, and to pairing of information. Correct outline structure will greatly enhance the writing of any paper.

Sample Outline:
Expository Essay with Four Major Points

I. Introduction: <u>Thesis statement</u> includes a listing or mention of four examples or supports and introduces the paper; use transitional words or phrases at the end of the paragraph.

II. Body
A. Example 1
   Application
   (transition words or phrases or sentences to the next topic)
B. Example 2
   Application
   (transition words or phrases or sentences to the next topic)
C. Example 3
   Application
   (transition words or phrases or sentences to the next topic)
D. Example 4
   Application
   (transition words or phrases or sentences to the conclusion)

III. Conclusion: Restatement of thesis, drawing from the evidence or applications used in the paper (do not use the words *in conclusion*—just conclude).

NOTE: For greater detail and explanation of outlining, refer to a composition handbook. Careful attention should be paid to parallel structure with words or phrases, to correct form with headings and subheadings, to punctuation, and to pairing of information. Correct outline structure will greatly enhance the writing of any paper.

The Thinking Challenge

The following chart is an example of a Thinking Challenge approach to Mark Twain's *The Adventures of Huckleberry Finn:*

The Problem or The Issue or The Question:

Should Huck turn in his escaped slave-friend Jim to the authorities?

State problem/issue in five sentences, then in two sentences, and, finally, in one sentence.

Five Sentences:
Huck runs away with Jim. He does so knowing that he is breaking the law. However, the lure of friendship overrides the perfidy he knows he is committing. As he floats down the Mississippi River, he finds it increasingly difficult to hide his friend from the authorities and to hide his feelings of ambivalence. Finally he manages to satisfy both ambiguities.

Two Sentences:
Huck intentionally helps his slave friend Jim escape from servitude. As Huck floats down the Mississippi River, he finds it increasingly difficult to hide his friend from the authorities and at the same time to hide his own feelings of ambivalence.

One Sentence:
After escaping with his slave-friend Jim and floating down the Mississippi River, Huck finds it increasingly difficult to hide his friend from the authorities and at the same time to hide his own feelings of ambivalence.

Name three or more subtopics of problem.
Are there times when we should disobey the law?
What responsibilities does Huck have to his family?
What should Huck do?

Name three or more subtopics of the subtopics.
Are there times when we should disobey the law?
Who determines what laws are unjust?
Should the law be disobeyed publicly?
Who is injured when we disobey the law?
What responsibilities does Huck have to his family?
Who is his family? Jim? His dad?
Is allegiance to them secondary to Jim's needs?
Should his family support his civil disobedience?

What should Huck do?
Turn in Jim?
Escape with Jim?
Both?

What information must be known?
Laws? Jim's character? If he is bad, then should Huck save him?

State the answer to the question/problem in five, two, and one sentence(s).

Five Sentences:
Huck can escape with Jim with profound feelings of guilt. After all, he is helping a slave escape. This is important because it shows that Huck is still a moral, if flawed, character. Jim's freedom does outweigh any other consideration—including the laws of the land and his family's wishes. As the story unfolds the reader sees that Huck is indeed a reluctant criminal, and the reader takes comfort in that fact.

Two Sentences:
Showing reluctance and ambivalence, Huck embarks on an arduous but moral adventure. Jim's freedom outweighs any other need or consideration.

One Sentence:
Putting Jim's freedom above all other considerations, Huck, the reluctant criminal, embarks on an arduous but moral adventure.

Once the Problem or Issue or Question is solved, what are one or two new problems that may arise? What if Huck is wrong? What consequences could Huck face?

Every essay has a beginning (introduction), a middle part (body), and an ending (conclusion). The introduction must draw the reader into the topic and usually presents the thesis to the reader. The body organizes the material and expounds on the thesis (a one sentence statement of purpose) in a cogent and inspiring way. The conclusion generally is a solution to the problem or issue or question or is sometimes a summary. Paragraphs in the body are connected with transitional words or phrases: *furthermore, therefore, in spite of.* Another effective transition technique is to mention in the first sentence of a new paragraph a thought or word that occurs in the last sentence of the previous paragraph. In any event, the body should be intentionally organized to advance the purposes of the paper. A disciplined writer *always* writes a rough draft. Using the well-thought-out outline composed during the pre-writing phase is an excellent way to begin the actual writing. The paper has already been processed mentally and only lacks the writing.

WRITING PHASE

The writer must make the first paragraph grab the reader's attention enough that the reader will want to continue reading.

The writer should write naturally, but not colloquially. In other words, the writer should not use clichés and everyday coded language. *The football players blew it* is too colloquial.

The writer should use as much visual imagery and precise detail as possible, should assume nothing, and should explain everything.

REWRITING PHASE

Despite however many rewrites are necessary, when the writer has effectively communicated the subject and corrected grammar and usage problems, she is ready to write the final copy.

Top Ten Most Frequent Essay Problems

Agreement between the Subject and Verb: Use singular forms of verbs with singular subjects and use plural forms of verbs with plural subjects.
WRONG: Everyone finished their homework.
RIGHT: Everyone finished his homework (*Everyone* is an indefinite singular pronoun).

Using the Second Person Pronoun—"you," "your" should rarely, if ever, be used in a formal essay.
WRONG: You know what I mean (Too informal).

Redundancy: Never use "I think" or "It seems to me"
WRONG: I think that is true.
RIGHT: That is true (We know you think it, or you would not write it!).

Tense consistency: Use the same tense (usually present) throughout the paper.
WRONG: I was ready to go, but my friend is tired.
RIGHT: I am ready to go but my friend is tired.

Misplaced Modifiers: Place the phrase or clause close to its modifier.
WRONG: The man drove the car with a bright smile into the garage.
RIGHT: The man with a bright smile drove the car into the garage.

Antecedent Pronoun Problems: Make sure pronouns match (agree) in number and gender with their antecedents.
WRONG: Mary and Susan both enjoyed her dinner.
RIGHT: Mary and Susan both enjoyed their dinners.

Parallelism: Make certain that your list/sentence includes similar phrase types.
WRONG: I like to take a walk and swimming.
RIGHT: I like walking and swimming

Affect vs. Effect: Affect is a verb; Effect is a noun unless it means to achieve.
WRONG: His mood effects me negatively.
RIGHT: His mood affects me negatively.
RIGHT: The effects of his mood are devastating.

Dangling Prepositions: Rarely end a sentence with an unmodified preposition.
WRONG: Who were you speaking to?
RIGHT: To whom were you speaking?

Transitions: Make certain that paragraphs are connected with transitions (e.g., furthermore, therefore, in spite of).
RIGHT: Furthermore, Jack London loves to describe animal behavior.

APPENDIX B

COMPOSITION EVALUATION EVALUATION TECHNIQUE #1

Based on 100 points: 85/B-

I. Grammar and Syntax: Is the composition grammatically correct?

(25 points) 15/25

Comments: See Corrections. Look up "Subject/Verb Agreement," "Run-on Sentences," "Verb Tense," "Parallel Structure," and "Use of the Possessive" in your grammar test; read about them, write the grammar rules on the back of your essay, and then correct these parts of your essay.

II. Organization: Does this composition exhibit well considered organization? Does it flow? Transitions? Introduction and a conclusion?

(25 points) 20/25

Comments: Good job with transitional phrases and with having a strong introduction. Your thesis statement gives me a clear idea about the content of your paper. Your conclusion explains your thesis very thoroughly. If you want to sermonize in your essay, be sure to mention that in the introduction.

III. Content: Does this composition answer the question, argue the point well, and/or persuade the reader?

(50 points) 50/50

Comments: Nice insights. You have used solid quotes from the poem to support your argument that Taylor uses nature elements to teach a moral view.

COMPOSITION EVALUATION TECHNIQUE #2

I. Organization
___ Is the writer's purpose stated clearly in the introduction? Is there a thesis sentence? What is it?
___ Does the writer answer the assignment?
___ Does the introduction grab the reader's attention?
___ Is the purpose advanced by each sentence and paragraph?
___ Does the body (middle) of the paper advance the purpose?
___ Does the conclusion accomplish its purpose?
Other helpful comments for the writer:

II. Mechanics
___ Does the writer use active voice?
___ Does the writer use the appropriate verb tense throughout the paper?
___ Is there agreement between all pronouns and antecedents?
___ Is there appropriately subject/verb agreement?
___ Are the transitions effective and appropriate?
Other mechanical trouble spots:

III. Argument
___ Are you persuaded by the arguments?
Other helpful comments for the writer:

COMPOSITION EVALUATION TECHNIQUE #3

Peer Checklist
(May Prefer to Use Evaluation Technique Forms One or Two)

I. Organization
___ Is the writer's purpose clearly introduced? What is it?
___ Does the organization of the paper coincide with the outline?
___ Does the writer answer the assignment?
___ Does the introduction grab the reader's attention?
___ Is the purpose advanced by each sentence and paragraph? (Are there sentences which don't seem to belong in the paragraphs?)
___ Does the body (middle) of the paper advance the purpose?
___ Does the conclusion solve the purpose of the paper?

Comments regarding organization:

II. Mechanics
___ Does the writer use active voice?
___ Does the writer use the appropriate verb tense throughout the paper?
___ Is there agreement between all pronouns and antecedents?
___ Are there effective and appropriately used transitions?

Comments regarding other mechanical problems:

III. Argument

___ Are you persuaded by the arguments?
___ Does the author need stronger arguments? More arguments?

Other helpful comments:

APPENDIX C

NOVEL REVIEW

BOOK _____ STUDENT _____

AUTHOR _____ DATE OF READING _____

I. BRIEFLY DESCRIBE:
PROTAGONIST—

ANTAGONIST—

OTHER CHARACTERS USED TO DEVELOP PROTAGONIST—

IF APPLICABLE, STATE WHY ANY OF THE BOOK'S CHARACTERS REMIND YOU OF SPECIFIC BIBLE CHARACTERS.

II. SETTING:

III. POINT OF VIEW: (CIRCLE ONE) FIRST PERSON, THIRD PERSON, THIRD PERSON OMNISCIENT

IV. BRIEF SUMMARY OF THE PLOT:

V. THEME (THE QUINTESSENTIAL MEANING/PURPOSE OF THE BOOK IN ONE OR TWO SENTENCES):

VI. AUTHOR'S WORLDVIEW: HOW DO YOU KNOW? WHAT BEHAVIORS DO(ES) THE CHARACTER(S) MANIFEST THAT LEAD YOU TO THIS CONCLUSION?

VII. WHY DID YOU LIKE/DISLIKE THIS BOOK?

VIII. THE NEXT LITERARY WORK I READ WILL BE . . .

SHORT STORY REVIEW

SHORT STORY _____ STUDENT _____

AUTHOR _____ DATE OF READING _____

I. BRIEFLY DESCRIBE
PROTAGONIST—

ANTAGONIST—

OTHER CHARACTERS USED TO DEVELOP PROTAGONIST—

IF APPLICABLE, STATE WHY ANY OF THE STORY'S CHARACTERS REMIND YOU OF SPECIFIC BIBLE CHARACTERS.

II. SETTING

III. POINT OF VIEW: (CIRCLE ONE) FIRST PERSON, THIRD PERSON, THIRD PERSON OMNISCIENT

IV. BRIEF SUMMARY OF THE PLOT

IDENTIFY THE CLIMAX OF THE SHORT STORY.

V. THEME (THE QUINTESSENTIAL MEANING/PURPOSE OF THE STORY IN ONE OR TWO SENTENCES):

VI. AUTHOR'S WORLDVIEW:
HOW DO YOU KNOW THIS? WHAT BEHAVIORS DO(ES) THE CHARACTER(S) MANIFEST THAT LEAD YOU TO THIS CONCLUSION?

VII. WHY DID YOU LIKE/DISLIKE THIS SHORT STORY?

VIII. THE NEXT LITERARY WORK I READ WILL BE . . .

DRAMA REVIEW

PLAY _____ STUDENT _____

AUTHOR _____ DATE OF READING _____

I. BRIEFLY DESCRIBE
PROTAGONIST—

ANTAGONIST—

IF APPLICABLE, STATE WHY ANY OF THE PLAY'S CHARACTERS REMIND YOU OF SPECIFIC BIBLE
CHARACTERS.

II. SETTING

III. POINT OF VIEW: (CIRCLE ONE) FIRST PERSON, THIRD PERSON, THIRD PERSON OMNISCIENT

IV. BRIEF SUMMARY OF THE PLOT

IDENTIFY THE CLIMAX OF THE PLAY.

V. THEME (THE QUINTESSENTIAL MEANING/PURPOSE OF THE PLAY IN ONE OR TWO SEN-TENCES)

VI. AUTHOR'S WORLDVIEW
HOW DO YOU KNOW THIS? WHAT BEHAVIORS DO(ES) THE CHARACTER(S) MANIFEST THAT LEAD YOU TO THIS CONCLUSION?

VII. WHY DID YOU LIKE/DISLIKE THIS PLAY?

VIII. THE NEXT LITERARY WORK I WILL READ WILL BE . . .

NON-FICTION REVIEW

LITERARY WORK _____ STUDENT _____

AUTHOR _____ DATE OF READING _____

I. WRITE A PRÉCIS OF THIS BOOK. IN YOUR PRÉCIS, CLEARLY STATE THE AUTHOR'S THESIS AND SUPPORTING ARGUMENTS.

II. ARE YOU PERSUADED? WHY OR WHY NOT?

III. WHY DID YOU LIKE/DISLIKE THIS BOOK?

IV. THE NEXT LITERARY WORK I READ WILL BE . . .

APPENDIX D

PRAYER JOURNAL GUIDE

Journal Guide Questions

Bible Passage(s): _____

_____

_____

1. Centering Time (a list of those things that I must do later):

2. Discipline of Silence (remain absolutely still and quiet).

3. Reading Scripture Passage (with notes on text):

4. Living in Scripture:

A. How does the passage affect the person mentioned in the passage? How does he/she feel?

B. How does the passage affect my life? What is the Lord saying to me through this passage?

5. Prayers of Adoration and Thanksgiving, Intercession, and Future Prayer Targets:

6. Discipline of Silence.

APPENDIX E

Book List for Supplemental Reading

Note:
Not all literature is suitable for all students; educators and students should choose literature appropriate to students' age, maturity, interests, and abilities.

Jane Austen, EMMA

Charlotte Brontë, JANE EYRE

Thomas Bulfinch, THE AGE OF FABLE

Pearl S. Buck, THE GOOD EARTH

John Bunyan, PILGRIM'S PROGRESS

Agatha Christie, AND THEN THERE WERE NONE

Samuel T. Coleridge, RIME OF THE ANCIENT MARINER

Jospeh Conrad, HEART OF DARKNESS, LORD JIM

James F. Cooper, THE LAST OF THE MOHICANS, DEERSLAYER

Stephen Crane, THE RED BADGE OF COURAGE

Clarence Day, LIFE WITH FATHER

Daniel Defoe, ROBINSON CRUSOE

Charles Dickens, GREAT EXPECTATIONS, A CHRISTMAS CAROL, A TALE OF TWO CITIES, OLIVER TWIST, NICHOLAS NICKLEBY

Arthur C. Doyle, THE ADVENTURES OF SHERLOCK HOLMES

Alexander Dumas, THE THREE MUSKETEERS

George Eliot, SILAS MARNER

T. S. Eliot, MURDER IN THE CATHEDRAL, SILAS MARNER

Anne Frank, THE DIARY OF ANNE FRANK

Oliver Goldsmith, THE VICAR OF WAKEFIELD

Edith Hamilton, MYTHOLOGY

Nathaniel Hawthorne, THE SCARLET LETTER, THE HOUSE OF THE SEVEN GABLES

Thor Heyerdahl, KON-TIKI

J. Hilton, LOST HORIZON, GOODBYE, MR. CHIPS

Homer, THE ODYSSEY, THE ILIAD

W. H. Hudson, GREEN MANSIONS

Victor Hugo, LES MISERABLES, THE HUNCHBACK OF NOTRE DAME

Zora Neale Hurston, THEIR EYES WERE WATCHING GOD

Washington Irving, THE SKETCH BOOK

Rudyard Kipling, CAPTAINS COURAGEOUS

Harper Lee, TO KILL A MOCKINGBIRD

Madeline L'Engle, A CIRCLE OF QUIET, THE SUMMER OF THE GREAT GRANDMOTHER, A WRINKLE IN TIME

C. S. Lewis, THE SCREWTAPE LETTERS, MERE CHRISTIANITY, CHRONICLES OF NARNIA

Jack London, THE CALL OF THE WILD, WHITE FANG

George MacDonald, CURATE'S AWAKENING, ETC.

Sir Thomas Malory, LE MORTE D'ARTHUR

Guy de Maupassant, SHORT STORIES

Herman Melville, BILLY BUDD, MOBY DICK

Monsarrat, THE CRUEL SEA

C. Nordhoff & Hall, MUTINY ON THE BOUNTY

Edgar Allen Poe, POEMS & SHORT STORIES

E. M.Remarque, ALL QUIET ON THE WESTERN FRONT

Anne Rinaldi, A BREAK WITH CHARITY: STORY OF THE SALEM WITCH TRIALS

Carl Sanburg, ABRAHAM LINCOLN

William Saroyan, THE HUMAN COMEDY

Sir Walter Scott, IVANHOE

William Shakespeare, HAMLET, MACBETH, JULIUS CAESAR, AS YOU LIKE IT, ROMEO AND JULIET, A MIDSUMMER NIGHT'S DREAM, ETC.

George Bernard Shaw, PYGMALION

Sophocles, ANTIGONE

Harriet Beecher Stowe, UNCLE TOM'S CABIN

John Steinbeck, OF MICE AND MEN, GRAPES OF WRATH

R. L. Stevenson, DR. JEKYLL AND MR. HYDE, TREASURE ISLAND, KIDNAPPED

Irving Stone, LUST FOR LIFE

Jonathan Swift, GULLIVER'S TRAVELS
Booth Tarkington, PENROD
J.R.R. Tolkien, THE LORD OF THE RINGS TRILOGY
Mark Twain, ADVENTURES OF HUCKLEBERRY FINN, THE ADVENTURES OF TOM SAWYER
Jules Verne, MASTER OF THE WORLD
Booker T. Washington, UP FROM SLAVERY
H. G. Wells, COLLECTED WORKS
Tennessee Williams, THE GLASS MENAGERIE

FOR OLDER STUDENTS

Chinua Achebe, THINGS FALL APART
Aristotle, POETICUS
Edward Bellamy, LOOKING BACKWARD
Jorge Luis Borges, VARIOUS SHORT STORIES
Stephen V. Benet, JOHN BROWN'S BODY
Charlotte Brontë, WUTHERING HEIGHTS
Camus, THE STRANGER
Chaucer, THE CANTERBURY TALES, BEOWULF
Willa Cather, MY ANTONIA
Miguel de Cervantes, DON QUIXOTE
Fyodor Dostovesky, CRIME AND PUNISHMENT, THE IDIOT, THE BROTHERS KARAMAZOV
William Faulkner, THE HAMLET TRIOLOGY
F. Scott Fitzgerald, THE GREAT GATSBY
John Galsworthy, THE FORSYTHE SAGA
Lorraine Hansberry, RAISIN IN THE SUN
Thomas Hardy, THE RETURN OF THE NATIVE, THE MAYOR OF CASTERBRIDGE

A. E. Housman, A SHROPSHIRE LAD
Henrik Ibsen, A DOLL'S HOUSE
Charles Lamb THE ESSAYS OF ELIA
Sinclair Lewis, BABBITT, ARROWSMITH
Kamala Markandaya, NECTAR IN A SIEVE
Gabriel Barcia Marquez, 100 YEARS OF SOLITUDE
John P. Marquand, THE LATE GEORGE APLEY
E. Lee Masters, A SPOON RIVER ANTHOLOGY
Somerset Maugham, OF HUMAN BONDAGE
Arthur Miller, THE CRUCIBLE, DEATH OF A SALESMAN
Eugene O'Neill, THE EMPEROR JONES
George Orwell, ANIMAL FARM, 1984
Thomas Paine, THE RIGHTS OF MAN
Alan Paton, CRY THE BELOVED COUNTRY
Plato, THE REPUBLIC
Plutarch, LIVES
O. E. Rolvaag, GIANTS IN THE EARTH
Edmund Rostand, CYRANO DE BERGERAC
Mary Shelley, FRANKENSTEIN
Sophocles, OEDIPUS REX
John Steinbeck, THE PEARL
Ivan Turgenev, FATHERS AND SONS
William Thackeray, VANITY FAIR
Leo Tolstoy, WAR AND PEACE
Edith Wharton, ETHAN FROME
Walt Whitman, LEAVES OF GRASS
Thornton Wilder, OUR TOWN
Thomas Wolfe, LOOK HOMEWARD ANGEL

APPENDIX F

GLOSSARY OF LITERARY TERMS

Allegory A story or tale with two or more levels of meaning—a literal level and one or more symbolic levels. The events, setting, and characters in an allegory are symbols for ideas or qualities.

Alliteration The repetition of initial consonant sounds. The repetition can be juxtaposed (side by side; e.g., simply sad). An example:

I conceive therefore, as to the business of being profound, that it is with writers, as with wells; a person with good eyes may see to the bottom of the deepest, provided any water be there; and that often, when there is nothing in the world at the bottom, besides dryness and dirt, though it be but a yard and a half under ground, it shall pass, however, for wondrous deep, upon no wiser a reason than because it is wondrous dark. (Jonathan Swift)

Allusion A casual and brief reference to a famous historical or literary figure or event:

You must borrow me Gargantua's mouth first. 'Tis a word too great for any mouth of this age's size. (Shakespeare)

Analogy The process by which new or less familiar words, constructions, or pronunciations conform to the pattern of older or more familiar (and often unrelated) ones; a comparison between two unlike things. The purpose of an analogy is to describe something unfamiliar by pointing out its similarities to something that is familiar.

Antagonist In a narrative, the character with whom the main character has the most conflict. In Jack London's "To Build a Fire" the antagonist is the extreme cold of the Yukon rather than a person or animal.

Archetype The original pattern or model from which all other things of the same kind are made; a perfect example of a type or group. (e.g. The biblical character Joseph is often considered an archetype of Jesus Christ.)

Argumentation The discourse in which the writer presents and logically supports a particular view or opinion; sometimes used interchangeably with *persuasion*.

Aside In a play an aside is a speech delivered by an actor in such a way that other characters on the stage are presumed not to hear it; an aside generally reveals a character's inner thoughts.

Autobiography A form of nonfiction in which a person tells his/her own life story. Notable examples of autobiography include those by Benjamin Franklin and Frederick Douglass.

Ballad A song or poem that tells a story in short stanzas and simple words with repetition, refrain, etc.

Biography A form of nonfiction in which a writer tells the life story of another person.

Character A person or an animal who takes part in the action of a literary work. The *main character* is the one on whom the work focuses. The person with whom the main character has the most conflict is the *antagonist*. He is the enemy of the main character (*protagonist*). For instance, in *The Scarlet Letter*, by Nathaniel Hawthorne, Chillingsworth is the antagonist. Hester is the protagonist. Characters who appear in the story may perform actions, speak to other characters, be described by the narrator, or be remembered. Characters introduced whose sole purpose is to develop the main character are called *foils*.

Classicism An approach to literature and the other arts that stresses reason, balance, clarity, ideal beauty, and orderly form in imitation of the arts of Greece and Rome.

Conflict A struggle between opposing forces; can be internal or external; when occurring within a character is called *internal conflict*. An example of this occurs in Mark Twain's *Adventures of Huckleberry Finn*. In this novel Huck is struggling in his mind about whether to return an escaped slave, his good friend Jim, to the authorities. An *external conflict* is normally an obvious conflict between the protagonist and antagonist(s). London's "To Build a Fire" illustrates conflict between a character and an outside force. Most plots develop from conflict, making conflict one of the primary elements of narrative literature.

Crisis or *Climax* The moment or event in the *plot* in which the conflict is most directly addressed: the main character "wins" or "loses"; the secret is revealed. After the climax, the *denouement* or falling action occurs.

Dialectic Examining opinions or ideas logically, often by the method of question and answer

Discourse, Forms of Various modes into which writing can be classified; traditionally, writing has been divided into the following modes:
Exposition Writing which presents information
Narration Writing which tells a story
Description Writing which portrays people, places, or things
Persuasion (sometimes also called *Argumentation*) Writing which attempts to convince people to think or act in a certain way

Drama A story written to be performed by actors; the playwright supplies dialogue for the characters to speak and stage directions that give information about costumes, lighting, scenery, properties, the setting, and the character's movements and ways of speaking.

Dramatic monologue A poem or speech in which an imaginary character speaks to a silent listener. Eliot's "The Love Song of J. Alfred Prufrock" is a dramatic monologue.

Elegy A solemn and formal lyric poem about death, often one that mourns the passing of some particular person; Whitman's "When Lilacs Last in the Dooryard Bloom'd" is an elegy lamenting the death of President Lincoln.

Essay A short, nonfiction work about a particular subject; *essay* comes from the Old French word *essai*, meaning "a trial or attempt"; meant to be explanatory, an essay is not meant to be an exhaustive treatment of a subject; can be classified as formal or informal, personal or impersonal; can also be classified according to purpose as either expository, argumentative, descriptive, persuasive, or narrative.

Figurative Language See *metaphor, simile, analogy*

Foil A character who provides a contrast to another character and whose purpose is to develop the main character.

Genre A division or type of literature; commonly divided into three major divisions, literature is either poetry, prose, or drama; each major genre can then be divided into smaller genres: poetry can be divided into lyric, concrete, dramatic, narrative, and epic poetry; prose can be divided into fiction (novels and short stories) and nonfiction (biography, autobiography, letters, essays, and reports); drama can be divided into serious drama, tragedy, comic drama, melodrama, and farce.

Gothic The use of primitive, medieval, wild, or mysterious elements in literature; Gothic elements offended 18th century classical writers but appealed to the Romantic writers who followed them. Gothic novels feature writers who use places like mysterious castles where horrifying supernatural events take place; Poe's "The Fall of the House of Usher" illustrates the influence of Gothic elements.

Harlem Renaissance Occurring during the 1920s, a time of African American artistic creativity centered in Harlem in New York City; Langston Hughes was a Harlem Renaissance writer.

Hyperbole A deliberate exaggeration or overstatement; in Mark Twain's "The Notorious Jumping From of Calaveras County," the claim that Jim Smiley would follow a bug as far as Mexico to win a bet is hyperbolic.

Idyll A poem or part of a poem that describes and idealizes country life; Whittier's "Snowbound" is an idyll.

Irony A method of humorous or subtly sarcastic expression in which the intended meanings of the words used is the direct opposite of their usual sense.

Journal A daily autobiographical account of events and personal reactions.

Kenning Indirect way of naming people or things; knowledge or recognition; in Old English poetry, a metaphorical name for something.

Literature All writings in prose or verse, especially those of an imaginative or critical character, without regard to their excellence and/or writings considered as having permanent value, excellence of form, great emotional effect, etc.

Metaphor (Figure of speech) A comparison which creatively identifies one thing with another dissimilar thing and transfers or ascribes to the first thing some of the qualities of the second. Unlike a *simile* or *analogy*, metaphor asserts that one thing is another thing—not just that one is like another. Very frequently a metaphor is invoked by the verb *to be*:

Affliction then is ours;
We are the trees whom shaking fastens more. (George Herbert)
Then Jesus declared, "I am the bread of life." (John 6:35)
Jesus answered, "I am the Way and the truth and the life." (John 14:6)

Meter A poem's rhythmical pattern, determined by the number and types of stresses, or beats, in each line; a certain number of *metrical feet* make up a *line* of verse; (pentameter denotes a line containing five metrical feet); the act of describing the meter of a poem is called *scanning* which involves marking the stressed and unstressed syllables, as follows:
   iamb A foot with one unstressed syllable followed by one stressed syllable, as in the word *abound*.
   trochee A foot with one stressed syllable followed by one unstressed syllable, as in the word *spoken*.
   anapest A foot with two unstressed syllables followed by one stressed syllable, as in the word *interrupt*.
   dactyl A foot with a stressed syllable followed by two unstressed syllables, as in the word *accident*.
   spondee Two stressed feet: *quicksand, heartbeat*; occurs only occasionally in English.

Motif A main idea element, feature; a main theme or subject to be elaborated on.

Narration The way the author chooses to tell the story.
   First Person Narration: A character and refers to himself or herself, using "I." Example: Huck Finn in *The Adventures of Huckleberry Finn* tells the story from his perspective. This is a creative way to bring humor into the plot.
   Second Person Narration: Addresses the reader and/or the main character as "you" (and may also use first person narration, but not necessarily). One example is the opening of each of Rudyard Kipling's *Just So Stories*, in which the narrator refers to the child listener as "O Best Beloved."
   Third Person Narration: Not a character in the story; refers to the story's characters as "he" and "she." This is probably the most common form of narration.
   Limited Narration: Only able to tell what one person is thinking or feeling. Example: in *A Separate Peace*, by John Knowles, we only see the story from Gene's perspective.
   Omniscient Narration: Charles Dickens employs this narration in most of his novels.
   Reliable Narration: Everything this Narration says is true, and the Narrator knows everything that is necessary to the story.
   Unreliable Narrator: May not know all the relevant information; may be intoxicated or mentally ill; may lie to the audience. Example: Edgar Allan Poe's narrators are frequently unreliable. Think of the delusions that the narrator of "The Tell-Tale Heart" has about the old man.

Narrative In story form.

Onomatopoeia. Use of words which, in their pronunciation, suggest their meaning. "Hiss," for example, when spoken is intended to resemble the sound of steam or of a snake. Other examples include these: *slam, buzz, screech, whirr, crush, sizzle, crunch, wring, wrench, gouge, grind, mangle, bang, blam, pow, zap, fizz, urp, roar, growl, blip, click, whimper,* and, of course, *snap, crackle, and pop.*

303

Parallelism Two or more balancing statements with phrases, clauses, or paragraphs of similar length and grammatical structure.

Plot Arrangement of the action in fiction or drama— events of the story in the order the story gives them. A typical plot has five parts: *Exposition, Rising Action, Crisis* or *Climax, Falling Action*, and *Resolution (*sometimes called *Denouement).*

Précis Summary of the plot of a literary piece.

Protagonist The enemy of the main character *(antagonist).*

Rhetoric Using words effectively in writing and speaking.

Setting The place(s) and time(s) of a story, including the historical period, social milieu of the characters, geographical location, descriptions of indoor and outdoor locales.

Scop An Old English poet or bard.

Simile A figure of speech in which one thing is likened to another dissimilar thing by the use of *like, as*, etc.

Sonnet A poem normally of fourteen lines in any of several fixed verse and rhyme schemes, typically in rhymed iambic pentameter; sonnets characteristically express a single theme or idea.

Structure The arrangement of details and scenes that make up a literary work.

Style An author's characteristic arrangement of words. A style may be colloquial, formal, terse, wordy, theoretical, subdued, colorful, poetic, or highly individual. Style is the arrangement of words in groups and sentences; *diction* on the other hand refers to the choice of individual words; the arrangement of details and scenes make up the *structure* of a literary work; all combine to influence the tone of the work; thus, diction, style, and structure make up the *form* of the literary work.

Theme The one-sentence, major meaning of a literary piece, rarely stated but implied. The theme is not a moral, which is a statement of the author's didactic purpose of his literary piece. A thesis statement is very similar to the theme.

Tone The attitude the author takes toward his subject; author's attitude is revealed through choice of details, through diction and style, and through the emphasis and comments that are made; like theme and style, tone is sometimes difficult to describe with a single word or phrase; often it varies in the same literary piece to suit the moods of the characters and the situations. For instance, the tone or mood of Poe's "Annabel Lee" is very somber.

Credits, Permissions, and Sources

Efforts have been made to conform to US Copyright Law. Any infringement is unintentional, and any file which infringes copyright, and about which the copyright claimant informs me, will be removed pending resolution.

All graphics are copyrighted by Clipart.com unless otherwise noted.

Most of the literature cited in this book is in the public domain. Much of it is available on the Internet through the following sites:

Bartleby.com, Great Books Online
Aeschylus, *Oresteia*
Budda, *The Bhagavad-Gîtââ*
Confucius, *The Sayings of Confucius*
Epictetus, *The golden sayings of Epictetus*, with the Hymn of Cleanthes; translated and arranged by Hastings Crossley
Mohammed, *Koran*
Plato, *Apology*
Unknown, *The Song of Roland*

Susan Wise Bauer, *Writing The Short Story* (Charles City, VA)

Classical Short Stories: The Best of the Genre (http://www.geocities.com/short_stories_page/index.html)
Leo Tolstoy, The Death of Ivan Ilych, Translated by Louise and Aylmer Maude.

Early Christian Writings (http://www.earlychristianwritings.com/justin.html)
Writings, by Polycarp, Justin Martyr, and Clement

Enuma Elish translated by N. K. Sanders (http://www.piney.com/Enuma.html)

Everypoet.com
Dante, *Inferno*

Gilgamesh Epic, translated by E. A. Speiser, in *Ancient Near Eastern Texts* (Princeton, 1950), pp. 60-72, as reprinted in Isaac Mendelsohn (ed.), *Religions of the Ancient Near East*, Library of Religion paperbook series (New York, 1955). PP. 100-6; notes by Mendolenson (http://www-relg-studies.scu.edu/netcours/rs011/restrict/gilflood.htm).

Herodotus, *Histories*. Translated by Rawlinson. (http://www.concordance.com/)

Herodotus and the Bible, Wayne Jackson (http://www.christiancourier.com/archives/)

http://www.cyberhymnal.org/htm/m/i/mightyfo.htm
Martin Luther, "A Mighty Fortress is Our God"

Infomotions, Inc. The Alex Catalogue of Electronic Texts (http://www.infomotions.com/alex/).

Infoplease.com. 2002 Family Education Network. (http://aolsvc.aol.infoplease.com/ipa/A0874987.html)

The Internet Classics Archive (http://classics.mit.edu/Aristotle/poetics.1.1.html)

Aristotle, *Poetics*

Internet Applications Laboratory at the University of Evansville
Plato, *Symposium*

The Library of Congress Collection (http://www.loc.gov/exhibits/gadd/)

Lecture on Sor Juana Ines de la Cruz (http://www.latin_american.cam.ac.uk/SorJuana/)
Sor Juana Ines de la Cruz, "May Heaven Serve as Plate for the Engraving" and "Yet if, for Singing your Praise."

National Park Service (http://www.nps.gov/edal/index.htm)

The Pachomius Library (http://www.ocf.org/OrthodoxPage/reading/St.Pachomius/Liturgical/didache.html)
Unknown, *The Didache*, edited by Friar Martin Fontenot Gonzalez

Shinto Creation Stories (http://www.wsu.edu/~dee/ANCJAPAN/CREAT2.HTM)
The Creation of the gods (Translated by W.G. Aston, Nihongi (London: Kegan, Paul, Trench, Trüübner, 1896), 1-2

Stephane Theroux. Classic Reader (http://classicreader.com/)
Anton Chekov, *The Sea Gull*
Andrew Barton Paterson, *The Man From Snowy River*

University of Oregon. (http://www.uoregon.edu)
Iliad, Homer. Translated by Samuel Butler.

University of Pennsylvania (www.sas.upenn.edu/)
Author Unknown, *Ani Papyrus: Book of the Dead*

University of Virginia. Browse E-Books by Author (http://etext.lib.virginia.edu/ebooks/Wlist.html).

University of Wisconsin, Milwaukee. The Classic Text: Traditions and Interpretations (http://www.uwm.edu/Library/special/exhibits/clastext/clshome.htm)

NOTES

NOTES

NOTES

NOTES

NOTES

NOTES